Design for Six Sigma as Strategic Experimentation

Also Available from ASQ Quality Press:

Computer-Based Robust Engineering: Essentials for DFSS
Genichi Taguchi, Jugulum Rajesh and Shin Taguchi

Simplified Project Management for the Quality Professional: How to Plan for and Manage Small and Medium-size Projects
Russell T. Westcott

The Certified Six Sigma Black Belt Handbook
Donald W. Benbow and T.M. Kubiak

Applied Statistics for the Six Sigma Greenbelt
Gupta Bhisham and H. Fred Walker

Six Sigma Project Management: A Pocket Guide
Jeffrey N. Lowenthal

Defining and Analyzing a Business Process: A Six Sigma Pocket Guide
Jeffrey N. Lowenthal

Six Sigma for the Shop Floor: A Pocket Guide
Roderick A. Munro

Design of Experiments with MINITAB
Paul Mathews

Failure Mode and Effect Analysis: FMEA From Theory to Execution, Second Edition
D. H. Stamatis

Lean Strategies for Product Development: Achieving Breakthrough Performance in Bringing Products to Market
Clifford Fiore

Decision Process Quality Management
William D. Mawby

To request a complimentary catalog of ASQ Quality Press publications, call 800-248-1946, or visit our Web site at http://qualitypress.asq.org.

Design for Six Sigma as Strategic Experimentation

Planning, Designing, and Building World-Class Products and Services

H. E. Cook

ASQ Quality Press
Milwaukee, Wisconsin

American Society for Quality, Quality Press, Milwaukee 53203
© 2005 by American Society for Quality
All rights reserved. Published 2005
Printed in the United States of America

12 11 10 09 08 07 06 05   5 4 3 2 1

Library of Congress Cataloging-in-Publication Data
Cook, H. E. (Harry E.)
  Design for six sigma as strategic experimentation : planning, designing, and building
world-class products
      and services / H. E. Cook.
        p. cm.
  Includes bibliographical references and index.
  ISBN 0-87389-645-9 (alk. paper)
  1. Product management.   I. Title.

  HF5415.15.C657   2005
  658.4′012—dc22   2004025739

ISBN 0-87389-645-9

Publisher: William A. Tony
Acquisitions Editor: Annemieke Hytinen
Project Editor: Paul O'Mara
Production Administrator: Randall Benson

ASQ Mission: The American Society for Quality advances individual, organizational,
and community excellence worldwide through learning, quality improvement, and
knowledge exchange.

Attention Bookstores, Wholesalers, Schools, and Corporations: ASQ Quality Press books,
videotapes, audiotapes, and software are available at quantity discounts with bulk
purchases for business, educational, or instructional use. For information, please contact
ASQ Quality Press at 800-248-1946, or write to ASQ Quality Press, P.O. Box 3005,
Milwaukee, WI 53201-3005.

Quality Press
600 N. Plankinton Avenue
Milwaukee, Wisconsin 53203
Call toll free 800-248-1946
Fax 414-272-1734
www.asq.org
http://qualitypress.asq.org
http://standardsgroup.asq.org
E-mail: authors@asq.org

To place orders or to request a free copy of the ASQ
Quality Press Publications Catalog, including ASQ
membership information, call 800-248-1946. Visit our
Web site at www.asq.org or http://qualitypress.asq.org.

∞ Printed on acid-free paper

To Valle

Contents

CD-ROM Contents

ReadMe File
Excel Macros
Excel SDWs (43)
Excel Templates (13)
Tutorials (12)
Raw Data
Camtasia Player

Figures and Tables

Preface

*D*esign for Six Sigma as Strategic Experimentation develops a practical, science-based methodology (DFSS/SE) for guiding the product realization process for highly competitive markets. Forecasts of cash flow, market share, and price are used to select the final design from among the alternatives considered. A single formalism is used to integrate the tasks and responsibilities of marketing research, product planning, finance, design, engineering, and manufacturing within the overall product realization process.

The targeted audiences for this book are graduate engineers, statisticians, and scientists who are or who soon will be involved in planning, designing, manufacturing, and servicing products for highly competitive markets. Portions of the book, as discussed below, should also be of interest to specialists in marketing research and finance as well as CEOs. The DFSS/SE methodology also applies to service industries as the word product can be replaced meaningfully by the word service almost everywhere in the text.

The basic assumptions for DFSS/SE are contained in the model used for forecasting product demand, price, and cash flow. These *bottom-line metrics* are defined in terms of the *fundamental metrics* of value to the customer, cost (variable, fixed, and investment), and the pace of innovation. The model used is the simplest possible for forecasting the bottom-line metrics. Because the performance of a new product is uncertain, forecasts are made in terms of the confidence ranges for cash flow and market share.

Strategic experimentation (SE) is an extension of Taguchi's seminal ideas for robust component design to all levels of design and manufacturing: system, subsystem, and component. System design is mostly about doing the right things, whereas subsystem and component design and manufacturing are mostly about doing the right things right. The analysis of a strategic experiment is done here in three steps. The first step examines the statistical significance of the individual factors studied in the experiment on the mean and variance of one or more product attributes of importance to the customer. The second step expresses the outcomes of the experiment in terms of the fundamental metrics. The third step converts the fundamental metrics into forecasts of the strategic significance of the factors on price, market share, and cash flow.

The influence of the control factors on the product attributes is solved for using matrix algebra because of its generality and the fact that matrix inversion has become an easy computational exercise using a personal computer. Two representations are used for the array elements in an experimental design. When the significance of an outcome is to be measured against an established baseline, which is almost always the case in new product development, a so-called lambda form is used. When there is no established baseline, the second form, noted as phi, is used with a default baseline given by the average outcome over all of the trials.

The topics treated here do not lend themselves to a full analysis using existing statistical software programs. However, all of the computations can be carried out using a spreadsheet program such as Excel. A collection of files and templates called Strategic Design Workbooks (SDWs) have been developed and made available on the CD-ROM included with this book for many of the common experimental designs to partially automate the computations. Monte Carlo methods are used to assess the significance of the factors on the bottom-line metrics. Not only does this method handle the messy statistics with ease, but it is also insightful and fast with today's personal computers. The normal probability plotting capability of the graphics software, KaleidaGraph, is used to display the Monte Carlo results.

A key engineering skill for making effective use of DFSS/SE is the ability to generate accurate *transfer functions* for connecting design changes at the component and subsystem levels to changes in attributes at the system level of importance to the customer. For example, how does a proposed design change to an automotive engine affect the vehicle's acceleration performance, stopping distance, interior noise level, fuel economy, handling, range, and manufacturing cost? My experience is that world-class engineering organizations know how to generate the transfer functions for their products.

It should be understood that DFSS/SE is not a substitute for good engineering, keen market insight, and world-class manufacturing capability. If a competitor is selecting its final design from a list of alternatives that are better than what you are considering, DFSS/SE will not turn the tide in your favor. But when combined with excellent design, engineering, marketing, and manufacturing expertise, DFSS/SE should provide the common language and strategic vision needed for successful continuous product improvement and innovation.

The first three chapters should be of interest to all involved in the product realization process, as they cover key elements of product planning, system design, and management. The remaining chapters should be of interest primarily to engineers, statisticians, and scientists. Chapter 4 reviews several basic statistical concepts, and Chapter 5 explores the role of variation on product value and cost. Chapter 6 introduces Monte Carlo simulation using the design of a shear pin as an example. Chapters 7 through 10 explore subsystem and component design at increasing levels of detail. Chapter 7 considers the statistical significance of the factors on the mean using pooled sample variances. Chapter 8 introduces Satterthwaite's approximate *t*-test for the significance of the factors on the mean when variance is inhomogeneous. Chapter 9 introduces several individual tests for the influence of the factors on log variance. Chapter 10, building upon the previous chapters, considers the strategic significance of the factors on value, price, cash flow, and market share.

Chapter 11 considers cases in which the experiment deviated from the desired plan and demonstrates how the generality afforded by matrix algebra and Monte Carlo simulation can often be used to extract a meaningful analysis of the outcomes. Chapters 12 and 13 focus on samples taken from lognormal, binomial, Poisson, and Weibull distributions. Chapter 14 considers the analysis of a sequence of experiments, which differ from one another by having different levels of a signal factor. This is the so-called dynamic problem first explored by Taguchi and co-workers. Chapter 15 briefly explores the development of strategic response surface maps using the central composite experimental design. Several appendices deal with special topics. In addition to the SDWs (see Appendix F), the CD-ROM also includes tutorials on selected Excel applications, templates to aid the generation of new SDWs, and the raw data used as input for the problems analyzed in the book.

Harry E. Cook
Breckenridge, Colorado

1

Product Management
and the Fundamental Metrics

Insight: Continuous improvement of the fundamental metrics forms the scientific basis for strategic experimentation and product management.

Key Topics

strategic experimentation	process analysis
fundamental metrics	target setting
DFSS versus TQM	standard work
guiding structure for product management	DFSS/SE roadmap

1.1 SIX SIGMA

The initial purpose of Six Sigma as stated by Motorola[1] was to "institutionalize quality within every step of business." Many firms have adopted the basics of the Six Sigma process, aligning the details to fit best their own needs. In doing so, Six Sigma has evolved into a strategic business process that uses well-designed experiments to implement business strategy and leadership. The purpose of Six Sigma today is to institutionalize competitiveness in every step of the business. Manufacturing firms particularly need such a process because they must continuously improve to survive and prosper in the hypercompetitive world economy. Service firms and organizations can also benefit from the process.

Six Sigma differs from traditional total quality management (TQM) as shown in Table 1.1[1, 2, 3], through its direct emphasis on business strategy and high-level, executive ownership. However, both Six Sigma and TQM focus on problem prevention rather than simply fixing problems. Experts experienced in the Six Sigma methodology and allied statistical

1

Table 1.1 Six Sigma versus traditional TQM.[1]

Six Sigma	Traditional TQM
Executive ownership	Self-directed work teams
Business strategy execution system	Quality initiative
Truly cross functional	Largely within a single function
Focused on training with verifiable return on investment	No mass training in statistics and quality
Business results oriented	Quality oriented
Problem prevention	Problem prevention

techniques are called "Black Belts" and train others in the process and consult with cross-functional teams.[4] A vital element in getting the full benefits of Six Sigma is the involvement of the CEO and the willingness of the next CEO to continue the process. Six Sigma is not merely delegated but also practiced and led by the CEO. It requires leadership through example and deep commitment to prevent it from being another fad. The ongoing challenge to Six Sigma practitioners is to understand better how improvements in the product or service improve customer satisfaction and to quantify better how improvements in customer satisfaction impact the bottom-line metrics of price, market share, and cash flow.

Strategic experimentation (SE) frames the outcomes of product design and manufacturing experiments in terms of what CEOs understand: price, market share, and cash flow. It is an extension of Taguchi's seminal idea of using experimentation to discover how to reduce the loss function, which he defined as the sum of two terms, one being the variable cost and the other the cost of inferior quality.[5] However, all levels of design—system, subsystem, and component—are covered here within a single formalism, whereas Taguchi focused on component design. Moreover, the word *product* can almost always be replaced by the word *service* wherever it appears in the text. But SE is only a support tool. The shared skills and responsibilities of engineering, manufacturing, finance, marketing, sales, and service must be integrated into a cross-functional team for it to be effective. The team must acquire a common understanding of the steps involved in strategic experimentation and share a common definition of the fundamental and bottom-line metrics that together form the full set of strategic metrics.

Cross-functional teams represent collectively the full skill set needed to plan, build, and service new high-tech products. However, if the disciplinary boundaries are too sharp, the team will likely be less effective than if there is an overlap of skill sets. With high-tech products, the burden falls more heavily on the engineers on the team to broaden their business skills. The reason is that nonengineers on the team will likely find it more difficult to keep up with the rapidly advancing technology than it will be for the engineers to pick up key business-side skills, which are more stable over time.

Not surprisingly, there is a growing movement among engineers in academia in developing system science as a quantitative, holistic "science of breadth" that embraces, tests, and integrates new ideas from all fields. In other words, engineers need one foot planted firmly on the technology side of product development and the other planted just as firmly on the business side. Engineers having the ability to frame their new product concepts in terms of a solid, quantitative business case should find it easier to gain corporate approval to take the new technologies to production. Companies employing these engineers stand to benefit immensely because they should be able to bring products to market faster with higher customer value, lower costs, and higher profits.

The integration of business models with design of experiments is a theme that runs through the Design for Six Sigma (DFSS) treatments by Creveling, Slutsky, and Antis[2], by Yang and El-Haik[3], and this book. The two earlier books included business and innovation matters through overviews of Taguchi's method for robust design,[5] Quality Function Deployment (QFD),[6] axiomatic design,[7] TRIZ,[8] and Pugh's methodology.[9] TRIZ is an exciting process for sparking innovation in a systematic manner. Suh's axiomatic design provides foundations for good designs based upon two axioms, one being to design so that functional requirements are uncoupled (independent) and the other being to design to minimize information content. Both QFD and Pugh's methodology are tools for selecting the right subsystem alternatives from the collection of those available at the concept and system level of design.

These tools, when employed wisely, can be very useful in generating ideas and making trade-off decisions during product design and development. However, they stop short of delivering quantitative predictions of price, cash flow, and market share. This means that a crisp, quantitative feedback loop is not available to check the accuracy of the planning methodologies against what actually happened in the market. The lack of quantitative checks limits the discovery of how to improve the planning process.

1.2 THE FUNDAMENTAL METRICS

The approach taken here to product planning and development is to make trade-off decisions between alternative subsystems based upon quantitative assessments of cash flow. Forecasts are generated by assessing first the fundamental metrics of value, cost, and the pace of innovation for each proposed alternative. These results are used to project the confidence level that each proposed subsystem has for improving the bottom-line metrics. The forecast for the subsystems eventually chosen for production should be tested against the actual technical and financial performance of the product once in production. As stated above, feedback of this nature tests the model and the assumptions and opens the way for improving them. Such a process is fundamental to having a scientific basis for product planning and design.

The key to making trustworthy bottom-line forecasts is the set of algorithms used for forecasting product demand and price. The sticking point is that trustworthiness is based upon rigor, but practicality is not. Thus, a balance has to be struck between rigor and simplicity. For demand, the S-model[10] expression will be used, as it is transparent and simple yet rigorous in the limit when the demand differences between competing products is not large. For price, the classical pricing model of Cournot/Bertrand will be used. It predicts two features of most real markets, one being that prices will fall as the number of competitors increases and the other being that products of higher value will command a higher price, all other things being equal. The combined models for demand and price used here do not rule out the use of the support tools described in references [2] and [3]. Indeed, the S-model builds upon Taguchi's seminal ideas, and features of the model have been coupled to the QFD process.[11]

The value changes associated with proposed product improvements are determined from the "neutral price," the price of the alternative at which potential buyers are indifferent collectively between the alternative and the baseline. The neutral price is determined in a straightforward manner from marketing research and is rather insensitive to the details of the demand model. Values determined from the neutral price can be directly inserted into the S-model for demand or into the logit model[12] for market share when higher order terms are important.

Total quality is defined here as the net value of the product to society.[13] When defined in this manner, total quality management transcends the traditional aspects of TQM as described in Table 1.1 and becomes synonymous with management of the entire firm. At this point, TQM and Six Sigma become one. Improving total quality becomes fully consistent with improving cash flow provided that the firm meets governmental regulations in regard to environmental quality, workplace safety, financial disclosure, and accounting practices, which today are a prerequisite to remaining in business. The connections between the stakeholders are clear. To stay in business, the firm needs to offer products valued by customers. Prices should be affordable but sufficiently above costs to generate the cash flow needed to fund future product improvements and reward shareholders. Defining *total quality* as the net value to society is the inverse of Taguchi's definition of the quality loss to society[14] due to "functional variation and harmful side effects."

In a highly competitive marketplace, the following will always be true:

1. Value: The value of the product is too low.

2. Cost: Its cost is too high.

3. Innovation: The pace of innovation is too slow.

Success in a competitive marketplace is thus derived from timely and continuous improvement of the product's three fundamental metrics. If they are improved at a rate higher than that of major competitors, the desired bottom-line metrics will follow and the company will remain in business. The strategic metrics are divided into their fundamental and bottom-line components in Table 1.2.

Table 1.2   The strategic metrics are divided into fundamental and bottom-line.

Strategic Metrics	
Fundamental	**Bottom-line**
Value to customer	Cash flow
Cost (variable, fixed, investment)	Market share
Pace of innovation	Price
	Return on investment
	Internal rate of return
	Breakeven time

The direct outcomes of replicated laboratory experiments performed at the component and subsystem design or manufacturing levels represent measurements of the means and variances of the attributes selected for study. However, the impact on customer satisfaction and cost and, ultimately, cash flow can only be forecast by projecting how the "critical to value" (CTV) product attributes at the full system level are affected. (In automotive companies, subsystems such as engine, body, and chassis are often referred to as systems. Here they are defined as a subsystem, the system being the fully assembled vehicle.) Transfer functions, usually derived from a math model or laboratory test, connect outcomes measured at the component and subsystem level to changes in system level performance. Only when the results of a manufacturing or product experiment have been translated into changes in the CTV attributes can they be used to project changes in the value, cost, and cash flow.

1.3 MANAGING THE ENTERPRISE

An effective organization plans *and* executes well. However, its actions and reactions are almost exclusively governed by paradigms, which may work well in one business environment but not in another. Because the business environment changes over time, the organization must make timely paradigm shifts to remain competitive. The continuing search for higher and higher effectiveness in planning, designing, building, and servicing of new products can be viewed as a series of linked, never-ending experiments. This represents a continuous learning process for the firm and is illustrated in Figures 1.1 and 1.2, where a response surface representing the effectiveness contours of the organization at a particular point in time is shown as a function of two order parameters, ρ_1 and ρ_2. The order parameters represent things that management can manage. Too little order leads to chaos, but too much order leads to inaction as a result of an excessive number of rules that restrict timely response and innovation.

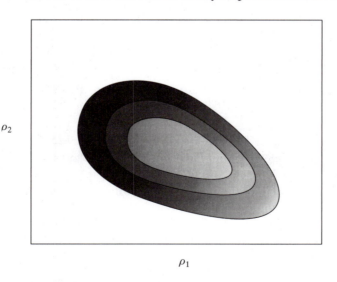

Figure 1.1   Effectiveness contours as a response surface, which is a function of two order
        parameters.

Source: Reprinted with permission from *Product Management: Value, Quality, Cost, Price, Profits, and Organization.* Amsterdam: Kluwer Academic Publishers, 1997.

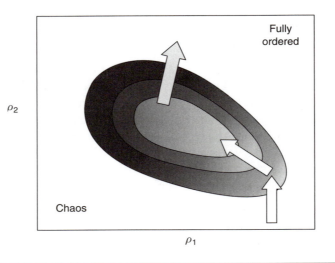

Figure 1.2 Path of two experiments to improve effectiveness. The maximum point moves over time.

Source: Reprinted with permission from *Product Management: Value, Quality Cost, Price, Profits, and Organization.* Amsterdam: Kluwer Academic Publishers, 1997.

The order parameters are not simply the attributes of the product being manufactured. For example, the order parameter ρ_2 could be the fraction of employees that are engineers and ρ_1 could be the fraction that are lawyers. In Figure 1.2, a sequence of arrows shows the progress of improvement made as the result of two experiments. Each experiment evaluated several paths and the one chosen was identified as best for improving the objective function. Initially, the organization was heavily involved with litigation over key patents. As a result of the experiments, the organization ended up with an increase in the fraction of engineers and a decrease in the fraction of lawyers as the patent positions were resolved. But the search for improving effectiveness never ends as the maximum moves over time. In this manner, the order parameters represent a general set of control factors whose strategic impact can be evaluated through designed experiments.

Unfortunately, changes in the business environment are seldom as simple and revealing as this example. Sometimes the right path is not recognized until it is too late to act or seen early enough but dismissed as being weak and unimportant because the experiment was not convincing due to its ad hoc nature or poor design. Often firms do not experiment but try to adopt what is working well for others without first testing the process on a local scale in their own environment. This is dangerous because a paradigm lifted from one company's environment may not work the same in another because of cultural and organizational differences.

As shown in Figure 1.3, the enterprise is managed by adjusting its order over time, which includes adjustments in its products, personnel, culture, organization, physical structure, core technologies, and core values. The nature of its order at any point determines how well the enterprise continuously improves the fundamental metrics of its products, which in turn drive the bottom line.

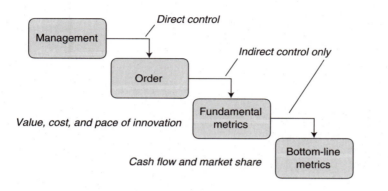

Figure 1.3   Management is three steps removed from managing the bottom line directly.

Source: Reprinted with permission from *Product Management: Value, Quality, Cost, Price, Profits, and Organization.* Amsterdam: Kluwer Academic Publishers, 1997.

To continuously develop and sell profitable products, the enterprise must clearly understand changing customer needs and react to them in a cost-effective and timely manner. Needs are quantified by establishing how customers value the CTV attributes of the product over its life cycle. An automobile, for example, has many attributes of importance to the customer, including the purchase experience and its levels of noise and vibration, operating costs, acceleration performance, visual appeal, roominess, ergonomics, resale price, and reliability. In setting out to improve one or more of these attributes, it is vital that planners and engineers measure the As-Is baseline attributes of the current vehicle. To arrive at consistent measurements of value, the proposed alternatives for a new product must be evaluated against the baseline. Moreover, every new product has a baseline no matter how innovative it is.

1.4 GUIDING DFSS/SE

1.4.1 The Coarse-grained DFSS/SE Roadmap

The task of developing a new product or service begins as an unstructured problem and the first step is to structure it by mapping the problem onto a solution template. The template shown in Figure 1.4[15] represents the coarse-grained roadmap which will be followed here as the guide for DFSS/SE. The customer and manufacturer loop on the right side starts with an identification of customer needs. These are coupled to the CTV attributes that best represent those needs. Marketing research is one of the major tools used to determine how customers value the improvements. The ongoing engineering challenge is to find cost effective ways to make the improvements that outdistance what competitors do.

The society and manufacturer loop on the left of Figure 1.4 introduces societal needs into the product realization process. Governmental requirements for the product, which extend over its life cycle from manufacture to disposal, controls much of what happens in this loop. The costs for meeting societal needs add to the overall cost for the product. It is essential, if the company is to remain in business, that its cash flow be sufficient to fund the development of new products to meet both customer and societal needs in the future.

In support of the DFSS/SE Roadmap are four key tasks that form the basis SE within the overall DFSS/SE structure:

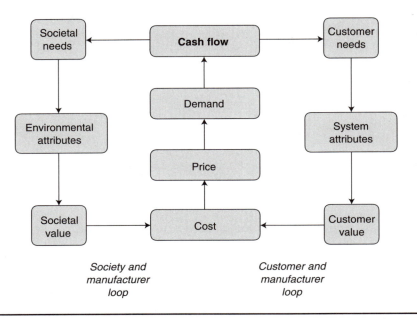

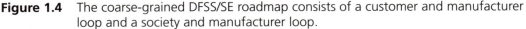

Figure 1.4 The coarse-grained DFSS/SE roadmap consists of a customer and manufacturer loop and a society and manufacturer loop.

Source: Res Eng Design 2001;13:42-52, reproduced with permission of Springer-Verlag London.

SE1: Setting financial targets

SE2: Multi-attribute value and cost analysis

SE3: Statistical analysis of designed experiments

SE4: Strategic analysis of designed experiments

The tasks are used collectively in traversing the two loops shown in Figure 1.4. The product plan sets the financial targets, SE1, which represent quantifiable bottom-line objectives. Multiattribute value and cost analysis, SE2, establishes the relationships between the CTV attributes and value and manufacturing cost. In task SE3, experiments are designed to show how new subsystem technologies affect these attributes. Value, cost, and investment are then combined to provide the confidence level for cash flow and return on investment, task SE4.

1.4.2 A Logical Management Process for DFSS/SE

The organization needs to have a work plan to follow the DFSS/SE Roadmap effectively. The plan must specify which part of the organization has the ultimate responsibility and authority for each waypoint in Figure 1.4.

The following is given as a logical management process for the generic organization structure shown in Figure 1.5 based upon a delineation of responsibility and authority along a system, subsystem, and component structure. The system organization has the responsibility for SE1, planning and setting financial targets for the product. The system organization is also responsible for SE2, multiattribute value and cost analysis, which entails assessing customer needs, identifying those needs in terms of the CTV attributes,

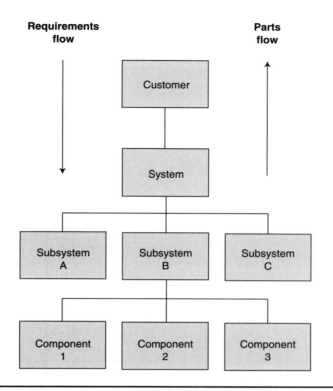

Requirements flow   **Parts flow**

Figure 1.5   A generic organization structure in which requirements flow sequentially from the customer to the system, subsystem, and component levels of design. The resulting flow of parts is also shown.

Source: Reprinted with permission from *Product Management: Value, Quality, Cost, Price, Profits, and Organization.* Amsterdam: Kluwer Academic Publishers, 1997.

and providing the algorithms for converting changes in the CTV attributes to value and cost. In addition, it has the responsibility and authority for final assembly, distribution, sales, and service. The system organization is supported by the subsystem organizations in assessing costs.

Each subsystem and component organization is responsible for the design of experiment tasks SE3 and SE4 associated with their own subsystems and components. The interrelationships between subsystems/components workflow and that for the system are outlined in Figure 1.6, the timeline being downward.

1.4.3 Descriptions of SE Tasks

The four SE tasks are coupled as shown in Figure 1.7. Also included are the chapter and section locations where the details of each task are discussed. Task SE1, the setting of financial targets, is listed first because of its criticality. Task SE2 generates the knowledge base for making trade-off decisions. Consequently, this task should be completed before tasks SE3 and SE4 are initiated and before SE1 is completed. The arrow from task SE2 to SE4 in Figure 1.7 represents the flow of information needed to convert the classical experimental outcomes from task SE3 to strategic outcomes. For example, task SE3 measures

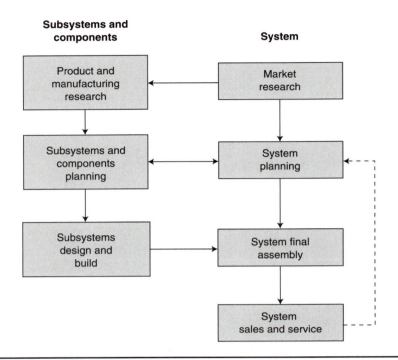

Figure 1.6 The interactions between component, subsystem, and system workflows that support the design and build of the system.

the mean and standard deviation of a CTV attribute relative to its baseline mean and standard deviation. Task SE4 converts these outcomes into the projected improvement in cash flow and its standard deviation using the marketing research information from SE2. Tasks SE2, SE3, and SE4 should be conducted, as already noted, in the research phase of product development.

The analyses of designed experiments are carried out here using a spreadsheet program, Excel. The primary reason is that there is no commercial software that will fully treat the new features introduced here as part of strategic experimentation. These include the following:

1. The *F* test method for assessing the influence of the factors on log variance, which is introduced in Chapter 9

2. The computations of the mean and variance for the strategic contrast between states, which are covered in Section 9.6

3. The determination of strategic significance of the factors on value and cash flow introduced in Chapter 10 using Monte Carlo simulation

The design and analysis of experiments are introduced here using a progression from Level 1 through Level 4 and covered, respectively, in Chapters 7 through 10. Dedicated, commercial design of experiment (DOE) software can be used to analyze the outcomes of Level 1, the assumption being that the population variance is constant for the trials.

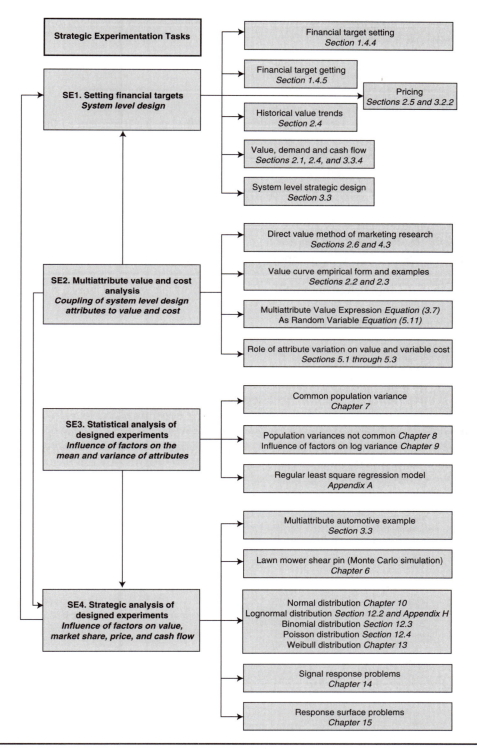

Figure 1.7   SE tasks and the locations within the text where discussed and applied.

Nevertheless, the spreadsheet is also used here for Level 1 to preserve continuity with Levels 2 through 4.

Level 2 relaxes the assumption that the populations have a common variance and incorporates Satterthwaite's method[16] for computing the degrees of freedom for sample variances measured in an experiment. The reason for this is that the assumption of a common population variance is highly unlikely to be correct because strategic experiments are robust design experiments, which search for factors that move the mean to the target *and* reduce variation. It follows that the statistical significance of the factors on both the mean and variance needs to be evaluated. This is covered in Level 3, which supports task SE3.

Level 4, which performs the strategic analysis of the statistical outcomes from Level 3, uses Monte Carlo simulation because accurate, simple statistical expressions are not available for assessing the confidence ranges in value and cash flow. Level 4 supports task SE4.

The burden of having to begin the analyses with a blank spreadsheet has been reduced considerably through the development of files termed Strategic Design Workbooks (SDWs) for many of the more commonly used experimental designs. Also, template files have been generated to lessen the effort in developing SDWs for other designs. These are discussed in Appendix F, and are included on the CD-ROM with this book.

1.4.4 Financial Target Setting

The flow diagram, Figure 1.8, for developing a new product's financial targets, task SE1, begins with situation analysis, which includes the study of the sales and value trends for the products competing in the segment and a projection of where these products are likely to be in the future. Target setting follows a direction opposite to the arrows shown in Figure 1.4, the first target being annual cash flow, A, which is constrained by investment level, M, and annual fixed cost, F_{Cost}. The total investment M is treated here like a mortgage paid out over the planning horizon, Y_{RS}, in years. Once the cash-flow target is set, *tentative* targets are set for annual demand (D); market share (m), and price (P).

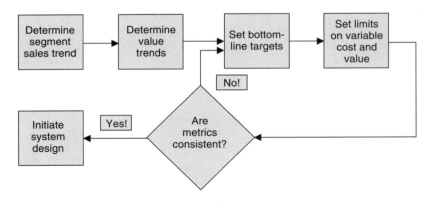

Figure 1.8 Flow diagram for situation analysis and financial target setting.

With the desired bottom-line targets in place, it follows from the equations for demand and cash flow that the *variable cost* must satisfy a lesser-than consistency relation in terms of the bottom-line metrics given by[17]

$$C \leq P - \frac{F_{Cost} + [M / Y_{RS}] + A}{D} \tag{1.1}$$

and that the *value* of the product to the customer must satisfy a greater-than consistency relationship given by

$$V \geq P + \frac{N\bar{P}[1 + m]}{[N + 1]E_2} \tag{1.2}$$

where N is the number of products competing against each other in the segment and $\bar{P}$ is their average price. The coefficient E_2 is the price elasticity of average demand when the prices of the N products are changed simultaneously by the same amount. At this juncture, the limiting conditions on variable cost and value need to be assessed to see if they are achievable. In other words, can the new technologies from research be integrated collectively into a new product that will deliver the bottom-line targets? If not, the targets need to be adjusted or the technologies improved.

Equation (1.1) or its equivalent is widely used for setting the target for variable cost. Equation (1.2) is relatively new, however, and therefore unfamiliar to many product planners. It is needed because the targets for demand and cash flow cannot be assured simply by setting a target price and target variable cost. The reason is that demand is controlled by price *and* value, not just price alone. Moreover, it is not just the price and value of the proposed new product that is of interest, as demand for a given product is also influenced by the prices and values of the $N–1$ products competing against it. Thus, in generating the financial plan for a new product, a careful assessment must be made of what competitors are likely to do and how the product plan should be positioned in response.

In deciding between several proposed alternatives for a new product, the full range of their projected cash flows over time need to be considered. The metric used for this is either breakeven time, or net present value (NPV), or internal rate of return (IRR). Breakeven time is the time period, *BE*, at which the sum of cash flows $A_{(j)}$ over time from $j = 0$ to BE goes from being negative, due to the investments needed to develop and tool the product, to zero:

$$\sum_{j=0}^{BE} A(j) = 0 \tag{1.3}$$

where

$$A(j) = D(j)[P(j) - C(j)] - F_{Cost}(j) - [M / Y_{RS}] \tag{1.4}$$

Breakeven time is widely used for its simplicity. Net present value is the discounted cash flow given by

$$NPV = \sum_{j=0}^{Y_{RS}} \left[\frac{A(j)}{[1 + I_R]^j} \right] \tag{1.5}$$

where I_R is the interest rate. The internal rate of return I_{RR} is the rate that makes the discounted cash flow over the product's time horizon equal to zero:

$$0 = \sum_{j=0}^{Y_{RS}} \left[\frac{A(j)}{\left[1+I_{RR}\right]^j} \right] \tag{1.6}$$

The I_{RR} can be considered as the projected interest that will be earned on the investment needed to design, build, assemble, and distribute the proposed new product. Both NPV and IRR are readily computed from spreadsheet functions. Although Equations (1.3), (1.5), and (1.6) evaluate the time value of cash flow, they do not convey directly the importance of speed to the product development process. In order to sustain cash flow over time, it is necessary that the product's universal metric, defined as[18]

$$U \equiv \frac{\delta(V-C)}{\delta t} \tag{1.7}$$

be equal to or greater than the universal metric for its best competitor in which δt is the time between product introductions; its reciprocal, $1/\delta t$, is the pace of innovation. Certain companies, Toyota being an excellent example,[19] excel at driving up value with high quality, driving down cost by reducing waste, and increasing the pace of innovation by reducing lead time.[20] Note that Equation (1.7) does not identify any of the three fundamental metrics as being more important than the others. There are constraints on applying Equation (1.7), however. The resulting price of the product has to remain affordable to the targeted buyer, and the investment and fixed costs have to be such that cash flow is positive. With these constraints, the universal metric guides the product development process such that the rate of cash flow over time, given by $\delta A/\delta t$, is both positive and sustainable.

1.4.5 Financial Target Getting

Once the targets for the bottom-line and fundamental metrics have been set, the next step is to discover how to select and integrate the subsystems so that the end product meets the targets through innovations in its design and manufacture. Ideally, strategic experiments for assessing new technology and new subsystems are run in the product and manufacturing research phase (see Figure 1.6), of new product development, well in advance of the setting of final system level requirements for the product. The results of task SE4 can be used by subsystem planners in assessing which of the new proposed subsystem alternatives are most promising. These can be transmitted to the system level planners for their assessment as to how the proposed new subsystems fit into the overall plan. Marketing research will have already transmitted information on customer needs to those responsible for the system and those responsible for the subsystems, so the entire organization should be on the same page in regard to customer needs and how value is generated.

Those people responsible for the system design act as the internal customer to the subsystem providers, which may be units within or outside the enterprise. As an internal customer, they transmit key subsystem requirements to the subsystem providers who in turn transmit key component requirements to component suppliers. Once the requirements are agreed to by all parties, the product plan can be approved, funded, and targeted for production. Ideally, at this juncture, all of the strategic experiments have been run and a projection has been made of cash flow and market share at a projected confidence level that meets the corporate guidelines for such investments. At a later specified time, subsystems flow to the system level for final assembly and delivery to the customer.

1.4.6 Process Analysis

Most managers feel that they have a good understanding of the existing design, validation, manufacturing, service, and business processes. However, when given the opportunity to fully review a process in detail, they may find their knowledge faulty if a mechanism for routinely mapping and updating all design and build processes has not been in place. Such maps (see Figure 1.9), represent the As-Is conditions for the interconnected tasks. Each task receives input and converts it into output, which becomes input to the next task. Those responsible for each task should have the responsibility of setting the requirements for the input to the task. The nature of the input, output, and tools required to do each task in a process need to be documented along with the details of the steps involved. Not only do the "whats" of the process need documentation, but so do the "whys," which explain the rationale for the actions.

Each task also has constraints or controls placed upon it by physical laws, corporate rules, and governmental regulations, and they too need to be described. Transfer functions for projecting the changes in the CTV attributes resulting from changes at the component and subsystem level need to be developed and verified. The firm needs an efficient and effective process for learning and translating what has been learned into practice on a continuous basis.

The full description of the sequence of tasks used for an existing design or manufacturing process is often called the "standard work" for the process.[21] The recipe provided by the

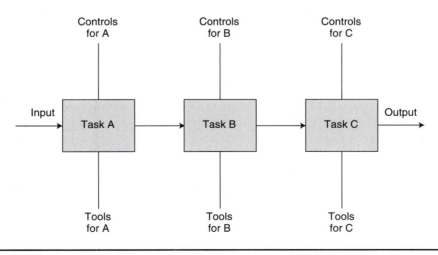

Figure 1.9 The interrelated task structure for a design, manufacturing, or business process.

standard work document is to be followed, as it represents the current best practice. Any proposed change to standard work needs to be fully validated before the proposal is accepted. The standard work document does not inhibit innovation but actually promotes innovation by fully describing the current best practice, readily exposing current practice to a critical assessment as to where its weaknesses are and thus where improvements are needed.

1.5 SUMMARY

Problem definition and its unchanging nature: In a highly competitive market, the current product will always be too low in value, too high in cost and its pace of innovation too slow. These represent the three fundamental metrics that must be continuously developed to drive the bottom-line metrics successfully.

System level action plan: The plan begins with an As-Is analysis of the strategic metrics, both fundamental and bottom line. It is imperative for the company to have agreed upon definitions and methods measuring the fundamental and bottom-line metrics. Standards are also needed for defining the system level attributes and the procedure for their measurement. Once these are in place, a host of important questions need to be answered: "What is the value trend of the product over time versus competition? What is the trend for variable cost over time, and how does the trend compare to the cost trends for the competition? What are the trends in cash flow and market share? What actions might competitors take to improve their products and reduce their costs? What should your response be? Given all of this, what should the total value of the new product be, and what CTV attributes need to be improved to achieve it? What must the targets for cost and investment be for the company to have high confidence that the targets for cash flow and market share will be met? What processes can be improved to reduce cost and speed up the pace of innovation?" These questions can be best answered using the risk management capability embodied in strategic experimentation.

Transmit requirements: The system plan is not complete until the set of requirements is transmitted to the subsystem providers and agreed upon by them. Subsystem providers need to develop the subsystem plan and transmit the key component-level specifications to the component providers. The set of requirements that flow from the system to the subsystem and component providers is not complete at any level. Included are only those specifications that assure with high confidence that the system-level requirements will be met by ensuring that the subsystems will work in harmony in bringing value to the customer at an affordable price.

Validation: New designs and processes at every level—system, subsystem, and component—need to be designed and built to validated processes. The current best practice or "standard work" for design and process activities should be documented and followed.

Produce: Controls must be in place during production to ensure that design and process intent is met continually. Problems should be prevented, and those that arise need to be resolved effectively and quickly.

Learn: Discrepancies between projections and actual performance, both good and bad, need to be understood by identifying the root causes for the differences. Document what has been learned with high confidence, what has been learned with moderate confidence, and what is still fuzzy but important to better understand. Things learned with high confidence need to be added to the enterprise's core body of knowledge and used to improve the bottom-line performance for the next product.

REFERENCES

1. M. Barney. May 2002. "Motorola's Second Generation," *Six Sigma Forum Magazine* 1, pp. 13–16.
2. C. M. Creveling, J. L. Slutsky, and D. Antis Jr. 2003. *Design for Six Sigma in Technology and Product Development*. Upper Saddle River, NJ: Prentice Hall.
3. K. Yang and B. El-Haik. 2003. *Design for Six Sigma: A Roadmap for Product Development*. New York: McGraw Hill.
4. *Certified Six Sigma Black Belt (CSSBB) Primer*. West Terre Haute, IN: Quality Council of Indiana, 2002.
5. G. Taguchi and Y. Wu. 1980. *Introduction to Off-line Quality Control*. Nagoya, Japan: Central Japan Quality Association.
6. Y. Akio (ed.). 1990. *Quality Function Deployment*. Cambridge, MA: Productivity Press.
7. N. Suh. 1990. *The Principles of Design*. New York: Oxford University Press.
8. G. Altschuller. 1999. *The Innovative Algorithm*. Worcester, PA: Technical Innovation Center.
9. S. Pugh. 1991. *Total Design: Integrated Methods for Successful Product Engineering*. Reading, MA: Addison-Wesley.
10. H. E. Cook. 1997. *Product Management: Value, Quality, Cost, Price, Profits, and Organization*. Amsterdam: Kluwer Academic Publishers (formerly Chapman & Hall, hereafter Kluwer).
11. H. E. Cook. 2000. *Enlarging QFD to Include Forecasts of Market Share and Profit in Making Trade-offs,* Transactions of the 12th QFD Symposium, Novi, MI. Ann Arbor, MI: QFD Institute, pp. 318–334.
12. M. Ben-Akiva and S. R. Lerman. 1985. *Discrete Choice Analysis: Theory and Applications to Travel Demand*. Cambridge, MA: MIT Press.
13. H. E. Cook and R. E. DeVor. 1991. "On Competitive Manufacturing Enterprises I: The S-Model and the Theory of Quality," *Manufacturing Review* 4:2, pp. 96–105.
14. M. S. Phadke, *Quality Engineering Using Robust Design*. 1989. Upper Saddler River, NJ: Prentice Hall, p. 4.
15. H. E. Cook and A. Wu. 2001. "On the Valuation of Goods and Selection of the Best Design Alternative," *Research in Engineering Design* 13, pp. 42–54.
16. F. E. Satterthwaite. 1946. "An Approximate Distribution of Estimates of Variance Components," *Biometrics Bulletin* 2, pp. 110–114.
17. H. E. Cook. 1997. *Product Management: Value, Quality, Cost, Price, Profits, and Organization*. Amsterdam: Kluwer, pp. 162–163.
18. Ibid., pp. 125–27.
19. S. Spear and H. K. Bowen. September–October 1999. "Decoding the DNA of the Toyota Production System," *Harvard Business Review,* pp. 96–106.
20. B. Bremner and C. Dawson. November 17, 2003. "Can Anything Stop Toyota?" *Business Week,* pp. 114–122.
21. H. K. Bowen. 2004. "Pratt & Whitney: Engineering Standard Work," *Harvard Business School Case* N2-604-084.

2

Product Value and Demand

Insight: Value to the customer can be estimated using marketing research techniques or economic analysis, depending upon the nature of the CTV attribute. A $1 increase in value has the same influence on demand as a $1 decrease in price.

Key Topics

value curves	direct value method of marketing research
values of automotive attributes and features	product demand
	S-model
historical value trends	logit model

There exist several definitions of value. Value engineers define *value* as functional worth divided by cost.[1] An object's utility, which can be computed using a lottery,[2] is often used as a measure of its value. Taguchi's "cost of inferior quality" is a measure of the loss in value due to a product specification being off its ideal point.[3] As mentioned in Chapter 1 and discussed in more detail in what follows, a phenomenological definition of value is used here based upon the S-model.[4] It allows value to be defined with minimal ambiguity and measured using straightforward marketing research methods. It also allows a computation of the total value of each of the products competing against one another from their demand and price trends. It is particularly important to document the value change when a product undergoes a major redesign to see if it is in line with the projections made and, if not, to ask why not.

2.1 MONOPOLY

The case of a monopoly is used to illustrate these concepts. Annual demand, D, is assumed to be a function of the value, V, of the product and its price, P:

$$D = f(V, P) \qquad (2.1)$$

If D is an analytic function of the two variables, it can be expanded in terms of a Taylor series about the demand, value, and price for the baseline or reference state defined as D_0, V_0, and P_0, respectively. When only the linear terms are kept, Equation (2.1) becomes:

$$D = K(V - P) \tag{2.2}$$

in the vicinity of D_0, V_0, and P_0. The negative slope of demand with price is given by $K = D_0 / [V_0 - P_0]$ for a monopoly. If value is held at its baseline level, V_0, and price increased toward the so-called reservation price, P_{RES}, where the linear demand function goes to zero, the reservation price is seen to equal to V_0, according to the phenomenological theory. Of course, the demand curve is likely not linear, in which case V_0 acts as a marginal quantity in that, if price changes by a large amount, value will also change. This does not usually pose a serious problem, as product prices and values are seldom changed by a large amount at any one time. The reason why value acts as a marginal quantity in practice is straightforward. When the price of a product is low, the product will have a variety of uses, many of them being marginal in the sense that if price increases by a significant amount those uses would be eliminated. Water is a good example. If it is cheap, we will water the lawn and wash the dog. If it is dear, we will use it to sustain life and not much else. The value of water is watered down when it is cheap!

The relationship between demand and value given by Equation (2.2) has been checked using the simulated purchase of two lottery tickets (Figure 2.1).[5] One ticket offered a 50% chance of winning $100 and the other offered an 80% chance of winning $100. The simulated demand curves for the two tickets are shown for a range of prices where the fractional demand was below 25%. The price intercepts at zero demand are near their respective expected economic values. Note that there was a risk taker for both tickets who offered more than the expected economic values. This discrepancy occurred at a very weak demand level, which would be of little interest for a real product. Figure 2.1 shows, as expected from Equation (2.2), that an increase in value shifts the demand curve. As long as the value change is relatively small, the change in the slope, $-K$, can be ignored.

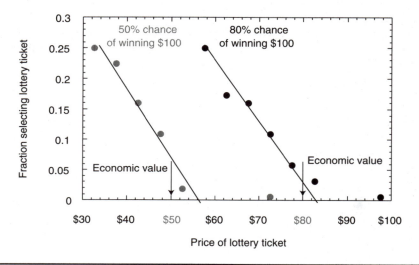

Figure 2.1   Demand curves for the simulated purchase of two lottery tickets.

Source: Res Eng Design 2001;13:42-52. Reproduced with permission of Springer-Verlag London.

2.2 VALUE CURVES AND THE COST OF INFERIOR QUALITY

2.2.1 Framing a Simple Strategic Problem: Filling a Cereal Box

Strategic problems are best framed around the fundamental metrics and how they couple to the bottom-line metrics. For illustration, consider the problem of filling a container with a quantity of oatmeal for consumer purchase. There are two basic ways in which the container can be filled. The customer can fill a bag from a bulk storage container at the grocery, or the cereal provider can fill a box at the processing plant.

When the customer fills the container, it is weighed at check-out and the customer pays according to the *exact* weight of oatmeal in the bag, which represents one of several CTV attributes associated with the purchase of the cereal. The value, price, and cost relationship for this activity is shown in Figure 2.2. Cost represents the variable cost, C, to the cereal provider to generate the product. For simplicity, assume that the cereal provider also owns the store, which eliminates the middleman.

When the cereal provider fills the container, the customer pays for the *nominal* weight of oatmeal in the container with the price of the oatmeal fixed (Figure 2.3). Variation in the filling process causes some boxes to be underweight and some overweight. If the weight is below target, customers receive less value and demand is reduced, as there is no reduction in price to compensate for the loss of oatmeal in the box. On the other hand, if the weight on average is above the target level, demand goes up but the net revenue per box sold, given by $P - C$, goes down because cost is higher. The behavior of demand and profit as a function of weight is shown schematically in Figure 2.4. The maximum in profit is obtained when the weight is exactly on target, g_0. Thus it follows from Figure 2.4 that variation about the nominal weight results in a loss of profit due to the fact that price was fixed.

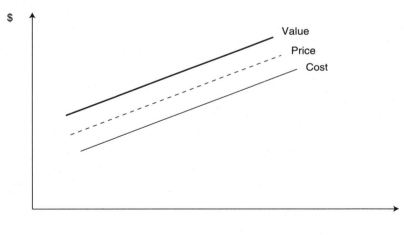

Figure 2.2   Value, price, and cost relationship for oatmeal filled and purchased in bulk by the customer.

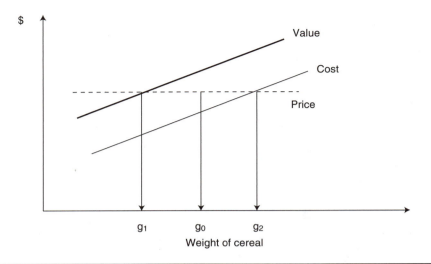

Figure 2.3 Value, price, and cost relationship for oatmeal filled by cereal provider.

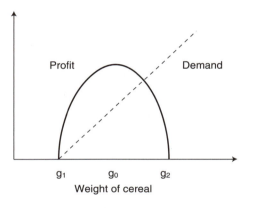
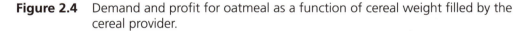

Figure 2.4 Demand and profit for oatmeal as a function of cereal weight filled by the cereal provider.

The value relationship shown in Figure 2.2 is a straight line. For many products, value will be concave with respect to the CTV attributes due to diminishing returns. If the value of a box of oatmeal as a function of its weight were fully explored, a concave value function with diminishing returns would likely also be found for several reasons—the customer has restricted storage space at home, the weight of the box becomes difficult to carry, and there is a finite shelf life for the product. As discussed in Chapter 5, variation of an attribute about its mean will reduce the average value of the product to the customer whenever the value function is concave.

2.2.2 An Empirical Form for Value Curves

If a CTV attribute g is continuous over a given range, for example the level of noise inside a car or the weight of a cell phone, the value of the product can be expressed as $V = V(g)$. If the baseline value of the product is V_0, then a *dimensionless value coefficient*

$$v(g) = \frac{V(g)}{V_0} \tag{2.3}$$

can be constructed to show the fractional value relative to the baseline. The functional relationship can usually be expressed empirically as

$$v(g) = f_V^\gamma \tag{2.4}$$

where

$$f_V = \left[\frac{\left[g_I - g_C \right]^2 - \left[g_I - g \right]^2}{\left[g_I - g_C \right]^2 - \left[g_I - g_0 \right]^2} \right] \tag{2.5}$$

represents a parabolic form as a function of the attribute g. The parameter γ in Equation (2.4) exponentially weights the parabolic form. The term g_I is the ideal specification for the attribute where value is a maximum; g_C is the critical specification where value goes to zero; and g_0 is the baseline specification (the mean value of the baseline attribute). The ideal and critical points can be estimated from human factor studies, from intuition, or from surveys, depending upon the nature of the CTV attribute.

When the natural logs of both sides of Equation 2.4 are taken, the expression becomes

$$Ln\left(\frac{V(g)}{V_0} \right) = \gamma Ln \left[\frac{\left[g_I - g_C \right]^2 - \left[g_I - g \right]^2}{\left[g_I - g_C \right]^2 - \left[g_I - g_0 \right]^2} \right] \tag{2.6}$$

It is possible using the direct value (DV) method described in Section 2.6 to determine $V(g)$ at discrete points $g = g(1), g(2),\ldots$ Thus the slope computed from a plot of $Ln(V(g)/V_0)$ versus

$$Ln\left\{ \left[\left[g_I - g_C \right]^2 - \left[g_I - g \right]^2 \right] / \left[\left[g_I - g_C \right]^2 - \left[g_I - g_0 \right]^2 \right] \right\}$$

over the attribute points at $g = g(1), g(2),\ldots$yields an estimate of the exponential weighting coefficient, γ, *which is expected to be approximately equal to the fraction of time that the attribute is important during the use of the product.*

The use of estimated ideal and critical points extends value curves beyond the range of measurements obtained by the DV method. The reason for doing this is not to enlarge the applicable range of the value curves but to provide better estimates for the weighting coefficient γ and the second derivative of the curve, which is important in estimating the loss in value when variation is present.

Value curves can be divided into three general types depending upon the position of the maximum in the curve. If it occurs at $g_I = 0$ and the attribute cannot be negative, it is known as a smaller is better (SIB) attribute. If the maximum is at $g_I = \infty$, it is known as a larger is better (LIB) attribute. If it occurs at a finite level, it is known as a nominal is best (NIB) attribute. Larger is better attributes, x, are usually converted to $g \equiv 1/x$, which transforms the value curve into the SIB form.

2.2.3 Cost of Inferior Quality

In their insightful discussion of the theory of quality and robust design, Taguchi and Wu[3] defined a quality loss function $L(g)$ as a sum of two functions, the cost of inferior quality (CIQ), $\Omega(g)$, and variable cost, $C(g)$:

$$L(g) = \Omega(g) + C(g) \qquad (2.7)$$

For a single attribute, they assumed that the CIQ was a parabolic function of g having a minimum equal to zero at $g = g_I$. As shown by Cook and DeVor,[6] the CIQ for an attribute can be defined in terms of the attribute's value curve from the relation:

$$\Omega(g) = V_I - V(g) \qquad (2.8)$$

where $V_I (= V(g_I))$ is the ideal (maximum) value for the attribute at $g = g_I$. (A graphical expression of this relationship is shown in Figure 5.2.)

The connection provided by Equation (2.8) between the CIQ and value is important for two reasons. First, it is a more general expression for computing $\Omega(g)$ than Taguchi's parabolic model. Second, it allows consideration of the full scope of the issues involved in planning and designing a new product including the making of complex trade-off decisions at the system and subsystem design levels involving potentially large variable cost and investment implications. By contrast, Taguchi focused on component design, a task where investment considerations are often not important. He also stressed evaluating only those component design alternatives that were variable cost neutral or a cost reduction.

2.3 EXAMPLES OF VALUE CURVES

2.3.1 Value of Acceleration Performance

The normalized value curve for vehicle acceleration is shown in Figure 2.5.[7] A baseline plus two other value points were determined from a DV survey in which respondents drove three vehicles through an urban test route 10 miles in length. The vehicles were identical except for their acceleration performance. A monitor rode with each respondent to provide the locations where the vehicle was to accelerate and decelerate from one speed to another at a rate determined by the respondent.

The value curve is seen to go to zero at 40 seconds, which was taken as the critical specification, as the vehicle was deemed so slow as to be unsafe for merging into freeway

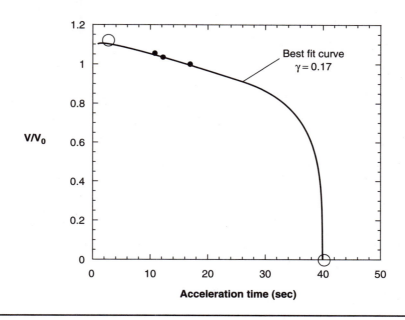

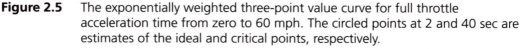

Figure 2.5   The exponentially weighted three-point value curve for full throttle acceleration time from zero to 60 mph. The circled points at 2 and 40 sec are estimates of the ideal and critical points, respectively.

Source: Reprinted with permission from SAE paper No. 960004 ca. 1996 SAE International.

traffic. The variable g was taken to be the logarithm of the reciprocal of the acceleration time with the belief that the driver senses the acceleration force as a psychometric variable. The ideal specification for the value of acceleration was taken as 2 seconds as the discomfort of the acceleration force of approximately $1g$ was seen as outweighing family sedan performance beyond this point.

Although the x axis in Figure 2.5 is the time t_{Accel} for the vehicle to accelerate from 0 to 60 mph at full throttle, $Ln(t_{Accel})$ was used for the CTV attribute in Equation (2.5) and the computation of the weighting coefficient in Equation (2.6). The log function was chosen based upon the assumption that a force acting upon the human body is experienced as a psychometric variable.

With these estimates, the empirical weighting coefficient γ for acceleration was found to be 0.17, as computed from the slope of the plot of Equation (2.6). This value for γ was discovered to be quite close to the amount of time the respondents on average spent accelerating while driving the test route, which suggests that the choice of the critical and ideal attributes were reasonable. The dimensionless acceleration value curve for sports cars is expected to have a higher γ.

In Figure 2.6, published acceleration times from 0 to 60 mph at full throttle are plotted against the ratio of horsepower to weight (in pounds) of the vehicles (all were V-6s). This plot represents the transfer function for connecting the ratio of horsepower/weight to a CTV attribute proportional to the force felt by the customer on full throttle acceleration. Figure 2.6 can be used in conjunction with Figure 2.5 to generate the relationship between value of acceleration performance and horsepower to weight, Figure 2.7. Changes, of course, in horsepower to weight also influence other CTV attributes such as fuel economy, handling, brake lining life, tire life and so forth.

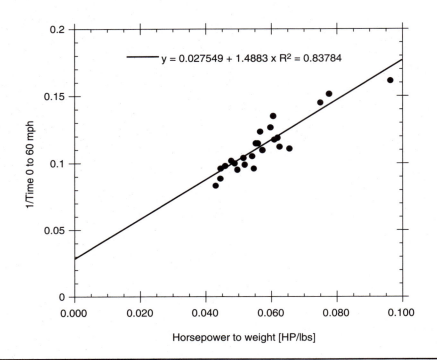

Figure 2.6   Plot of reciprocal 0 to 60 mph time versus horsepower to weight for V-6s.

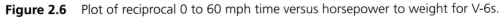

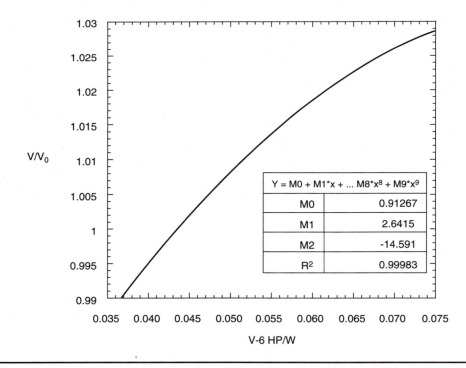

Figure 2.7   Normalized vehicle value due to changes in acceleration performance as a function of horsepower to weight (in pounds).

2.3.2 Value of Interior Noise

The normalized value curve for vehicle interior noise is shown in Figure 2.8.[8] The points on the curve were determined from a DV survey in which respondents wore headphones and could switch between listening to the noise level of the baseline vehicle, which was fixed at 66 dBA, and the noise of the alternative vehicle, which was identical except for its noise level. The noise of the alternative was set at 11 different levels from 55 to 78 dBA. The value difference from baseline was determined from the neutral price determined for each noise level. The critical specification was taken as 110 dBA as human factor studies have shown that this is the threshold of pain. The ideal specification was taken as 40 dBA as human factor studies have shown that individuals sense the environment as being too quiet below this level.[9]

The exponential weighting coefficient determined from the slope of $Ln(V(g)/V_0)$ versus $Ln(f_V)$ was found to be 0.59. The fraction of time that persons drive at highway speeds is approximately 0.4, according to the EPA. So there is rough agreement between this fraction of time and γ estimated from survey results.

Audible noise represents unwanted sounds; other sounds can be desirable. For example, during full throttle acceleration of a sports car a "throaty" sound may be preferred, and similarly a special sound may be valued during engine/transmission braking and during the closure of a door. Such sounds are more complex than the white noise evaluated in Figure 2.8 and will generally not be amenable to a value assessment in terms of a continuous, physical parameter. Nevertheless the value differences in the sound quality of different exhaust/muffler designs during acceleration, for example, can be evaluated versus a baseline condition using

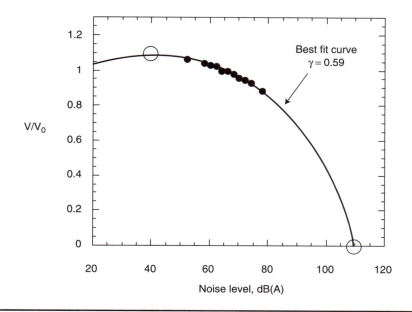

Figure 2.8 The exponentially weighted three-point value curve for interior noise at 70 mph. The circled points at 40 and 110 dBA are estimates of the ideal and critical points, respectively, taken from published human factor studies.

Source: Reprinted with permission from SAE paper No. 980621 ca. 1998 SAE International.

the DV method. In addition, it is also important to evaluate the interior noise levels for the different mufflers while cruising as they will also influence this attribute.

2.3.3 Value of Fuel Economy

The respondents who participated in the vehicle acceleration survey also responded to questions designed to assess the value of fuel economy over the range of g_{FE} from 18 to 26 mpg versus a baseline level of $g_{FE,0} = 22$ mpg. The findings could be fitted to a discounted cash-flow model having a time period of $Y_D = 7$ years and a discount rate I_D of 5%. Two assumptions were that respondents drove an average of 12,000 miles per year and paid $1.20 per gallon for fuel. The annual flow of value V_{FE} to the customer associated with fuel economy is given by

$$V_{FE}(g) = -\Phi P_{fuel} / g_{FE} \qquad (2.9)$$

where Φ is the average number of miles driven per year and P_{fuel} is the price of fuel in $ per gallon. The general model for discounted cash flow for the value added due to improvements in fuel economy relative to a baseline fuel economy level of $g_{FE,0}$ is given by[10]

$$\Delta V_{FE} = \Phi P_{fuel} \left[\frac{1}{g_{FE,0}} - \frac{1}{g_{FE}} \right] \sum_{i=1}^{Y_D} \frac{1}{[1+I_D]^i} \qquad (2.10)$$

For simplicity, the cash flow is assumed to take place at the end of each year. With the assumptions for Φ, P_{fuel}, and $g_{FE,0}$, Equation (2.10) was used to obtain the parameters for I_D by adjusting and I_D with $Y_D = 7$ in trial-and-error fashion to achieve a best fit to the values from DV survey. By having the value curves for both fuel economy and acceleration, the classic trade-off between the two attributes can be evaluated. For example, the value of improved acceleration performance of a new engine can be evaluated vis-à-vis its reduction in fuel economy value for a projected range of fuel prices in the future.

2.3.4 Value of Seating Capacity

The value of seating capacity has been estimated relative to the seating capacity of a five-passenger sedan using the expression[11]

$$\frac{V(C_P)}{V(C_P = 5)} = \frac{\displaystyle\sum_{j=1}^{C_P} jt_j}{\displaystyle\sum_{j=1}^{5} jt_j} \qquad (2.11)$$

in which j is the number of passengers and t_j is the fraction of time on average that persons occupy a vehicle.

Table 2.1 Fractional occupation times.

Number of occupants	Time fraction for occupancy
1	0.671
2	0.216
3	0.065
4	0.031
5	0.0113
6	0.0039

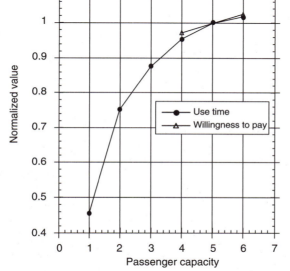

Figure 2.9 Normalized vehicle value versus passenger capacity, the value of a five passenger vehicle being taken as equal to unity.

Source: Reprinted with permission from SAE paper 960002 ca. 1996 SAE International.

Table 2.1 lists the empirical values for t_j.[12] The dimensionless value curve for the fractional added value of going from a 4- to a 6-passenger vehicle in Figure 2.9[11] shows that there is a reasonable agreement between the two slopes.

2.3.5 Value of Interior Room

If all other factors are held constant, the value of a vehicle will increase if one or more of the interior dimensions are increased to accommodate better leg room, shoulder room, or head room. No other attribute is assumed to change. For example, the value curve for shoulder room is constructed assuming that overall vehicle width does not change, even though this may be physically impossible if a large change in shoulder room is made. The value for changing both attributes would be computed from their respective value curves using the multi-attribute expression given in Chapter 3 in Equation 3.1.

The value for improving interior room has been estimated using empirical forms for the value functions in conjunction with the known frequency distributions for the key dimensions of the adult human body. The process used for estimating the value of legroom is shown schematically in Figure 2.10. The value function is equal to unity (its maximum) for persons, whose leg dimension is equal to or less than the legroom, L, in the vehicle. Persons whose legs are longer than L are cramped and value falls off gradually going to zero at some critical dimension beyond L. A schematic of the population distribution is also shown in Figure 2.10. For this particular vehicle, only a small fraction of the population, given by the integral under the distribution curve from minus infinity to L, could be satisfied with the legroom provided. A similar process was used for estimating the value of headroom and shoulder room.

The SAE standard for key interior seating dimensions are shown schematically in Figure 2.11. These dimensions are reported by the manufacturers using the 95% male mannequin and can be obtained from various manufacturing associations.

Examples of value curves estimated in this manner are shown in Figure 2.12 through Figure 2.16 for headroom, legroom, rear knee room, two-person shoulder room, and three-person shoulder room, respectively. The curves are directional only. Moreover, adjustments to the reported dimensions need to be made for legroom, knee room, and headroom. The original papers by Simek and Cook[11] and by Phillipart et al.[13] should be consulted for details.

A more rigorous way to determine the value curves for interior room would be to run the DV survey using an adjustable seating buck. The directional curves provided here should be useful in selecting the price for the alternative seating dimensions versus the baseline.

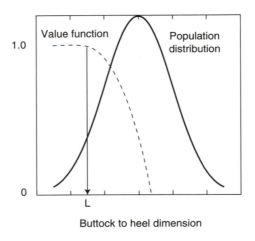

Figure 2.10   Schematic representation of the process used to estimate the value of leg room.

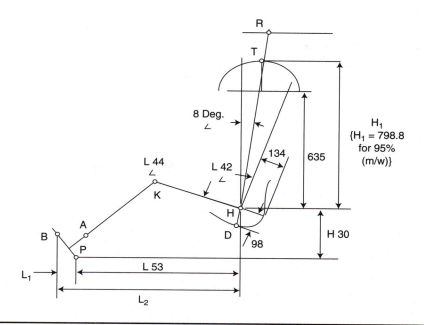

Figure 2.11 Seating dimensions for SAE standard using the seated mannequin.
Source: Reprinted with permission from SAE paper 960002 ca. 1996 SAE International.

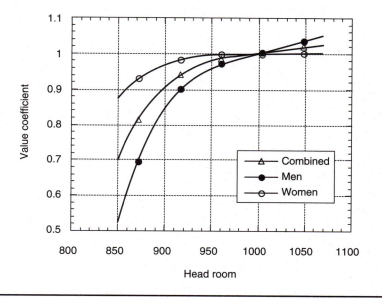

Figure 2.12 Value of headroom.
Source: Reprinted with permission from SAE paper 960002 ca. 1996 SAE International.

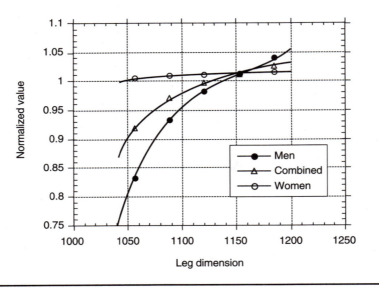

Figure 2.13   Value of front legroom.

Source: Reprinted with permission from SAE paper 960002 ca. 1996 Society of Automotive Engineers.

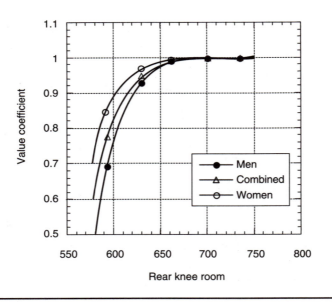

Figure 2.14   Value of rear knee room.

Source: Reprinted with permission from SAE paper 960002 ca. 1996 SAE International.

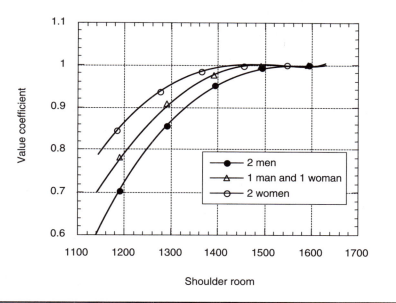

Figure 2.15 Value of shoulder room for two persons.

Source: Reprinted with permission from SAE paper 960002 ca. 1996 SAE International.

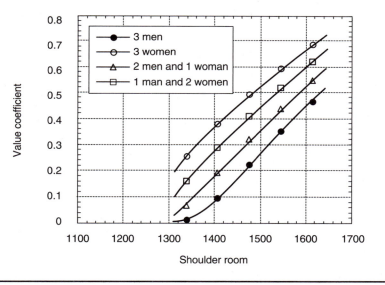

Figure 2.16 Value of shoulder room for three persons.

Source: Reprinted with permission from SAE paper 960002 ca. 1996 SAE International.

2.3.6 Value of Reliability

Reliability, or the lack of it, can have a large influence on the value of a product. Companies often quantify the cost of poor reliability in terms of the warranty costs that they pay. But this cost simply adds to the cost of manufacture and does not represent the loss in value to the customer due to a repair, which must include the loss of use value due to the time the product was out of service and the associated "collateral damage" due to missed appointments and other losses. If the product is out of warranty coverage, then the cost of the repair must be paid by the customer. When this is the case, the cost directly subtracts from value.

It is not clear at this juncture what the correct functional relationship is between value and the number of repairs experienced over the life of the product. The simplest model for the change in value due to a change in the number of repairs $\tilde{R}$ over the lifetime for a vehicle (lifetime taken approximately as 7 years) is given by

$$\delta V = V_{\tilde{R}} \delta \tilde{R} \tag{2.12}$$

The size of empirical parameter $V_{\tilde{R}}$ for the loss in value for one additional repair for a midsized vehicle in the mid-1990s priced around \$15,000 was approximately –\$300.[14] If this result is extrapolated, boldly, to other segments, prices (P), and time periods, Equation (2.12) becomes a rule of thumb given by

$$\delta V \cong -0.02 P \delta \tilde{R} \tag{2.13}$$

2.3.7 Value of Vehicle Range

If the range that a vehicle can cover before refueling is improved, it adds value because it eliminates time lost in taking a trip. The value of range computed for 100,000 miles of driving can be computed as[10]

$$V_{Range} \cong -\frac{10^5 \dot{V}_D}{3600 g_{FE}} \left[S_{Pump} + S_{Stop} \right] \tag{2.14}$$

where $\dot{V}_D$ is the value of one hour of a person's time, S_{Pump} is the time in seconds to pump one gallon of fuel, and S_{Stop} is the added time in seconds per gallon pumped for the time spent getting off of the road and back. Simek[10] estimated that S_{Pump} is typically 6.8 seconds and $S_{Stop} \cong 214/[0.8 T_{Vol}]$, where T_{Vol} is the volume of the fuel tank in gallons. The factor of 0.8 assumes that a refueling stop begins when 80% of the fuel capacity has been used. The minus sign in Equation (2.14) signifies that operating costs are involved and thus contribute negatively to value. Better fuel economy and a larger fuel tank increase value by reducing the number of stops to refuel and the time for refueling.

2.4 DEMAND AND PRICE ANALYSIS FOR VALUE TRENDS OF PRODUCTS IN A SEGMENT

The usual competitive environment for manufacturers is not a monopoly situation, which has the demand expression given by Equation (2.2), but an oligopoly of N manufacturers competing within a given product segment. Competing firms, by definition, are targeting the same customers and as a consequence their products generally have similar values and prices but with some differentiation. When this is the case, product demand, using the dummy index, $i = 1,2,...N$, is set equal to a Taylor expansion about a cartel point in which the N products are assumed to be identical, having the same value, price, and demand.[15] The outcome is the S-model demand expression given by N simultaneous equations of the form:

$$D_i = K \left\{ V_i - P_i - \frac{1}{N} \sum_{j \neq i} [V_j - P_j] \right\} = K \left\{ \frac{N+1}{N} [V_i - P_i] - [\bar{V} - \bar{P}] \right\} \qquad (2.15)$$

where V_i and P_i are the value and price of product i, which are near but assumed away from the value and price at the cartel point. The terms $\bar{V}$ and $\bar{P}$ are the average value and average price, respectively, over the N competing products. The value, price, and demand for the cartel point are constructed by averaging the values, prices, and demands for the N products across a reference or baseline state. For example, the issue could be the planning of a new product, which is to be in production in four years. The baseline state might be constructed from the values, prices, and demands for the N products in the current year. The term K represents the negative slope of demand with price at the cartel point. It is estimated from the baseline state using the expression

$$K = \frac{D_{T,0}}{\bar{V}_0 - \bar{P}_0} = \frac{D_{T,0} E_2}{\bar{P}_0} \qquad (2.16)$$

The terms $\bar{V}_0$ and $\bar{P}_0$ are the value and price averaged over the values ($V_{0,i}$) and prices ($P_{0,i}$) of the products for i from one to N in the baseline state. (When it is clear which product is being referred to, the subscript i will be dropped in what follows.) The term $D_{T,0}$ is the total demand for the reference state, and E_2 equal to $\bar{P}_0 / (\bar{V}_0 - \bar{P}_0)$ is taken as the price elasticity of average demand, as discussed earlier, when each of the competitors change price by the same amount, δP.

Equation (2.15) can be used to forecast future demand based upon the values and prices projected for the future products. It can also be used in a retrospective manner to trace how the values of competing products have changed over time. This application involves solving the system of simultaneous equations for the past values of the products in terms of their past prices and demands, which is given by

$$V_i = \frac{N[D_i + D_T]}{K[N+1]} + P_i \qquad (2.17)$$

where

$$D_T = \sum_{i=1}^{N} D_i$$

and it follows from Equation (2.15) that $D_T = K[\bar{V} - \bar{P}]$.

An application of Equation (2.17) is shown in Figure 2.17 for two minivans (mvA and mvB). The industry value leader at the start of this time period, mvA, had front-wheel drive and carlike ride and handling. The competitor, mvB, initially had rear-wheel drive and represented a scaled-down full-size van. The manufacturer of mvB introduced a new minivan during the 1994 and 1995 model years. It also had front-wheel drive, carlike ride and handling, and fresher styling than mvA. However, in the 1996 model year, the manufacturer of mvA introduced an all-new design, with added roominess, fresh styling, and a second rear sliding door. These changes restored mvA to its value leadership position. Without a second rear sliding door, mvB lost its short-lived value leadership. The company immediately began an expensive redesign and retooling of its product to regain its competitiveness. A national DV survey of minivan owners found that that the second rear sliding door had a value of $1225,[16] which was almost half of the value advantage of mvA over mvB in the 1996 model year.

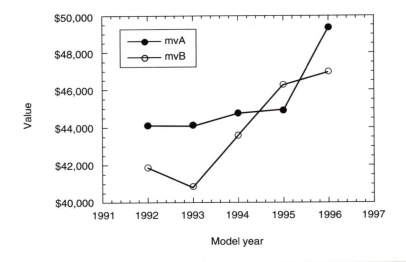

Figure 2.17 The values of two minivans computed over time using Equation (2.15).

Source: Res Eng Design 2001;13:42-52. Reproduced with permission of Springer-Verlag London.

When the demand and price differences are large, the difference between the values for competitors i and j can be estimated using the aggregate, linear-in-attributes, multinomial logit model[17, 19] (the *logit model*, for simplicity) using the following relationship:

$$V_i - V_j = \left[\frac{\bar{P}_0}{[N+1]E_2}\right] Ln\left[\frac{D_i}{D_j}\right] + P_i - P_j$$

This expression is derived by first considering the two analytical models in the limit of small departures in market share from $1/N$ and small differences in price and value. In this limit, the linear model is dominant as it represents the exact analytical model. Thus, the theoretical expressions for the coupling coefficients in the logit model can be determined by comparing the analytic form of the logit model in this limit to the S-model.[15] An expression for V_i itself (as opposed to a value difference) that is consistent with both the S-model (within its limits) and the logit model can be written as

$$V_i = \left[\frac{\bar{V}_0 - \bar{P}_0}{[N+1]}\right] Ln\left[\frac{D_i}{\bar{D}}\right] + P_i + c \tag{2.18}$$

The term $\bar{D}$ is the average demand and c is a normalization constant that ensures that

$$\sum_{i=1}^{N} D_i = N\bar{D}$$

If Equation (2.17) or (2.18) correspond to the baseline state for product i, V_i can be taken as the baseline value $V_{0,i}$ for product i. Equation (2.18) yields the logit form given by

$$D_i = \bar{D} \exp\left(\left[\frac{N+1}{\bar{V}_0 - \bar{P}_0}\right][V_i - P_i - c]\right) \tag{2.19}$$

The coefficient c is solved for from the log of the expression

$$\exp\left(-\left[\frac{N+1}{\bar{V}_0 - \bar{P}_0}\right]c\right) = \frac{N}{\sum_{j=1}^{N} \exp\left(\left[\frac{N+1}{\bar{V}_0 - \bar{P}_0}\right][V_j - P_j]\right)}$$

It is important to understand that average demand, $\bar{D}$, is not fixed for real markets when using Equation (2.19). Demand, as opposed simply to market share, can be estimated using the logit model by generating a nested arrangement that divides the initial purchase decision between buying a product in the segment under consideration and not buying.[18]

For simplicity when using Equation (2.18) to examine historical total value trends (as opposed to values relative to those for another competitor as a baseline), the constant can be approximated as $c \cong \bar{P}_0 / E_2$ when N is small (less than five) and each P_i is within $\pm$ 10% of $\bar{P}_0$. Often the price elasticity E_2 will be known, and Equation 2.19 can be written as

$$D_i = \bar{D} \exp\left(\left[\frac{[N+1]E_2}{\bar{P}_0}\right]\left[V_i - P_i - c\right]\right) \qquad (2.20)$$

The recommendation here is to use Equation (2.18) only to analyze values of products competing within a product segment. The total values found for each product can be entered into a regression model to generate estimates of the values associated with the product attributes. Caution is advised in applying Equation (2.18) across product segments, the issues in doing so having been described by Boyd and Mellman[19] in their analysis of automobile purchases in the late 1970s. For example, the value coefficient found for reducing the 0 to 60 mph acceleration time is the same for an entry level sedan as for a high-performance sports car when the computation is averaged across product lines. There is also the problem of collinearity between attributes, which is a serious issue common to all regression models of historical data.

It is important to vet the coefficients found in the regression analysis against independent assessments. For example, according to the S-model, the coefficient for price, as shown in Equation (2.19), is equal to $[N+1]/[\bar{V}_0 - \bar{P}_0] = [N+1]E_2/\bar{P}_0$. Assuming that customers consider $N = 4$ cars on average within a segment (the minimum being one and maximum likely being seven) and taking $0.5 \leq E_2 \leq 1$, this coefficient is expected to lie between 5.5 and 11×10^{-4}/$ for the Boyd and Mellman study[19] with $\bar{P}_0$ =\$4,360 (the reported 1977 U.S. market average car price). This is two to four times the result of 2.9×10^{-4} /$ found using the logit regression model.[19] If the logit result truly represents a large underestimate of the price coefficient, this may be the explanation for the large *overestimates* of value reported by Boyd and Mellman for almost all of the attributes evaluated in their regression model.

2.5 EMPIRICAL PRICE AND VALUE RANGES FOR A SEGMENT

Each market segment has a reasonably well-defined price and value ranges for the products competing within the segment. This can be seen in Figure 2.18, where the normalized value is plotted versus price for four family sedan segments for the 1993 model year.[20] The values were computed for the individual vehicles in each segment using Equation 2.17. The plots show strong correlation between value and price within and between segments. It is worth noting that the brand with the highest value in each segment was almost always the highest quality product in the segment based upon its *Consumer Report* five-point rating.

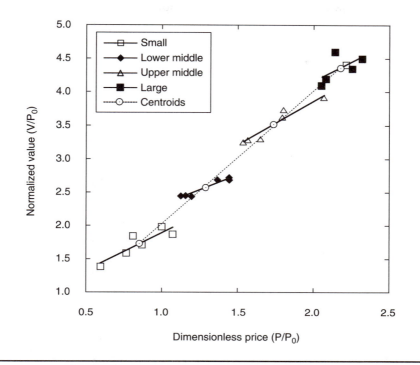

Because the value and price ranges in each segment lie within a value-price envelope, caution should be exercised when the value and price position for a proposed new product falls outside the envelope, apart from normal trend movements over time due to continuous improvement and inflation. The most obvious problem is that consumers who limit their shopping to products within the established value and price range for the segment may see the new product as simply too expensive in spite of the fact that it is offset with added value. Also, if the price and value change is too large, the product may receive competition from those products in a higher segment and also cannibalize sales from the firm's own product in the higher segment.

2.6 DIRECT VALUE (DV) METHOD

Given a baseline product at price P_0 and an alternative that is similar except for one attribute, g, which is different from the baseline level g_0, Equation (2.15) shows that a neutral price, P_N, for the alternative exists such that the baseline demand, $D_0(= D(g_0))$, will be equal to the demand of the alternative, $D_{ALT}(= D(g))$. When the two demands are equal, the relation

$$V_{ALT} - V_0 = V(g) - V_0 = P_N - P_0 \qquad (2.21)$$

follows where $V(g_0) = V_0$. Equation (2.21) states that the value difference between the two is equal to the price difference, an assumption being that K is approximately the same for both. As already stated, this will be true if the value change is not too large. Although Equation (2.21) was derived from a Taylor expansion of demand, the same identity is found using the logit model and the probit model, which indicates that the relationship is not highly sensitive to the demand model.

The form of Equation (2.21) is the basis of the DV method of marketing research.[5,14] Based upon stated choice theory,[21] the DV method uses price in a unique manner to assess the neutral price and then determine value from it using Equation (2.21). As a result, respondents need only to make paired comparisons. This reduces their cognitive stress in taking the survey. It also uses a fixed baseline for assessing the value of alternatives in a given problem. The need for a fixed baseline comes from prospect theory.[22, 23] The alternative being evaluated can be represented by a single attribute or by a combination of attributes. Preference conjoint methods cannot be used to assess value reliably because there is not a clear connection between stated preferences and demand.[21]

The DV method has been used in proprietary applications to assess the value improvements for automobiles, farm equipment, forest products, and the value of the name of selected manufacturers of automobiles and manufacturers of motor-generator sets. Convenience surveys, in which respondents were not chosen at random from a segment of buyers, have been used to evaluate the methodology for assessing a variety of features and attributes, including the value of lottery tickets with known pay-off probabilities,[5] vehicle acceleration performance,[7] interior noise in a luxury vehicle,[8] automotive fuel economy,[7] four-wheel drive,[24] and a truck's extended cab.[24] The survey itself can be a printed form, which is mailed to the respondents, or it can be presented on the screen of a computer, which lends itself to exploring a wider range of attributes and features. Computer surveys facilitate automatic data analysis and are adaptive in that they allow for interaction with the respondent in the presentation of the sequence of survey questions.

A sample of a DV survey form for assessing the value of the name of manufacturer B versus A is shown in Figure 2.19. Respondents are asked to assume that they are in the market to buy a new midsized vehicle similar to the type shown in the picture. A preference, noted by checking either the box on the left or the right, is to be made for each paired comparison. The baseline product is the one on the left and its price, and all attributes remain fixed for each comparison. The alternative product on the right has one or more different attributes (the name of the manufacturer) and a different price for each comparison.

Once the survey has been completed, the results are analyzed to determine the neutral price, P_N. The difference between the neutral price and the baseline price, P_0, yields the value of the attribute relative to the baseline condition as already discussed.

The outcomes for each of the $z = 4$ trials of the hypothetical survey are shown in Table 2.2. The column P lists the four prices of the alternative that appeared in the survey. Column Select lists the number of respondents out of the assumed $n = 600$ returned surveys that selected the alternative for each price point. Column f is the fraction of respondents at the price

Survey

Assume that you are in the market to purchase a midsized sedan vehicle, and that you have a choice of a vehicle manufactured by company A or a vehicle manufactured by company B. The two vehicles are built to the same performance specifications and have the same interior and exterior styles and appearance. Four paired comparisons are shown below. For each of the four comparisons, please select either the vehicle on the left or the one on the right. The vehicle manufactured by A is offered at the same price for each comparison, whereas vehicle manufactured by B is offered at a different price for each comparison.

Midsized Sedans

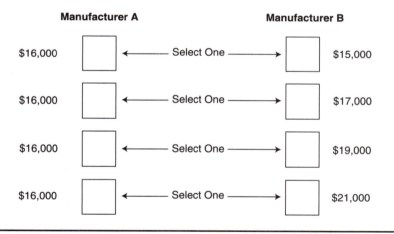

Figure 2.19   A hypothetical survey form for assessing the value of manufacturer B versus A for a midsized sedan.

levels that selected the alternative. Column Y is the logit form given by $Ln(f/(1-f))$, which is used because this functional relationship generally gives a better linear fit with price than f alone does for the large ranges of f usually found in the DV survey.

The logit plot of the outcomes is shown in Figure 2.20. The neutral price is seen to be $17,905. When the baseline price of $16,000 is subtracted, the value of the name of manufacturer B is $1,905 versus manufacturer A. The uncertainty in the measurement of the value of the attribute using the DV method is discussed in Chapter 4.

Table 2.2 Hypothetical outcomes for the DV survey shown in Figure 2.19.

Trial	P	Select	f	Y
1	15000	403	0.672	0.716
2	17000	353	0.588	0.357
3	19000	258	0.430	-0.282
4	21000	174	0.290	-0.895
		f = Select/n		Y = LN(f/(1 - f))

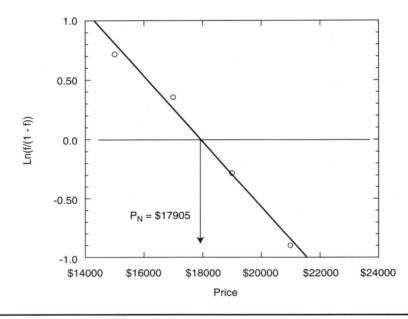

Figure 2.20 Logit plot of results from hypothetical survey yielding a neutral price of $17,905.

As surveys ask for demographic information such as age, household income, gender, education level, and so forth, the survey findings can be divided into subgroups and the values for each can be determined. *Another important subgroup division is between those that view an attribute as an economic good and those that do not.* A particularly strong value dispersion of this type was found by McConville and Cook[25] for the automatic transmission for buyers of Mustang vehicles, with half viewing it as an economic good and the other half needing to be paid to accept it. Clearly, such an attribute should not be made standard equipment for this brand. The value of the automatic transmission as an option for those viewing it as an economic good was computed using only the fraction of respondents willing to pay for it, suitably renormalized to one at the original or aggregate neutral price.[25]

2.7 INTUITIVELY ESTIMATED VALUE CURVES

When considering improving a CTV attribute whose value curve has not been generated, persons familiar with customer needs in relation to the product can be used to generate an intuitive estimate of the value curve. If the intuitive value curve looks promising versus the cost of changing the attribute, a full market survey of the type described in Figure 2.19 can be developed.

An intuitively estimated value curve (Figure 2.21) in the form of Equation 2.4 can be generated as a function of the continuous specification variable g as follows:

1. Assemble a value curve team of six to eight persons who are familiar with customer needs.

2. Decide if the attribute in question corresponds to SIB, NIB, or LIB.

3. Identify the baseline specification, g_0, for the attribute.

4. Identify the critical specification, g_C, at which no one would buy the product at any price because it would be valueless or unsafe for its intended use. For a NIB attribute, there will be two critical specifications on either side of the maximum in value unless the attribute cannot be negative, in which case the curve may be finite at $g = 0$. As stated earlier, the LIB attribute, x, is often converted to a SIB attribute using the $g = 1/x$ transformation.

5. Identify the ideal attribute specification, g_I, at which value should be at a maximum.

6. Sketch out the normalized value curve for V/V_0 similar to the one shown in Figure 2.21.

7. Survey each team member using a form similar to the one shown in Figure 2.19 to identify the neutral price $P_N(g^*)$ for the attribute g^* relative to the baseline attribute g_0 at the baseline price P_0. The neutral price determined by the team is the price $P_N(g^*)$ of the alternative at which half of the team would buy the alternative at this price and the other half would buy the baseline at price P_0.

8. If the elasticity E_2 is not known, set the baseline value $V_0 \approx 2P_0$ (making the assumption that $E_2 \approx 1$). Thus $V(g^*) = 2P_0 + [P_N(g^*)-P_0] P_0 + P_N(g)$.

9. The team then computes the exponential weighting coefficient by taking the natural log of Equation 2.4 which on rearranging yields

$$\gamma = \frac{Ln\left(V(g^*)/V_0\right)}{Ln\left[\dfrac{[g_I - g_C]^2 - [g_I - g^*]^2}{[g_I - g_C]^2 - [g_I - g_0]^2}\right]}$$

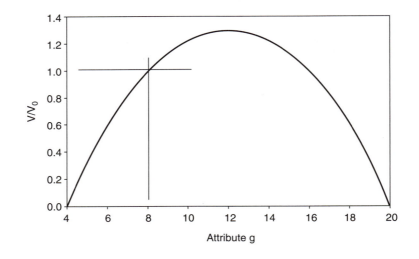

Figure 2.21   Sketch of intuitively constructed value curve for a baseline attribute of 8, critical attributes at 4 and 20, and an ideal attribute at 12.

With these parameters now in place, the team can plot the intuitively estimated, quantified value curve, $V(g)$ versus g. This value curve provides an initial estimate of how value is expected to change as a function of the attribute. If the potential value improvements look promising versus the expected cost changes, then a random survey of potential buyers will likely be in order to more accurately assess how value is expected to change with a change in the attribute. The values provided by the estimated curve in Figure 2.21 are used to set up the prices and attribute changes for a preliminary survey. The findings from the preliminary survey are then used to develop the final survey.

2.8 SUMMARY

Product demand: The demand for a product is a function of its price and value to the customer and the prices and values of the products competing against it. Value is measured in the same units as price. A change in value by an amount x shifts the demand curve versus price by x.

Value curves: The value curve for a product as a function of a continuous, CTV attribute, g, is the mirror image of Taguchi and Wu's cost of inferior quality. Value curves can be fitted with exponentially weighted parabolic functions.

Value trends: Changes in product value over time can be computed from the prices and demands (set equal to sales) of the products competing in a market segment. It is important to use actual transaction prices instead of list prices. Also, sales will not be representative of demand if the product is in scarce supply and there is a waiting list of customers.

Direct Value method of marketing research: The DV method uses demand theory, choice theory, and prospect theory to assess the value of a product alternative versus a fixed baseline product. The objective of the survey is to determine the neutral price of the product where half of the respondents choose it and the other half choose the baseline. The difference between the neutral price and the baseline price is equal to the value of the alternative. No parameters enter the computation of value apart from the two prices. The method can be used for discrete or continuous attributes as well as attributes that are quantifiable such as acceleration performance or subjective such as the appearance of a cell phone or the value of the name of a manufacturer.

REFERENCES

1. T.C. Fowler. 1990. *Value Analysis in Design*. New York: Van Nostrand Reinhold.
2. J. von Neumann and O. Morgenstern. 1944. *Theory of Games and Economic Behavior.* Princeton, NJ: Princeton University Press.
3. G. Taguchi and Y. Wu. 1980. *Introduction to Off-line Quality Control*. Nagoya, Japan: Central Japan Quality Association.
4. H. E. Cook. 1997. *Product Management: Value, Quality, Cost, Price, Profits, and Organization*. Amsterdam: Kluwer.
5. H. E. Cook and A. Wu. 2001. "On the Valuation of Goods and Selection of the Best Design Alternative," *Research in Engineering Design* 13, pp. 42–54.
6. H. E. Cook and R.E. DeVor. 1991. "On Competitive Manufacturing Enterprises I: The S-Model and the Theory of Quality," *Manufacturing Review* 4:2, pp. 96–105.
7. G. P. McConville and H. E. Cook. 1996. "Estimating the Value Trade-Off Between Automobile Performance and Fuel Economy," SAE 1996 Transactions, *Journal of Materials & Manufacturing* 105, pp. 37–45.
8. M. Pozar and H. E. Cook. 1998. "On Determining the Relationship Between Vehicle Value and Interior Noise," SAE 1997 Transactions, *Journal of Passenger Cars* 106, pp. 391–401.
9. W. E. Woodson, B. Tillman, and P.L. Tillman. 1992. *Human Factors Design Handbook,* 2nd edition. New York: McGraw-Hill,p. 606.
10. M. E. Simek. 1994. "Human Factors Value Modeling Applied to Vehicle Analysis and Development," M.S. Thesis, University of Illinois.
11. M. E. Simek and H. E. Cook. 1996. "A Methodology for Estimating the Value of Interior Room in Automobiles," SAE 1996 Transactions, *Journal of Materials & Manufacturing* 105, pp. 13–26.
12. Office of Highway Information Management. 1990. *NPTS Data Book, Volume II*. Washington, DC: Federal Highway Administration.
13. N. L. Phillipart, R. W. Roe, A. J. Arnold, and T. J. Kuchenmeister. 1984. *Driver Selected Seat Position Model,* SAE Technical Paper 840508, Society of Automotive Engineers, Warrendale, PA.
14. J. Donndelinger and H. E. Cook. 1997. "Methods for Analyzing the Value of Automobiles," SAE 1997 Transactions, *Journal of Passenger Cars* 106, pp. 1263–1281.
15. H. E. Cook. 1997. *Product Management: Value, Quality, Cost, Price, Profits, and Organization*. Amsterdam: Kluwer, pp. 62–63.
16. A. Wu. 1998. *Value Benchmarking the Minivan Segment,* M.S. Thesis, Department of Mechanical and Industrial Engineering, University of Illinois at Urbana-Champaign.

17. M. Ben-Akiva and S. R. Lerman. 1985. *Discrete Choice Analysis: Theory and Applications to Travel Demand*, Cambridge, MA: MIT Press.
18. D. Besanko, S. Gupta, and D. Jain. 1998. "Logit Demand Estimation under Competitive Pricing Behavior: An Equilibrium Framework," *Management Science* 44, Part 1 of 2, pp. 1533–1547.
19. J. H. Boyd and R. E. Mellman. 1980. "The Effect of Fuel Economy Standards on the U.S. Automotive Market: An Hedonic Demand Analysis," Transportation Research A 14, pp. 367–378.
20. E. M. Monroe, R. L. Silver, and H. E. Cook. 1997. *Value Versus Price Segmentation of Family Automobiles,* SAE International Congress, Detroit, MI. Warrendale, PA: Society of Automotive Engineers, SAE Paper 970765.
21. J. Louviere and G. Woodworth. 1983. "Design and Analysis of Simulated Consumer Choice or Allocation Experiments: An Approach Based on Aggregate Data," *Journal of Marketing Research* 20, pp. 350–357.
22. D. Kahneman and A. Tversky. 1979. "Prospect Theory: An Analysis of Decision Under Risk," *Econometrica* 47, pp. 263–291.
23. A. Tversky and D. Kahneman. 1981. "The Framing of Decisions and Psychology of Choice," *Science* 211, pp. 453–458.
24. E. M. Monroe and H. E. Cook. 1997. "Determining the Value of Vehicle Attributes Using a PC Based Tool," SAE International Congress, Detroit, MI. Warrendale, PA: Society of Automotive Engineers, SAE Paper 970764.
25. G. P. McConville and H. E. Cook. 1997. "Evaluating Mail Surveys to Determine the Value of Vehicle Options," SAE Transactions, *Journal of Passenger Cars* 106, pp. 1290–1297.

3

System Level Design and Strategic Experimentation

Insight: *The price of a product is a function of the total number of products competing in the segment and their values and variable costs.*

Key Topics

entrepreneurial engineering

systems viewpoint

systems architecture

pricing

design and analysis of a strategic experiment

3.1 ENTREPRENEURIAL ENGINEERING AND THE SYSTEMS VIEWPOINT

The traditional engineering skill set focuses on how to take an innovative concept to technical feasibility. Engineers today, however, need to understand the requirements for commercial feasibility (Figure 3.1), in addition to technical feasibility. In fact today's global marketplace is so competitive that the words "commercial feasibility" should be replaced by "commercial superiority."

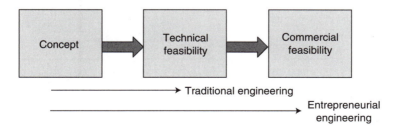

Figure 3.1   The traditional engineer is trained to design technical feasibility into a new product. The entrepreneurial engineer is trained to fully assess both technical and commercial feasibiilty in the development of a new product.

This broader vision has been called "entrepreneurial engineering." The entrepreneurial engineer or statistician or scientist needs to be a holistic thinker having a wide skill set to grasp the complex interrelationships between customer needs and the artifacts, technologies, and services that help in satisfying those needs. The wants and desires of multiple stakeholders have to be satisfied simultaneously. A systems viewpoint and interdisciplinary skills are required to mold a successful product plan out of the complexity[1] presented by the conflicting needs of the customer, the seller, the final assembler, the supply chain, and all persons who are impacted by the product's externalities through its manufacture, use, and disposal.

The challenge to the entrepreneurial engineer is to design products and services so that customer needs are aligned smartly with the needs of the firm and society. The customer judges the worth of a product through its CTV attributes, which are determined by how well the components and subsystems perform within the system architecture. Thus, good and timely design capability rests on being able to project (1) how a proposed design change at the component level will affect the CTV attributes and environmental quality at the system level and (2) how CTV changes affect market share and cash flow (Figure 3.2).

A system is a set of integrated subsystems, as illustrated in Figure 3.3 for a desktop computer. Within the subsystems are sub-subsystems and components (Figure 3.4). Systems are linked to network support structures and must function harmoniously within these networks. Typical systems and their respective networks are shown in Table 3.1. Desktop computer systems, for example, are connected to local area networks (Figure 3.5), which, in turn, are linked to a wide area network (Figure 3.6).

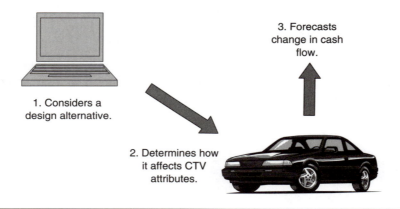

1. Considers a design alternative.

2. Determines how it affects CTV attributes.

3. Forecasts change in cash flow.

Figure 3.2   A schematic illustration of the entrepreneurial engineer translating a proposed design change at the component level to the CTV attribute changes and then to the changes in cash flow.

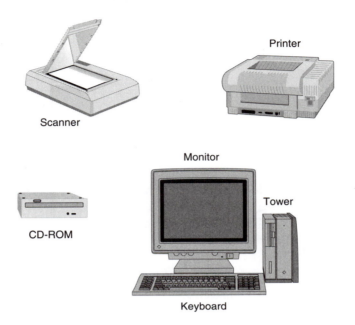

Figure 3.3   A desktop computer system consists of an integrated set of subsystems.

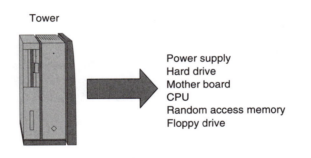

Figure 3.4   Each subsystem is a collection of sub-subsystems and components.

Table 3.1   Examples of product systems and the networks in which they function

Product System	Network(s)
Cell phone	Wireless voice communication
Laptop computer	Local area or wide area data network
Automobile	Highway system
Airplane	Air traffic control system
House	Power grid, communication network, highway system

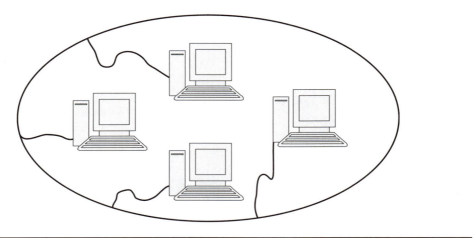

Figure 3.5 Desktop computers are shown linked in a local area network.

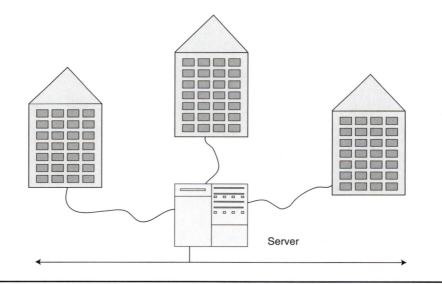

Server

Figure 3.6 Local area networks are linked to a wide area network.

Thus, system design involves not only the interfacing of subsystems and components but also the design of the connections that link the system to the network. The network must also be well designed and administered effectively so that it is robust and trustworthy. Homes and businesses require reliable, on-demand power from a nation's electrical grid. The nation's highways need to be well maintained if efficient use is to be made of this distribution system for manufactured goods and produce.

3.2 SYSTEM ARCHITECTURE

The system for an automobile is divided into its key subsystems in Figure 3.7. Also shown is the division of the chassis subsystem into its sub-subsystems. These are the basic building blocks of the system architecture for automobiles, which has remained unchanged for many years. However, the full expression of system architecture is much more than the basic block diagram formed by the division of a system into its subsystems. It includes:

1. Full requirements for system level performance.

2. Key performance requirements of subsystems.

3. Amount and timing for delivery of components and subsystems.

4. Cost, weight, and investment requirements for each subsystem and the total system.

5. Warranty and life-cycle costs and serviceability.

6. Interface management requirements (e.g., attaching points, electrical impedance, heat flow, air flow, etc.).

7. Verification of processes for design, manufacturing, assembly, and delivery.

8. Projected demand and cash flow forecasts over the product's life cycle.

9. Means for product disposal at end of lifetime.

10. Adherence to societal and governmental requirements and obligations.

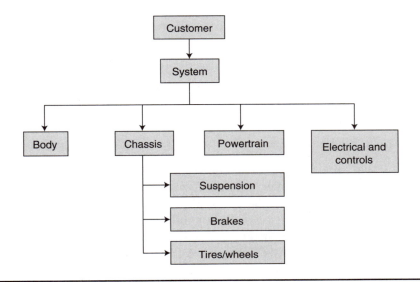

Figure 3.7   The division of an automotive system into its key subsystems represents the basic building blocks for the system architecture.

3.1.1 Task Structure

Task structures exist within each of the blocks shown in Figure 3.7. The incomplete list of subtasks within the system, subsystem, and component levels of design are shown in Table 3.2. Those having the responsibility for a task should be sure that they also have the capability and authority to do the task.

Table 3.2 The incomplete listing of subtasks.

Included in system task
Marketing research
System financial analysis
System design
System final assembly
Marketing
Distribution
Warranty
Service
Disposal
Included in subsystem tasks
Subsystem financial analysis
Subsystem design
Subsystem assembly
Subsystem distribution
Included in component tasks
Component financial analysis
Component design
Component manufacture
Component distribution

3.2.2 Pricing the System

The system is usually priced either to maximize cash flow or to improve market share to a given level. In a competitive market, price theory[2, 3] is not trivial, as pricing is highly influenced by the prices and values of the competing products. Nevertheless, the straightforward Cournot/Bertrand (CB) pricing model illuminates very well the issues involved in a quantitative manner. The mathematical formulation of the CB postulate is that each competitor i in a product segment prices to maximize its cash flow A_i assuming that the other $N - 1$ competitors will not change their prices. Since each would be actually making the same assumption, erroneously, the mathematical expression of the CB model is a set of linear simultaneous equations formed by setting to zero the partial derivative of the cash flow expression for each competitor with respect to its own price, P_i. When the S-model demand expression for product i given by Equation (2.15) is substituted into Equation (1.4) and its partial derivative with respect to P_i is taken, the CB price[4] for each is obtained:

$$P_{CB,i} = \frac{\left[N^2 + 2N\right]C_i + \left[N^2 + N + 1\right]V_i + \left[N^2 - N\right]\left[\bar{C}_{Cmpt} - \bar{V}_{Cmpt}\right]}{2N^2 + 3N + 1} \qquad (3.1)$$

The terms $\bar{C}_{Cmpt}$ and $\bar{V}_{Cmpt}$ are the average variable cost and value, respectively, of the other N - 1 products. If the price for product i were being considered, then

$$\bar{C}_{Cmpt} = \left[1/(N-1)\right]\sum_{j \neq i} C_j .$$

To illustrate the properties of this expression, consider the problem of N competitors in a segment making identical products for the same cost and selling them for the same price given by Equation (3.1). The outcome is shown in Figure 3.8 as a function of the number of competitors, having a limiting price as N goes to infinity equal to variable cost. Note, although it is not plotted, the market share of each competitor is equal to $1/N$. Thus, as the number of competitors increase, *both price and market share drop,* but total demand actually increases due to the price reductions. The model shows in theory what is seen in practice, which is that the emergence of the global marketplace has made competition considerably tougher. The one silver lining is that by becoming global, a firm makes its products available to a larger market and can source components at lower cost.

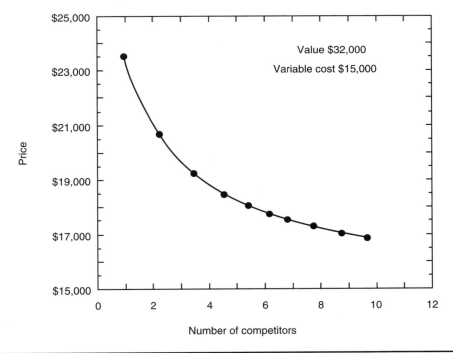

Figure 3.8   The CB price as a function of the number of competitors selling the identical product having a value of $32,000 and a variable cost of $15,000.

It is farfetched to believe that any firm knowingly sets prices using Equation (3.1), so why should it be expected to provide an approximate model for pricing in a highly competitive market? The reason is that the CB prices represent the theoretical set of prices where a price war stops because there is no short-term advantage for any competitor to reduce price any further.[5] As such it is a Nash equilibrium. To maximize profits, the firms need to display cooperative behavior, for example, by letting one firm act as the price leader.

When only price *changes* are of interest, the variational form of the CB price given by

$$\delta P_{CB,i} = \frac{\left[N^2 + 2N\right]\delta C_i + \left[N^2 + N + 1\right]\delta V_i + \left[N^2 - N\right]\left[\delta \bar{C}_{Cmpt} - \delta \bar{V}_{Cmpt}\right]}{2N^2 + 3N + 1} \tag{3.2}$$

should be used to project a price change based upon changes in the fundamental metrics. For a monopoly, Equation 3.2 becomes

$$\delta P_{CB,i} = \frac{\delta C_i + \delta V_i}{2} \tag{3.3}$$

This expression also holds approximately for the case $N > 1$, provided that competitors do not change their variable cost or value.

Note, price is not a direct function of fixed cost or of investment level in any of the above expressions. Investment affects price by how it affects value and cost. If fixed cost or investment level changes, price remains unaffected unless value or variable cost is affected. In other words, you cannot recover an increase in fixed costs through pricing.

3.3 STRATEGIC EXPERIMENT EXAMPLE

Consider, as an exercise, the system level technology and financial planning for the major redesign of a car. The current, baseline vehicle has a 4-cylinder engine and a steel body. It has a price $P_0 = \$22,000$, variable cost $C_0 = \$14,000$, value $V_0 = \$30,000$, fixed cost $F_{Cost} = F_0 = \$200,000,000$, and demand $D_0 = 200,000$ annual units. Two alternatives or *control factors* are to be evaluated, replacement of the 4-cylinder with a V-6 and replacement of the steel body with aluminum. For simplicity, the vehicle is assumed to have no competitors. Also, for this exercise, the role of product variation on value and cash flow is ignored.

3.3.1 Experimental Design and Multiple Attribute Outcomes

The experimental design chosen for study has four trials as expressed by the design array of 1s and 0s shown in Table 3.3. The design displays how the vehicles are to be evaluated: The first column in the design is reserved for the baseline and is always a column of ones. To the right of the baseline column are the columns for the off-baseline control factors. If a zero is in a factor column for a given trial, that factor is not present for the trial. If a one appears, the factor is present. Thus, the baseline 4-cylinder engine is used in trials 1 and 2 and the V-6 in trials 3 and 4. The steel body is used in trials 1 and 3, and the aluminum body is used in trials 2 and 4. Elements of the baseline vehicle, noted by the column of ones, represent the starting point for each trial, which is then modified by changes in certain subsystems as specified by the 0s and 1s in the columns for the off-baseline control factors.

The average acceleration performance, interior noise, and fuel economy outcomes for each trial shown in Table 3.3 represents a multiple attribute outcome matrix, Y. It is given by a linear regression model of the form (see Appendix C):

$$\mathbf{Y} = \mathbf{X}\boldsymbol{\beta} + \mathbf{e} \tag{3.4}$$

For convenience, the name of the spreadsheet function will typically be listed in parentheses after the algebraic expression is introduced, for example, Y (Y). For this specific problem, the last three columns and four rows on the RHS of Table 3.3 represent Y, and the array of 1s and 0s in Table 3.3 represent the design matrix $\mathbf{X}$ (X). The spreadsheet name Y was assigned to design matrix $\mathbf{Y}$ by highlighting the area in the spreadsheet occupied by it and then typing "Y" into the Name Box in the upper left corner of the spreadsheet, as shown in Figure 3.9. The matrix β is the general form for an array of coefficients that represent the contribution made by each of the control factors to the outcomes. The vector e represents random error. The symbol $\hat{\beta}$ is used for the regular least square estimate for the β coefficients. They are computed from the relation

$$\hat{\boldsymbol{\beta}} = \mathbf{X}_S \mathbf{Y} \tag{3.5}$$

in which X_s (XS) is the solution matrix given by

$$\mathbf{X}_S = [\mathbf{X}'\mathbf{X}]^{-1}\mathbf{X}'$$

=MMULT(MINVERSE(MMULT(TRANSPOSE(X),X)),TRANSPOSE(X))   (3.6)

where $\mathbf{X}'$ is the transpose of $\mathbf{X}$ and $[\mathbf{X}'\,\mathbf{X}]^{-1}$ is the inverse of the matrix multiplication $[\mathbf{X}'\,\mathbf{X}]$. When samples are taken from populations having a common variance σ^2, the product

Table 3.3   The experimental design (X) having four trials and two off-baseline factors. Also shown are the average outcomes (Y) for three CTV attributes (0 to 60 mph acceleration, interior noise, and fuel economy). The solution matrix (XS) is also shown.

| | | X | | | | Y | | | |
| | | | | | | | g | | |
Trial	Base Vehicle	V-6 Engine	Aluminum Body	Trial	0–60 mph Accel Time sec	0–60 mph Accel Time LOG(sec)	Interior Noise dBA	Fuel Economy mpg	
1	1	0	0	1	12.8	1.1072	70.2	28	
2	1	0	1	2	11.5	1.0607	68.7	30.5	
3	1	1	0	3	11.2	1.0492	66.5	26.2	
4	1	1	1	4	9.8	0.9912	65.2	27.8	

| | XS | | | |
	1	2	3	4
Baseline	0.75	0.25	0.25	-0.25
V-6	-0.5	-0.5	0.5	0.5
Aluminum body	-0.5	0.5	-0.5	0.5

=MMULT(MINVERSE(MMULT(TRANSPOSE(X),X)),TRANSPOSE(X))

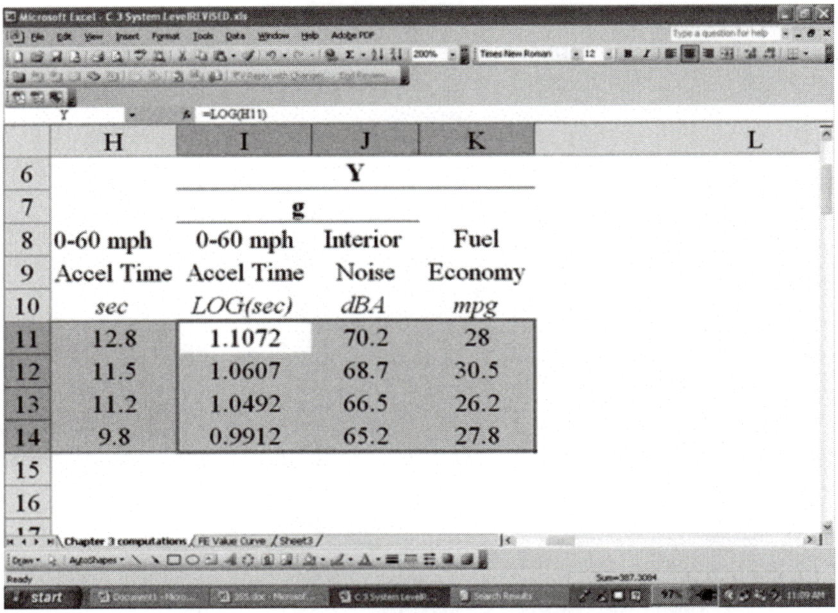

Figure 3.9 Process for entering the name for the outcomes array by highlighting the area and typing in the name "Y" in the Name Box to the left of the Formula Bar.

$\sigma^2[\mathbf{X'\,X}]^{-1}$ is known as the variance-covariance matrix, as its elements represent the covariance between the doubly indexed factors ij and kl. Strictly speaking, $[\mathbf{X'\,X}]^{-1}$ represents a unit variance, variance-covariance matrix. However, in what follows, $[\mathbf{X'\,X}]^{-1}$ will be called simply the covariance matrix.

The spreadsheet expression is listed to the right of the formula in Equation 3.6 and also at the bottom of Table 3.3. Because the formula for the solution matrix is needed often, the macro SolMatrix() was recorded to compute it automatically from the design array, name X. The location and the size of the region for XS has to be selected before the macro is run. The procedure for recording a macro is described fully in the Help menu of the spreadsheet. If the design matrix is named something other than X, say XX, the macro can still be used by entering its keyboard shortcut and then pasting over the entries for X in the Formula Bar with the correct name XX, clicking on the new expression in the Formula Bar, holding down the **Shift>Ctrl** keys, and hitting **Enter**. (All array formulas are computed by holding down the **Shift>Ctrl** keys and hitting **Enter**.)

As described in Appendix A, when the baseline used for the design array is trial 1 (this is the case in Table 3.3), the $\hat{\boldsymbol{\beta}}$ coefficients will be written as λ. If the baseline is the average of all of the trials, the $\hat{\boldsymbol{\beta}}$ will be written as φ. The model or predicted outcomes for the trial model are written as $\hat{\mathbf{Y}}\ (=\mathbf{X}\hat{\boldsymbol{\beta}})$.

The experiments used to determine the system-level performance levels involve the testing of real prototypes or virtual math models of fully assembled vehicles having the mix of subsystems for a given trial as specified by the experimental design. Use of prototypes in product development will generally be more expensive and time consuming compared to simulation, but there is no alternative if the math model does not have sufficient fidelity. As already stated, the math model must provide a transfer function that accurately predicts the impact of each component design change on all of the CTV attributes that are important to the customer.

3.3.2 Converting Attribute Changes to Value Changes

The acceleration times in seconds were converted into a psychometric variable proportional to −1 times the log of the acceleration force for modeling the sensation of acceleration on value, the assumption behind this choice being that the sensation felt from the acceleration force is proportional to the log of the force rather than the force itself. (It is unimportant to keep track of the minus sign, however, as all of the terms in Equation (2.4) end up being squared in the analysis.) The parameters used in constructing the value curves for acceleration time and interior noise are listed in Table 3.4.

   Improvements in fuel economy reduce the operating cost of the vehicle to the customer and thereby add value. The discounted cash flow computations used to compute the value for the different fuel economies are shown in Table 3.5. The costs are based upon $1.50/gallon of fuel, driving 12,000 miles per year, and a discount rate of 5% annually over 7 years. The sum of the costs suitably discounted over the 7 years of expected usage was used to

Table 3.4   The critical, ideal, and baseline specifications and the weighting coefficients GAMMA used in constructing the value curves for LOG base 10 acceleration time and interior noise.

	Acceleration time Log(seconds)	Interior noise dBA
gC	1.602	110
gI	0.301	40
G0	1.107	70.2
GAMMA	0.170	0.59

Table 3.5   Discounted cash-flow computations for computing the values of fuel economy and the resulting value coefficients for fuel economy as determined from differences in discounted operating costs.

N	O	P	Q	R	S	T	U	V	W	X	Y	Z	AA
			Discounted annual operating costs by year								Sum discounted	Deviation from	
Trial	MPG	AnnualCost	1	2	3	4	5	6	7	Trial	costs	baseline	FEValCoeff
1	28	$643	$612	$583	$555	$529	$504	$480	$457	1	$3,720	$-	1
2	30.5	$590	$562	$535	$510	$486	$462	$440	$419	2	$3,415	$305	1.010
3	26.2	$687	$654	$623	$593	$565	$538	$513	$488	3	$3,975	$(256)	0.991
4	27.8	$647	$617	$587	$559	$533	$507	$483	$460	4	$3,747	$(27)	0.999
		=MilesDriven*FuelCost/MPG									=SUM(Q21:W21)		
			=AnnualCost/(1+DiscountRate)^YEAR									=$Y$21-Y21	
												=(V0+Z21)/V0	

compute the value deviations δV from baseline for fuel economy in Table 3.5. The fuel economy value coefficients v_{FE} for the trials are from the changes in fuel economy value δV_{FE} from baseline using the expression $v_{FE} = [V_0 + \delta V_{FE}] / V_0$.

The dimensionless value coefficients for each of the three attributes for each trial are shown in Table 3.6. The coefficients for acceleration time and interior noise were computed in the spreadsheet using Equation (2.4) in the form

$$v(g)=(((gI\text{-}gC)\char`^2\text{-}(gI\text{-}g)\char`^2)/((gI\text{-}gC)\char`^2\text{-}(gI\text{-}g0)\char`^2))\char`^{GAMMA}$$

and the named parameters listed in Table 3.4, each of which include the two columns in a single row.

The resulting total value for each vehicle evaluated is also shown in the next to last column in Table 3.6. A multi-attribute value expression was used to compute the total values given by

$$V(g_1,g_2,g_3,...) = V_0 v(g_1)v(g_2)v(g_3)... \tag{3.7}$$

This empirical form is chosen because the total value of a product will go to zero if the specification of any one of its CTV attributes is at its critical level. For example, if the interior noise level were at the threshold of pain, the value of the vehicle would be zero even if the other specifications were at their ideal levels. Similarly, if a laptop computer were perfect in every way except that the screen displayed zero contrast, it would have no value. The variable cost for each trial is listed in the final column. (Assume that an analyst estimated the costs shown after reviewing the details of the proposed design changes.) The array of two columns by four rows was given the name FUNMET, shorthand for *fundamental metrics*.

Table 3.6 The value coefficients and the resulting values for the vehicles tested and their variable cost.

	B	C	D	E	F	G	H	I	J
31								FUNMET	
32				Value Coefficients					
33		**Trial**	**AccelTime**	**Noise**		**FuelEcon**	**Trial**	**VALUE**	**COST**
34		1	1	1		1	1	$ 30,000	$ 14,000
35		2	1.012	1.013		1.010	2	$ 31,054	$ 14,400
36		3	1.014	1.031		0.991	3	$ 31,093	$ 14,200
37		4	1.027	1.040		0.999	4	$ 32,012	$ 14,600
38	D34:E37	=(((gI-gC)^2-(gI-g)^2)/((gI-gC)^2-(gI-g0)^2))^GAMMA					**VALUE**	=V0*AccelTime*Noise*FuelEcon	
39	F34:F37	=FEValCoeff					**COST**	*from analyst*	

3.3.3 Lambda Coefficients for Value and Variable Cost

The spreadsheet expression

$$=MMULT(XS,FUNMET)$$

represents the matrix multiplication of the solution matrix in Table 3.3 times the two columns of fundamental metrics (FUNMET) in Table 3.6. The outcome is the array, shown as Table 3.7 whose elements represent the lambda coefficients for value and variable cost. The forecast improvements in value for the V-6 engine and the aluminum body are seen to be $1,026 and $986, respectively.

The individual, off-baseline, lambda coefficients are best represented using a double subscript index, the first representing the type of factor and the second its level. In terms of the double subscripted coefficients using the arguments V and C for value and cost, the elements in Table 3.7 would be represented as:

$$\lambda_0(V) = \$30,034 \quad \lambda_0(C) = \$14,000$$

$$\lambda_{21}(V) = \$986 \quad \lambda_{21}(C) = \$400$$

$$\lambda_{11}(V) = \$1,026 \quad \lambda_{11}(C) = \$200$$

$$\lambda_{10}(V) = \lambda_{10}(C) = \lambda_{20}(V) = \lambda_{20}(C) = 0$$

Note that the value of the baseline lambda coefficient in Table 3.7 is slightly off the $30,000 amount in Table 3.6. This is a result of the random error term in Equation (3.5) and the fact that Equation (2.8) is a regular least square solution (RLS), which provides a best fit (not a perfect fit) to the outcomes when there are more trials than unknowns, which was the case here. This is similar, in principle, to constructing a best straight line to fit three or more data points. The best line will not go through each data point due to random error.

Table 3.7   Results of the computations for the lambda coefficients for the contributions of each factor to the value and cost of the vehicles.

	Value	Variable cost
Base	$ 30,034	$ 14,000
4 Cyl to V-6	$ 1,026	$ 200
Steel to alum.	$ 986	$ 400

=MMULT(XS,FUNMET)

Although trade-off decisions should be made based upon fine-grained, component-by-component, subsystem-by-subsystem considerations of cost versus the benefit in value for each alternative, *there may be times where it is strategically sound to implement a value-adding feature even if the associated cost is greater than the added value.* Why should such an action be taken that defies economic logic? First of all, it should delight your customers! It will also protect your product against having one or more of your competitors introduce the feature and catching your product without it, because adding a major feature after a design is in production is usually very costly, if not prohibitive, due to the tear-up of the existing design and a substantial investment for new tools. The caveat in making such a decision is that *the overall product cost should be at or below target (find the cost savings elsewhere), or there should be high confidence that, after production begins, the learning process will discover a way to reduce the cost of the new subsystem.*

A very long view in this regard was taken by Toyota in bringing the Prius strong hybrid vehicle into production.[6] The Prius represents a learning experience. Its monetary losses are covered by very large profits from other vehicles. What is game-changing is not the vehicle itself (all automotive companies know how to design and build a strong hybrid), but the decision to release a product as a learning experience well before it would be profitable to do so by any short-term accounting analysis.

3.3.4 Forecast of Future Demand and Cash Flow

The sum divided by two of the added value and added cost in Table 3.7 represents a rule-of-thumb, Equation (3.3), for the price premium of the proposed new product relative to the baseline product. With this rule and Equation (2.2), the demand change for the proposed new vehicle sold by the monopoly is given by

$$\delta D = \frac{D_0}{V_0 - P_0} \left[\frac{\delta V - \delta C}{2} \right] \tag{3.8}$$

and the annual cash flow before taxes is given by

$$A = D(P - C) - F_{Cost} - (M / Y_{RS}) \tag{3.9}$$

The term M is the total investment including any interest and, as already stated, it is assumed paid out as a mortgage in equal M / Y_{RS} amounts over the time horizon Y_{RS} in years, which was taken as 6 for this problem. Using the baseline financial parameters in Table 3.8, the cash flow for the current product is $1,400,000,000, assuming the investments are paid at the end of each year. The forecast change in demand for the proposed new product versus baseline computed from Equation (3.8) is 17,645 units annually. When this amount is added to D_0 and the changes in price and variable cost are added to their baseline amounts, the annual cash flow forecast for the future product is $1,528,103,061, for a total investment level of $M = \$1,000,000,000$ paid in equal increments over the time horizon of $Y_{RS} = 6$.

Table 3.8 Baseline financial parameters.

D0=	200,000
P0=	$22,000
V0=	$30,000
C0=	$14,000
F0=	$200,000,000
M0=	$0
E2=	2.75
K=	25.00

3.3.5 Lambda Coefficients for Future Demand, Investment, Price, and Cash Flow

The above analysis evaluated the financial merits for the combination of the two factors. Their individual merits should, in fact, have been evaluated first by computing the bottom-line financial parameters (BOTTOMLINES) for each trial, as shown in Table 3.9. The lambda coefficients for each of the financial parameters are shown in Table 3.10. They were computed using the RLS expression, Equation (3.6). Table 3.10 shows that both factors are forecast to contribute positively to cash flow, with the change from the 4-cylinder to V-6 having the larger impact.

Table 3.9 Financial parameters for each trial. The name of each array is shown in bold at the top of each column. Cash flow does not represent a name for its column, as it is not used alone in subsequent computations.

	BOTTOM LINES			
Trial	DEMAND	INVEST	PRICE	Cash flow
1	200000	0	$ 22,000	$ 1,400,000,000
2	208170	$ 500,000,000	$ 22,727	$ 1,450,058,942
3	211164	$ 500,000,000	$ 22,647	$ 1,500,270,448
4	217645	$1,000,000,000	$ 23,306	$ 1,528,103,061

DEMAND	=D0+K*(VALUE-V0-(COST-C0))/2
PRICE	=P0+(VALUE-V0+(COST-C0))/2
Cash flow	=DEMAND*(PRICE-COST)-F0-INVEST/6

Table 3.10 Attribute lambda coefficients for each of the bottom-line financial parameters.

	Demand	Investment	Price	Cash flow
Base	200422	$ -	$ 22,017	$ 1,405,556,582
4 Cyl to V-6	10319	$ 500,000,000	$ 613	$ 89,157,284
Steel to alum.	7326	$ 500,000,000	$ 693	$ 38,945,777

=MMULT(XS,BOTTOMLINES)

3.4 SUMMARY

Entrepreneurial engineering: The skill set of engineers participating in the highly competitive, global market should include a keen understanding of the requirements for commercial superiority as well as an understanding of how to achieve technical feasibility.

Systems viewpoint: The systems viewpoint must be holistic, being sensitive to the needs of all stakeholders and the capability of new technologies to fill those needs in a cost-effective and timely manner.

System pricing: The CB pricing model for a highly competitive market predicts that a product's price depends upon its value and variable cost as well as the values and variable costs of the products competing against it. It does not depend directly upon fixed cost and investment level. They influence price only indirectly through their influence on value and/or variable cost. The CB price is also a function of the number of products competing in the segment.

Multiple factors and multiple attributes: In a major product design change, multiple factors are changed and each can affect multiple CTV attributes of the product that are important to the customer. In the automotive example, there were two major changes in subsystem content considered, and each affected several attributes.

Connecting attribute changes to value changes: The changes in CTV attributes were translated into changes in value to the customer, variable cost, and investment. The changes in the dimensionless value coefficients determined elsewhere for 0 to 60 mph acceleration performance[7] and interior noise[8] were used. The dimensionless value curves were converted into dollars by multiplying them times the baseline value of the family sedan in question. The value changes for fuel economy were computed from the discounted cash flow over the expected period of use of the vehicle.

Linear model: A linear regression model is used to examine the impact of the factors on both the fundamental and bottom-line metrics using the S-model expressions. The changes in the metrics are referenced against a common baseline represented by trial 1.

REFERENCES

1. R. L. Flood and E. R. Carlson. 1993. *Dealing with Complexity An Introduction to the Theory and Application of Systems Science,* 2nd ed. New York: Plenum Press, pp. 97–140.
2. H. Simon. 1989. *Price Management.* Amsterdam: North-Holland.
3. K. B. Monroe. 2003. *Pricing Making Profitable Decisions.* Boston: McGraw-Hill Irwin.
4. E. M. Monroe, R. L. Silver, and H. E. Cook. 1997. *Value Versus Price Segmentation of Family Automobiles,* SAE International Congress, Detroit, MI. Warrendale, PA: Society of Automotive Engineers, SAE Paper 970765.
5. H. E. Cook. 1997. *Product Management: Value, Quality, Cost, Price, Profits, and Organization.* Amsterdam: Kluwer, Chapter 3.
6. Motor Trend. November 20, 2003. *Motor Trend Announces 2004 Car of the Year.* http://motortrend.com/oftheyear/car/index.html
7. G. P. McConville and H. E. Cook. 1996. "Estimating the Value Trade-Off Between Automobile Performance and Fuel Economy," SAE 1996 Transactions, *Journal of Materials & Manufacturing* 105, pp. 37–45.
8. M. Pozar and H. E. Cook. 1998. "On Determining the Relationship Between Vehicle Value and Interior Noise," SAE 1997 Transactions, *Journal of Passenger Cars* 106, pp. 391–401.

4

Statistics

Insight: The statistics of interest are those for the population. However, we are limited to relatively small sample sizes and can form confidence levels only for the ranges of the population statistics.

Key Topics

statistical distributions (normal, t, chi-square, Weibull, Poisson, binomial, and uniform)

Central Limit Theorem

"Law of Variances"

statistics for DV surveys

4.1 STATISTICAL DISTRIBUTIONS[1]

4.1.1 Normal Distribution

Nature introduces randomness at every opportunity, ensuring that no two artifacts are identical. Yet, when a large number of measurements are made of a property, Y, from a collection of manufactured products built to the same nominal specifications, the measurements often generate a smooth function if the frequency distribution given by

$$f(Y) = N^*(Y) / N_T^*$$

is plotted where $N^*(Y)$ is the number of times that a measurement falls in the intervals of Y and $Y + \Delta Y$ and N_T^* is the total number of things measured over the full range.

The smooth, bell-shaped frequency distribution

$$f(Y) = \frac{1}{\sigma\sqrt{2\pi}} \exp\left[\frac{-[Y-\mu]^2}{2\sigma^2}\right] \qquad (4.1)$$

shown in Figure 4.1 is for the normal distribution having a mean value μ equal to ten and a standard deviation σ of one. The standard normal distribution, Z, which has a mean of zero and a standard deviation of one is shown in Figure 4.2. The normally distributed variable Y can be transformed into the standard normal form using the relation $Z = [Y - \mu]/\sigma$ and $f(Z) = f(Y)[\partial Y / \partial Z]$.

Frequency distributions can be continuous or discrete, depending upon the nature of the variable Y. The integral of a continuous frequency distribution from $-\infty$ to ∞ is unity (one). Likewise the sum of a discrete frequency distribution over its entire range is unity.

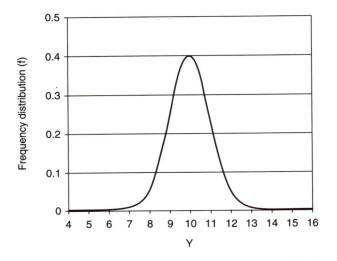

Figure 4.1 Normal distribution with mean ten and standard deviation one.

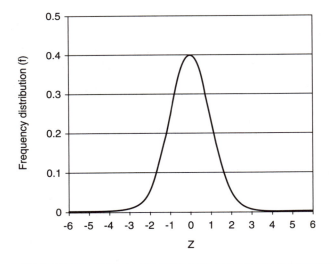

Figure 4.2 The standard normal distribution having mean zero and standard deviation of one.

The expected value $E(Y)$ for a continuous distribution is its mean given by

$$\mu = E(Y) \equiv \int_{-\infty}^{\infty} f(Y)YdY \tag{4.2}$$

The standard deviation, σ, is the square root of the variance σ^2, which for a continuous distribution is given by

$$\sigma^2 = E\left(\left[Y-\mu\right]^2\right) \equiv \int_{-\infty}^{\infty} f(Y)\left[Y-\mu\right]^2 dY \tag{4.3}$$

The mean for a discrete distribution is given by

$$\mu = \frac{1}{N_T^*}\sum_{r=1}^{N_T^*} Y(r) \tag{4.4}$$

having a variance

$$\sigma^2 = \frac{1}{N_T^*}\sum_{r=1}^{N_T^*}\left[Y(r)-\mu\right]^2 \tag{4.5}$$

When samples are randomly selected from a larger population, the sample mean for a sample of size n is given by

$$\bar{Y} = \frac{1}{n}\sum_{r=1}^{n} Y(r) \tag{4.6}$$

and the sample standard deviation, s, is equal to the square root of the unbiased sample variance given by

$$s^2 = \frac{1}{n-1}\sum_{r=1}^{n}\left[Y(r)-\bar{Y}\right]^2 \tag{4.7}$$

The properties of the frequency distribution of interest are often only four: the mean, the standard deviation (or variance), the standard deviation of the mean, and the nature of the distribution (normal, lognormal, chi-square, binomial, Weibull, etc.).

The integral of the frequency distribution from $-\infty$ to $Y = Y^*$ is equal to the cumulative distribution, $F_C(Y^*)$, for Y at Y^*. The integral of the standard normal frequency distribution over the range from -6 to $+6$ contains all but 2 billionths of the area equal to 1 under the full distribution. If the allowable upper limit, Y_{UL}, and allowable lower limit, Y_{LL}, on a part dimension were centered symmetrically about the mean μ specified for the part and if $6\sigma \leq [Y_{UL} - Y_{LL}]/2$, the manufacturing process would have ideal Six Sigma capability, with only two parts per billion being outside of the limits. Practical Six Sigma capability is only 4.5σ as the sample mean, $\overline{Y}$, has a range itself of roughly 1.5σ for the sample sizes typically used in statistical process control.

4.1.2 The Central Limit Theorem[2]

The variance of the sample mean for a normal distribution is equal to the population variance divided by the sample size:

$$\sigma_{\overline{Y}}^2 = \frac{\sigma^2}{n} \tag{4.8}$$

Moreover, this relationship holds approximately for any distribution if the sample size is large as a result of the Central Limit Theorem, which states:

If a random sample of size n is repeatedly taken from a population with mean μ and variance σ^2, then the resulting distribution of the sample means, $\overline{Y}$, will be normally distributed about the mean μ having a variance of σ^2/n as the sample size n approaches infinity:

$$\overline{Y} = \mu + Z\sqrt{\sigma^2 / n} \quad Lim\ n \to \infty$$

It follows from the theorem, that the sum

$$g(q,n) \equiv \frac{1}{\sigma\sqrt{n}} \sum_{r=1}^{n} [Y(q,r) - \mu] = Z \quad Lim\ n \to \infty \tag{4.9}$$

is also normally distributed with zero mean and unit variance where $Y(q,r)$ is replication r for trial q in an experiment. The mean of the replications for a trial

$$\overline{Y}(q) \equiv \frac{1}{n} \sum_{r=1}^{n} Y(q,r)$$

will be written as $Y(q)$ for simplicity in notation, it being understood that with the single argument q, $Y(q) \equiv \bar{Y}(q)$.

4.1.3 *t* Distribution

The time and expense in generating and analyzing large sample sizes forces the use of small sample sizes in most studies, in which case Equation 4.8 cannot be used to compute the variance of the sample average. However, if the population is normal, the sample standard deviation can be substituted for population standard deviation thereby converting the Z statistic into the *t* statistic:

$$t(q,v) \equiv \frac{Y(q) - \mu(q)}{s(q)/\sqrt{n}} \tag{4.10}$$

The *t* statistic is a function of the degrees of freedom (df), defined as

$$v(q) = n(q) - 1 \tag{4.11}$$

The t distributions for 2 df and 30 df are shown in Figure 4.3 and Figure 4.4, respectively. The 30 df t distribution closely follows the standard normal distribution in Figure 4.2, which is expected from the Central Limit Theorem. However, the t distribution is seen to be broadened considerably for 2 df. If Equation 4.10 is rearranged as

$$\mu(q) = Y(q) + t(q,v)s(q)/\sqrt{n} \tag{4.12}$$

the population mean itself becomes a statistic for a given measured sample mean and variance having a confidence range given by

$$Y(q) - t_{\alpha/2}(q,v)s(q)/\sqrt{n} < \mu(q) < Y(q) + t_{\alpha/2}(q,v)s(q)/\sqrt{n} \tag{4.13}$$

where α is the significance level specified by the investigator. The percent confidence level that the mean lies in this range is equal to $100 \times (1 - \alpha)$, where $t_{\alpha/2}$ is the lower limit of the integral that satisfies the expression

$$\frac{\alpha}{2} = \int_{t_{\alpha/2}}^{\infty} f(t)dt \tag{4.14}$$

The two-tailed, critical region for the confidence range consists of two regions. One is on the left side from $-\infty$ to $-t_{\alpha/2}$, and the other is on the right side from $t_{\alpha/2}$ to $+\infty$. For a given value of α, $t_{\alpha/2}$ can be computed as

$$t_{\alpha/2} = \text{TINV}(\alpha, v) \tag{4.15}$$

The term TIN V(α, v) is the spreadsheet function for computing the t statistic for the critical region. When t for a single-tail critical region is desired, α in Equation 4.15 is replaced by 2α. Descriptions of the more common statistical functions available in Excel are shown in Table 4.1.

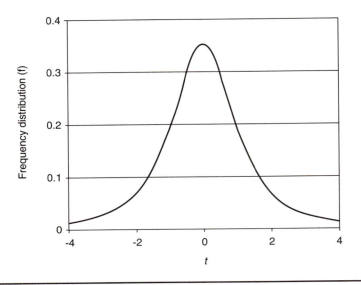

Figure 4.3 t distribution for 2 df.

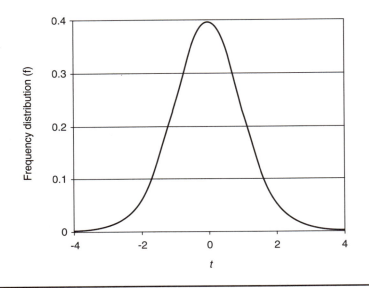

Figure 4.4 t distribution for 30 df.

Table 4.1 A list of the more common statistical functions and their Excel names.

Description	Excel function
Cumulative distribution for F ratio of two sample variances	=1–FDIST(F=var1/var2, df1, df2)
Tail of cumulative distribution for F ratio	=FDIST(F=var1/var2, df1, df2)
F ratio given alpha	=FINV(alpha, degrees of freedom 1, degrees of freedom 2)
Cumulative distribution for Normal variable at x	=NORMDIST(x, mean, standard deviation, 1)
Frequency distribution for Normal variable at x	=NORMDIST(x, mean, standard deviation, 0)
Position x given value for Normal cumulative distribution	=NORMINV(cumulative distribution, mean, standard deviation)
Single tail Type I error t distribution	=TDIST(t, df,1)
Two tail Type I error t distribution	=TDIST(t, df, 2)
Value of t for two tail Type I error	=TINV(alpha, df)
Value for t for single tail Type I error	=TINV(2*alpha, df)
Single tail error for value of chi-square distribution	=CHIDIST(χ2, df)
Value of chi-square for single tail Type I error	=CHIINV(alpha, df)
Cumulative distribution for Weibull	=WEIBULL(x,alpha,beta,1)
Frequency distribution for Weibull	=WEIBULL(x,alpha,beta,0)
Cumulative distribution for Poisson	=POISSON(x,mean,1)
Frequency distribution for Poisson	=POISSON(x,mean,0)

Statistical inferences are made by forming a null hypothesis with the random variable of interest and comparing it against the likelihood of an alternative hypothesis. For example, the null hypothesis that $Y(q)$ is equal to $\mu(q)$ in Equation 4.10 can be formed and compared to the alternative that $Y(q) \neq \mu(q)$. (A value must be chosen for $\mu(q)$ to form the test!) The alternative is assumed true if t is in the critical region. The rate for *incorrectly* inferring that $Y(q) \neq \mu(q)$ is known as the Type I error and is equal to TDIST(t,df,2) for the t statistic (see Table 4.1). A so-called Type II error results when it is inferred that the null hypothesis is correct when it is not. In almost every situation, the size of the critical region is chosen to bias against making Type I errors. For the above two-tailed distribution, the Type II error would be 1 – TDIST(t,df,2). When the null hypothesis is being tested against the alternative that $Y(q) > \mu(q)$, the positive tail of the distribution is considered and the Type I error is given by TDIST(t,df,1), the Type II error being 1 – TDIST(t,df,1). If the alternative hypothesis is $Y(q) < \mu(q)$, the negative tail of the distribution is considered. Note that the *absolute value* of t needs to be entered into the TDIST function.

The t distribution for the difference between the averages of two samples having the same df but taken from two different populations having the same population variance is given by

$$t(1,2; v = 2n-2) \equiv \frac{Y(2) - Y(1) + \mu(2) - \mu(1)}{\sqrt{(s^2(1) + s^2(2))/n}} \tag{4.16}$$

Often the null hypothesis that the two population means are equal is formed, which results in Equation (4.16) becoming

$$t(1,2; v = 2n - 2) \equiv \frac{Y(2) - Y(1)}{\sqrt{(s^2(1) + s^2(2))/n}} \qquad (4.17)$$

When the value for t from Equation (4.17) is inserted into the function TDIST(t,df,2), the Type I *pairwise error* (PWE) for assuming $\mu(2) \neq \mu(1)$ is computed from the difference between two sample averages. Of course, the null hypothesis could be made for a finite value for the difference between the two population means using Equation (4.16). The PWE for assuming $\mu(2) > \mu(1)$ is given by single-tail expression, TDIST(t,df,1). The PWE as defined here is more commonly known as the *p-value*. A t statistic can be formed for the difference between the means for a pair of *states* as defined in Appendix C, Equation (C.32).

4.1.4 Chi-square Distribution

The sample and population variances for a normally distributed population are connected through the chi-square statistic:

$$\chi^2 = \frac{vs^2}{\sigma^2} \qquad (4.18)$$

The mean of the chi-square distribution is the df = v, and its variance is $2v$. For small df, the distribution has a long tail, as can be seen in Figure 4.5. When the df is large (Figure 4.6), the distribution is approximately normal about its mean of 30 but, nevertheless, with a not insignificant tail on the RHS.

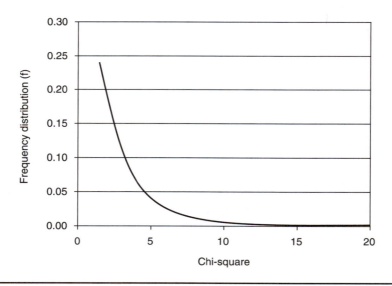

Figure 4.5   The chi-square distribution for 2 df.

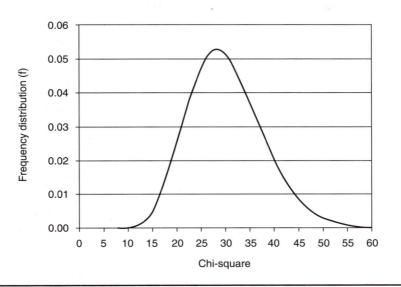

Figure 4.6   The chi-square distribution for 30 df.

4.1.5 The *F* Ratio and *F* Distribution

The sample variances from two different normally distributed populations are compared using the *F* distribution. The *F* ratio is given by

$$F = \left[\frac{s_1^2 / \sigma_1^2}{s_2^2 / \sigma_2^2} \right] \tag{4.19}$$

   Plots of the frequency distribution for *F* are shown in Figure 4.7 and Figure 4.8 for the cases where the two population variances are equal and the two sample variances have the same df of 2 and 30, respectively. The mean of the *F* distribution is equal to $n / [n - 2]$ and thus not defined for a sample size of 2, although the distribution itself is well defined. Both the chi-square and the *F* distributions illustrate that there is considerable uncertainty in the population variance when the sample variance is measured using a small sample size. In Figure 4.8, the two df are the same and relatively large (equal to 30). As a result the distribution is approximately centered about 1 and appears approximately normal except for the tail again on the RHS. Often the null hypothesis is invoked that the two population variances are equal in which case Equation (4.19) becomes

$$F = \left[\frac{s_1^2}{s_2^2} \right] \tag{4.20}$$

Standard convention is to place the larger of the two sample variances in the numerator, the value of the cumulative distribution for *F* being the probability that $\sigma_1^2 > \sigma_2^2$.

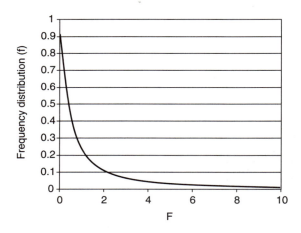

Figure 4.7   The *F* distribution for $v_1 = v_2 = 2$.

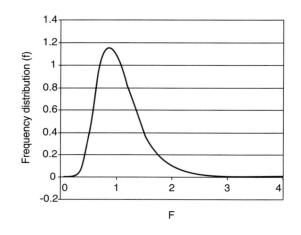

Figure 4.8   The *F* distribution for $v_1 = v_2 = 30$.

4.1.6 The Weibull Distribution

The distribution of failures over time can often be fitted to a Weibull distribution having a cumulative distribution of the form

$$F_C(Y) = 1 - \exp(-(Y / \beta_W)^{\alpha_W}) \tag{4.21}$$

The frequency distribution is obtained by taking the derivative of Equation (4.21). The coefficient β_W represents the location parameter and α_W represents the shape parameter for the distribution. Figure 4.9 shows the distribution for $\alpha_W = \beta_W = 2$. The shape parameter is increased to 10 in Figure 4.10, which makes the shape more symmetrical and moves the tail from the high to the low side of the distribution.

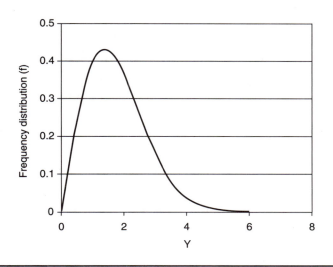

Figure 4.9   Weibull distribution for $\alpha_w = \beta_w = 2$.

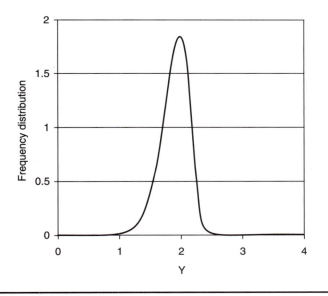

Figure 4.10   Weibull distribution for $\alpha_w = 10$ and $\beta_w = 2$.

4.1.7 Poisson and Binomial Distributions

The number of random events that occur within a fixed time interval often follow the Poisson distribution. Its frequency distribution is discrete and is given by

$$f(Y) = \frac{\mu^Y \exp(-\mu)}{Y!} \tag{4.22}$$

The distribution with $\mu = 4$ is shown in Figure 4.11. The variance of the Poisson distribution is equal to the mean.

The binomial distribution is associated with outcomes for a sample (series) of n replications of a Bernoulli trial in which each trial has one of two outcomes, a and b. Outcome a for any given trial has the probability κ and outcome b has the probability $1 - \kappa$, a series of tosses of a weighted coin being a good example. The frequency distribution for Y representing the number of outcomes for $n = 10$ and $\kappa = 0.5$ is shown in Figure 4.12. The general expression for the frequency distribution is given by

$$f(Y) = \left(\frac{n!}{(n-Y)!Y!} \right) \kappa^Y (1-\kappa)^{n-Y} \tag{4.23}$$

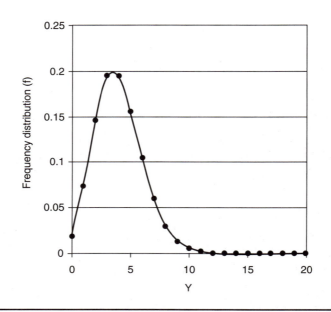

Figure 4.11　Poisson distribution for mean equal to 4. The filled circles represent the discrete points. The curve is drawn as an aid to the eye.

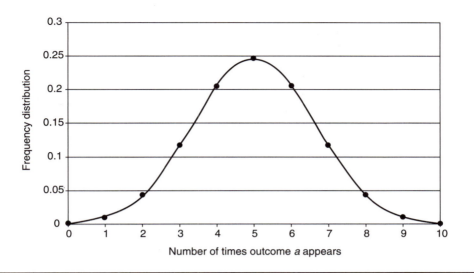

Number of times outcome *a* appears

Figure 4.12 Binomial distribution for ten trials with $\kappa = 0.5$. The circles represent the discrete points. The curve is drawn as an aid to the eye.

4.1.8 The Uniform Distribution

The frequency distribution for the uniform distribution for Y over its range L is constant over this range with $f(Y) = 1/L$. The variance of the uniform distribution is $L^2/3$ as computed from Equation (4.3). Although this distribution is seldom found in practice, it plays a key role in the Monte Carlo simulation process, where numbers, randomly selected from the uniform distribution between 0 and 1, are set equal to the cumulative distribution for the population under investigation. This selection is accomplished for a given experimental trial q and simulation r using the expression $F_C (Y(q,r)) = RAND()$, where RAND() is a pseudo random number function.

When the uniform distribution is centered about 0 having a range from –0.5 to 0.5, its cumulative distribution is given by

$$F_C(Y(q,r)) = Y(q,r) + 0.5 \tag{4.24}$$

When F_C is set equal to RAND(), it follows that

$$Y(q,r) = RAND() - 0.5 \tag{4.25}$$

When the sum in Equation (4.9) is divided by the standard deviation equal to $\sqrt{(0.5)^2/3}$ for the uniform distributions between –0.5 and 0.5, the random variable is given by

$$g(n) = \sqrt{\frac{12}{n} \sum_{j=1}^{n} \left[RAND() - 0.5 \right]_j} \tag{4.26}$$

The ± range for $g(n)$ is given by

$$R(n) = \frac{n}{2}\left[\frac{12}{n}\right]^{0.5} = \sqrt{3n} \qquad (4.27)$$

Samples from two distributions shown in Figure 4.13 are plotted on normal probability paper, the percentage axis being the cumulative distribution in % estimated for the points. One distribution is for $n = 1$ and the other is for $n = 80$. The $n = 80$ distribution is shown to be quite linear reflecting the behavior for a normal distribution as a result of the Central Limit Theorem. The $n = 1$ distribution is seen to be highly nonlinear, particularly near the ends of its range at +/– 1.73. The percentage values are computed automatically by KaleidaGraph using an estimate given by $100(i - 0.5)/n$ for the n random numbers after listing them in ascending order and indexing by i from 1 to n.

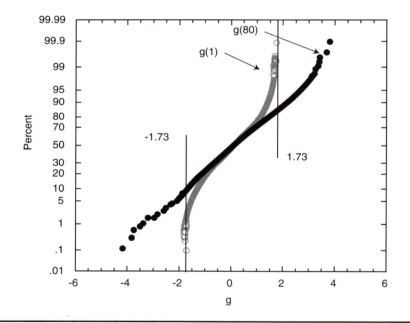

Figure 4.13   Results of 500 simulations for the sum $g(n)$ of the n random variables RAND()-0.5 for $n = 1$ and $n = 80$.

4.2 "LAW OF VARIANCES"

The need often arises to evaluate the variance of a function equal to a sum of independent random variables. For example, an overall dimension L_{Total} may be the sum of several other dimensions L_i, for $i = 1$ to n, which are statistically independent. It follows that the variance of L_{Total} is the sum of the variances of the individual L_i. For the more complex case in which $Y = Y(x_1,x_2, ...)$ is the function whose variance is of interest, an approximate computation can be made by expressing Y as a Taylor expansion including only zeroth and first order terms:

$$Y \cong \mu + \sum_i \partial Y / \partial x_i \big|_{\mu_i} [x_i - \mu_i]$$

This relationship can also be written in terms of the differentials from the means:

$$\delta Y \cong \sum_i \partial Y / \partial x_i \big|_{\mu_i} \delta x_i \tag{4.28}$$

When the variance of both sides equal to the expected value of the square of both sides is taken, the outcome for *statistically independent* random variables is the well-known expression for the "Law of Variances":

$$E(\delta Y^2) \equiv VAR(Y) \cong \sum_i [\partial Y / \partial x_i]^2 \big|_{\mu_i} VAR(x_i) \tag{4.29}$$

When the random variables are *not* statistically independent, Equation (4.29) becomes

$$VAR(Y) \cong \sum_{i,j} \left[\left[\frac{\partial Y}{\partial x_i} \right] \left[\frac{\partial Y}{\partial x_j} \right] \Big|_{\mu_i, \mu_j} E([x_i - \mu_i][x_j - \mu_j]) \right]$$

Of course, Equation (4.29) is not a law but a very useful approximation. As an example, consider the variance of $Y = Ln(u)$ in the vicinity of $\mu_u = 3$. From Equation (4.28), it follows that

$$\delta Y \cong \frac{1}{u} \Big|_{\mu_u} \delta u$$

$$VAR(Y) \cong \left[\frac{1}{\mu_u} \right]^2 \sigma_u^2 = \frac{\sigma_u^2}{9}$$

where σ_u^2 is the variance of u. Consider another example, the acceleration a_{accel} of an automobile given approximately by the relation $a_{accel} = C\tau / W$, where τ is the engine torque, W is the weight of the vehicle, and C is a constant. From Equations (4.28) and (4.29), it follows that the standard deviation of acceleration is given by

$$\sigma_{accel} \cong C\sqrt{\sigma_\tau^2/\mu_W^2 + \mu_\tau^2\sigma_W^2/\mu_W^4}$$

4.3 DV SURVEY STATISTICS

The DV survey[3] was discussed in Chapter 2 as a means for assessing the value of proposed attribute improvements. The survey form used in Chapter 2 is repeated here as Figure 4.14 showing how a typical respondent out of the 600 total might have checked off the boxes in the series of paired comparisons. The goal is to use the survey to determine the value of an attribute improvement and its uncertainty. There are three basic steps involved. First, the neutral price, P_N (PN) is determined. Then the value improvement, ΔV, relative to the baseline condition is computed by subtracting the baseline price, P_0 (P0), from the neutral price, $\Delta V = P_N - P_0$. Finally, the standard deviation, S_{P_N}, of the neutral price is computed, which is equal to the standard deviation of the value change. The 95% confidence range about the point estimate for ΔV is approximately $2S_{P_N}$.

The outcomes for each of the $z = 4$ trials of the hypothetical survey are expanded in Table 4.2 to include a computation of the standard deviation S_Y of $Y = Ln(f/(1-f))$ in column (and name) SDY and the standard deviation of the price, column (and name) SDP. As stated in Chapter 2, the column labeled Select is the number of hypothetical respondents that selected the alternative out of 600, the others having selected the baseline. The logit plot is shown in Figure 4.15. The vertical error bars in Figure 4.15 are computed from the binomial distribution for a 95% confidence range. (The horizontal error bars are those that result if the logit function standard deviations are transformed into an effective standard deviation for the prices.)

Table 4.2   Outcomes from a direct value survey for measuring relative brand value (hypothetical).

PO	n	z
16000	600	4

Trial	P	Select	f	Y	SDY	SDP
1	15000	403	0.672	0.716	0.087	318
2	17000	353	0.588	0.357	0.083	303
3	19000	258	0.430	-0.282	0.082	301
4	21000	174	0.290	-0.895	0.090	329
		f =Select/n		SDY	=SQRT(1/(f*(1-f)*n))	
		Y =LN(f/(1-f))		SDP	=ABS(SDY/b)	

Survey

Assume that you are in the market to purchase a midsized sedan vehicle,
and that you have a choice of a vehicle manufactured by company A or a
vehicle manufactured by company B. The two vehicles are built to the
same performance specifications and have the same interior and
exterior styles and appearance. Four paired comparisons are shown below.
For each of the four comparisons, please select either the vehicle on the
left or the one on the right. The vehicle manufactured by A is offered at the
same price for each comparison, whereas vehicle manufactured by B is
offered at a different price for each comparison.

Midsized Sedans

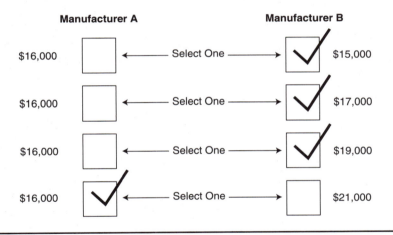

Figure 4.14   A completed hypothetical survey form for assessing the value of manufacturer
B versus A for a midsized sedan.

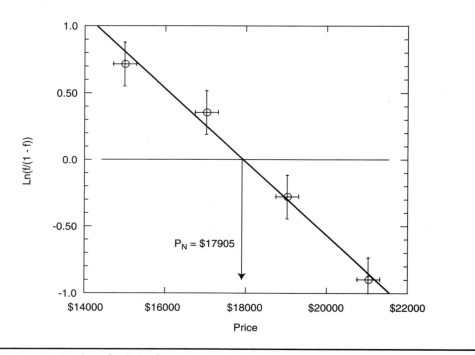

Figure 4.15   Logit plot of results from hypothetical survey.

4.3.1 Theoretical Error in Neutral Price for a Binomial Distribution

The steps involved in computing a theoretical value for S_{P_N} are given here as they provide insight into the variables that influence the error in value obtained from the survey. First, the logit function is expanded about a nominal value of $f = \bar{f} + \delta f$ using only terms up to and including first order, which yields (see section 4.2)

$$Ln\left(\frac{f}{1-f}\right) \cong Ln\left(\frac{\bar{f}}{1-\bar{f}}\right) + \left[\frac{1}{\bar{f}} + \frac{1}{1-\bar{f}}\right]\delta f$$

$$\cong Ln\left(\frac{\bar{f}}{1-\bar{f}}\right) + \frac{\delta f}{\bar{f}\left[1-\bar{f}\right]}$$

(4.30)

The variance is given by

$$VAR\left(Ln\left(\frac{f}{1-f}\right)\right) \cong \left[\frac{1}{\bar{f}\left[1-\bar{f}\right]}\right]^2 VAR(\delta f)$$

$$\cong \frac{1}{\bar{f}\left[1-\bar{f}\right]n}$$

(4.31)

because the statistics for f should follow a binomial distribution with the variance of f being $f(1-f)/n$. The logit function standard deviations, S_Y, computed from the variances are listed in column SDY of Table 4.2.

The linear form $Y(q) = \hat{Y}(q)$ where

$$\hat{Y} = Ln\left(\left[f/\left[1-f\right]\right]\right)$$

is used to model the outcomes where

$$\hat{Y} = a + bP \tag{4.32}$$

The linear regression plot is shown in Figure 4.15. A *lower bound* for the standard deviation for the price points is given by

$$S_{Price} = \left|s_Y / b\right| \tag{4.33}$$

It follows from Equation (4.33) and from the well-known linear regression formula for the standard error of the mean of Y that the lower bound can be written as

$$S_{\bar{P}} = \frac{s_Y}{|b|}\sqrt{\frac{1}{z} + \frac{\left[Y(P)-\bar{\bar{Y}}\right]^2}{SSY}} \tag{4.34}$$

The term SSY is equal to the sum of the squares of the differences between $Y(P)$ and the mean of the means $\bar{Y}$. At $P = P_N$, $Y(P_N) = 0$ and the lower bound for the standard deviation S_{P_N} (SDPN) of the neutral price is given by

$$S_{P_N} = \frac{2}{|b|\sqrt{n}}\sqrt{\frac{1}{z} + \frac{\bar{\bar{Y}}^2}{SSY}} \quad \text{at } P = P_N \tag{4.35}$$

The coefficients a and b for the model were computed using the INTERCEPT and SLOPE functions in the spreadsheet, as shown in the first two rows of Table 4.3. The computations of the neutral price and the added value, named DeltaV, of manufacturer B relative to A are also shown.

The 95% confidence range for the mean price at P_N is obtained by setting the name variable Alpha equal to 0.05, computing t in terms of the spreadsheet expression TINV(Alpha,n–1), and multiplying the result times SDPN. The resulting uncertainty, named ERRORPN estimated to be $293 as a lower bound, is listed at the bottom of Table 4.3.

The theoretical lower bound of $293 for the confidence range for value is directional, the actual measurement from the sample data being generated by the inverse logit plot in which price is on the y-axis and $Ln(f/[1 - f])$ is on the x-axis as shown in Figure 4.16. When the LINEST spreadsheet function is used with inverse plot, the standard error for the neutral price, and thus value was computed as $186. This direct computation, which

Table 4.3 Computation of the lower bound for the standard deviation and 95% confidence range of the mean of the neutral price.

a	4.90	=INTERCEPT(Y,P)
b	-2.7E-04	=SLOPE(Y,P)
PN	17905	=-(a/b)
DeltaV	1905	=PN-P0
Alpha	0.05	
t	1.96	=TINV(Alpha,n-1)
YBAR	-0.0261	=AVERAGE(Y)
SSY	1.518	=SUMSQ(Y-YBAR)
SDPN	149	=ABS((2/(b*SQRT(n))))*
		SQRT(1/z+(0-YBAR)^2/SSY)
ERRORPN	293	=t*SDPN

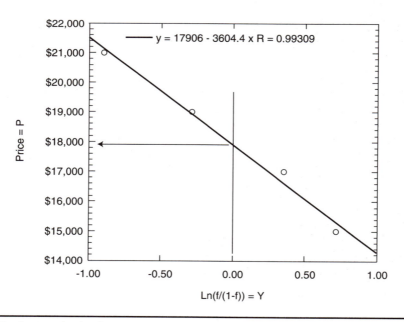

$$y = 17906 - 3604.4 \; x \quad R = 0.99309$$

Price = P (y-axis): $22,000; $21,000; $20,000; $19,000; $18,000; $17,000; $16,000; $15,000; $14,000

x-axis: -1.00; -0.50; 0.00; 0.50; 1.00

$Ln(f/(1-f)) = Y$

Figure 4.16   Inverse logit plot.

avoids the need to use the lower bound approximation, converts to a 95% confidence range of \$365.

4.4 SUMMARY

Six Sigma capability: What is usually reported as 6 σ capability is, in fact, 4.5 σ capability. This is a result of the typical variation in the sample mean used in statistical process control.

Central Limit Theorem: The key property of the Central Limit theorem of interest to us here is that the distribution of the sample means taken from an arbitrary distribution will be normally distributed for a large sample size having a standard deviation equal to the population standard deviation divided by the square root of the sample size.

t *distribution:* The statistic given by $(\bar{Y}-\mu)/\sqrt{s^2/n}$ for samples taken from a normally distributed populations follows a t distribution, which is symmetric about zero. The t distribution is characterized by the degrees of freedom, df, equal to $n-1$ in which n is the sample size used in measuring the sample variance, s^2.

Statistical inference: The statistics for the two populations from which sample measurements were taken are assumed to differ if the sample measurement of the alternative is in the critical region.

Uncertainty in a measurement of value using the DV method: The standard error (standard deviation) in value determined by the DV method is equal to the standard error in the neutral price as determined from a plot of price of the alternative versus $Ln(f/(1-f))$.

REFERENCES

1. W. Mendenhall and T. Sincich. 1995. *Statistics for Engineering and the Sciences,* 4th ed. Upper Saddle River, NJ: Prentice Hall, pp. 143–251.
2. Ibid., p. 311.
3. H. E. Cook. 1997. Product Management: Value, Quality, Cost, Price, Profits, and Organization. Amsterdam: Kluwer, pp. 93–99.

5

Role of Variation on Product Value

Insight: Robust designs take advantage of nonlinear relationships between CTV attributes and one or more manufacturing parameters to reduce the sensitivity of value on variation.

Key Topics

value curves	scaling factors
target specification	outer arrays
Taguchi methods	population versus sample statistics
robustness	

5.1 INTRODUCTION

When a value curve for a product has *negative* curvature (is concave) as a function of a CTV attribute g, variations in g reduce quality by reducing the average value of the product sold to customers. This is illustrated in Figure 5.1, where variation, noted by the line with arrows on both ends, is shown dropping the average from the maximum on the curve to a lower level. Taguchi first made this observation in terms of the loss function and, in doing so, laid the foundation for robust design and modern quality theory. If the value curve is parabolic, the loss due to a given amount of variation is constant and independent of g. Negative curvature for the value function generates a positive curvature in Taguchi's loss function and CIQ, Equation (2.8). The mirror image relationship between a value curve and the corresponding CIQ curve is shown graphically for a nominal is best attribute in Figure 5.2.

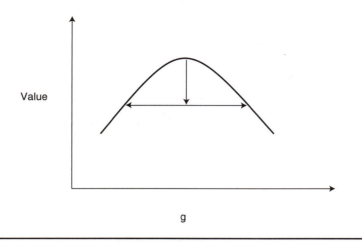

Figure 5.1 Variation in the attribute leads to a reduction in value.

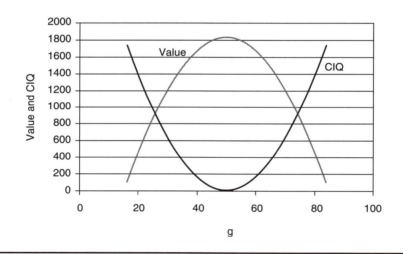

Figure 5.2 Relationship between value and CIQ for a NIB attribute.

5.2 UNWEIGHTED VALUE CURVES

In addition to nominal is best (NIB), there are two other types of value curves, smaller is better (SIB) and larger is better (LIB), as discussed in Chapter 2. Examples of the three types are shown in Figure 5.3. The empirical forms of the mathematical expressions for each are listed in Table 5.1. The LIB curve in Figure 5.3 is shown using the notation x as the natural form for the variable. In the first row of Table 5.1 the natural form of the LIB variable is transformed to $g = 1/x$, which, as noted in Chapter 2, converts the LIB expression to a form identical to that for SIB. The baseline value, V_0 for product i, is computed using Equation (2.14). The ideal value, V_I, represents the maximum value that appears at

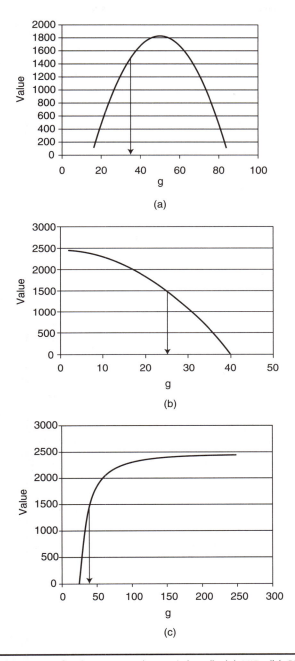

Figure 5.3   The three types of value curves (unweighted): (a) NIB; (b) SIB; (c) LIB for three attributes for the same product. Note that each of the curves has the same value (the total value of the product) when each attribute is at its baseline value.

Table 5.1 Unweighted expressions for the three types of value curves.

Condition	$f_V(g) =$	Ideal value relation $V_I =$
SIB & LIB (g=1/x)	$\dfrac{g_C^2 - g^2}{g_C^2 - g_0^2}$	$V_0 \dfrac{g_C^2}{g_C^2 - g_0^2}$
NIB	$\dfrac{\left[g_C - g_I\right]^2 - \left[g - g_I\right]^2}{\left[g_C - g_I\right]^2 - \left[g_0 - g_I\right]^2}$	$\dfrac{V_0}{1 - \dfrac{\left[g_0 - g_I\right]^2}{\left[g_C - g_I\right]^2}}$
LIB(x)	$\dfrac{1 - \dfrac{x_C^2}{x^2}}{1 - \dfrac{x_C^2}{x_0^2}}$	$\dfrac{V_0}{1 - \dfrac{x_C^2}{x_0^2}}$

the ideal specification, g_I. For the LIB case, the ideal specification is at infinity in the natural variable x and zero when transformed to $1/x$.

5.3 WEIGHTED PARABOLIC EXPRESSION FOR THE VALUE OF A DISTRIBUTION FOR TRIAL (q)

The weighted parabolic expression given by Equation (2.4) is a more general form for the empirical curves than given in Figure 5.3 and Table 5.1. The weighting coefficient γ is computed as an empirical constant from the best fit to the points on the value curve as described in Chapter 2. A rough estimate can be made by setting γ equal to the fraction of time, based upon a jury evaluation, that the attribute is important when using the product.

5.3.1 Quantifying the Value Loss Due to Variation

For a specific experimental trial q, the benefit to the customer for the product alternative under examination can be expressed in terms of the value $V(q)$ for the trial, which is equal to the integral over g from minus to plus ∞ of the frequency distribution for trial q times the value function:

$$V(q) = \int_{-\infty}^{\infty} f(g(q))V(g)dg \tag{5.1}$$

When there is only one attribute of interest $g(q,r)$ and it is measured over a relatively large number of replications $r = 1$ to $n > 30$, a reliable estimate of $V(q)$ could be obtained simply by summing the value $V(q,r)$ for each replication using the expression

$$V(q,r) = V_0 \left[\frac{\left[g_I - g_C\right]^2 - \left[g_I - g(q,r)\right]^2}{\left[g_I - g_C\right]^2 - \left[g_I - g_0\right]^2} \right]^\gamma$$

obtained from Equation (2.4) and dividing by n.

A more useful closed form expression for $V(q)$ is found by expanding $V(g)$ on the RHS of Equation (5.1) in a Taylor series about the mean $g = \mu(q)$ of the distribution. When terms up to second order are included, the expression for $V(q)$ for a population mean $\mu(q)$ and a population variance $\sigma^2(q)$ is given by

$$V(q) = V\left(\mu(q), \sigma^2(q)\right) \cong V_0 \left[\frac{\left[g_I - g_C\right]^2 - \left[g_I - \mu(q)\right]^2}{\left[g_I - g_C\right]^2 - \left[g_I - g_0\right]^2} \right]^\gamma - k_T \sigma^2(q) \qquad (5.2)$$

where

$$k_T = \frac{-V_0}{2} \left\{ \gamma[\gamma-1] f_V^{\gamma-2} \left[\frac{4\left[\mu(q) - g_I\right]^2}{\left[\left[g_I - g_C\right]^2 - \left[g_I - g_0\right]^2\right]^2} \right] - \frac{2\gamma f_V^{\gamma-1}}{\left[g_I - g_C\right]^2 - \left[g_I - g_0\right]^2} \right\} \qquad (5.3)$$

is minus one times one-half the second derivative of the value function evaluated at $g = \mu(q)$. The function f_V is the same as the NIB function in Table 5.1 given by

$$f_V(\mu(q)) = \left[\frac{\left[g_I - g_C\right]^2 - \left[g_I - \mu(q)\right]^2}{\left[g_I - g_C\right]^2 - \left[g_I - g_0\right]^2} \right] \qquad (5.4)$$

The NIB expression in Equation (5.4) is sufficiently general to apply also to SIB and LIB, with $g_I = 0$ (note that $g = 1/x$ for LIB). A wide class of robust design problems can be evaluated by using Equation (5.2) to express value as a function of the mean and variance of the population. The key assumptions in using Equation (5.2) are as follows: (1) the value function, $V(g)$, is analytic in g; (2) the frequency distribution in Equation (5.1) is representative of what is being *shipped* to customers; and (3) customers are using the product shipped to them without repair even though some may not be satisfied with the attribute g of their product. Although Equation (5.2) is complex, it can be evaluated quickly using the Value Curve Plotter worksheet described in Appendix F.

When the exponential weighting coefficient γ is equal to unity, $k_T = k_T^*$, the expression given by Equation (5.2) becomes

$$V(\mu(q),\sigma^2(q)) \cong k_T^* \left\{ \left[g_I - g_C \right]^2 - \left[g_I - \mu(q) \right]^2 - \sigma^2 \right\}$$ (5.5)

where

$$k_T^* = \frac{V_0}{\left[g_I - g_C \right]^2 - \left[g_I - g_0 \right]^2}$$ (5.6)

is independent of g. Thus, in the presence of variation and with $\gamma = 1$, the CIQ reduces to

$$\Omega(\mu(q),\sigma^2(q)) = k_T^* \left[\left[\mu(q) - g_I \right]^2 + \sigma^2(q) \right]$$ (5.7)

Equation (5.7) is similar in form to Taguchi's loss function, except that the ideal specification, g_P, appears in the CIQ in place of the target specification, g_T, in the loss function, $L(g) = \Omega(g) + C(g)$. A different form of Equation (5.2) applies for the NIB case (termed NIB1 here) when a *scaling factor* is used to move the mean found for each trial q to the target, g_T. NIB1 is explored more fully at the end of Chapter 5 in considering the design of a shear pin. Taguchi called minus ten times the log of the loss function the "signal to noise ratio," which is accurate in a literal sense only for NIB1 problems, where the scaling factor is used to place the mean on target. The interest here is on the log of the CIQ, defined here as SN_Ω, not on the log of the loss function. Point estimates given in Appendix I for the three types of SN_Ω can be used as an aid in selecting the sample size when planning an experiment and as an order of magnitude check against more involved computations for SN_Ω based upon Monte Carlo simulations.

5.3.2 Uncertainty in Value Curves for Continuous CTV Attributes

The statistical uncertainty in value for a discrete change in an attribute was discussed in Section 4.3, where it was shown that the standard deviation for value was equal to the standard deviation in the neutral price. The change in the style of an automobile and the change in a sound system of a movie theatre are examples of discrete changes. For CTV attributes that can be varied in a continuous manner, the variation in value is computed from multiattribute expression Equation (3.7). The variation in value due to the multiple attributes varying from their mean, baseline positions is given by

$$\delta V(g_1, g_2, g_3, \ldots) \cong V_0 \sum_i \delta Ln\big(v(g_i)\big)$$ (5.8)

Thus the variance of value at a specific point g_1, g_2, g_3,...is given by

$$\sigma_V^2 \cong V_o^2 \sum_i \sigma_{Ln(v(g_i))}^2$$ (5.9)

The term $\sigma^2_{Ln(v(g_i))}$ is the variance of $Ln(v(g_i))$ and it follows from Equation (2.6) that

$$\sigma^2_{Ln(v(g_i))} = \left[Ln \left[\frac{\left[g_{I,i} - g_{C,i} \right]^2 - \left[g_{I,i} - g_i \right]^2}{\left[g_{I,i} - g_{C,i} \right]^2 - \left[g_{I,i} - g_{0,i} \right]^2} \right] \right]^2 \sigma^2_{\gamma_i} \tag{5.10}$$

where $\sigma^2_{\gamma_i}$ is the variance of γ_i. Equation (5.10) is defined only for the region where value is positive and in the vicinity of the baseline point. The sample measurement $s^2_{\gamma_i}$ of this variance can be determined from the uncertainty in the slope for the best straight line in plots of $Ln(v(g_i))$ versus the log of the function f_V for attribute i as described in Section 2.2.2. The expression for f_V is given by Equations (2.5) and (5.4). The uncertainty in value about its mean is assumed to follow a t distribution having $z - 2$ df. Thus the range for value is given by

$$v(g_1)v(g_2).. - \left| t \right| \sqrt{\sum_i s^2_{Ln(v(g_i))}} < \frac{V(g_1, g_2, ...)}{V_0} < v(g_1)v(g_2).. + \left| t \right| \sqrt{\sum_i s^2_{Ln(v(g_i))}} \tag{5.11}$$

The variances in the summation under the square root sign are given by Equation (5.10). As might be expected, the uncertainty in value increases as the attributes move away from their baseline specifications in either a positive or negative direction.

5.3.3 Influence of Variation on the Variable Cost

It is customary for practitioners of Taguchi's methodology to set the loss due to variation equal to the variance times one-half of the second derivative of the loss function with respect to the attribute g. *Use of the entire loss function, however, leads to a double counting of a portion of the variable cost.* The reason is that the variable cost for a manufacturing process is computed for a fixed process capability, which is defined by a set of nominal values for the mean and variance of the attribute of interest. Thus, the effect of product variation on variable cost is already accounted for when establishing the cost for the process at its stated capability. If the process capability is changed, then the variable cost, of course, may change. To avoid a double counting error, the loss due to variation should be computed from the variance times k_T, which is equal to one half of the second derivative of the CIQ, Equation (5.3) instead of the second derivative of the entire loss function equal to the sum of the CIQ and variable cost. Variable cost can, of course, be uncertain due to uncertainties in labor rates, material costs, shipping costs, and so forth. This uncertainty is not related, however, to the second derivative of $C(g)$ with respect to g.

5.4 ANALYSIS OF SHAFT AND BEARING

Consider the performance of the shaft and bearing shown in Figure 5.4. Assume it generates a baseline amount of value V_0 if it reaches its normal service life T without fatigue failure. Thus, it creates value at an average rate of V_0/T during use. Over a time period dt the value created is equal to $[V_0/T]dt$ times the probability $1 - F_C$ that the shaft has not failed, where F_C is the cumulative distribution function for the fatigue life of the shaft. Thus, the value of the assembly on average is given by

$$V = \int_0^T \frac{V_0}{T}\left[1 - F_C\right]dt$$

$$= V_0\left[1 - \frac{1}{T}\int_0^T F_C(t)dt\right]$$

(5.12)

If no shaft has failed, F_C is equal to zero, and if all have failed, it is equal to 1. An assumption made for simplicity in writing Equation (5.12) is that fatigue failure of the shaft causes no collateral damage.

The cumulative distribution over time can be taken as a Weibull function of the stress level, which is proportional to the inverse of the square of the nominal diameter of the shaft. A typical value curve for the shaft computed in this manner using Equation (5.12) is shown in Figure 5.5. The cost of the shaft can be taken as proportional to the square of its nominal diameter. The location of the maximum difference between the value and cost curves yields the target diameter for the shaft, g_T (≈ 6). Taguchi's loss function is at a minimum at g_T.

The value curve does not follow the $1/x^2$ LIB empirical form of Table 5.1 but follows instead a $1/x^{1.37}$ form. Thus the LIB empirical equation in Table 5.1 is not a general form and should be used with a degree of caution.

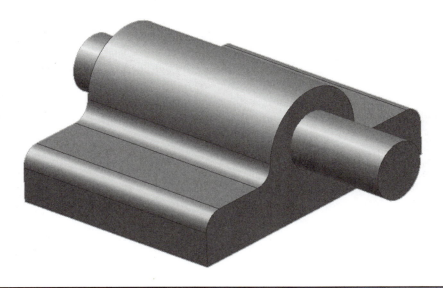

Figure 5.4   Shaft and bearing.

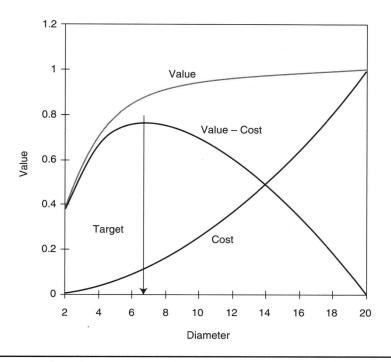

Figure 5.5   Curves for value, cost, and value minus cost for the shaft as a function of its diameter.

This problem is special because the losses in value due to variation are *not* related to the curvature of value as a function of the attribute, thereby voiding the use of Equation (5.2) to compute the loss due to variation. The reason for this is that the shaft diameter was constrained by the bearing. Consequently, a small increase in the shaft diameter relative to its nominal dimension could cause it to freeze within the bearing, and a small decrease in its diameter could cause it to run loosely in the bearing. Thus, if the standard deviation of the bearing is fixed, the value of the shaft is a decreasing function of its standard deviation, as shown in Figure 5.6. The functional relationship can be expressed approximately as

$$V = V_T - k_d E\left(\left[\mu_S + \delta g_S - [\mu_B + \delta g_B] - \Delta_I\right]^2\right)$$

$$= V_T - k_d\left\{\sigma_S^2 + \sigma_B^2 + \left[\mu_S - \mu_B - \Delta_I\right]^2\right\}$$

(5.13)

where σ_S^2 and σ_B^2 are the shaft and bearing variances, respectively, μ_S and μ_B are the shaft and bearing mean diameters, respectively; and δg_S and δg_B are the deviations from the mean diameters for the shaft and bearing. The term Δ_I is the ideal clearance between the shaft and bearing. The term V_T is the value at the target in Figure 5.5, and k_d is an empirical constant.

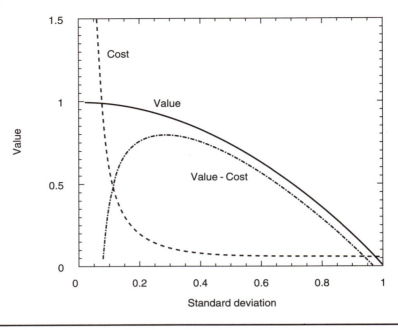

Figure 5.6   Value and cost as a function of the standard deviation of the shaft.

With σ_B^2, μ_S, μ_B, and Δ_I fixed, a critical standard deviation of one for the shaft diameter is taken arbitrarily as the point where the design ceases to function, the point where $V = 0$. The manufacturing cost as a function of the standard deviation is singular as the standard deviation approaches zero. The target for the standard deviation for the shaft is the point at which value minus cost in Figure 5.6 is at a maximum with $\partial V / \partial g = \partial C / \partial g$. This problem shows how tolerance can be set on the basis of strategic considerations.

Although cost is shown as a continuous function of the variables in Figure 5.5 and Figure 5.6, this is an idealization for most attributes, as different manufacturing processes usually come into play when an attribute is changed over a large range. When this is the case, cost becomes a discontinuous function of the attribute. Value curves, however, act as *state functions* of an attribute, being independent of the manufacturing process used to obtain the attribute.

5.5 ROBUSTNESS

A central element of Taguchi's methodology is to generate design and manufacturing processes (DMPs) that are robust in the sense of being relatively insensitive to variation in the design and manufacturing variables[1]. Robustness is illustrated in Figure 5.7 using three value curves. Curve A is seen to be most sensitive to variation, so it is the least robust; curve C is least sensitive and most robust. The design variable g shown in Figure 5.7 is not a CTV attribute of direct importance to the customer but a secondary DMP variable that couples to a CTV attribute. The key CTV attribute for Figure 5.7 could be the brightness of a computer screen, and the secondary design variable g could be the line voltage. Three different

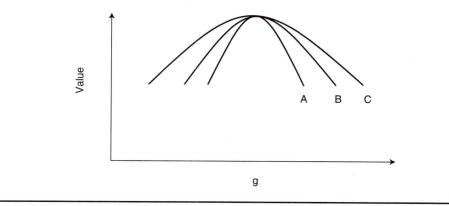

Figure 5.7 Robustness increases from A to B to C.

DMPs yield three different curves of value versus *g*, but there remains just one curve for value versus brightness. Brightness for design A is most sensitive to changes in line voltage and is least robust.

5.5.1 Scaling Factor for Certain NIB Problems

The scaling factor for the NIB1 problem allows the mean to be shifted to the target specification. The diameter of the shear pin in Figure 5.8 is an example of a scaling factor. Given

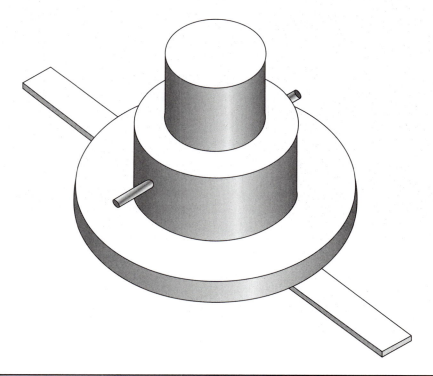

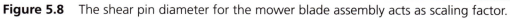

Figure 5.8 The shear pin diameter for the mower blade assembly acts as scaling factor.

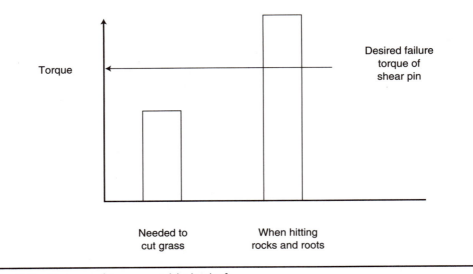

Figure 5.9   Ranges of torque on blade shaft.

the mechanical properties of the material, the diameter can be set to place the nominal shear strength of the pin at its ideal level midway between the upper and lower allowable torque ranges, as shown in Figure 5.9.

Robustness can be introduced if the material's shear strength is a *nonlinear* function of the annealing temperature of the manufacturing process, as shown in Figure 5.10. The variation in annealing temperature (shown schematically at the lower part of the plot) is seen to give a larger variation in strength for a high-temperature anneal than it does for a low-temperature anneal. Thus, for robustness considerations, the lower annealing temperature should be chosen. The larger material strength at the lower temperature is compensated for by choosing a smaller pin diameter, thereby keeping the mean strength of the pin in the center of the desired range shown in Figure 5.9.

Do not confuse the plot in Figure 5.10 with the variation of an attribute with the value function, Equations (5.1) and (5.2). What is being considered in Equation (5.1) is the effect of the variation for a CTV attribute on *average* value. What is being considered in Figure 5.10 is the effect of the variation of a manufacturing factor (annealing temperature) on the *variance* $\sigma^2_{Strength}$ of shear strength, a CTV attribute. A Taylor expansion shows that

$$\sigma^2_{Strength} \cong \left[\text{Slope} \right]^2 \sigma^2_{Temperature}$$

where Slope is the slope of strength versus temperature, which is a function of temperature in Figure 5.10.

5.5.2 Value for a NIB1 Problem

The scaling factor, which is implemented after the experiments have been run, can be used to translate any mean constructed from an arbitrary combination of control factors to the *target position* g_T. The target for the attribute can be taken as the point where value minus variable cost is at a maximum with respect to g. However, the better strategic choice for the

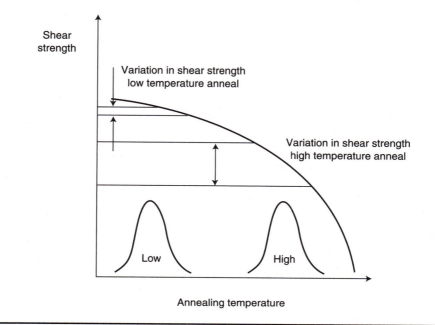

Shear strength

Variation in shear strength
low temperature anneal

Variation in shear strength
high temperature anneal

Low

High

Annealing temperature

Figure 5.10 Schematic representation of shear strength of the material with annealing temperature.

target is the point where cash flow A in Equation (3.6) is at a maximum. The two choices can be different due to differences in fixed cost and investment for a given DMP and the fact that the DMP that yields the maximum in cash flow may provide only a finite range for g. Over this limited range $\partial V / \partial g$ may never be equal to $\partial C / \partial g$.

The modification for Equation (5.2) for the NIB1 case is given by

$$V(\mu(q),\sigma^2(q)) = V(\mu_T) - \frac{k_T g_T^2 \sigma^2(q)}{\mu^2(q)} \tag{5.14}$$

Note that the mean, $\mu(q)$, and variance, $\sigma^2(q)$, in Equation (5.14) are the population mean and variance found for experimental trial q *before* the scaling factor is used to shift the mean to the target specification, g_T. Multiplication of the variance $\sigma^2(q)$ in Equation (5.14) by the ratio $g_T^2 / \mu^2(q)$ converts the trial variance into the variance for the target position. This is simply a size effect correction for variance as a result of applying the scaling factor. Note that if variance were unaffected, the goal would be to make the mean as large as possible before applying the scaling factor to bring the mean to target.

The coefficient k_T in Equation (5.14) is evaluated from Equations (5.3) and (5.4) on replacing $g(q)$ with g_T. The NIB2 expression, Equation (5.2), is a parabolic function of the mean, $\mu(q)$, and special care needs to be taken in interpreting the outcomes of NIB2 experiments as value is not monotonic in $\mu(q)$, in contrast to Equation (5.14) for NIB1. Moreover, the mean cannot be placed exactly at the target specification in a NIB2 experiment due to the absence of the scaling factor. The NIB2 experiment, like SIB and LIB, searches for the combination of factors that provides the maximum in cash flow, Equation (3.9), without the benefit of a scaling factor.

5.5.3 Using an Outer Array to Design for Robustness

Among Taguchi's many contributions to modern quality theory and practice is his invention of the "outer array" or "crossed array" for systematically introducing noise variables into an experiment in a controlled manner. The noise variables are not controllable in production but are controllable during the experiment. An outer array is shown in Table 5.2 for the experimental design shown in Table 3.1. The notations AT, IN, and FE are abbreviations for acceleration time in seconds from 0 to 60 mph, interior noise level in dBA, and fuel economy in mpg, respectively.

The outer array in Table 5.2 is an $L_4(2^3)$ orthogonal array of 0s and 1s rotated 90 degrees counterclockwise to its normal position. Because there are three attributes, each column is repeated three times for data entry, resulting in 12 entries for each trial. The titles of the three rows running from left to right are the names of the three noise factors, which in this case are fuel type (87 and 93 octane), altitude of test (sea level and 7,000 feet), and season of test (summer and winter).

The noise variables chosen for the problem in Table 5.2 are representative of the range of operating conditions experienced in typical driving conditions. The range chosen for continuous noise variables (e.g. the temperature of a heat treat furnace) should be centered about the mean level of the noise expected, μ_η, and the deviation from the mean should be such that the standard deviation for the noise variable in the working environment, σ_η, is reproduced. Thus, if the noise factor is introduced at only two levels, it follows on setting the population variance equal to the variance computed from the noise factor settings that

$$\sigma_\eta^2 = [1/2] \sum_{i=-1,1} \left[\mu_\eta + i\tilde{\alpha}\sigma_\eta - \mu_\eta \right]^2$$

where $\tilde{\alpha}$, which is equal to one for this expression, is a weighting factor that adjusts the noise factor levels to agree with the known variance. Thus, the setting for level −1 should be $\mu_\eta - \sigma_\eta$ and level 1 should be $\mu_\eta + \sigma_\eta$. With three levels,

$$\sigma_\eta^2 = [1/3] \sum_{i=-1,0,1} \left[\mu_\eta + i\tilde{\alpha}\sigma_\eta - \mu_\eta \right]^2_i$$

which has the solution $\tilde{\alpha} = \sqrt{3/2}$. Thus, the settings should be $\mu_\eta - \sigma_\eta\sqrt{3/2}$, μ_η, and $\mu_\eta + \sigma_\eta\sqrt{3/2}$ for levels −1, 0, and 1, respectively.

The rows of the outer array display the settings for each of the noise factors for each replication (repeat) of each experimental trial. The repeats are not true replications as the noise factors are different for each. The outcomes of the hypothetical experiment are shown in Table 5.3 generating four replications per trial for computing the mean and variance of each of the three CTV attributes. For example, the noise factors of fuel, altitude, and sea-

Table 5.2　The 0s and 1s of an outer array have been added to the experimental design shown in Table 3.1.

				Outer array												
		Inner array		0	0	0	1	1	1	1	1	1	0	0	0	Fuel
	Base	V-6	Aluminum	0	0	0	1	1	1	0	0	0	1	1	1	Altitude
	vehicle	engine	body	0	0	0	0	0	0	1	1	1	1	1	1	Season
Trial				AT	IN	FE	AT	IN	FE	AT	IN	FE	AT	IN	FE	
1	1	0	0													
2	1	0	1													
3	1	1	0													
4	1	1	1													

Table 5.3　Hypothetical outcomes for each trial in Table 5.2.

	Outer array													Mean			Variance		
	0	0	0	1	1	1	1	1	1	0	0	0	Fuel						
	0	0	0	1	1	1	0	0	0	1	1	1	Altitude						
	0	0	0	0	0	0	1	1	1	1	1	1	Season						
Trial	AT	IN	FE	AT	IN	FE	AT	IN	FE	AT	IN	FE		AT	IN	FE	AT	IN	FE
1	12	70	28	12.9	68	26	13.2	72	26	14.3	72	25		13.1	71	26.3	0.9	3.7	1.6
2	10.9	69	30	12.1	67	28	11.8	70	28	12.8	70	27		11.9	69	28.3	0.6	2.0	1.6
3	11	66	26	12.2	67	24	12.1	69	24	12.8	70	24		12.03	68	24.5	0.6	3.3	1.0
4	10.2	65	28	10.8	63	25	10.9	68	25	12.1	68	26		11	66	26	0.6	6.0	2.0

son are at their 0 or baseline levels for the first replication. The attributes for AT, IN, and FE are recorded in the appropriate columns for each replication in Table 5.3. The sample mean, $g_i(q)$, and sample variance, $s_i^2(q)$, for each are then computed for each attribute $i = 1$ to 3 for each trial q and shown in the array to the right of the replications. The use of the outer array in this manner allows the influence of the control factors to be evaluated for robustness in the presence of variation expected in the manufacturing and use environment.

The outer array of noise factors can be transposed and incorporated in the inner array as additional columns of control factors, which are not controlled in production. The folding of the outer array in Table 5.3 into the inner array of Table 5.2 is shown in Table 5.4. There can be several reasons for doing this. In certain problems, one or more noise factors may offer the possibility of being controlled, usually at additional expense. Treating these noise factors as potential control factors allows their influence on the outcomes to be directly measured and thus a cost/benefit analysis can be made to see if it is prudent to establish control. Additional degrees of freedom are used when noise factors are placed in the inner array. Interactions between the true control factors and the noise factors can be measured, which provides added insight. However, the use of noise factors as control factors[2,3,4,5] is not uniformly supported. The issues are discussed more fully in Chapter 15.

Table 5.4 Placement of the noise factors in the outer array of Table 5.3 in a new inner array.

Trial	Base vehicle	V-6 engine	Al body	Fuel	Altitude	Season
1	1	0	0	0	0	0
2	1	0	1	0	0	0
3	1	1	0	0	0	0
4	1	1	1	0	0	0
5	1	0	0	1	1	0
6	1	0	1	1	1	0
7	1	1	0	1	1	0
8	1	1	1	1	1	0
9	1	0	0	1	0	1
10	1	0	1	1	0	1
11	1	1	0	1	0	1
12	1	1	1	1	0	1
13	1	0	0	0	1	1
14	1	0	1	0	1	1
15	1	1	0	0	1	1
16	1	1	1	0	1	1

5.6 UNCERTAINTY IN POPULATION STATISTICS

The means and variances of the three attributes shown in Table 5.3 are sample statistics, whereas Equation (5.2) for SIB, NIB2, and LIB and Equation (5.14) for NIB1 are written in terms of the population means and variances. Although it is tempting to substitute the sample statistics for the population statistics, the errors can be substantial when the sample size is small. As discussed in what follows, it is preferable to use instead the confidence ranges for the mean and variance for the population.

The expected value of the average of m sample variance measurements as m approaches infinity is equal to the population variance:

$$E(s^2(q)) = \sigma^2(q) \tag{5.15}$$

and the expected value of a measurement of sample mean is equal to the population mean:

$$E(g(q)) = \mu(q) \tag{5.16}$$

But only a *single* measurement of the sample variance and a *single* measurement of the sample mean are measured for each experimental trial. Statistical inferences are then generated from them for the ranges for the population mean and variance. In regard to variance, an assessment is needed for the frequency distribution $f(\sigma_S^2)$ of the possible population variances $\sigma_S^2(q)$ associated with a single, measured sample variance. When the attributes are normally distributed, the relationship between the two variances is given by

$$\sigma_S^2(q) = \frac{v(q)s^2(q)}{\chi^2} \tag{5.17}$$

The expected value for $\sigma_S^2(q)$ is therefore given by

$$E(\sigma_S^2(q)) = v(q)s^2(q)E\left(\frac{1}{\chi^2}\right)$$
$$= \frac{v(q)s^2(q)}{v(q)-2} \tag{5.18}$$

Note that when $v(q) \leq 2$, the expected value for $\sigma_S^2(q)$ does not exist. Nevertheless, the distribution for $\sigma_S^2(q)$ is well defined through Equation (5.17). This emphasizes that the use of a point estimate to express the outcome of an experiment is inferior to expressing the outcome in terms of the frequency or cumulative distribution.

A similar situation arises when considering a point estimate of the square of the mean

$$E(\mu_S^2(q)) = E\left(\left[g(q) + t_S\sqrt{\frac{s^2(q)}{n}}\right]^2\right) \tag{5.19}$$

versus its distribution function. When the terms in brackets are squared,

$$E(\mu_S^2(q)) = g^2(q) + 2g(q)\sqrt{\frac{s^2(q)}{n}}E(t) + \frac{s^2(q)E(t^2)}{n}$$
$$= g^2(q) + \frac{v(q)s^2(q)}{[v(q)-2]n} \tag{5.20}$$

The results $E(t) = 0$ and $E(t^2) = v/[v-2]$ were used in writing Equation (5.20). Again, when $v(q) \leq 2$, the expected value of $\mu_S^2(q)$ does not exist, but the distribution obtained from the t statistic given by

$$\mu_S^2(q) = \left[g(q) + t_S \sqrt{\frac{s^2(q)}{n}} \right]^2 \tag{5.21}$$

is well defined.

To illustrate these important points, the results of 1000 simulations of $\sigma_S^2(q)$ given by Equation (5.17) are shown as normal probability plots, Figure 5.11 and Figure 5.12, for 30 and 2 df, respectively. The sample variance, $s^2(q)$, for both was the same and equal to one. The distributions for both exist and the average for $\sigma_S^2(q)$ is approximately equal to the sample variance for 30 df but much larger, 10.5, for the 2 df case. If the number of simulations for the 2 df case are increased, the average would likely increase as the expected value is not defined. The simulations for $\sigma_S^2(q)$ were made using 1000 repeats of the spreadsheet function

$$\sigma_S^2(q) = df * SVAR/CHIINV(1-RAND(),df) \tag{5.22}$$

in which SVAR represented the sample variance equal to unity and RAND() generates pseudo-random numbers uniformly between 0 and 1. For completeness, the results for an intermediate df, $v = 4$, are shown in Figure 5.13. The simulated result for the variance is surprisingly close to its expected value of 2.

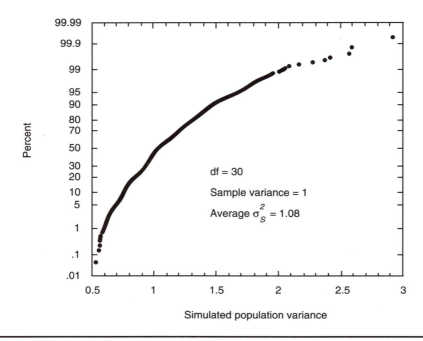

Figure 5.11 Simulated distribution for the population variance: $s^2(q) = 1$ and $v(q) = 30$.

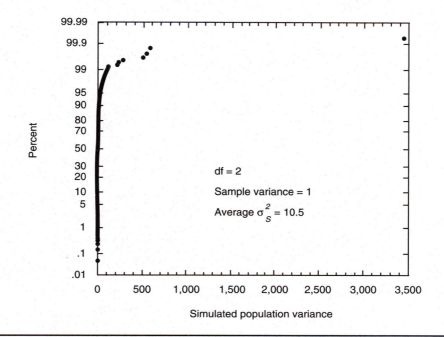

Figure 5.12   Simulated distribution for the population variance: $s^2(q) = 1$ and $v(q) = 2$.

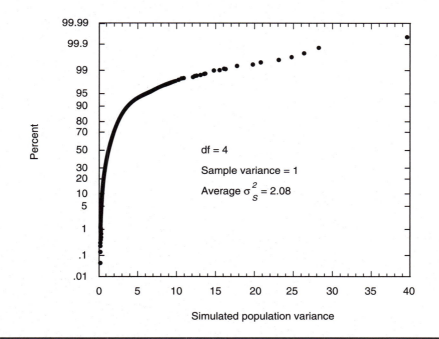

Figure 5.13   Simulated distribution for the population variance: $s^2(q) = 1$ and $v(q) = 4$.

5.7 SUMMARY

Types of value curves: Three types of value curve exist: smaller is better (SIB), larger is better (LIB), and nominal is best (NIB). NIB divides into NIB1, which has a scaling factor, and NIB2, which does not.

Weighted parabolic expression: A weighted parabolic function is used to express the value curves. The weighting coefficient, γ, is an empirical constant, which is expected to be roughly equal to the fraction of time that the attribute is important during the use of the product.

Constrained value curves: The loss of value due to variation of an attribute will not be proportional to the second derivative of value with respect to the attribute if there are constraints. The example used to show this was the value for the diameter of a shaft constrained by a bearing.

Robustness: The design and build of robust products, whose performance is insensitive to environmental and part variation, is central to modern quality theory.

Outer array for noise factors: Noise is introduced in a controlled manner using an outer array for factors not controllable in production. Selection of the level of noise should be done in a manner that replicates the variation seen in production.

Scaling factor: The adjustment of the scaling factor for NIB1 attributes is made after the optimal settings deemed best at reducing the CIQ have been selected.

Sample and population statistics: Sample statistics measured in an experiment are used to assess the confidence ranges for the population statistics.

REFERENCES

1. M. S. Phadke. 1989. *Quality Engineering Using Robust Design*. Englewood Cliffs, NJ: Prentice Hall, pp. 13–39.
2. V. N. Nair (ed.). 1992. "Taguchi's Parameter Design: A Panel Discussion," *Technometrics* 34, pp. 127–161.
3. G. E. P. Box. 1988. "Signal to Noise Ratios, Performance Criteria, and Transformations," *Technometrics* 30, pp. 146–147.
4. R. H. Myers and D.C. Montgomery. 2002. *Response Surface Methodology Process and Product Optimization Using Designed Experiments*. New York: John Wiley & Sons, pp. 539–552.
5. C. F. J. Wu and M. Hamada. 2000. *Experiments Planning, Analysis, and Parameter Design Optimization*. New York: John Wiley & Sons, pp. 436–473.

6

Design of Shear Pin Using Monte Carlo Simulation

> *Insight: Monte Carlo simulation is a powerful tool for translating sample statistics into confidence ranges for the financial metrics.*

Key Topics

Monte Carlo simulation	value improvement
Prospect Theory	scaling factor

6.1 NATURE OF PROBLEM

The design of the shear pin in Figure 5.8 is used here to illustrate (1) how component variation can contribute to product failure, (2) how value is affected when failure occurs, and (3) how Monte Carlo simulation can be used to develop confidence levels for the financial metrics. The shear pin will fail 100% of the time if the torque resistance of the pin falls below the torque of 4 needed to cut grass. On the other hand, if it exceeds the torque strength of 5 for the cast iron crankshaft, the crankshaft will fail instead of the pin if the blade hits a root or rock. The problem is that the baseline heat treatment generates large variation in the pin's shear strength that will lead to failures in the field.

The situation is illustrated in Figure 6.1 by the superposition of a hypothetical frequency distribution of pin shear strengths f on the rectangular value curve V/V_0 for the problem, being equal to one in the safe zone from 4 to 5 and zero outside. Because the curve is not an analytic function of the shear strength g of the pin, Equation (5.2), based upon a Taylor expansion, cannot be used to study this problem, leading us to use Monte Carlo simulation.

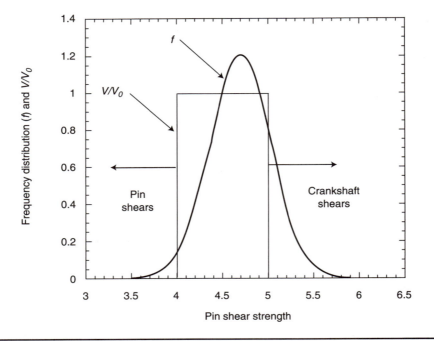

Figure 6.1   Superposition of the frequency distribution of pin shear strengths on the value
curve, illustrating the two failure modes.

6.2 COMPUTING VALUE LOSSES

The loss in value is total for both failure modes, as the mower ceases to function for each
case. However, the customer can restore value as follows: When the shear pin fails, the customer on average needs two hours to insert a replacement pin, which comes with the mower
and has a shear strength between 4 and 5. A person's time is assumed to be worth $25 per
hour, which makes the net value loss $50 for a single failure. The average value loss per
mower sold is $50 times the probability that the shear strength of the pin is below 4.

When the crankshaft fails, the loss in value comes from several sources. First there
is the loss of the value of the entire mower. The customer can restore this loss by buying
a new mower at a price of $600. In addition there is a loss in value associated with the
time of three hours taken over a period of a week to dispose of the old mower and purchase a new mower. Plus there is a loss in value equal to the payment of $25 to a lawn
service to cut the lawn once before the new mower is available. Thus the total loss in
value for a single crankshaft failure is the sum of the four terms:

1. $1200, equal to the total value loss of the mower (taken as twice its price
   assuming $E_2 = 1$)

2. A payment (loss) of $600 for a new mower, which restores the $1200 value
   loss listed in item 1

3. A loss of value of $75 for time lost

4. A payment of $25 to have someone cut the lawn once

The average loss in value per mower sold for crankshaft failure is equal to $700 times the probability that the shear strength of the pin is above 5 times the probability that a root or rock will be hit by the average customer during the mower's lifetime. Assume that historical records show that the probability is 20% for hitting a root or rock.

6.3 SCALING FACTOR

As this is a NIB1 problem, value loss is minimized by adjusting of the diameter the shear pin to place its shear strength optimally between the lower and upper torque limits. Although the bias should be to the low torque side of the midpoint, based upon the loss of value arguments discussed above, for simplicity, the pin diameter is adjusted to set the target at the midpoint (4.5) of the acceptable torque range.

6.4 MONTE CARLO CONSIDERATIONS

The average loss of value per mower for both failure modes is equal to

$$\Delta V = -50F_L - 140F_H \tag{6.1}$$

where F_L is equal to the fraction of pins whose shear strength g is less than 4 and F_H is equal to the fraction of pins whose shear strength g is greater than 5. Equation (6.1) represents the *transfer function* for this problem. It follows that

$$F_L = F_C(g = 4)$$

and

$$F_H = 1 - F_C(g = 5)$$

where $F_C(g)$ is cumulative distribution for the pin's shear strength at g.

Monte Carlo simulation can be used to assess the fraction of mowers expected to fail by either shear pin failure or crankshaft failure based upon sample measurements of the strength of the pin. A total of $n = 5$ replicated measurements of pin strength were made for the baseline and alternate heat treatments. The samples are assumed to have been taken randomly from a normal population; thus the distribution of the possible means for the population for a given heat treatment is given in terms of the t statistic:

$$\mu_s = g(q) + t\sqrt{\frac{s^2(q)}{n}} \tag{6.2}$$

The distribution of the possible variances for the population as a function of the measured sample variance is given by Equation (5.17).

With the Monte Carlo method, a value for the population mean is computed using Equation (6.2) in two steps. The first is to choose a value for the cumulative t-distribution by setting it equal to a pseudo-random number RN = RAND( ) in the spreadsheet, between 0 and 1:

$$F_C(t) = \text{RAND}() \tag{6.3}$$

The second step is to compute the value for the t statistic corresponding to $F_C(t)$, using the TINV function (which returns the magnitude of t) suitably modified using IF statements:

$$t = \text{IF}(RN > 0.5, 1, -1) * \text{TINV}(\text{IF}(RN > 0.5, 2 * (1 - RN), 2 * RN), n-1) \qquad (6.4)$$

The IF statements in Equation (6.4) are needed to work around a shortcoming in the spreadsheet due to the TINV function accepting only the positive tail times 2 of a point on cumulative distribution $F_C(t)$. The first IF statement controls the sign of t and is interpreted as follows: "If $RN = F_C(t)$ is greater than 1/2, then the logic function equals one, otherwise it is equal to minus one." The second IF statement forces the first argument in TINV to be evaluated using the positive tail of the distribution. The last argument for TINV is the df equal to n − 1. Note, it would be improper to replace each RN in Equation (6.4) with a RAND( ) function, as the RAND( ) functions would not be the same.

A complete listing of the named variables used in the Monte Carlo simulations for the alternative heat treatment and their respective spreadsheet expressions is given in Table 6.1. SVAR and SAVG are the names for the cells containing the hypothetical measurements of the sample variance and sample mean, respectively. The same variables were used for the baseline heat treatment except that SVAR was 0.10. TORQLO and TORQHI refer to the low and high torque limits of 4 and 5, respectively, in Figure 6.1.

The last four names in Table 6.1 are random variables determined by computer simulation, their values changing with each simulation. The spreadsheet expressions for these variables are also shown in Table 6.1 to the right of the cell in which the computation was made. SIMPOPVAR and SIMPOPAVG represent the names for the simulated population variance and mean, respectively. They are the spreadsheet versions of Equations (5.17) and (6.2). The name SIMPOPVARC represents the "corrected" simulated population variance on implementing the scaling factor for this NIB1 problem, the assumption being that the variance of the shaft diameter is proportional to the square of the diameter.

Table 6.1 Named variables and spreadsheet equations for a single simulation of the alternative heat treatment.

RN	0.633002	=RAND()
TORQLO	4	
TORQHI	5	
SVAR	0.01	
SAVG	4.5	
TARGET	4.5	
n	5	
SIMPOPVAR	0.00474	=(n-1)*SVAR/CHIINV(1-RAND(),n-1)
t	0.364414	=IF(RN>0.5,1,-1)*TINV(IF(RN>0.5,2*(1-RN),2*RN),n-1)
SIMPOPAVG	4.516297	=TARGET+t*SQRT(SVAR/n)
SIMPOPVARC	0.004706	=SIMPOPVAR*TARGET^2/SIMPOPAVG^2

Next, the expressions for the fractions below and above the safe torque strength range were computed from the spreadsheet expression given by

$$F_L = \text{NORMDIST(TORQLO,SIMPOPAVG,SQRT(SIMPOPVARC),1)} \qquad (6.5)$$

$$F_H = 1\text{-NORMDIST(TORQHI,SIMPOPAVG,SQRT(SIMPOPVARC),1)} \qquad (6.6)$$

The NORMDIST function (see Table 4.1) returns the normal cumulative distribution when the last of its four arguments is unity. Its first argument is the value at which the distribution is computed, the second is the population average, and the third is the population standard deviation. The uncertainty in the fraction of pins falling outside of the safe region comes from the fact that both the population mean and the population variance are uncertain because the mean and variance were obtained from a small sample size.

Finally, F_L and F_H computed from Equations (6.5) and (6.6), respectively, were substituted into Equation (6.1) to compute the value loss ΔV for each simulation. A macro, SimPasteDown(), which performs 100 simulations, was used to compute F_L, F_H and ΔV. It was run six times quickly to obtain 600 simulations by holding down the Shift Ctrl keys and hitting the + key six times in succession.

The cumulative distribution for the fraction of times the strength falls outside the safe zone for the baseline heat treatment is shown in Figure 6.2. The distribution is very poor for

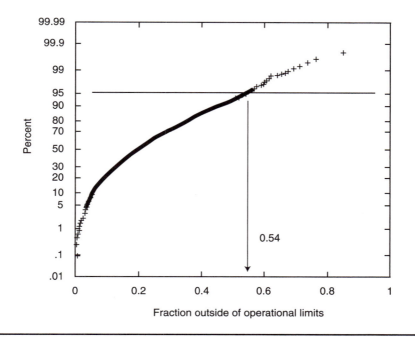

Figure 6.2 The cumulative distribution for strengths outside the operational limits for a sample variance of 0.1.

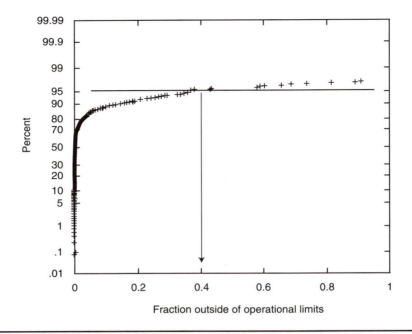

Figure 6.3 The cumulative distribution for strengths outside the operational limits for a sample variance of 0.01.

the product in that there is 95% confidence that only 46% of the pins will have strengths that fall inside of the operational limits. The computations were made assuming that the probabilities were low enough to ignore repeat failures after repair or replacement. The Monte Carlo results for the lower annealing temperature are shown in Figure 6.3, where there is 95% confidence that 96% of the pins will fall inside the operational limits.

6.5 VALUE IMPROVEMENT

The distribution function for value improvement for the revised heat treatment relative to the baseline was computed as follows: for each simulation number n_s from 1 to 600, the negative loss in value $\Delta V_{0.1}(n_S)$ for the baseline variance of 0.1 was subtracted from the value loss $\Delta V_{0.01}(n_S)$ for the alternative variance of 0.01. The resulting distribution is shown in Figure 6.4. The median improvement is seen to be $17.20, and there is 95% confidence that the value improvement will be better than $2.25 (95% of the points are greater than $2.25). The so-called Type I error (see Appendix B) that the value improvement is not greater than a null hypothesis of $0 is approximately 1% (only 1% of the points are less than zero).

Ideally the quality problem associated with the variance of the pin's shear strength would be found and resolved before production began. If the problem were discovered after production began, the aggregate perceived value of the mower would drop over time as customers experienced the two types of failure modes. The resulting change in value can be

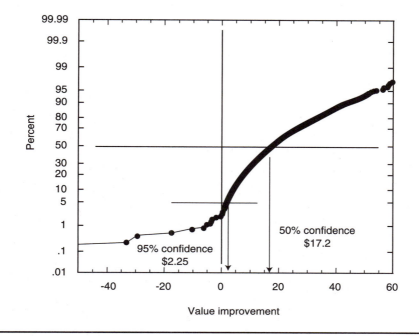

Figure 6.4   Distribution for value improvement.

substituted into the expression for demand to project the expected change in demand. The variation of the general linear demand expression, Equation (4.1), is given by

$$\delta D_i = K \left\{ \delta V_i - \delta P_i - \frac{1}{N} \sum_{j \neq i} \left[\delta V_j - \delta P_j \right] \right\} \tag{6.7}$$

The prices of the $N-1$ competing products are unlikely to change as a result of the quality problem. Moreover, the values of the competing products will be unaffected by the quality problem of a competitor. Thus Equation (6.7) can be written as

$$\delta D_i = K \left\{ \delta V_i - \delta P_i \right\} \tag{6.8}$$

Because the change in value is an unexpected loss, $\delta V_i < 0$, the perceived loss in value may be twice as high as computed here based upon findings from Prospect Theory[1]! Thus, the relationship in Equation (6.8) becomes

$$\delta D_i \cong K \left\{ 2\delta V_i - \delta P_i \right\} \tag{6.9}$$

Prospect Theory highlights the need to avoid problems in the field. When a field failure does occur, the problem must be fixed quickly and the affected customer must be compensated for his or her losses to restore full confidence in the product. In the above example, a customer who has experienced a pin failure should be compensated by approximately \$100 (twice the monetary loss). A customer whose mower has experienced a crankshaft failure should be compensated by approximately \$240 and given a new mower. When a company chooses to address the entire scope of value losses in this manner, the financial implications of field failures force it to maintain a high vigilance in regard to quality, thereby avoiding an erosion of confidence in the product and a decline in market share.

The magnitude of the pin's value loss was implicitly assumed to be much larger than the variable cost and investment implications needed to facilitate the change in the heat treatment process. If the variation in pin strength had been small, it would have been appropriate to consider the full implications on a bottom-line metric using Equations (1.5) or (1.6), respectively, for NPV or IRR in seeking which pin to use. Cash flows are computed for a pin with the baseline heat treatment and for a pin with the alternative heat treatment but having added variable cost and investment. The original demand target of D_0 is reduced by an amount approximately equal to $2K\delta V_i$ for the baseline pin, as customers will not expect pin failures to be a normal part of the operation of the mower. With the alternative pin, demand would be D_0, variable cost would be $C_0 + \delta C_i$, and investment would be $M + \delta M_i$. Price is assumed to remain constant. It follows that NPV or IRR for the two pins can be computed from their projected cash flows over the time horizon Y_{RS} to determine which pin should be used.

6.6 SUMMARY

Robust design using Monte Carlo simulation:

1. Sample means and variances are measured for a baseline and an alternate component.

2. The assumption is made from experience or conjecture that the population is normally distributed or is transformed in a manner to make it approximately normally distributed. Other distributions can also be used but require special considerations. (See Chapters 12 and 13 and Appendices D and E.)

3. Repeated simulations are used to compute the range of uncertainty in the population variance using Equation (5.17), the value for the chi-square statistic being determined from its cumulative distribution equal to a pseudo-random number selected between 0 and 1.

4. Similarly, repeated simulations are used to compute the range of uncertainty in the population mean using Equation (6.2), the value for the *t* statistic being determined from its cumulative distribution equal to a random number selected between 0 and 1 and independent of the random number selected in step 3.

5. A transfer function is constructed and used to compute customer value from the simulated population mean and variance for the component in question for each simulation.

6. The range of value differences is plotted on normal probability paper to determine the degree of confidence for assuming that the alternative offers a value improvement over the baseline.

7. If a value improvement is found, then a bottom-line metric reflecting variable cost and investment implications is used to assess the confidence level that the proposed design change represents a sound financial investment.

Note: The population means and variances are not correlated for a normally distributed population. This property, which was used in steps 3 and 4, will not necessarily be true for other distributions.

REFERENCE

1. A. Tversky and D. Kahneman. 1981. "The Framing of Decisions and Psychology of Choice," *Science* 211, pp. 453–458.

7

Level 1: Multiple Regression with Pooled Variances

> *Insight: Well-designed, controlled experiments offer greater precision than regression analysis of historical data, which often show strong collinearity between factors.*

Key Topics

RLS model

use of spreadsheet to design and analyze experiments

pooled variance

lack of fit analysis

hierarchical rules of thumb

residuals

7.1 HISTORICAL ANALYSIS VERSUS CONTROLLED EXPERIMENTATION

A factory manager has noticed cyclical fluctuations in the quality of the product shipped over the past month. She wisely begins her search for corrective action by talking to the people working on the factory floor, explaining the problem, and asking what might be the cause. The suggestions could include changes in the suppliers of parts, changes in line speed, turnover in personnel, unusual variations in ambient temperature and humidity, changes in machine performance, and changes in raw material. Was there any correlation with quality when parts from supplier G were used versus K? When the line speed was changed from the standard rate, was quality affected?

If this information has been recorded, a linear regression model can be used as an aid in forming inferences about the possible causes and their effects. The model provides a general set of coefficients, β_{ij}, that couple the potential causes X_{ij} to the effect, Y. The coefficients are defined mathematically as $\beta_{ij} = \delta Y / \delta X_{ij}$, the dummy index i representing the type of factor and j representing its level.

Instead of mining historical data, planned experiments can be used to form inferences about cause-and-effect relationships. If due care is taken in choosing the design, the planned experiment will almost always provide a more sensitive measure of the β_{ij} than a regression analysis of historical trends. The main reason for this is that when the factors change naturally over time, their movements are often highly correlated. This makes it difficult to assess the sensitivity of the factors on the outcomes. Well-designed experiments, on the other hand, can entirely eliminate correlation between certain factors. However, it takes extra time and resources to run an experiment and, for some problems, a controlled experiment is simply impossible. Macroeconomists, for example, cannot run controlled experiments to see which factors influence the gross national product. They must form inferences from the analysis of historical data. However, microeconomists can run highly informative, controlled experiments[1].

7.2 LEVELS OF ANALYSIS

The analysis levels shown in Table 7.1 represent degrees of insight in examining the outcomes of an experiment. Level 1 assumes that the samples came from populations having a common variance and uses the *t*-test for assessing the significance of the factors on the sample means. Level 2 takes the opposite and more realistic assumption, which is that the samples did not come from populations having a common variance, and Satterthwaite's approximate *t*-test is used to assess the significance of the factors on the sample means[2]. (Satterthwaite actually used an ANOVA approach employing an approximate *F* test.) Level 3 considers the influence of the factors on the sample means *and* variances, and Level 4 considers, in addition, the influence of the factors on strategic metrics such as cash flow and market share using Monte Carlo (bootstrapping) techniques. Level 1 analysis can be carried out using most any commercial statistical package, including the regression tool in Excel's data analysis tool pack.

However, Levels 2, 3, and 4 require the use of one or more algorithms not included in most commercial packages. Fortunately, the needed range and flexibility can be handled

Table 7.1 Levels of analysis for examining the outcomes of an experiment.

Level	n	Sample Variance	Significance Test for Mean	Significance Test for Variance	Strategic Significance Test
1	Constant or not constant	Pooled	Yes regular t-test	No	No
2	Constant or not constant	Not pooled	Yes Satterthwaite's t-test	No	No
3	Constant or not constant	Not pooled	Yes Satterthwaite's t-test	Yes individual test	No
4	Constant or not constant	Not pooled	Yes Satterthwaite's t-test	Yes individual test	Yes Monte Carlo method

using commercial spreadsheet programs having statistical functions and matrix algebra capabilities. The spreadsheet is also used for the Level 1 analysis to provide continuity and a seamless transition to Levels 2, 3, and 4.

7.3 THE REGULAR LEAST SQUARE (RLS) LINEAR REGRESSION MODEL

The outcomes Y are assumed to be connected to the causes $X\beta$ by a set of linear simultaneous equations of the form

$$\mathbf{Y} = \mathbf{X}\boldsymbol{\beta} + \mathbf{e} \tag{7.1}$$

Pure error is represented by e. The matrix $\mathbf{X}$ is the model or design matrix, ideally chosen on the basis of being as efficient as possible for solving the problem at hand. The number of columns in $\mathbf{X}$ must equal the number of rows in $\boldsymbol{\beta}$, and the number of rows in $\mathbf{X}$ must equal the number of rows in $\mathbf{Y}$. The number of columns in Y must equal the number of columns in β.

The random error term makes it impossible to obtain a precise determination of the w unknown coefficients $\boldsymbol{\beta}$. Instead $\hat{\boldsymbol{\beta}}$, the regular least square (RLS) estimate for β, is computed using the relation

$$\hat{\boldsymbol{\beta}} = \mathbf{X}_S \mathbf{Y} \tag{7.2}$$

where X_s is the solution matrix given by Equation (3.6). When $\boldsymbol{\beta}$ is a column vector, which is often the case, its transpose, β', becomes the row vector:

$$\boldsymbol{\beta}' = (\beta_0 (= \beta_{00}), \beta_{11}, \beta_{12}, \ldots \beta_{21}, \ldots) \tag{7.3}$$

The subscript 0 denotes the baseline coefficient. Although not shown in the above expression, the coefficient for the interaction between a pair of factors ij and kl is written as β_{ijkl}.

It is useful to divide experimental designs into one of two types, lambda or phi. (See Appendix A.) The lambda form, which is often called the "relationship" design, measures the control factors relative to a baseline trial. The baseline is often taken to be trial 1 for convenience. The phi form, often called the "effects" design, measures the control factors relative to a baseline represented by the average of all the trials. The phi design can also be used for strategic experiments but extra steps need to be taken to compute the differences between the trial 1 baseline and alternate states.

When a lambda matrix is used, the array $\boldsymbol{\beta}$ will be written as λ, and when a phi matrix is used the array will be written as φ. For simplicity in notation, λ and the φ are shown without "hats," it being understood that they are always RLS estimates.

7.4 USE OF THE SPREADSHEET

The first step in using a spreadsheet to support the design and analysis of an experiment is to enter the design matrix and its cohorts. A suggested organization of these matrices within a spreadsheet is shown in Figure 7.1. If the design matrix has r rows and c columns, its transpose will have c rows and r columns. The covariance matrix, $[\mathbf{X}'\mathbf{X}]^{-1}$, will always

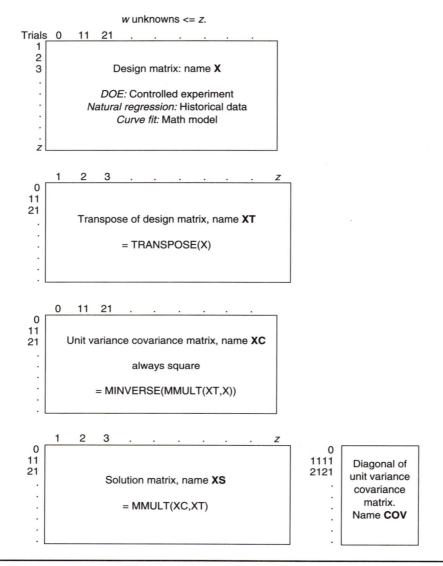

Figure 7.1 Suggested organization of matrices within the spreadsheet.

be square and have c rows and c columns. The solution matrix will always have c rows and r columns like the transpose. *It is good practice to label the rows and columns of each matrix.* The formats used to display some experimental designs need to be translated into the proper mathematical form before matrix operations can be performed. The procedure for transforming orthogonal arrays (OA) represented by Taguchi and Konishi's format[3] is described in Appendix A.

Each of the steps needed to perform the analyses for Levels 1 through 4 will be presented in a deliberate manner to illuminate the process. However, much of the actual work needed to analyze the outcomes of strategic experiments can be automated if the design is already included in the SDW library, Appendix F, which contains some of the more commonly used experimental designs. Templates also exist to aid in creating designs not yet in the library.

It is good practice to give the matrices array names that indicate what they represent. For example, the names X, XT, XC, and XS are logical for the design, transpose, covariance, and solution matrices, respectively (Figure 7.1). Once these choices are made, the names cannot be used for another matrix in the same workbook. When multiple design matrices are being used in a single workbook, it is tempting to use the names X1, X2, and so forth for the design matrix. However, the spreadsheet is already using these names for cells. Consequently, names such as XX1 and XX2 or X_1 and X_2 should be used instead. Names such as XPHI and XLAM are obvious choices for the design matrices when using phi and lambda matrices in the same workbook.

Consider the regression problem in which the effect was believed to have three possible causes and there was no random error. In year 1, the effect was 8 and causes 0, 11, and 21 were, respectively 1, 2, and 5. The effects in years 2 and 3 were 12 and 4 and the causes were 1, 3, and 8 and 1, 0, and 4, respectively. The problem is expressed in terms of three simultaneous regression equations given by

$$\beta_0 + 2\beta_{11} + 5\beta_{21} = 8$$
$$\beta_0 + 3\beta_{11} + 8\beta_{21} = 12$$
$$\beta_0 + 0\beta_{11} + 4\beta_{21} = 4$$

The resulting design matrix for this problem and the outcomes vector were keyed into the spreadsheet in Table 7.2. The outcome vector Y is also shown as a column to the right of the design matrix. The transpose, covariance, and solution matrices are listed in order below the design matrix.

The 3×3 design matrix was named X. The transpose of this matrix, named XT, was computed as follows: A 3×3 region where XT was to be placed was highlighted. Then the function for the transpose,

XT = TRANSPOSE(X)

was typed into the formula bar followed by hitting the Enter key *while holding down the Shift and Ctrl keys* (Shift + Ctrl → Enter). While the region was still highlighted, the name XT was typed into the Name Box. The covariance matrix, named XC, was computed similarly using the relationship

XC = MINVERSE(MMULT(XT,X))

Table 7.2 Development of the design, transpose, covariance, and solution matrices.

Design matrix

	0	11	21	Y
1	1	2	5	8
2	1	3	8	12
3	1	0	4	4

Transpose

	1	2	3
0	1	1	1
11	2	3	0
21	5	8	4

Covariance matrix

	0	11	21
0	8.360	2.120	−2.040
11	2.120	1.040	−0.680
21	−2.040	−0.680	0.560

Solution matrix

	1	2	3
0	2.400	−1.600	0.200
11	0.800	−0.200	−0.600
21	−0.600	0.400	0.200

The solution matrix named XS was then computed:

$$XS = MMULT(XC,XT)$$

When the **X** matrix is square (when the number of rows and columns are equal), the solution matrix is simply the inverse of **X** given by XS=MINVERSE(X). The solution matrix can also be computed directly from the design matrix as discussed in Chapter 3 and Appendix C using the direct expression for the regular least square solution given by

$$XS = MMULT(MINVERSE(MMULT(TRANSPOSE(X),X)),TRANSPOSE(X))$$

A word of caution is advised when using this expression. It is possible to have, unwittingly, a design matrix that has fewer independent trials than unknowns and to compute, using the direct expression listed above, what appears to be a well-defined solution matrix.

This rare but very unfortunate situation, which arises from round-off error, can be caught by computing the solution matrix using the expression XS = MMULT(XC,XT), which requires the preliminary step of computing the covariance matrix as a check. It will not compute when the number of unknowns exceed the number of independent equations. Thus, it is highly recommended to check the existence of the covariance matrix for the experimental design to ensure that the number of independent equations are sufficient to solve for the unknown coefficients before starting the experiment if the design chosen is a departure from the standard fare.

The array of unknown coefficients $\boldsymbol{\beta}$ having elements β_{ij} was represented on the spreadsheet as the matrix variable BETA. These unknowns were computed from the matrix operation = MMULT(XS,Y) which yielded

BETA

0	4/5
11	1 3/5
21	4/5

The elements of the covariance matrix are written as $\text{cov}_{ij\,kl}$ and the elements of the solution matrix are written as $\omega_{ij}(q)$ where ij is the row and q is the column in $\mathbf{X}_s$. The row argument q runs from 1 to z. Within the total number of equations, z, $w \leq z$ must be linearly independent to solve for the w unknown coefficients. The elements of the *sample average outcome vector* $\mathbf{Y}$ are defined as

$$Y(q) = \frac{1}{n(q)} \sum_{r=1}^{n(q)} Y(q,r) \tag{7.4}$$

where $Y(q,r)$ is replication r for trial q and $n(q)$ is the number of replications for trial q. The sample variance $s^2(q)$ is given by

$$s^2(q) = \frac{1}{n(q)-1} \sum_{r=1}^{n(q)} \left[Y(q,r) - Y(q) \right]^2 \tag{7.5}$$

As discussed in Chapter 4, the population variance and average are written as $\sigma^2(q)$ and $\mu(q)$, respectively. When the sample variances are known to come from populations having a common variance, σ^2, they are replaced by a *pooled variance* equal to the weighted average of the sample variances over the z trials:

$$s_P^2 = \frac{\sum_{q=1}^{z} [n(q)-1]s^2(q)}{\sum_{q=1}^{z} [n(q)-1]} \tag{7.6}$$

having a pooled df given by

$$v_P = \sum_{q=1}^{z} [n(q) - 1] \qquad (7.7)$$

However, a common population variance is often *assumed* without solid evidence to support it. The resulting pooled df may be generously overstated, leading to a false level of confidence in the significance of the factors on the mean. When it is not clear that there is a common population variance, the general form of Satterthwaite's approximate solution for assessing the significance of the mean should be used as described in Chapter 8.

7.5 LEVEL 1 ANALYSIS

There are various ways at arriving at an experimental design for a problem. The simplest is to use a design already worked out by someone else that fits your problem. Two popular designs are full factorial (FF) designs and orthogonal arrays (OAs), which are a form of fractional factorial designs. The American Supplier Institute publishes a collection of orthogonal arrays compiled by Taguchi and Konishi.[3] Wu and Hamada have provided an extensive review of a wide range of experimental designs.[4] Also software packages such as MINITAB or Design Ease can be used to explore a wide range of designs.

A full factorial design provides the opportunity for determining the main effect coefficient for each factor and all possible interactions between the main effects. Orthogonal arrays saturated with main effects (no interactions) are often used when it is believed that the interactions between main effects are weak, as more main effects can be evaluated for the same number of experimental trials. The risk in doing so is that interactions are confounded with main effects. For example, between the FF and saturated or nearly saturated OA designs are fractional factorial designs having an intermediate number of main effects that are not confounded with pairwise interactions.

7.5.1 Example

Walpole and Myers[5] reported an experiment that investigated the influence of two factors ($i = 1, 2$) on the burn rates of solid rocket fuels. One factor, A ($i = 1$), had three levels—A1 (10), A2 (11), and A3 (12)—and the other, B ($i = 2$), had four levels—B1 (20), B2 (21), B3 (22), and B4 (23)—yielding a total of $z = 3 \times 4 = 12$ trials. Assume that the objective was to determine which factors, if any, chosen for investigation *reduce* the burn rate relative to the baseline. Also assume that there is good evidence that the variances can be pooled and trial 1 is the baseline reference.

The lambda form for the design matrix shown in Table 7.3 is taken from the Design & Outcomes worksheet of the L12(3^1,4^1) FF SDW. Columns with double indices *ij* are for

Table 7.3 The design matrix, lambda form, for the problem.

	0	A1 11	A2 12	B1 21	B2 22	B3 23	A1B1 1121	A1B2 1122	A1B3 1123	A2B1 1221	A2B2 1222	A2B3 1223
1	1	0	0	0	0	0	0	0	0	0	0	0
2	1	0	0	1	0	0	0	0	0	0	0	0
3	1	0	0	0	1	0	0	0	0	0	0	0
4	1	0	0	0	0	1	0	0	0	0	0	0
5	1	1	0	0	0	0	0	0	0	0	0	0
6	1	1	0	1	0	0	1	0	0	0	0	0
7	1	1	0	0	1	0	0	1	0	0	0	0
8	1	1	0	0	0	1	0	0	1	0	0	0
9	1	0	1	0	0	0	0	0	0	0	0	0
10	1	0	1	1	0	0	0	0	0	1	0	0
11	1	0	1	0	1	0	0	0	0	0	1	0
12	1	0	1	0	0	1	0	0	0	0	0	1

the main effects. Each row represents a specific experimental trial (q). When a one is present in main effect column ij for trial (q), factor i is at level j. The baseline for factor i is written as $i0$. However, a separate column is not shown for each $i0$ as all are included in the baseline column, which is always labeled 0. When a zero is present for each level $j = 1, 2, \ldots$ of factor i in row (q), factor i must be at its baseline level $j = 0$ *as it is not at any other level.* If an array is keyed in, it is important to error check the entries by summing each row and column to see if one or more sums deviate from the others. Another check is to examine the elements along the diagonal of the covariance matrix to see if they differ. If they do, should they?

Column $ijkl$ represents the pairwise interaction between factors ij and kl. The number in column $ijkl$ for trial (q) is equal to the product of the number in column ij times the number in column kl for trial (q). *To avoid keystroke errors, the ijkl interactions should be entered as equations in terms of the product of the number entered for factor ij in the row times the number entered for factor kl.* The same procedure should be followed for all higher order interactions. Compute interactions; do not key them in.

Table 7.3 shows that all of the factors are at their baseline levels for trial 1, as intended. Factor 1 is at its level 0 (baseline) for trials 1 through 4, at level 1 for trials 5 through 8, and at level 2 for trials 9 through 12. Factor 2 goes through each of its four levels, while factor 1 is being held fixed over each sequence of trials.

7.5.2 Analyzing Outcomes Using Pooled Pure Error Variance

Two replications were made of the burn rate for each of the 12 trials. The computations of the averages and variances for each are shown in Table 7.4, along with a computation of the pooled variance of 1.24. These were taken from the same worksheet as in Table 7.3. The named array variables n, Y and SVAR represent, respectively, the number of replications per trial, the average of the replications for each trial, and the sample variances for each trial. The pooled sample variance is named PSVAR; and the pooled df is named PDF. The

Table 7.4 Outcomes for the experiment as displayed in the SDW.

					z	w
					12	12

REPLICATIONS (leave blank if no entry)

1	2	3	4	5	6	7	8	9	10	n	Trial	Y
34.0	32.7									2	1	33.35
30.1	32.8									2	2	31.45
29.8	26.7									2	3	28.25
29.0	28.9									2	4	28.95
32.0	33.2									2	5	32.60
30.2	29.8									2	6	30.00
28.7	28.1									2	7	28.40
27.6	27.8									2	8	27.70
28.4	29.3									2	9	28.85
27.3	28.9									2	10	28.10
29.7	27.3									2	11	28.50
28.8	29.1									2	12	28.95

				SVAR
1.24	12	2	1	0.84
PSVAR	**PDF**	**AVGn**	2	3.64
			3	4.81
PSVAR	=SUM((n-1)*SVAR)/SUM(n-1)		4	0.01
PDF	=SUM(n-1)		5	0.72
AVGn	=AVERAGE(n)		6	0.08
			7	0.18
			8	0.02
			9	0.40
			10	1.28
			11	2.88
			12	0.04

scalar, AVGn, is the average number of replications per trial and is used to interpolate between the upper and lower PWE bounds for the influence of the factors on log variance when the sample size is not constant (see Chapter 9).

7.5.3 Computation of the Unknown Coefficients and *t*-Statistics

The unknown lambda coefficients, λ_{ij}, shown in Table 7.5 were given the name LAM. The *t* statistic for coefficient *ij* and its spreadsheet expression are given by

$$t_{ij} = \frac{\lambda_{ij}}{\sqrt{s_{ij}^2}} t = \text{LAM/SDij} \qquad (7.8)$$

Although $S_{ij} = \sqrt{s_{ij}^2}$ (SDij) is known as the *standard error* for the coefficient λ_{ij}, it will be referred to here as the standard deviation for factor ij in keeping with the description that

$$s_{ij}^2 = \sum_{q=1}^{z} \frac{\omega_{ij}^2(q)s^2(q)}{n(q)} \qquad\qquad \text{VARij = MMULT(XS\^2,SVAR/n)} \qquad (7.9)$$

is the variance of λ_{ij}. The expression for the t statistic in Equation (7.8) assumes implicitly that the null hypothesis for the population mean, μ_{ij}, for the factor ij is $\mu_{ij} = 0$. When the assumption of a common population variance is made, Equation (7.9) becomes

$$s_{ij}^2 = \sum_{q=1}^{z} \omega_{ij}^2(q)\frac{s_P^2}{n(q)} \qquad\qquad \text{VARij = MMULT(XS\^2,PSVAR/n)} \qquad (7.10)$$

When the sample size is constant, it reduces to $s_{ij}^2 = s_P^2 \text{cov}_{ij\,ij} / n$ where the term $\text{cov}_{ij\,ij}$ is the element in row ij and column ij along the diagonal of the covariance matrix. This result follows from Equation (7.9) because the term $\text{cov}_{ij\,ij}$ is equal to the sum of the square of the elements ω_{ij} along row ij of the solution matrix. When n is constant, the spreadsheet expression for the column vector of factor standard deviations (SDij) can be written as SDij=SQRT(PSVAR*COV/n), the column vector representing the $\text{cov}_{ij\,ij}$ being named COV. For this problem, the sample df is 1, which makes the uncertainty in a measured sample variance rather large. The solution matrix, $\mathbf{X}_s$, for this problem was computed from the inverse of the $\mathbf{X}$ matrix and is shown in Table 7.6 along with the diagonal elements of the covariance matrix. This method of computation for $\text{cov}_{ij\,ij}$ is preferred when using the spreadsheet because it places the elements in a column for easier access than in their usual place on the diagonal of the covariance matrix.

Three main effects, 12, 22, and 23, are seen to decrease burn rate at an experiment-wise error (EWE) of less than 5%. (See Appendix B for Bonferroni's approximate method for computing EWE.) Two interactions, 1222 and 1223, are significant at less than 10% EWE. The pooled df represented by V_P (PDF) is equal to the sum of the df for each trial, Equation (7.7). The usual pairwise error (PWE) is computed from the spreadsheet function TDIST (see Table 4.1). The EWE is 11 times the PWE using Bonferroni's approximate method because there are 11 off-baseline unknown coefficients. The EWE is the expected number of times *per experiment* that a Type I error would be made by rejecting the null hypothesis that the coefficient was zero. The spreadsheet expressions used in making the computations are listed at the bottom of Table 7.5. Bonferroni's method for converting PWE to EWE is exact in the limit when deviations of the coefficients from zero are nothing more than random error. This estimate provides a conservative (larger) estimate of EWE when this is not the case. The significance of a factor in the SIGNIFICANCE column is judged against the value for the single tail alpha in Cell L7, which is entered into the spreadsheet by the analyst.

Table 7.5 Computation of the unknown coefficients and their EWE as taken from the Level 1 worksheet.

	E	F	G	H	I	J	K	L	M
6								Level 1 alpha	
7								0.1	
8									
9			LAM	SDij	PDF	t	PWE	EWE	SIGNIFICANCE
10	0	0	33.4	0.79	12.0	42.31	0.000	0.000	significant
11	A1	11	−0.8	1.11	12.0	−0.67	0.257	2.826	NOT
12	A2	12	−4.5	1.11	12.0	−4.04	0.001	0.009	significant
13	B1	21	−1.9	1.11	12.0	−1.70	0.057	0.627	NOT
14	B2	22	−5.1	1.11	12.0	−4.58	0.000	0.004	significant
15	B3	23	−4.4	1.11	12.0	−3.95	0.001	0.011	significant
16	A1B1	1121	−0.7	1.58	12.0	−0.44	0.332	3.657	NOT
17	A1B2	1122	0.9	1.58	12.0	0.57	0.289	3.182	NOT
18	A1B3	1123	−0.5	1.58	12.0	−0.32	0.378	4.161	NOT
19	A2B1	1221	1.1	1.58	12.0	0.73	0.240	2.638	NOT
20	A2B2	1222	4.7	1.58	12.0	3.01	0.005	0.059	significant
21	A2B3	1223	4.5	1.58	12.0	2.85	0.007	0.080	significant
22									
23		LAM	=MMULT(XS,Y)						
24		SDij	=SQRT(MMULT(XS^2,PSVAR/n))						
25		PDF	PDF						
26		t	=LAM/H10:H21						
27		PWE	=TDIST(ABS(J10:J21),PDF,1)						
28	*Off baseline*	EWE	=K11*(w-1)		*Drag Down*				
29		SIGNIFICANCE	=IF(L10<$L$7,"significant","NOT")				*Drag Down*		

Table 7.6 The solution matrix and the diagonal elements of the covariance matrix.

		1	2	3	4	5	6	7	8	9	10	11	12	COV
0	0	1	0	0	0	0	0	0	0	0	0	0	0	1
A1	11	−1	0	0	0	1	0	0	0	0	0	0	0	2
A2	12	−1	0	0	0	0	0	0	0	1	0	0	0	2
B1	21	−1	1	0	0	0	0	0	0	0	0	0	0	2
B2	22	−1	0	1	0	0	0	0	0	0	0	0	0	2
B3	23	−1	0	0	1	0	0	0	0	0	0	0	0	2
A1B1	1121	1	−1	0	0	−1	1	0	0	0	0	0	0	4
A1B2	1122	1	0	−1	0	−1	0	1	0	0	0	0	0	4
A1B3	1123	1	0	0	−1	−1	0	0	1	0	0	0	0	4
A2B1	1221	1	−1	0	0	0	0	0	0	−1	1	0	0	4
A2B2	1222	1	0	−1	0	0	0	0	0	−1	0	1	0	4
A2B3	1223	1	0	0	−1	0	0	0	0	−1	0	0	1	4

7.5.4 The Reduced Model and R^2

With alpha set at 10% or less EWE, the default reduced model shown as REDLAM_1 in Table 7.7 is automatically constructed in the Level 1 worksheet by setting the nonsignificant coefficients to zero. The 1222 and 1223 interactions would need to be included even if alpha had been set at 5% as a result of the hierarchical rules discussed in what follows. Omission of these interaction terms would generate an overly favorable bias for reducing the burn rate. The model outcomes $\hat{Y}$(YMODEL_1) were then constructed for comparison to the measured outcomes Y listed in Table 7.4. The spreadsheet expression for $\hat{Y}$ is YMODEL_1 = MMULT(X,REDLAM_1).

The coefficient of determination, $R^2 = 1 - SSE / SSY$, is shown in Table 7.7 as R^2_1 equal to 0.45. It represents one of several measures available for assessing the fidelity of a model. The term *SSE* (SSE_1) is known as the residual sum of the squared errors and *SSY* (SSY_1) is known as the total sum of squared errors. SSE is computed in two steps in Table 7.7. First the differences between the model outcomes and the replications are squared and summed across the row for each trial. Then the resulting column is summed to arrive at *SSE*. *SSY* is computed in a similar manner but with the single, average value of the outcomes over all of the trials used in place of the model values.

The result for R^2 indicates that only 45% of the *variation about the mean of the observations* is explained by the reduced model for alpha equal to 0.1. When all of the coeffi-

Table 7.7 The model for coefficients deemed significant using the EWE test and the resulting Level 1 model averages (YMODEL_1) as taken from the Level 1 worksheet. The computation of R^2 is also shown.

	N	O	P	Q	R	S	T	U
8							Sum across rows	
9			REDLAM_1	Trials	YMODEL_1		SSE	SSY
10	0	0	33.35	1	33.35		0.84	29.10
11	A1	11	0.00	2	33.35		10.87	10.55
12	A2	12	−4.50	3	28.25		4.81	8.41
13	B1	21	0.00	4	28.95		0.01	0.83
14	B2	22	−5.10	5	33.35		1.85	18.82
15	B3	23	−4.40	6	33.35		22.53	0.41
16	A1B1	1121	0.00	7	28.25		0.22	3.02
17	A1B2	1122	0.00	8	28.95		3.15	7.18
18	A1B3	1123	0.00	9	28.85		0.41	1.51
19	A2B1	1221	0.00	10	28.85		2.41	5.73
20	A2B2	1222	4.75	11	28.50		2.88	5.26
21	A2B3	1223	4.50	12	28.95		0.05	0.87
22							50.00	91.7
23	REDLAM_1	=G10*IF(M10="significant",1,0)					SSE_1	SSY_1
24	YMODEL_1	=MMULT(X,REDLAM_1)					R^2_1	0.45
25							=1-SSE_1/SSY_1	

cients obtained from the full factorial model are used, R^2 becomes 0.84 but, of course, several of the coefficients used in making this computation were highly insignificant.

It is important to note that the lambda form chosen for this problem is designed to explain the variation about the baseline, trial 1. Thus, for lambda designs, it is appropriate in assessing model fidelity to replace R^2 by $R_B^2 \equiv 1 - SSE/SSB$ where SSB is the total sum of the squared errors about the *baseline*. When this is done, R_B^2 is found to be 0.88 for the reduced model and to 0.97 for the full model.

7.6 LOF ANALYSIS

When there is only one replication per trial and $w = z$, significance can be examined using the lack of fit (LOF) analysis worksheet in the SDW. The LOF variance S_{LOf}^2 (SSLOFvar) is defined as

$$s_{LOF}^2 = \sum_q n(q) \left[Y(q) - \hat{Y}_{LOF}(q) \right]^2 / \left[z - w_{LOF} \right] \qquad \begin{matrix} \text{=SUM(n*(Y-REDLOFY)^2/} \\ \text{(z-SUM(KEEP))} \end{matrix} \qquad (7.11)$$

having $z - w_{LOF}$ df. The terms $\hat{Y}_{LOF}$ (REDLOFY) and w_{LOF} are the reduced LOF model and reduced number of unknowns, respectively. The reduced LOF model is constructed by eliminating one or more unknowns in a systematic manner with $w_{LOF} < z$. The named array KEEP is a column vector of 1s and 0s. The 1s identify the coefficients that are to be kept in the reduced model. The term w_{LOF} is equal to SUM(KEEP). The LOF variance given by Equation (7.11) provides a estimate for the pooled variance, S_P^2, and we should generally expect it to be conservative with $S_{LOf}^2 > S_P^2$. It follows from Equations (7.10) and Equation (7.11) that the LOF approximation for S_{ij}^2 is given by

$$s_{ij}^2 \cong \sum_{q=1}^z \omega_{ij}^2(q) \frac{s_{LOF}^2}{n(q)} \qquad \text{=MMULT(XS^2,SSLOFvar/n)} \qquad (7.12)$$

The initial KEEP vector should be a column of 1s. The first step in generating the final reduced model for this problem shown in Table 7.8 is to set the lambda coefficient with the smallest absolute value to zero. This is done by entering a zero in the cell of the KEEP vector that is in the same row as this coefficient.

Next the coefficient for the factor with the largest EWE is set to zero by entering another 0 appropriately in the KEEP vector. The effectiveness of the model evolving from this iterative process is evaluated by monitoring the EWE for the most significant factors. The final model is taken to be the one that gives the minimum in EWE for the largest lambda coefficient in absolute value.

When there is more than one replication per trial providing for a direct computation for the pooled variance, another measure of the fidelity of the reduced model (in addition to R^2)

Table 7.8 Lack of Fit final model (KEEPLAM) formed by setting the weaker coefficients to zero until a minimum is reached in the EWE column for the most influential factors as taken from the LOF worksheet.

	LAM	KEEP	KEEPLAM	Trials	Y	REDLOFY		REDLOFSDij	tLOF	PWE	EWE
0　0	33.35	1	33.35	1	33.35	33.35	0　0	1.06	31.6	3E-07	3.0E-07
A1　11	−0.75	0	0.00	2	31.45	31.45	A1　11	1.49	0.0	0.500	3.00
A2　12	−4.50	1	−4.50	3	28.25	28.25	A2　12	1.49	−3.0	0.015	0.09
B1　21	−1.90	1	−1.90	4	28.95	28.95	B1　21	1.49	−1.3	0.130	0.78
B2　22	−5.10	1	−5.10	5	32.60	33.35	B2　22	1.49	−3.4	0.009	0.06
B3　23	−4.40	1	−4.40	6	30.00	31.45	B3　23	1.49	−2.9	0.016	0.10
A1B1　1121	−0.70	0	0.00	7	28.40	28.25	A1B1　1121	2.11	0.0	0.500	3.00
A1B2　1122	0.90	0	0.00	8	27.70	28.95	A1B2　1122	2.11	0.0	0.500	3.00
A1B3　1123	−0.50	0	0.00	9	28.85	28.85	A1B3　1123	2.11	0.0	0.500	3.00
A2B1　1221	1.15	0	0.00	10	28.10	26.95	A2B1　1221	2.11	0.0	0.500	3.00
A2B2　1222	4.75	1	4.75	11	28.50	28.50	A2B2　1222	2.11	2.2	0.037	0.22
A2B3　1223	4.50	1	4.50	12	28.95	28.95	A2B3　1223	2.11	2.1	0.043	0.26

7	Y　=Y
=SUM(KEEP)	REDLOFY　=MMULT(X,KEEPLAM)
	REDLOFSDij　=SQRT(MMULT(XS^2,SSLOFvar/n))
	tLOF　=KEEPLAM/REDLOFSDij
	PWE　=TDIST(ABS(tLOF),z-SUM(KEEP),1)

can be generated by constructing a LOF F ratio given by $F_{LOF} = S^2_{LOf} / S^2_P$ (=SSLOFvar/PSVAR). If the model is representative, the LOF Type I error computed from F_{LOF} will be *large* because the two variances will be approximately equal. The results for the LOF F ratio test are shown in Table 7.9. The Type I error reported in Table 7.9 suggests that the model is moderately representative.

The final model in Table 7.8 has seven nonzero coefficients, whereas only six coefficients were deemed significant in Table 7.5 based upon an alpha of 10%. Moreover, the EWEs for the factors in Table 7.5 are much smaller than those found using the LOF analysis. Only factors 12, 22, and 23 would be taken as significant at 10% EWE. Although factor 21 was found to be important in building the model shown in Table 7.8, this same factor was found to be insignificant at 0.627 EWE in Table 7.5. There is a plausible explanation of why this seemingly insignificant factor is important in building a representative model. The Bonferroni correction

Table 7.9 *F* ratio Type I error for the sum square of the LOF variance and the pooled sample variance for the final model.

SSLOFvar	PSVAR	Type I Error
2.229	1.2425	0.189

=SUM(n*(Y-REDLOFY)^2)/(z-SUM(KEEP))

=FDIST(SSLOFvar/PSVAR,z-SUM(KEEP),SUM(n-1))

is exact only in the null hypothesis limit when the values for the coefficients come simply from random error about their expected value of zero. However, based upon the EWE outcomes in Table 7.5, the five off-baseline coefficients were assumed significant, which leaves only six (11–5) off-baseline coefficients assumed caused by random error about an expected value of zero for the null hypothesis. The proper Bonferroni multiple for these six remaining coefficients is now six, not 11. The EWE for factor 21 thus is reduced from 0.627 to 0.34. With this change, the odds are somewhat better that factor 21 is different from zero.

The above method for arriving at the final model differs from the standard *stepwise regression* process because the design and solution matrices were not restructured here by removing the column for a factor when its value was set to zero (deemed insignificant). In support of this approach, Monte Carlo simulations by Altman and Andersen[6] have shown that the confidence levels for coefficients determined by the standard stepwise regression process were too narrow (overly optimistic). Altman and Andersen also reported that "broadly similar results" were found by Chen and George[7]. The method used here avoided this problem. Moreover, the EWE for the coefficients in the final LOF model were, in fact, *larger* than the EWE for the Level 1 default model for alpha of 0.1.

7.6.1 One Outcome per Trial Example

The following simulated problem, Table 7.10, examines three types of factors on crop yield: farmers (three), seeds (two types) and fertilizer (three levels). There is one outcome per trial and $w<<z$. The baseline was for farmer A, seed 1, and moderate fertilizer having a yield of 35 (shown enclosed in a box). The first step in constructing the analysis was to transform the information in Table 7.10 into a design array and an outcome vector for the trials. Trial 1 was for farmer A, seed 1, and low fertilizer, having an outcome of 30 (one replication). The subsequent trials worked down the first column, then to the top of the next column then down, and so forth until trial 18 was reached, having the outcome of 22. Note the baseline is trial 2, which differs from the default choice. This is immaterial to the analysis.

The lambda design matrix for this problem is shown in Table 7.11, along with the outcomes and the results of the model for the outcomes (YMODEL), which is computed as MMULT(X,LAM). The lambda coefficients (LAM) are computed as shown in Table 7.12. The solution matrix is shown in Table 7.13. As there was only one replication per trial, the LOF variance was used as an approximation to the pooled variance. The baseline seed and baseline fertilizer are seen to be superior to their alternatives. Farmer C is seen to generate a larger yield than farmer A, which was significant at better than 5% EWE. Farmer B is pro-

Table 7.10 Simulated crop yield as a function of farmer, seed type, and fertilizer.

Farmer	A		B		C	
	Seed 1	Seed 2	Seed 1	Seed 2	Seed 1	Seed 2
Fertilizer						
Low	30	20	28	16	34	26
Moderate	35	22	36	19	40	25
High	36	18	34	18	38	22

Table 7.11   Design matrix, crop yield, and model of yield.

TRIALS	0	Farmer B 11	Farmer C 12	Crop Seed 2 21	Fertilizer Low 31	Fertilizer High 32	z 18 n	w 6 Yield Y	YMODEL
1	1	0	0	0	1	0	1	30	31.83
2	1	0	0	0	0	0	1	35	35.67
3	1	0	0	0	0	1	1	36	33.83
4	1	0	0	1	1	0	1	20	17.94
5	1	0	0	1	0	0	1	22	21.78
6	1	0	0	1	0	1	1	18	19.94
7	1	1	0	0	1	0	1	28	30.17
8	1	1	0	0	0	0	1	36	34.00
9	1	1	0	0	0	1	1	34	32.17
10	1	1	0	1	1	0	1	16	16.28
11	1	1	0	1	0	0	1	19	20.11
12	1	1	0	1	0	1	1	18	18.28
13	1	0	1	0	1	0	1	34	35.83
14	1	0	1	0	0	0	1	40	39.67
15	1	0	1	0	0	1	1	38	37.83
16	1	0	1	1	1	0	1	26	21.94
17	1	0	1	1	0	0	1	25	25.78
18	1	0	1	1	0	1	1	22	23.94

Table 7.12   Analysis of the lambda coefficients and their EWE.

		LAM	SD ij	t	PWE	EWE
0	0	35.67	1.23	29.03	8.68E-13	
B	11	−1.67	1.23	−1.36	0.100	0.500
C	12	4.00	1.23	3.26	0.003	0.017
Seed 2	21	−13.89	1.00	−13.85	5E-09	2E-08
Low	31	−3.83	1.23	−3.12	0.004	0.022
High	32	−1.83	1.23	−1.49	0.081	0.404

SSLOFvar   4.527778   =SUM(n*(Y-YMODEL)^2)/(z-w)

LAM   =MMULT(XS,Y)

SD ij   =SQRT(MMULT(XS^2,SSLOFvar/n))

t   =LAM/(SDij)

PWE   =TDIST(ABS(t),z-w,1)

Table 7.13 Solution matrix (XS) computed from the crop yield design matrix.

	1	2	3	4	5	6	7	8	9	10	11	12	13	14	15	16	17	18
0	1/6	1/3	1/6	0	2/9	0	0	1/6	0	−1/9	0	−1/9	0	1/6	0	−1/9	0	−1/9
11	−1/6	−1/6	−1/6	−1/6	−1/6	−1/6	1/6	1/6	1/6	1/6	1/6	1/6	0	0	0	0	0	0
12	−1/6	−1/6	−1/6	−1/6	−1/6	−1/6	0	0	0	0	0	0	1/6	1/6	1/6	1/6	1/6	1/6
21	−1/9	−1/9	−1/9	1/9	1/9	1/9	−1/9	−1/9	−1/9	1/9	1/9	1/9	−1/9	−1/9	−1/9	1/9	1/9	1/9
31	1/6	−1/6	0	1/6	−1/6	0	1/6	−1/6	0	1/6	−1/6	0	1/6	−1/6	0	1/6	−1/6	0
32	0	−1/6	1/6	0	−1/6	1/6	0	−1/6	1/6	0	−1/6	1/6	0	−1/6	1/6	0	−1/6	1/6

jected to have a smaller yield than A, the amount being judged as not significant from zero with EWE equal to 0.5 (one Type I error per two experiments). The use of seed 2 is seen to generate a large significant loss in yield versus the baseline.

7.7 HIERARCHICAL RULES OF THUMB

Rules of thumb exist for the inclusion of coefficients in a reduced model. If the pairwise interaction coefficient $ijkl$ is included, for example, then the adjoining main effects ij and kl should also be included independent of whether their PWE or EWE meets the condition set for significance. When coefficients for both the mean and variance are being considered, which occurs in levels 3 and 4, the coefficient ij for the mean should be included if coefficient ij for the variance is taken as being significant and vice versa. For example, if the main effect coefficient for the mean ij is deemed significant and thus included in the model, the main effect for coefficient ij for the variance (actually log variance) should also be included. In following these hierarchical rules, a conservative bias can also be imposed by including adjoining coefficients deemed insignificant on their own merits only if they make the outcome less favorable.

7.8 EXAMINATION OF RESIDUALS

The differences, known as *residuals,* between the replications and the values for YMODEL_1 in Table 7.7 are shown in Table 7.14 for each of the trials, q. Also shown are the outcome averages, $Y(q)$, for the trials. The residuals are plotted against $Y(q)$ in Figure 7.2 to provide a visual aid for identifying possible irregularities. The pattern suggests a possibility of nonrandom behavior in the middle of the plot between 30 and 32. But this trend is weak and is taken to be no more than a statistical aberration. The normal probability plot of the residuals is shown in Figure 7.3. The plot is approximately linear, which supports the assumption that the random errors are normally distributed.

Table 7.14 Residuals determined from the difference between outcomes and prediction given by the reduced model in Table 7.7.

Trial	Y	Residuals	
1	33.35	0.65	-0.65
2	31.45	-3.25	-0.55
3	28.25	1.55	-1.55
4	28.95	0.05	-0.05
5	32.6	-1.35	-0.15
6	30	-3.15	-3.55
7	28.4	0.45	-0.15
8	27.7	-1.35	-1.15
9	28.85	-0.45	0.45
10	28.1	-1.55	0.05
11	28.5	1.2	-1.2
12	28.95	-0.15	0.15

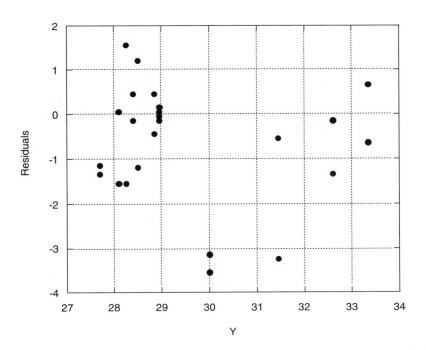

Figure 7.2 Plot of the residuals as a function of the average of the outcomes, $Y(q)$.

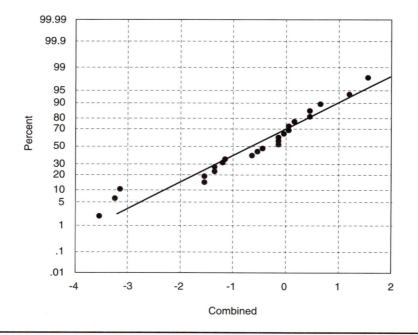

Figure 7.3 Normal probability plot of the residuals.

7.9 SUMMARY

Controlled experiments versus regression of historical data: Insight into the factors affecting the value of products can be obtained from controlled experiments and from an analysis of historical data. The two approaches provide complementary perspectives. Controlled experiments have higher sensitivity and greater flexibility and can be used to evaluate novel, new concepts not part of the historical record.

Strategic experimentation: Three things need to be in place to make strategic experiments viable: (1) appropriate transfer functions, (2) value relationships for the CTV attributes, and (3) financial information on variable cost, fixed cost, and investment.

Level 1 Analysis: Level 1 analysis makes the simplifying assumption that the population variances are the same for the experimental trials. Although this may never be the case for strategic experiments where reduction of variance is generally an important goal, the Level 1 analysis can be done quickly and can be used as a check against more involved, higher level analyses.

Matrix method solution of linear system of equations: Matrix algebra provides a flexible, robust, and powerful tool for solving for the unknown coefficients in the linear model.

Experiment-wise error: It is important in strategic experiments to use experiment-wise error to minimize the likelihood of inferring that a coefficient was significant when, in fact, it was large in absolute value solely as a result of random error. The likelihood of such an error increases in proportion to the number of factors being considered per experiment. Bonferroni's technique is an easy but approximate method for converting pairwise error to experiment-wise error.

Model fidelity: The coefficient of determination, R^2, is a useful measure of the fidelity of a model in fitting the observed variation about the mean of the experimental outcomes. It is not a good measure of fidelity when the coefficients are measured relative to a given trial as a baseline, which is the case when using a lambda design array. The size of the Type I error computed from the LOF F ratio also provides a measure of model fidelity. The larger the Type I error the better the model, provided that the LOF variance is not less than the pooled variance.

Stepwise regression: Caution is advised in using stepwise regression, as Monte Carlo simulations elsewhere have shown that the confidence levels found are too narrow.

Strategic Design Workbooks (SDWs): Workbooks can partially automate several aspects of the analysis of strategic experiments.

REFERENCES

1. V. L. Smith and A. W. Williams. December 1992. "Experimental Market Economics," *Scientific American,* pp. 116–121.
2. F. E. Satterthwaite. 1946. "An Approximate Distribution of Estimates of Variance Components," *Biometrics Bulletin* 2, pp. 110–114.
3. G. Taguchi and S. Konishi. 1987. *Taguchi Methods Orthogonal Arrays and Linear Graphs.* Milwaukee, WI: American Supplier Institute, ASI Press.
4. C .F. J. Wu and M. Hamada. 2000. *Experiments Planning, Analysis, and Parameter Design Optimization.* New York: John Wiley & Sons.
5. R. E. Walpole and R. H. Myers. 1993. *Probability and Statistics for Engineers and Scientists*, 5th ed. New York: Macmillan, p. 541.
6. D. G. Altman and P. K. Andersen. 1989. "Bootstrap Investigation of the Stability of a Cox Regression Model," *Statistics in Medicine* 8, pp. 771–783.
7. H. Chen and S. L. George. 1985. "The Bootstrap and Identification of Prognostic Factors via Cox's Proportional Hazards Regression Model," *Statistics in Medicine* 4, pp. 39–46.

8

Level 2: Satterthwaite's df and Approximate *t*-Test

> *Insight: The population variance will seldom be constant for each of the trials in a strategic experiment, which leads to the use of Satterthwaite's df and approximate t-test.*

Key Topics

Satterthwaite's df   approximate t-test

8.1 FLOW CHART FOR LEVEL 2 ANALYSIS

Level 1 analysis assumed that none of the factors (control factors) influenced variance. This led to pooling of the variances, and their df and the *t*-test was used to assess the significance of the factors on the mean. However, for strategic experiments, factors are chosen for their likelihood of improving customer satisfaction by reducing product variation in addition to moving CTV attributes toward their ideal positions in a cost-effective manner. Thus, when examining the outcomes of strategic experiments, it is unlikely that the population variances were constant for the experimental trials.

Level 2 analysis assumes that the samples were taken from populations having different variances, which requires that the regular *t*-test is replaced with Satterthwaite's approximate *t*-test[1]. Instead of pooling variances and their df, a factor standard deviation, s_{ij}, and factor df, v_{ij}, are computed for each doubly indexed factor ij in the experiment. Each factor df is less than the pooled df, but usually each will be larger than $\bar{n} - 1$, where $\bar{n}$ is the average number of replications per trial.

The Level 2 analysis flow chart is shown in Figure 8.1. After the design matrix and the replications are entered into the appropriate SDW, the remaining steps in Figure 8.1 are generated automatically across several worksheets. For example, the number of replications for each trial is placed in a column to the right of the replications in a Design and

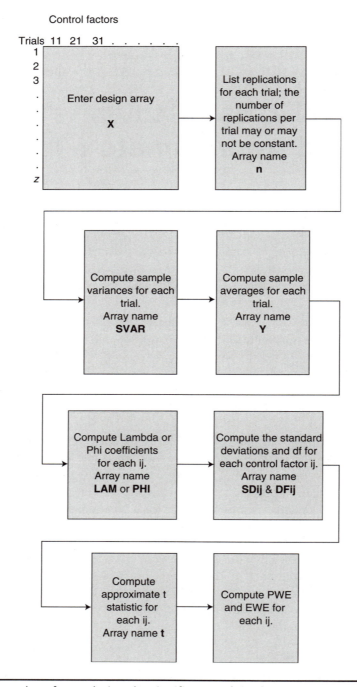

Figure 8.1 Flow chart for analyzing the significance of the factors on the mean.

Outcomes worksheet and given the array name n. The sample averages and variances, which are given the array names Y and SVAR, respectively, are also generated in the Design and Outcomes worksheet. The remaining computations for the coefficients (LAM or PHI) and their *t* statistics, PWE and EWE, are generated in the Lambda Coefficients worksheet.

8.2 SATTERTHWAITE'S APPROXIMATE *T*-TEST

The factor variances s_{ij}^2 for each of the coefficients are computed from Equation (7.9), and Satterthwaite's factor df are computed from the expression

$$v_{ij} = \frac{\left[s_{ij}^2\right]^2}{d_{ij}} \qquad \text{DFij = (MMULT(XS\^2,SVAR/n))\^2/Dij} \qquad (8.1)$$

where

$$d_{ij} = \sum_{q=1}^{z} \frac{\omega_{ij}^4(q)s_i^4(q)}{n^2(q)[n(q)-1]} \qquad \text{Dij = MMULT(XS\^4,(SVAR/n)\^2/(n-1))} \qquad (8.2)$$

If the difference $\lambda_{11} = Y(2) - Y(1)$ between just two sample means is being considered, Equation (8.1) reduces to the familiar form for computing the factor df when the population variance is not constant. In this limit, the design matrix and the solution matrix are given, respectively, by

$$\mathbf{X} = \begin{array}{c} \\ 1 \\ 2 \end{array}\begin{array}{c} 0 \quad 11 \\ \begin{bmatrix} 1 & 0 \\ 1 & 1 \end{bmatrix} \end{array}$$

and

$$\mathbf{X}_s = \begin{array}{c} \\ 0 \\ 11 \end{array}\begin{array}{c} 1 \quad 2 \\ \begin{bmatrix} 1 & 0 \\ -1 & 1 \end{bmatrix} \end{array}$$

Thus, it follows from Equation (7.9) that

$$s_{11}^2 = \frac{s^2(1)}{n(1)} + \frac{s^2(2)}{n(2)} \tag{8.3}$$

has the df given by

$$v_{11} = \frac{\left[\dfrac{s^2(1)}{n(1)} + \dfrac{s^2(2)}{n(2)} \right]^2}{\left[\dfrac{\left[s^2(1)/n(1) \right]^2}{n(1)-1} + \dfrac{\left[s^2(2)/n(2) \right]^2}{n(2)-1} \right]} \tag{8.4}$$

as computed from Equation (8.1). The result given by Equation (8.4) is found in introductory texts on statistics.

8.3 LEVEL 2 EXAMPLE

8.3.1 $L_4(2^3)$ OA

To illustrate Level 2 analysis, consider an $L_4(2^3)$ OA experiment, the design and solution matrices being shown in Table 8.1 as taken from the L4(2^3) SDW. The outcomes, shown in Table 8.2, have four replications for trials 1 and 2 and three replications for trials 3 and 4. The objective was to consider proposed alternatives singly or in concert for making the outcome **Y** as large as possible while making the variance in Y as small as possible.

Table 8.1 $L_4(2^3)$ lambda design and solution matrices and diagonal of covariance matrix.

Trial	Base 0	A 11	B 21	C 31
1	1	0	0	0
2	1	0	1	1
3	1	1	0	1
4	1	1	1	0

	1	2	3	4	COV
0	1.00	0.00	0.00	0.00	1
11	-0.50	-0.50	0.50	0.50	1
21	-0.50	0.50	-0.50	0.50	1
31	-0.50	0.50	0.50	-0.50	1

Table 8.2 Replications and outcomes of experiment as taken from the L4(2^3) SDW.

#	AJ	AK	AL	AM	AN	AO	AP	AQ	AR	AS	AT	AU	AV	AW	AX	AY	AZ	BA
7											z	w				4.4	10	3.5
8											4	4				PSVAR	PDF	AVGn
9						REPLICATIONS												
10	1	2	3	4	5	6	7	8	9	10	n	Trial	Y	YMODEL		SSELIST	SSYLIST	
11	24.0	17.1	21.1	17.5							4	1	19.93	19.93		31.85	56.19	
12	25.2	24.9	25.3	24.9							4	2	25.08	25.02		0.14	28.93	
13	23.8	25.5	25.1								3	3	24.80	25.02		1.72	18.98	
14	17.8	22.2	19.3								3	4	19.77	19.93		10.08	30.68	
15																43.8	134.8	
16												Trial	SVAR	SVARMODEL		SSE	SSY	
17												1	10.62	10.62				
18												2	0.04	0.27		R^2		
19												3	0.79	0.27		0.68	=1-SSE/SSY	
20												4	5.00	10.62				

Y =AVERAGE(AJ11:AS11)
YMODEL =MMULT(X,REDLAM)
SVAR =VAR(AJ11:AS11)
SVARMODEL =10^(-MMULT(X,REDXI)/10)

SSE =SUM(SSELIST)
SSY =SUM(SSYLIST)
PSVAR =SUM((n-1)*SVAR)/SUM(n-1)
PDF =SUM(n-1)
AVGn =AVERAGE(n)

The replications were taken from simulated populations whose means were 20, 25, 25, and 20, respectively for trials 1 through 4. The population variances were 10, 1, 1, and 10. The array names for the variables computed for the analysis and their respective Excel expressions are shown in Table 8.2.

8.3.2 Satterthwaite's df

The computations for the test of significance of the coefficients using Satterthwaite's model are given in Table 8.3. The factor variance s_{ij}^2 given by Equation (7.9) was represented in the spreadsheet by the square root of this quantity, s_{ij}, (SDij). Note in Table 8.3 that the expressions for SDij and DFij are expressed in terms of matrix algebra operations. The factor df are seen to be constant and equal to 5.6, which were rounded down automatically to 5.0 in the computations for the t statistic. If the variances for this problem had been pooled, the df would have been 10, thereby underestimating the Type I error for the coefficients.

8.3.3 Converting PWE to EWE

The pairwise errors for the three off-baseline coefficients in Table 8.3 were computed using the spreadsheet function for the t distribution given by = TDIST(ABS(t), DFij,1). (See

Table 8.3   Analysis of significance of the lambda coefficients as taken from the Lambda Coefficients worksheet.

	E	F	G	H	I	J	K	L	M	N	O	P
7								**ALPHALAM**				
8								0.05				
9												
10			**LAM**	**SDij**	**DFij**	**t**	**PWE2**	**EWE**	**SIGLAM**			**REDLAM**
11	**Base**	0	19.93	1.63	3.00	12.23	0.003	0.00	significant	**Base**	0	19.93
12	**A**	11	-0.22	1.07	5.60	-0.20	0.424	1.27	NOT	**A**	11	0.000
13	**B**	21	0.06	1.07	5.60	0.05	0.479	1.44	NOT	**B**	21	0.000
14	**C**	31	5.09	1.07	5.60	4.75	0.003	0.01	significant	**C**	31	5.092
15			**LAM**	=MMULT(XS,Y)								
16			**SDij**	=SQRT(MMULT(XS^2,SVAR/n))								
17			**DFij**	=SDij^4/MMULT(XS^4,(SVAR/n)^2/(n-1))								
18			**t**	=LAM/SDij								
19			**PWE2**	=TDIST(ABS(t),DFij, *Off baseline*								
20			**EWE**	=PWE2*(w-1)								
21			**SIGLAM**	=IF(L11<ALPHALAM,"significant","NOT")			*Drag*					
22		P12	**REDLAM**	=G12*IF(M12="significant",1,0) *Off baseline drag*								

Chapter 4 for a description of the statistical functions.) The last argument in TDIST should be either a 1 for a single-tail error or a 2 for a two-tail error. The *t* statistic, which is symmetric about zero, has to be expressed as an absolute value, ABS(t), because negative values are not accepted by this function. The EWE for the off-baseline coefficients, based upon Bonferroni's method, is *w* - 1 times the PWE, which for this case is 3 times the PWE. The PWE for the baseline coefficient simply expresses the Type I error for assuming that this coefficient is different from zero. The real interest is almost always in the significance of the off-baseline coefficients.

8.3.4 Model Fidelity

The column of the significant coefficients in Table 8.3 named REDLAM represents the default, reduced model used to compute $\hat{Y}$ from the relation YMODEL = MMULT(X,REDLAM) in Table 8.2. The fidelity of the model can be checked using the result for R^2 shown in Table 8.2, which was computed from the expression

$$R^2 \equiv 1\text{-SSE/SSY} \tag{8.5}$$

The value of 0.68 for R^2 may appear low (only 68% of the variance of the replications about the mean of the means is explained by the model) because the coefficient, 31, had been identified correctly as being significant and 11 and 21 had been identified correctly as being insignificant. But keep in mind that the regression coefficients model the averages of the trials and not the individual replications from which the averages are computed. Thus, there is an inherent limit on R^2 dictated by the size of the pure error in the replications. In other words, the model could fit the mean outcomes exactly but R^2 would still be less than 1.

To understand how the outcomes affect cash flow, the transfer function must exist to transform the component and subsystem attributes to the CTV attributes of importance to the customer. Value curves for the CTV attributes must also be in place, along with the changes in variable costs for the alternatives under consideration.

8.3.5 Residuals

The plot of residuals (added by the user to the Lambda Coefficients worksheet of the SDW) is shown in Figure 8.2. The scatter is observed to be higher for trials 1 and 4. This is a result of the variance for the populations for those two trials being 10 compared to one for trials 2 and 3. The nature of the distribution of the variance coincides with the movements in the level of factor 31. (This factor was, in fact, found to be significant on log variance based upon the individual *F* test for the factors. This test, which is generated in the XI Coefficients worksheet of the SDW, is described in Chapter 9.)

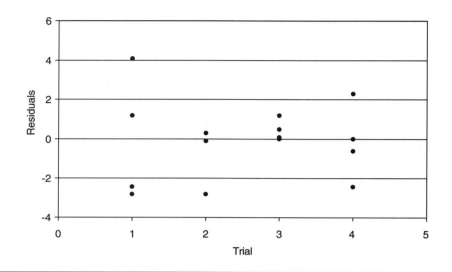

Figure 8.2   Plot of residuals showing higher scatter for trials 1 and 4.

8.4 LEVEL 1 ANALYSIS

It is useful to compare the Level 2 analysis of this problem with its Level 1 analysis, shown in Table 8.4. These results were taken from the Level 1 worksheet of the SDW for this problem. The lambda coefficients, of course, are identical. The standard deviations differ somewhat because the sample size is not constant. However, the main difference between it and Satterthwaite's test comes from the differences in the degrees of freedom. After round-off, the Level 1 pooled df are twice as large. The disparities between the pooled and the Satterthwaite df will generate appreciable differences in the Type I EWE when considering small alphas. This is compounded as the number of off-baseline coefficients increase.

Table 8.4 Outcomes for Level 1 analysis.

	E	F	G	H	I	J	K	L	M	N	O	P	Q	R
7								**Level 1 alpha**						
8								0.05						
9														
10			LAM	SDij	PDF	t	PWE	EWE	SIGLAM_1	**Base**		**REDLAM_1**		**YMODEL_1**
11	**Base**	**0**	19.93	1.04	10	19.09	0.000	0.000	significant	**A**	**0**	19.93		19.93
12	**A**	**11**	-0.22	1.13	10	-0.19	0.426	1.277	NOT	**B**	**11**	0.00		25.02
13	**B**	**21**	0.058	1.13	10	0.05	0.480	1.440	NOT	**C**	**21**	0.00		25.02
14	**C**	**31**	5.092	1.13	10	4.52	0.001	0.002	significant		**31**	5.09		19.93
15			LAM =MMULT(XS,Y)											
16			SDij =SQRT(MMULT(XS^2,PSVAR/n))											
17			PDF =PDF											
18			t =G11/H11 *Drag*											
19			PWE =TDIST(ABS(J11),PDF,1) *Drag*											
20			EWE =K12*(w-1) *Off baseline Drag*											
21			**SIGLAM_1** =IF(L11<$L$8,"significant","NOT")						*Off baseline drag*					

8.5 SUMMARY

Level 2 Analysis: The assumption made here for all Level 2 and above strategic experiments is that the population variances are not the same for any of the trials.

Satterthwaite's df: When the population variances are not the same, the coefficients for the control factors should not be evaluated by the usual pooled variances and pooled df. Instead, Satterthwaite's df should be computed and used in the *t*-test, which is then approximate.

REFERENCE

1. F. E. Satterthwaite. 1946. "An Approximate Distribution of Estimates of Variance Components," *Biometrics Bulletin* 2, pp. 110–114.

9

Level 3: Influence of the Factors on the Mean and Variance

Insight: There are four complementary methods for measuring the influence of the control factors on the log variance: an F test, a normal test, a graphical test, and Monte Carlo simulation.

Key Topics

influence of control factors on variance   Monte Carlo simulation

double-half-normal plots   contrasts

9.1 FLOW DIAGRAM FOR LEVEL 3

Levels 1 and 2 examined the significance of the factors on the mean, the difference being that the population variances were assumed to be the same for the trials in Level 1 and not the same in Level 2. Level 3 also assumes that the populations do not have a common variance. In addition, it provides an assessment of the significance of the individual factors on variance shown as element A in the Level 3 flow chart, Figure 9.1.

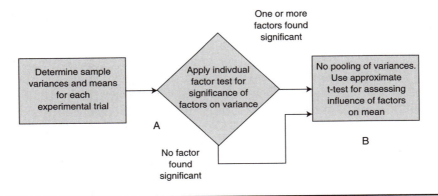

Figure 9.1 The flow diagram for assessing the influence of factors on sample variance. For either outcome in A, there is no pooling of variances.

The several individual tests available for use in block A examine the same question, which is: "What is the Type I error for assuming that a specific factor reduces variance?" However, if no factor is found to have a significant influence on variance, this is not taken as sufficient proof that the populations had a common variance. Instead, the conservative assumption is made that one or more factors did influence variance but the effect was not large enough to be deemed significant. Thus, the populations are never assumed here to have a common variance, and Satterthwaite's df and approximate *t*-test are always used to assess the significance of the factors on the mean.

Two formal tests, half-normal plots, and Monte Carlo simulation represent complementary methods for assessing the Type I error. The formal *F* test for the influence of the individual factors on log variance (the individual *F* test) is exact when the conditions for its use exist. The other formal test, noted here as the individual *Z* test method, is approximate but less restrictive in its application. The half-normal test and Monte Carlo simulation are least restrictive for analyzing Type I error.

9.2 *F* TEST METHOD FOR THE INFLUENCE OF THE FACTORS ON LOG VARIANCE

There are three conditions for using the individual *F* test for the influence of the factors on log of variance:[1]

1. The samples should be taken from a normally distributed population.

2. The sample size must be constant for each trial.

3. The solution matrix must be balanced in that for every positive element $\omega_{ij}(q)$ a negative element $\omega_{ij}(q')$ must exist having the same the same absolute value.

In regard to condition 1, populations that are not normal can often be made to be approximately so by making a log transformation of the measurements. Condition 2 is good practice. Condition 3 is always satisfied for two-level orthogonal arrays. The lambda form of main-effects-only orthogonal arrays also satisfies this condition when factors have more than two levels. When condition 2 is not satisfied because the sample size is not constant, an upper and lower bound for the Type I error is assessed when using a SDW. When condition 3 is not satisfied, the *F* test appears robust enough to provide a reasonable estimate of the Type I error based upon comparisons with Monte Carlo simulation results. When conditions 2 and 3 are not met, the *Z* test method (described later in this chapter) represents a good approximation if the sample sizes are 10 or greater. Finally, Monte Carlo simulation can be used to quantify the significance of the individual factors when none of the conditions is satisfied, provided that the form of the distribution is known.

The first step in employing the individual *F* test is to take –10 times the base 10 logarithm of each sample variance and use the results as the outcomes in the linear model. (Taguchi used this form of the log transformation for generating his signal to noise ratio. The natural log transformation can also be taken for a direct comparison with the Z test method outcomes.) A feature of this transformation is that a positive coefficient is good in that it reduces variation. The coefficients for -10 log variance are written as ξ_{ij} (Greek Xi) and are solved for in the standard manner:

$$\xi_{ij} = -\sum_q \omega_{ij}(q)10Log_{10}\left(s^2(q)\right) \quad = \text{MMULT(XS, } -10 * \text{LOG(SVAR))} \tag{9.1}$$

The PWE for the individual coefficients ξ_{ij} are computed from the F distribution

$$F_{ij} = 10^{|G_{ij}|} \tag{9.2}$$

where

$$G_{ij} = \frac{\xi_{ij}}{\sqrt{50\,\text{cov}_{ijij}}} \quad = \text{XIij / SQRT(50 * COVij)} \tag{9.3}$$

The derivation of Equation $(9.2)^1$ is given again here in Appendix G. Each of the two df needed to evaluate F are equal to $n-1$. When n is not constant, the PWE is estimated in the SDW by interpolating between an upper and lower bound. The lower bound is computed using a df equal to the maximum in $n-1$ and the upper bound uses the minimum in $n-1$.

If the natural log transformation of the sample variances is used, the coefficients are given by

$$\xi_{ij,Ln} = -\sum_q \omega_{ij}(q)Ln\left(s^2(q)\right) \tag{9.4}$$

and the expression for F_{ij} becomes

$$F_{ij} = \exp\left[\frac{|\xi_{ij,Ln}|}{\sqrt{\text{cov}_{ijij}/2}}\right] \tag{9.5}$$

In direct comparisons (unpublished), Bartlett's test[2] generally provides greater power than the individual test. This is expected because Bartlett's test does not attempt to identify the individual factors that are significant for influencing variance. The power of the individual test could, therefore, be improved for a single, borderline significant factor by assessing the Type I error using Bartlett's test for homogeneity of variance. (It is important to restate that the null hypothesis of a common population variance is always rejected here for strategic experiments independent of the Type I error found for the individual test or for Bartlett's test.)

9.2.1 Application of the *F* Test for the Influence of the Factors on Variance

A Level 3 simulated experiment based upon a $L_8(2^7)$ OA was chosen for illustration (Table 9.1). Its solution matrix and the diagonal elements of the covariance matrix, Table 9.2, were copied from the L8(2^7) SDW used to perform the computations. As noted earlier, the diagonal elements were constructed in the column format by summing the square of the elements along each row of the solution matrix. Factors 0 (baseline), 11, and 41 were taken to be contributing to both the mean and log variance, all other factors having no effect. The population mean and variances were constructed by first selecting values for the λ_{ij} and ξ_{ij} coefficients for the population mean and -10 log population variance, respectively. The values chosen for these coefficients for the *populations* are listed in columns PLAM and PXIij, respectively, of Table 9.3. The population variances and mean for the individual trials were then constructed from these coefficients using the general model, Equation (7.1) with zero error. These are listed in columns POPMEAN and POPVAR in Table 9.4

A total of five replications were chosen for each of the eight trials. The sample measurements were simulated by highlighting an eight-row by five-column rectangle in the spreadsheet and typing in the expression

$$= \text{NORMINV(RAND(),POPMEAN,SQRT(POPVAR))}$$

Table 9.1 The lambda form of the $L_8(2^7)$ OA used as the experimental design.

	Base	A	B	C	D	E	F	G
Trial	0	11	21	31	41	51	61	71
1	1	0	0	0	0	0	0	0
2	1	0	0	0	1	1	1	1
3	1	0	1	1	0	0	1	1
4	1	0	1	1	1	1	0	0
5	1	1	0	1	0	1	0	1
6	1	1	0	1	1	0	1	0
7	1	1	1	0	0	1	1	0
8	1	1	1	0	1	0	0	1

Table 9.2 The solution matrix for the lambda form of the $L_8(2^7)$ OA and the diagonal elements of the covariance matrix.

		1	2	3	4	5	6	7	8	COV
Base	0	1	0	0	0	0	0	0	0	1
A	11	-0.25	-0.25	-0.25	-0.25	0.25	0.25	0.25	0.25	0.5
B	21	-0.25	-0.25	0.25	0.25	-0.25	-0.25	0.25	0.25	0.5
C	31	-0.25	-0.25	0.25	0.25	0.25	0.25	-0.25	-0.25	0.5
D	41	-0.25	0.25	-0.25	0.25	-0.25	0.25	-0.25	0.25	0.5
E	51	-0.25	0.25	-0.25	0.25	0.25	-0.25	0.25	-0.25	0.5
F	61	-0.25	0.25	0.25	-0.25	-0.25	0.25	0.25	-0.25	0.5
G	71	-0.25	0.25	0.25	-0.25	0.25	-0.25	-0.25	0.25	0.5

Table 9.3 Coefficients chosen for the mean (PLAM) and −10 log variance (PXI) for the populations.

	ij	PLAM	PXI
Base	0	8.00	−8.000
A	11	3.00	10.000
B	21	0.00	0.000
C	31	0.00	0.000
D	41	5.00	10.000
E	51	0.00	0.000
F	61	0.00	0.000
G	71	0.00	0.000

Table 9.4 Population means and variances constructed from the coefficients for the mean and −10 log variance in Table 9.3.

Trial	POPMEAN	POPVAR
1	8	6.310
2	13	0.631
3	8	6.310
4	13	0.631
5	11	0.631
6	16	0.063
7	11	0.631
8	16	0.063

which was entered by holding down the Shift and Ctrl keys and hitting Enter. The RAND() function changes each time a computation is made, thereby changing the replications. Several repeated computations are made and a "typical" set of replications were then copied and pasted using the Paste Special Value spreadsheet command, which fixes them from changing in future computations.

The resulting simulated replications and outcomes used in the analysis shown in Table 9.5 were entered into the Design and Outcomes worksheet of the SDW. The array names n, SVAR, and Y are used for the sample size, sample variance, and sample mean, respectively. The name PSVAR is used for the pooled sample variance, and z and w are used for the number of trials and number of unknown coefficients. Default models are generated by the SDW for Y and SVAR based upon the single-tail alphas entered in the worksheets for the mean and variance, respectively.

The results for the individual F test are shown in Table 9.6 as taken from the XI coefficients worksheet. The array variables XIij and Gij are used to represent the ξ_{ij} coefficients and G_{ij}, respectively. The expressions used in the computations are listed at the bottom of Table 9.6. The experiment-wise error is computed from the PWE distribution, using the multiplication factor of $w - 1$ for the off-baseline coefficients following Bonferroni's transformation of PWE to EWE. The PWE in Cell N11 represents a linear interpolation between the two PWE outcomes in columns I and L in row 11 computed as

$$= IF(MAX(n) = MIN(n),L11,I11-(I11-L11)*(AVGn-MIN(n)) / (MAX(n) - MIN(n)))$$

which is then dragged down. The interpolation is scaled according to the relative location of the average value for *n* (AVGn) between the minimum and maximum values of *n*. The interpolated EWE is $(w - 1)$ times this PWE. The logic statement handles the condition when MIN(n) = MAX(n). Of course for this problem, the interpolation computations were redundant because *n* was constant.

The lambda coefficients, the standard deviations s_{ij} (SDij), and effective df v_{ij} (DFij) are shown Table 9.7, as taken from the Lambda Coefficients worksheet. The specific

Table 9.5 Simulated outcomes used in the analysis provided by the L8(2^7) SDW. The vector Y lists the sample variances, and YMODEL is the default model for Y generated by the vector (REDLAM) of significant lambda coefficients for the alpha shown. The vector SVAR lists the sample variances, and SVARMODEL is the default model for the sample variances generated by the vector (REDXI) of the significant XI coefficients for the alpha shown.

| | | | | | | | | | | | | Z 8 | W 8 | | alpha 0.05 |

| REPLICATIONS | | | | | | | | | | | | | | |
1	2	3	4	5	6	7	8	9	10	n	Trials	Y	YMODEL
9.8	9.4	6.2	10.9	6.5						5	1	8.56	8.56
13.9	13.4	12.4	13.1	13.1						5	2	13.18	13.56
4.7	6.7	12.6	6.7	7.7						5	3	7.68	8.56
12.9	12.4	11.9	13.3	11.9						5	4	12.48	13.56
11.0	11.3	10.9	10.6	10.1						5	5	10.78	11.43
16.2	15.8	15.9	16.4	15.6						5	6	15.98	16.43
11.2	8.4	10.9	11.0	11.6						5	7	10.62	11.43
16.3	15.7	16.1	16.2	15.7						5	8	16.00	16.43

| | | alpha 0.05 |
Trial	SVAR	SVARMODEL
1	4.38	4.38
2	0.30	0.40
3	8.75	4.38
4	0.38	0.40
5	0.21	0.69
6	0.10	0.06
7	1.61	0.69
8	0.08	0.06

expressions used in the computations are shown at the bottom of Table 9.7. Satterthwaite's effective df for each off-baseline coefficient is seen to be 10.14, which will automatically be rounded down to 10 in subsequent computations. The results found for the lambda coefficients and experiment-wise error based upon the single-tailed *t*-test are also shown in Table 9.7. The named variable PWE2 is defined only for the off-baseline coefficients. The EWE shows that factors 11 and 41 have a 0.00 Type I error. The results in Table 9.6 and Table 9.7 are expected because of the population statistics. The default reduced model, REDLAM, for the lambda coefficients is given on the right of Table 9.7 and used to compute YMODEL in Table 9.5. Because dragging down the second expression in the REDLAM column generates the model, it is straightforward to change it to include more or fewer factors as desired.

In summary, the Level 3 analysis has identified two factors judged to significantly influence both the mean and variance (specifically –10 log of variance). Because a lambda form has been used for the OA, the coefficients are measured relative to the trial 1 baseline.

Table 9.6 Results of the individual test of the significance of the factors on log variance, as taken from the Xi Coefficients worksheet.

	E	F	G	H	I	J	K	L	M	N	O	P	Q	R	S	T	U
8																	
9							**ALPHAXI**										
10					MIN(n)		0.1	MAX(n)		Interpolated					**REDXI**		
			XI	**Gij**	**PWE**	**EWE**		**PWE**	**EWE**	**PWE**	**EWE**	**SIGXI**					
11		Base	−6.42	−0.91	0.0337	0.03		0.0337	0.03	0.03	0.03	significant	Base	0	−6.42		
12		A	8.01	1.60	0.0018	0.01		0.0018	0.01	0.00	0.01	significant	A	11	8.01		
13		B	−2.99	−0.60	0.1055	0.74		0.1055	0.74	0.11	0.74	NOT	B	21	0.00		
14		C	0.94	0.19	0.3425	2.40		0.3425	2.40	0.34	2.40	NOT	C	31	0.00		
15		D	10.35	2.07	0.0002	0.00		0.0002	0.00	0.00	0.00	significant	D	41	10.35		
16		E	2.29	0.46	0.1654	1.16		0.1654	1.16	0.17	1.16	NOT	E	51	0.00		
17		F	−2.97	−0.59	0.1069	0.75		0.1069	0.75	0.11	0.75	NOT	F	61	0.00		
18		G	2.01	0.40	0.1954	1.37		0.1954	1.37	0.20	1.37	NOT	G	71	0.00		
19																	

Cell formula definitions:

Row		
20	XI =MMULT(XS,-10*LOG(SVAR))	PWE =FDIST(10^ABS(Gij),MAX(n)-1,MAX(n)-1)
21	Gij =XI/SQRT(50*COV)	EWE =(w-1)*L12 Off baseline
22	PWE =FDIST(10^ABS(Gij),MIN(n)-1,MIN(n)-1) Off baseline	PWE =IF(MAX(n)=MIN(n),L11,I11-(I11-L11)*(AVGn-MIN(n))/(MAX(n)-MIN(n))) Drag N11
23	EWE =PWE*(w-1) Off baseline	EWE =(w-1)*N12 Off baseline
24		SIGXI =IF(O11<ALPHAXI,"significant","NOT")
25		S11 REDXI =G11
26		S12 REDXI =G12*IF(P12="significant",1,0)
27		

Table 9.7 Computations of Satterthwaite's effective df and EWE for the lambda coefficients as taken from the Lambda Coefficients worksheet.

	E	F	G	H	I	J	K	L	M	N	O	P
6								ALPHALAM				
7								0.05				
8												
9			LAM	SDij	DFij	t	PWE2	EWE				REDLAM
10	**Base**	0	8.56	0.94	4.00	9.14	0.00	0.00	significant	**Base**	**0**	8.560
11	**A**	11	2.87	0.44	10.14	6.45	0.00	0.00	significant	**A**	**11**	2.870
12	**B**	21	−0.43	0.44	10.14	−0.97	0.18	1.25	NOT	**B**	**21**	0.000
13	**C**	31	−0.36	0.44	10.14	−0.81	0.22	1.53	NOT	**C**	**31**	0.000
14	**D**	41	5.00	0.44	10.14	11.25	0.00	0.00	significant	**D**	**41**	5.000
15	**E**	51	−0.29	0.44	10.14	−0.65	0.26	1.85	NOT	**E**	**51**	0.000
16	**F**	61	−0.09	0.44	10.14	−0.20	0.42	2.95	NOT	**F**	**61**	0.000
17	**G**	71	0.00	0.44	10.14	0.00	0.50	3.50	NOT	**G**	**71**	0.000
18												
19			**LAM**	=MMULT(XS,Y)					P10	**REDLAM** =G10		
20			**SDij**	=SQRT(MMULT(XS^2,SVAR/n))					P11	**REDLAM** =G11*IF(M11="significant",1,0)		
21			**DFij**	=SDij^4/MMULT(XS^4,(SVAR/n)^2/(n-1))								
22			**t**	=LAM/SDij								
23			**PWE2**	=TDIST(ABS(t),DFij,1)								
24			**EWE**	=PWE2*(w-1) *Off baseline*								

It follows from Chapters 3, 5, and 6 that this information can be used to compute how the factors influence value to the customer provided that the transfer functions that couple changes in the component level attributes to changes in the CTV attributes are known.

9.2.2 Influence of Several Factors on Variance

When the ξ_{ij} coefficients for the factors have been determined, the expected sample variance for a combination of factors *ij, kl, mn, . . .* may also be of interest. For a lambda model, this is given by the expression

$$s^2_{ij,kl,mn,...} = 10^{-[\xi_0 + \xi_{ij} + \xi_{kl} + \xi_{mn} + ...]/10} \tag{9.6}$$

The $1 - \alpha$ confidence range for the population variance is obtained by substituting the expression given by Equation (9.6) for the sample variance on the RHS of Equation (5.17). The chi-square statistic in the denominator of Equation (5.17) is then used to establish the two limits.

9.3 *Z* TEST (NORMAL APPROXIMATION TEST) FOR THE INFLUENCE OF THE FACTORS ON VARIANCE

The Z or normal approximation test for the influence of the individual factors on variance uses the result that $Ln(\chi^2 / v(q))$ for trial q is approximately normally distributed for $n(q) \geq 10$ having a standard deviation $\sigma_{NA} = \sqrt{2/v(q)} = \sqrt{2/(n(q)-1)}^3$. From Equation (9.4), $\xi_{ij,Ln}$ is seen to be equal to the sum of $q = 1$ to z normally distributed parameters with weights $\omega_{ij}(q)$ and variance $2/(n(q) - 1)$. It follows that the variance of $\xi_{ij,Ln}$ is given by

$$\text{var}\left(\xi_{ij,Ln}\right) = 2\sum_q \frac{\omega_{ij}^2(q)}{n(q)-1} \qquad = 2 * \text{MMULT(XS^2,1 / (n-1))} \qquad (9.7)$$

which leads to the normal statistic

$$Z_{ij} = \frac{\xi_{ij,Ln}}{\sqrt{2\sum_q \dfrac{\omega_{ij}^2(q)}{n(q)-1}}} \qquad (9.8)$$

The results of the Z test for the influence of the factors on Ln variance for the above problem are shown in Table 9.8. The outcomes for the single-tail EWE are shown and compared to the results for $\xi_{ij,Ln}$ listed in the last column, which were computed from the independent F test. The coefficients $\xi_{ij,Ln}$ and their variances are expressed as the name arrays XILN and VARXILN, respectively. The expressions used in the spreadsheet computations are shown at the bottom of Table 9.8. Because the sample size of 5 for each trial is much smaller than the recommended level of 10 or greater for applying the Z test, close agreement is not expected between the two EWE associated with the tails of the distribution.

Table 9.8 Results of the computations for the significance of the factors on the Ln variance based upon the Z test approximation. The last column shows the EWE significance for $\xi_{ij,Ln}$ from the F test for comparison.

	V	W	X	Y	Z	AA	AB
9						Z	F
10			**XILN**	**VARXILN**	**PWE**	**EWE**	**EWE**
11	**Base**	0	-1.478	0.50	0.02	0.018	0.034
12	**A**	11	1.844	0.25	0.00	0.001	0.012
13	**B**	21	-0.688	0.25	0.08	0.590	0.739
14	**C**	31	0.217	0.25	0.33	2.327	2.397
15	**D**	41	2.384	0.25	0.00	0.000	0.001
16	**E**	51	0.528	0.25	0.15	1.018	1.158
17	**F**	61	-0.684	0.25	0.09	0.600	0.748
18	**G**	71	0.464	0.25	0.18	1.237	1.368
19		**XILN**	=MMULT(XS,-LN(SVAR))				
20		**VARXILN**	=2*MMULT(XS^2,1/(n-1))				
21		**PWE**	=1-NORMDIST(ABS(XILN),0,SQRT(VARXILN),1)				
22		**EWE**	=(w-1)*Z12		*Off baseline*		

9.4 USING HALF-NORMAL PLOTS FOR ASSESSING SIGNIFICANCE

In addition to the two formal, quantitative tests, half-normal plots can be used to judge the significance of multiple factors on the outcomes of an experiment[4]. However, when using software such as KaleidaGraph, it is simpler and equally insightful to make a double-half-normal plot. The transformation of the data to make such a plot is shown in Table 9.9 for the off-baseline outcomes for XILN in Table 9.8. The plot was made as follows. First, the off-baseline coefficients were copied and placed in a column. Then each of their values times minus one were listed below them, thereby doubling the length of the column. This list was then copied and placed in KaleidaGraph to construct the normal probability plot, shown here as Figure 9.2. When n is not constant or designs having mixed levels are used, the spreadsheet function XILN/SQRT(VARXILN) should be plotted.

Table 9.9 Preparation of data for making a double-half-normal plot of the off-baseline XILN results shown in Table 9.8.

	AD	AE
12	**11**	1.844
13	**21**	-0.688
14	**31**	0.217
15	**41**	2.384
16	**51**	0.528
17	**61**	-0.684
18	**71**	0.464
19	**-11**	-1.844
20	**-21**	0.688
21	**-31**	-0.217
22	**-41**	-2.384
23	**-51**	-0.528
24	**-61**	0.684
25	**-71**	-0.464

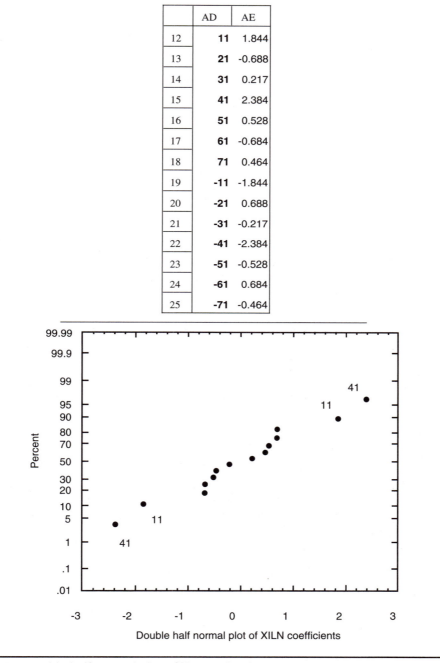

Figure 9.2 Double-half-normal plot of the results shown in Table 9.9.

If none of the factors influenced log variance, then the plot would be approximately normal and the points would lie roughly along a straight line passing through the origin. This is seen not to be the case as the points for 11 and 41 break away from the remainder of the other points at both ends of the plot. It is reasonable to infer that factors 11 and 41 influence the natural log of variance in a significant manner in agreement with the findings in Table 9.6.

Because all of the off-baseline coefficients are considered when evaluating a half-normal plot, experiment-wise error is accounted for. However, the amount of Type I error cannot be quantified as readily as with the two formal methods. When assessing the significance of multiple factors on the log variance, it is wise to use both the analytical and graphical techniques, as they provide a cross-check to each other.

9.5 MONTE CARLO SIMULATION EVALUATION OF THE INFLUENCE OF THE FACTORS ON LOG VARIANCE

As already discussed, the F and Z tests for the influence of the individual factors on log variance have conditions on their use. When they are not satisfied, Monte Carlo simulation can be used to arrive at a quantitative measure of significance. Although the conditions are fully satisfied for the use of the F test with the problem at hand, it is useful to demonstrate the Monte Carlo procedure and compare its results with those from the F test.

The outcomes of 1000 simulations for the XI coefficients are shown in Figure 9.3. The XI coefficients for a single simulation are shown in Table 9.10. The expressions used are shown at the bottom of the table. The column for the simulated XI was transposed to an adjacent row and 10 repeats of the macro were used to generate the 1000 simulations. More than 100,000 simulations would be needed to have the points for 11 and 41 cross the vertical line through zero in Figure 9.3.

A normal distribution line was fit to the simulated outcomes for 11 and 41, the resulting mean and standard deviation for each being shown at the top of Figure 9.3. The mean values of 8.0 and 10.5 for the two variances are in good agreement with the values of 8.01 and 10.35 for the 11 and 41 coefficients, respectively, in Table 9.6. The predicted Type I errors of 0.18% and 0.02%, respectively, for 11 and 41 from Table 9.6 for the F test method are shown by the horizontal lines in Figure 9.3. The extrapolated intercept of the line through the 11 distribution with the vertical line at zero is in reasonable agreement with the value from the independent test. The intercept of the line through the 41 distribution falls well below the Type I error prediction from Table 9.6, but considering the degree of extrapolation this cannot be taken as a serious disagreement.

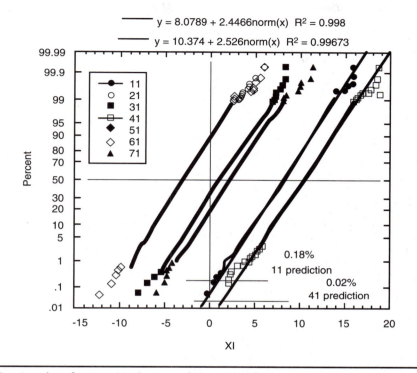

Figure 9.3   Results of 1000 simulations of the XI coefficients.

Table 9.10   Outcomes for a single Monte Carlo simulation of the XI coefficients.

	D	E	F	G	H	I	J	K	L
40					Simulated				
41					Pop			Simulated	
42				RAND()	Var	ʼ		XI	
43			1	0.288	8.242	**Base**	0	−9.16	
44			2	0.072	1.361	A	11	9.24	
45			3	0.192	21.789	B	21	0.52	
46			4	0.836	0.235	C	31	1.19	
47			5	0.581	0.212	D	41	9.38	
48			6	0.081	0.434	E	51	4.37	
49			7	0.596	1.606	F	61	−7.03	
50			8	0.608	0.078	G	71	1.10	
51									
52		*Simulated population variances*			=(n-1)*SVAR/CHIINV(1-G43:G50,n-1)				
53			*Simulated XI*	=MMULT(XS,-10*LOG(H43:H50))					

9.6 CONTRASTS FOR A PAIR OF STATES

In addition to considering the outcomes associated with the individual control factors and their significance, the general case for the significance between states formed by combinations of control factors needs to be considered. This occurs, for example, when a phi design is used but the amount and its significance need to be computed for changing from the trial 1 baseline to an alternate state. It also occurs when the significance between any two alternative states needs to be computed. The expressions for applying Satterthwaite's df model to the contrast problem are summarized below with the full derivation being given in Appendix C.

The combinations of states ij,kl that can occur for a 3^2 FF design are illustrated in Figure 9.4. The origin for the lambda design is shown as 10,20 representing trial 1. The phi origin, for purposes of illustration, is placed in the middle of the first square. The outcome for an arbitrary site on the lattice is written as $Y(R)$ and is equal to a linear combination of the coefficients $\hat{\beta}_{ij}$ given by the expression

$$\hat{Y}(R) = \sum_{ij} c_{ij}(R)\hat{\beta}_{ij} \tag{9.9}$$

The difference or contrast between the outcomes of sites R and R^* is given by

$$\hat{Y}(R,R^*) = \mathbf{C}\hat{\beta} \tag{9.10}$$

The matrix $\mathbf{C}$ (CRR) has elements

$$c_{ij}(R,R^*) = c_{ij}(R) - c_{ij}(R^*) \tag{9.11}$$

The row vector c(R,R*) represented by the horizontal arrow from 10,20 to 11,20 is shown in Figure 9.4.

The computation of the contrast between the baseline and the state with factor 11 alone at its second level is shown in Table 9.11, taken from the Contrasts worksheet for the problem being considered here, and is in agreement with the results for this factor in Table 9.7. The variance $s^2_{\hat{Y}(R,R^*)}$ (VARRRstar in Table 9.11) of $\hat{Y}(R,R^*)$ is given by

$$s^2_{\hat{Y}(R,R^*)} = \mathbf{X}_\psi \mathbf{S} \tag{9.12}$$

where the matrix $\mathbf{X}_\psi$ (PSIQ) is a row vector whose elements $\psi(R,R^*,q)$ are given by Equation (C.26) and $\mathbf{S}$ is a column vector whose elements from $q = 1$ to z are equal to

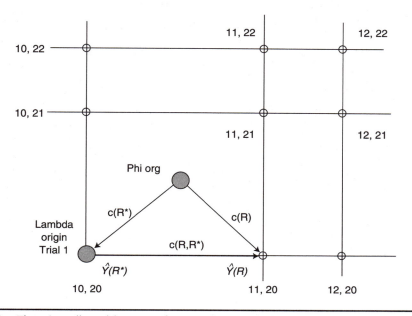

Figure 9.4 The nine allowable states for two factors at three levels each forming a 3^2 FF design.

$s^2(q)/n(q)$. The t statistic is given by Equation (C.32). Satterthwaite's df $v(R,R^*)$ (dfRRstar) for $s^2_{\hat{Y}(R,R^*)}$ is given by

$$v(R,R^*) = \frac{s^4_{\hat{Y}(R,R^*)}}{d(R,R^*)} \tag{9.13}$$

where $d(R,R^*)$ is given by Equation (C.30). The spreadsheet expressions for the named variables are listed in Table 9.11 for completeness.

In summary, the Contrasts worksheet facilitates Level 2 computations of the statistics between arbitrary pairs of states. When using a phi design, the worksheet can be used to compute (1) the size and the Type I error significance of the phi baseline coefficients (e.g., φ_{i0}, φ_{i0kl}, etc.) and (2) to compute the significance of an arbitrary state relative to a baseline set as specific trial (by default, trial 1), thereby yielding the lambda coefficient for the state and its significance. To avoid data entry blunders when interactions are included in the CR and CRstar vectors, compute the interactions from the main effects; do not key them into the columns. Also, it is quite helpful when using the Contrasts worksheet to sketch out the vectors involved, as illustrated in Figure 9.4, before keying in the numbers (zeros, ones, and minus ones) for the main effects.

Table 9.11   Computation of a contrast vector $c(R,R*)$ between the baseline and factor 11 at its off-baseline level as taken from the Contrasts worksheet. Its PWE is given by PWERRstar.

	CR	**CRstar**	**CRR**				
Base	0	1	1	0	**YRRstar**	2.87	=MMULT(TRANSPOSE(CRR),LAM)
A	11	1	0	1	**VARRRstar**	0.20	=MMULT(PSIQ,SVAR/n)
B	21	0	0	0	**SDRRstar**	0.44	=SQRT(VARRRstar)
C	31	0	0	0	**tRRstar**	6.45	=YRRstar/SDRRstar
D	41	0	0	0	**dfRRstar**	10.14	=VARRRstar^2/MMULT(PSIQ^2,(SVAR/n)^2/(n-1))
E	51	0	0	0	**PWERRstar**	4E-05	=TDIST(ABS(tRRstar),dfRRstar,1)
F	61	0	0	0			
G	71	0	0	0			

	PSIQ	=TRANSPOSE(MMULT(TRANSPOSE(XS),CRR))^2					
1	**2**	**3**	**4**	**5**	**6**	**7**	**8**
0.0625	0.0625	0.0625	0.0625	0.0625	0.0625	0.0625	0.0625

9.7 SUMMARY

Influence of factors on variance: In addition to their influence on the mean, assessing the influence of the factors on variance is also important because both the mean and variance affect the outcomes of strategic experiments.

F test method: The *F* test method for the influence of the individual factors on variance is exact when (1) samples be taken from a normal distribution, (2) the sample size is constant, and (3) the solution matrix is balanced in that for every positive element along a row there is a negative element having the same absolute value. When the sample size is not constant, an upper and lower bound for the Type I error is computed. Results from computer simulations show that the model is not too sensitive to the condition that the solution matrix be balanced.

Z test method: The *Z* test method for the influence of the individual factors on variance also requires that the samples be taken from a normally distributed population but does not require that the sample size be constant for the trials and places no conditions on the elements of the solution matrix. However, it is an approximate expression and requires that the sample size be roughly 10 or greater.

Half-normal plots: Normal probability plots of the G_{ij} statistic are a graphical means of assessing the significance of factors on log variance. It should be used with the other tests as it provides an important visual complement to the *F* and *Z* tests.

Monte Carlo simulation: When the conditions do not apply for using either the *F* or the *Z* test, Monte Carlo simulation provides a quantitative method for assessing the significance of the factors on log variance.

Contrast between states: Often several factors at levels that differ from the baseline state may be of interest based upon the outcomes of an experiment. The differences between the means between two states and their PWE are computed on the Contrasts worksheet of the SDW.

REFERENCES

1. H. E. Cook, 1997. *Product Management: Value, Quality, Cost, Price, Profits, and Organization.* Amsterdam: Kluwer, pp. 360–362.
2. M. S. Bartlett. 1937. "Properties of Sufficiency and Statistical Tests," *Proceedings Royal Society.* A 160, pp. 262–282.
3. C. F. J. Wu and M. Hamada. 2000. *Experiments Planning, Analysis, and Parameter Design Optimization.* New York: John Wiley & Sons, pp. 117–118.
4. R. H. Myers and D. C. Montgomery. 2002. *Response Surface Methodology Process and Product Optimization Using Designed Experiments.* New York: John Wiley & Sons, pp. 114–116.

10

Level 4: Testing for Strategic Significance

> *Insight: Strategic significance is influenced by the range of uncertainty in both the mean and variance for the CTV attribute of interest.*

Key Topics

Strategic significance	variable cost
Monte Carlo simulation	CIQ

10.1 STRATEGIC VERSUS STATISTICAL SIGNIFICANCE

The Type I error evaluations in Chapters 7 through 9 represented tests of the statistical significance of the coefficients on the mean and variance of the attributes. They do not, however, provide a direct measure of the *strategic significance* that the factors had on the financial metrics needed for a product planner to assess whether or not to implement a control factor (new technology) in production. For example, an experiment may show that the Type I error for assuming that factor 21 favorably improves the mean of an attribute is 5%. This is not the same as saying that the factor is projected to favorably improve value or cash flow with only a 5% Type I error.

The reason is that other considerations come into play, such as the factor's influence on variance, on other attributes, on variable cost, and on investment. Moreover, strategic significance[1] involves considering the uncertainty associated with a population mean and variance combination, which will generally have greater uncertainty than found for either the population mean or population variance. Nevertheless, the tests for statistical significance considered in Chapters 7 through 9 are a vital first step in assessing strategic significance.

10.2 PROBLEM OF COMPUTER MONITOR ILLUMINATION INTENSITY

Consider the problem of improving the illumination of a computer screen. Assume that the value of illumination follows the nominal-is-best curve shown in Figure 10.1. Such a curve could be determined using the DV survey described in Chapters 2 and 4. Also shown are curves for cost (variable cost per unit) and value minus cost. The parameters listed in Table 10.1 define the value curve used by the SDW to compute value and the CIQ. The value curve is generated in the Value Curve Plotter worksheet of the SDW.

The value curve was constructed with g_0 equal to 8. Value at this point was set at 10 and the exponential weighting factor γ, GAMMA, was taken to be 0.9. These parameters represent a convenient starting point for constructing the value curve based upon Equation (5.1). The value $V(g_0) = V_0$ does not represent the value for trial 1 in the experiment. The attribute g_0 equal to 10 was simply a convenient starting point for constructing the curve. It is not equal to the expected value for g for trial one given by $\mu(1)$.

Assume that the linear cost curve arises from the power needed to operate the monitor as a function of its illumination, g. The function f_v is evaluated at g_T for every $g(q)$ because a scaling factor is assumed to exist; it is used to transform $g(q)$ to g_T for each trial. The slope of the cost curve is equal to the slope of the value curve at the target given by $g_T = 11.5$, which is just to the low side of the maximum in value at g_I.

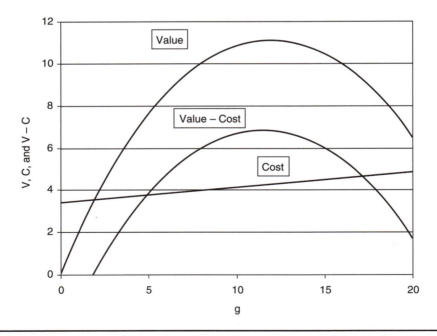

Figure 10.1 Value and cost curves (hypothetical) as a function of the attribute *g*.

Table 10.1 Parameters used to construct the value and cost curves.

Parameter	Name	Spreadsheet Value or Expression
Value at g=8	V0	10
Exp. weighting	GAMMA	0.9
Ideal attribute	gI	12
Critical attribute	gC	0
Baseline attribute	g0	8
Target attribute	gT	11.5
f_v	fv	1.12305 =((gI-gC)^2-(gI-gT)^2)/((gI-gC)^2-(gI-g0)^2)
Value curve		
slope at target	SLOPE	0.0695 =2*V0*GAMMA*fv^(GAMMA-1)*(gI-gT)/((gI-gC)^2-(gI-g0)^2)
Cost at g=8	c0	4
Cost at g	cT	* =c0+SLOPE*(g-g0)

Seven two-level factors were evaluated, and the sample average and sample variance outcomes were those for the example in Chapter 9, Table 9.5. Thus, based upon the findings in Chapter 9, factors 11 and 41 are known to be significant for increasing the degree of illumination and reducing variation, both of which aid in solving a NIB1 problem with a value function defined by Equation (5.14) as both reduce variation on implementing the scaling factor. The first term on the RHS of Equation (5.14) is a constant and equal to $V(g_T)$ = V_T. It follows from the definition given by Equation (2.8) that minus one times the second term on the RHS of Equation (5.14) is equal to $\Omega(g(q))$ for the NIB1 problem:

$$\Omega(g(q)) = \frac{k_T g_T^2 \sigma^2(q)}{\mu^2(q)} \, \text{NIB1} \tag{10.1}$$

Taguchi defines the SN ratio for trial q as -10 times the log of the loss function determined from the distribution for trial q, which is equal to the sum of $\Omega(g(q))$ and cost, $C(q)$. As discussed in Chapter 5, his definition is modified here by defining SN_Ω as the log of CIQ only:

$$Y_\Omega(q) \equiv SN_\Omega = -10 Log(\Omega(g(q))) \tag{10.2}$$

Cost is not included at this juncture. This does not mean that cost is known precisely. It is just that the variance in g has been accounted for in arriving at the cost estimate.

The reason for taking the log of the CIQ is to improve the additivity of the coefficients determined from the linear model. This transformation is also in keeping with the linear model used for the log of the variance, which has theoretical support for normally distrib-uted populations. The minus sign is used for convenience in that a positive coefficient reduces the CIQ (improves value). The factor of 10 is simply for improved sizing of the coefficients. The same type of log transformation was used to set up the linear model for variance in Chapter 9.

10.3 MONTE CARLO SIMULATION

The bottom-line metrics of cash flow and demand, when projected from experiments as described in Chapter 3, represent random variables whose statistics have not been devel-oped in closed form. The same holds true for Taguchi's CIQ, $\Omega(g(q))$. However, the random variables can often be expressed in terms of combinations of statistics that are well charac-terized, allowing Monte Carlo simulation to be used to evaluate the significance of the fac-tors on the bottom-line metrics.

As outlined in Chapter 6, the Monte Carlo process treats the population mean and vari-ance as random variables. For each simulation for each trial q, a possible population mean is computed using Equation (6.2) from the sample mean, sample variance, sample size, and t statistic. A possible population variance is computed from the sample variances $s^2(q)$, the df, and the chi-square statistic using Equation (5.17). The coefficients are then determined from Equation (7.2) on replacing $Y(q)$ with $Y_\Omega(q) = SN_\Omega$. Point estimates of the variance of SN_Ω, which are given in Appendix I, can be used as cross checks against the outcomes of the Monte Carlo simulations.

The array names and the spreadsheet expressions used in the simulations are shown in Table 10.2. Two random numbers, RN1 and RN2, were generated, RN1 being used to select a point from the chi-square cumulative distribution and RN2 being used to select a point from the t cumulative distribution. The name used for the simulated population variance was POPVARSIM, which was computed in terms of the df (DFij) and sample variances (SVAR) from Chapter 9 and the reciprocal of the chi-square statistic. The population mean (POPYSIM) was simulated using the t statistic (tSIM) and the sample variance divided by the sample size (SVAR/n).

The parameters f_V (fvSIM1) and k_T (kTSIM1) for the value curve were computed from Equations (5.4) and (5.3), respectively. The value, V_I, at the ideal position (VIDEAL) was computed because it is useful as a reference and because it is also insightful to compute the CIQ by subtracting the value at the location of interest from V_I. The expressions for kTSIM1 and VALUESIM1 defined as "Macro" were entered using macros because they were too tedious to key in routinely. These expressions are fully displayed in the SDW. The simulated values for $\Omega(q)$ (CIQSIM1) were computed by subtracting VALUESIM1 from VIDEAL. Finally the lambda coefficients $\lambda_{ij}(\Omega)$ (LAMSN1) for SN_Ω were computed using the spreadsheet expression

$$\lambda_{ij}(\Omega) = -\text{MMULT}(XS, 10*\text{LOG}(\text{CIQSIM1}))$$

which results in coefficients being positive that reduce the CIQ.

Table 10.2 Parameters used in the Monte Carlo simulations.

RN1	=RAND()
POPVARSIM	=(n-1)*SVAR/CHIINV(1-RN1,n-1)
RN2	=RAND()
tSIM	=IF(RN2>0.5,1,-1)*TINV(IF(RN2>0.5,2*(1-RN2),2*RN2),n-1)
POPYSIM	=Y+tSIM*SQRT(SVAR/n)
fvSIM1	=((gI-gC)^2-(gI-(1-SF)*POPYSIM-SF*gT)^2)/((gI-gC)^2-(gI-g0)^2)
ktSIM1	Macro
VIDEAL	=V0*(((gI-gC)^2-(gI-gI)^2)/((gI-gC)^2-(gI-g0)^2))^GAMMA
VALUESIM1	Macro
CIQSIM1	=VIDEAL-VALUESIM1
LAMSN1	=-MMULT(XS,10*LOG(CIQSIM1))

Table 10.3 Outcomes from a single simulation.

Trials	RN1	POPVARSIM	RN2	tSIM	POPYSIM
1	0.63	4.10	0.75	0.73	9.24
2	0.80	0.20	0.27	-0.66	13.02
3	0.25	18.40	0.14	-1.26	6.01
4	0.17	1.04	0.45	-0.12	12.45
5	0.90	0.11	0.23	-0.83	10.61
6	0.77	0.07	0.84	1.12	16.14
7	0.91	0.79	0.57	0.19	10.73
8	0.02	0.70	0.76	0.77	16.10

Trials	fvSIM1	ktSIM1	VIDEAL	VALUESIM1	CIQSIM1			LAMSN1
1	1.1230	0.0695	11.12	10.66	0.458	Base	0	3.39
2	1.1230	0.0695	11.12	11.09	0.028	A	11	8.59
3	1.1230	0.0695	11.12	6.42	4.702	B	21	-5.69
4	1.1230	0.0695	11.12	11.04	0.079	C	31	-1.61
5	1.1230	0.0695	11.12	11.09	0.026	D	41	8.46
6	1.1230	0.0695	11.12	11.10	0.020	E	51	6.46
7	1.1230	0.0695	11.12	11.04	0.081	F	61	-1.81
8	1.1230	0.0695	11.12	11.08	0.042	G	71	-0.99

Typical outcomes for a single simulation are shown in Table 10.3 and Table 10.4. A total of 1000 simulations were made and the results were plotted on normal probability paper in Figure 10.2. The L8(2^7) SDW used to run the simulations has the LAMSN1 coefficients transposed to a row to facilitate making the simulations. Note that the distribution for factors 11, 41, and 51 in Figure 10.2 are displaced positively from the others and all of the curves are approximately normal (linear).

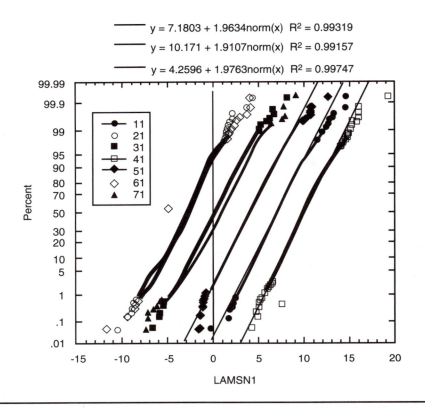

$y = 7.1803 + 1.9634\text{norm}(x)$ $R^2 = 0.99319$

$y = 10.171 + 1.9107\text{norm}(x)$ $R^2 = 0.99157$

$y = 4.2596 + 1.9763\text{norm}(x)$ $R^2 = 0.99747$

Figure 10.2 Normal probability plot of the SN ratio lambda coefficients determined from the Monte Carlo simulations.

The intercept of the line of points with the vertical line through zero represents the single-tail Type I PWE for a distribution if the median is positive. If the median is negative, the intercept needs to be subtracted from unity. The intercepts for 11 and 41 are quite small, less than 0.1%. The EWE is seven times the intercept, which is still very small, less than 0.7%. Thus, there is high confidence that the two coefficients are larger than zero, the null hypothesis. The PWE intercept for factor 51 is 1.7%, which converts to 12% EWE. However, because factors 11 and 41 are deemed significant, the Bonferroni multiplier can be reduced from 7 to 5, which reduces the EWE for factor 51 to 8.5%, which is still above our 5% cutoff.

As two factors have already been deemed as significant in reducing variance, the addition of a marginal factor will make little difference on the strategic outcomes. Thus, factor 51 is not taken as being significant. However, this generates a Type II error. Although this factor does not influence the log variance, it does influence variance, which can be seen by computing the coefficients of the population variance directly from Table 9.4 without taking the log transformation.

10.4 CONVERTING THE $\lambda_{ij}(\Omega)$ COEFFICIENTS TO PROJECTED IMPROVEMENT IN VALUE

Once the coefficients $\lambda_{ij}(\Omega)$ that are favorable for reducing the log of the CIQ have been identified, the results need to be converted into the projected improvement in value to the customer. The change in value is equal to minus one times the change in the CIQ. The CIQ for the projected best improvement is given by

$$\Omega_{BEST} = 10^{-\lambda_{(BEST)}/10} \tag{10.3}$$

For this problem, the best combination is taken as

$$\lambda_{(BEST)} = \lambda_0(\Omega) + \lambda_{11}(\Omega) + \lambda_{41}(\Omega) \tag{10.4}$$

The change in value is therefore given by

$$\Delta V_{BEST} = -\left[10^{-\lambda_{(BEST)}/10} - 10^{-\lambda_0/10}\right] \tag{10.5}$$

The values of the 11 and 41 coefficients for a point estimate can be taken from their medians in Figure 10.2, which are 7.1 and 10.1, respectively. The median for the baseline coefficient, $\lambda_0(\Omega)$, which was not plotted, was 1.81. Thus the value improvement on going from the trial 1 baseline to a condition with factors 11 and 41 in place is 0.64. This is also seen in the value distributions in Figure 10.3. The combination of the two factors has diminishing returns, as the combined distribution is only slightly better than that for factor 41 alone, which has a median value of 0.59. Figure 10.3 shows that the 95% confidence level for the combined factors is approximately 0.25.

10.5 STRATEGIC CONSIDERATIONS

The variable cost trend shown in Figure 10.1 as a function of the CTV attribute *g* will generally not be the only contributor to the variable cost. For example, one of the unspecified factors could have been a change in the sensitivity of a voltage regulator resulting in a cost increase. As stated earlier, the second derivative of the cost curve does not contribute to the loss function. However, cost needs to be considered in evaluating the strategic significance of each factor on *net value,* defined as added value less added variable cost. Moreover, if the cost estimate is uncertain, then that uncertainty should be included as part of the Monte Carlo simulation for cash flow. Also, as described in Chapter 5, there is uncertainty in the

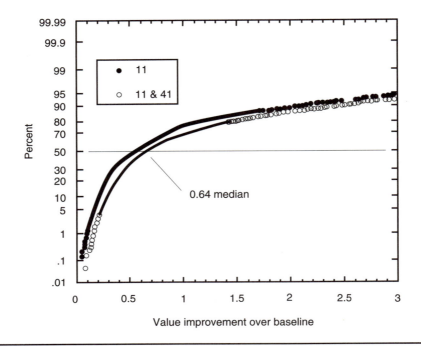

Figure 10.3 Distributions for ΔV_{11}, and $\Delta V_{11,41}$, which is the distribution for the combined 11 and 41 factors. The distribution for ΔV_{41} is not plotted, as it is just to left of the combined distribution.

change in value from baseline as one or more attributes move away from their baseline specifications. These uncertainties can be included in the Monte Carlo simulations by expressing cost and value as normally distributed parameters about their means. The range of uncertainty in value is given by Equation (5.11). The standard deviation for variable cost needs to be supplied by the cost analyst. However, for simplicity in what follows, the uncertainties in value and cost are assumed small enough to be ignored.

If the added variable cost is less than 0.25, then, from Figure 10.3, there is 95% confidence that it is exceeded by the combined value of the two factors. However, the analysis of strategic significance is still incomplete, as there can be investment and fixed-cost implications. When this is the case, the next step is to arrive at a price change in keeping with the change in net value. The rule of thumb given by Equation (3.3) is that the increment in price over its baseline amount is equal to one-half the sum of the value change plus the variable cost change. If the combined variable cost increase for the two factors relative to trial 1, for example, were 0.2, this is added to the median of 0.64 for the combined value distribution, resulting in a theoretical price increase of 0.42.

Next the value and price change need to be used to project the change in demand. The demand expression for a monopoly is given by Equation (2.2) and the expression for an oligopoly is given by Equation (2.15). When Equation (2.15) is used, an assessment needs to be made of what competitors might do by the time the design change represented by factors 11 and 41 is implemented. The use of demand price analysis, as described in Chapter

2 for assessing competitive value trends, can be helpful in projecting the values of future products. A more reliable measure may in fact be generated from an analysis as to what changes you would make if you were the product planner at your strongest competitor. With demand, pricing, and cost information at hand, Equation (3.9) can be used to project the cash flow for the proposed product redesign.

10.6 SUMMARY

Strategic significance: The Type I error found for the significance of a factor on the mean or variance will not necessarily be the same as the Type I error that the factor has on a strategic outcome such as value or cash flow. In most cases, the strategic Type I error will be greater because it is a function of the combined uncertainties in the mean and variance. In addition, there will be uncertainties in variable cost and value.

Variable cost: As discussed in Chapter 5, the second derivative of a variable cost curve does not contribute to the loss in cash flow, as process capability has already been accounted for in arriving at the quote for variable cost. However, if the cost estimate is uncertain, its uncertainty should be included as part of the Monte Carlo simulation used to project cash flow.

Monte Carlo simulation: The simulation progresses by converting the sample variances and means into ranges for the population variances and means. These are converted into value and/or CIQ. The price change can be estimated roughly using the rule of thumb that it is equal to ½ of value plus cost. Equation (3.2) can be used for a more refined estimate for highly competitive markets. Once value, cost, and price have been estimated, they can be substituted into the expressions for demand and cash flow.

REFERENCE

1. H. E. Cook. 1997. *Product Management: Value, Quality, Cost, Price, Profits, and Organization.* Amsterdam: Kluwer, pp. 214–245.

11

When Plans Have Been
Modified or Need to Be

Insight: Although things can go wrong in planned experiments, often there are means for recovery.

Key Topics

Problems in planning and running	interactions
experiments	nonregular designs

11.1 TYPICAL PROBLEMS

When planning and running an experiment, the following types of problems can arise:

1. The design needed was not available as one of the standard forms.

2. The parts available for testing for one or more trials was less than the number of planned replications, n.

3. The design chosen, for whatever reason, was not followed precisely.

4. Interactions between factors were assumed to be negligible but, on running a confirmation experiment, it was discovered that the assumption was likely incorrect.

Fortunately, steps can often be taken to mitigate these problems. To illustrate, consider an experiment to reduce the variance of the line widths on an integrated circuit on a silicon wafer. Each of the three manufacturing control factors is to be evaluated at three levels using a $L_9(3^3)$ design matrix, as shown in Table 11.1. This matrix was formed by eliminating the two columns for factor 4 in the SDW for the $L_9(3^4)$ OA. The resulting solution matrix is shown in Table 11.2. The column labeled COV lists the sum of the squares of the elements across each row *ij* which are equal to elements cov$_{ijij}$ along the diagonal of the covariance matrix.

Due to an oversight, trial 7 was not set up properly in that factor 1 was not at level 2 as required in Table 11.1 but at its baseline, level 0, as shown in Table 11.3. All of the replications were run in this manner for trial 7. Also two of the silicon wafers for trial 3 were broken in handling and could not be used.

Table 11.1 Lambda form of L$_9$(3^3) design matrix.

	0	11	12	21	22	31	32
1	1	0	0	0	0	0	0
2	1	0	0	1	0	1	0
3	1	0	0	0	1	0	1
4	1	1	0	0	0	1	0
5	1	1	0	1	0	0	1
6	1	1	0	0	1	0	0
7	1	0	1	0	0	0	1
8	1	0	1	1	0	0	0
9	1	0	1	0	1	1	0

Table 11.2 Solution matrix and diagonal of covariance matrix for design matrix in Table 11.1.

	1	2	3	4	5	6	7	8	9	COV
0	0.7778	0.1111	0.1111	0.1111	−0.222	0.1111	0.1111	0.1111	−0.222	0.7778
11	−0.333	−0.333	−0.333	0.3333	0.3333	0.3333	0	0	0	0.6667
12	−0.333	−0.333	−0.333	0	0	0	0.3333	0.3333	0.3333	0.6667
21	−0.333	0.3333	0	−0.333	0.3333	0	−0.333	0.3333	0	0.6667
22	−0.333	0	0.3333	−0.333	0	0.3333	−0.333	0	0.3333	0.6667
31	−0.333	0.3333	0	0.3333	0	−0.333	0	−0.333	0.3333	0.6667
32	−0.333	0	0.3333	0	0.3333	−0.333	0.3333	−0.333	0	0.6667

Table 11.3 The design matrix actually used in the experiment.

Trials	0	11	12	21	22	31	32
1	1	0	0	0	0	0	0
2	1	0	0	1	0	1	0
3	1	0	0	0	1	0	1
4	1	1	0	0	0	1	0
5	1	1	0	1	0	0	1
6	1	1	0	0	1	0	0
7	1	0	0	0	0	0	1
8	1	0	1	1	0	0	0
9	1	0	1	0	1	1	0

The first thing to do after recognizing what has happened is to check to see if the solution matrix exists for the design in Table 11.3 that was actually used. The computation shown in Table 11.4 confirms that the solution matrix does, in fact, exist. However, one important additional check needs to be made, which is verification that the full covariance matrix exists (there should be no large elements of size 10^{16}) as Excel can arrive at a solution matrix due to round-off error when, in fact, it does not exist. Next check how the elements of the solution matrix were affected. In Table 11.2, each element in each row of off-baseline coefficients is seen to have an element that is equal in absolute value but opposite in sign. This is not the case in Table 11.4, which means that the independent test for the significance of the factors on -10 log variance will not be exact if used. Thus, this example fails to support on two counts the requirements for using the independent test for the influence of factors on variance (see Chapter 9) because (1) the solution matrix was not balanced and (2) a constant df was not used for the trials as shown in Table 11.5, which was taken from the Design and Outcomes worksheet for the SDW.

Table 11.4 Solution matrix and diagonal of covariance matrix for the design matrix in Table 11.3.

	1	2	3	4	5	6	7	8	9	COV
0	0.67	0.08	0.00	0.08	−0.25	0.17	0.25	0.17	−0.17	0.667
11	−0.25	−0.38	−0.25	0.38	0.38	0.25	−0.13	0.00	0.00	0.625
12	−0.25	−0.63	−0.25	0.13	0.13	−0.25	0.13	0.50	0.50	1.125
21	−0.25	0.54	0.08	−0.38	0.29	0.08	−0.38	0.17	−0.17	0.792
22	−0.25	0.21	0.42	−0.38	−0.04	0.42	−0.38	−0.17	0.17	0.792
31	−0.33	0.33	0.00	0.33	0.00	−0.33	0.00	−0.33	0.33	0.667
32	−0.42	−0.21	0.25	0.04	0.38	−0.42	0.38	−0.17	0.17	0.792

Table 11.5 Results of the simulated tests.

Trial	1	2	3	4	5	6789#	n	Trial	Y	YMODEL	SSELIST	SSYLIST	PSVAR	PDF	AVGn
			REPLICATIONS										0.20	34	4.8
1	9.50	9.88	10.10	10.33	10.18		5	1	10.00	9.95	0.44	47.08			
2	14.01	13.91	14.03	14.35	13.44		5	2	13.95	13.91	0.44	4.44			
3	10.50	10.39	10.08				3	3	10.32	9.95	0.51	22.47	8.54	391.40	
4	19.09	19.03	19.05	19.10	18.95		5	4	19.04	18.89	0.13	179.51	SSE	SSY	
5	14.87	15.19	15.24	15.11	15.13		5	5	15.11	14.93	0.24	21.21			
6	14.95	14.81	14.61	14.73	15.16		5	6	14.85	14.93	0.21	16.41	R^2	0.98	
7	8.41	10.52	9.98	10.50	9.73		5	7	9.83	9.95	3.03	54.94			
8	10.54	8.97	10.30	11.16	10.60		5	8	10.31	9.95	3.33	40.20			
9	13.88	14.05	14.22	13.94	14.20		5	9	14.06	13.91	0.20	5.14			

Z 9
W 7

Trial	SVAR	SVARMODEL
1	0.11	0.30
2	0.11	0.04
3	0.05	0.30
4	0.00	0.00
5	0.02	0.03
6	0.05	0.03
7	0.74	0.30
8	0.67	0.30
9	0.02	0.04

The average of the elements in column COV in Table 11.2 for the desired orthogonal array is roughly 0.68. The average for COV in Table 11.4 is 0.78. As the *t* statistic for each experiment is proportional to the reciprocal of the square root of this quantity, the sensitivity is lower for the non-orthogonal design in Table 11.3. Also note in Table 11.4 that the brunt of the loss in accuracy involves factor 12, which is not surprising since it was this factor that was missing in trial 7.

The deviations from the requirements, however, appear relatively minor as only one factor level was off in Table 11.3 from the desired design and only one set of replications in nine trials did not follow the desired number of five, Table 11.5. Thus, the analysis proceeds as if the requirements for the independent test were met. Nevertheless, caution should be exercised by checking the results against those generated by Monte Carlo simulation, which, importantly, is not limited by the need to use a balanced solution matrix or to use a constant df for the trials. The nature of the distribution for the population must be known, however.

The array variables Y and SVAR in Table 11.5 list the sample means and sample variances, respectively. The next step in the process is to use the individual test to see if the specific factors influencing variance can be identified based upon the outcomes of the ξ_{ij} coefficients, Equation (9.3). The results taken from the XI coefficients worksheet in the SDW are shown in Table 11.6, where two separate sets of df (2 and 2 df and 4 and 4 df) were used to form a range of estimates of the EWE of the factors on log variance using the *F* test method. The 2 df results provide an upper bound on the Type I error and the 4 df results provide a lower bound. A single tail was chosen for the significance test because the goal was to see if one or more factors could reduce variance from its baseline level. Table 11.6 shows that two off-baseline factors (11 and 31) are significant at better than 5% EWE using the interpolated EWE. The PWE interpolation expression used in Cell N11 is shown in Table 11.6. It was dragged down to generate the other computations.

The outcomes for a typical Monte Carlo simulation used to vet the results are shown in Table 11.7. The spreadsheet expressions used are shown at the bottom of Table 11.7. The coefficients ξ_{ij} computed from the simulation are shown in the column XIijSIM.

A total of 1000 simulations were made to obtain the distributions for the ξ_{ij}. The first 10 simulations are listed in Table 11.8, and all of the simulation results are shown graphically in Figure 11.1; they were copied from the SDW and pasted into a KaleidaGraph file for normal probability plotting. Factors 11 and 31 are shown as being favorable for reducing variance and are significant at better than 0.1% PWE based upon the fractional intercepts (% intercept/100) of 0.0006 and 0.001 for factors 11 and 31, respectively. The interpolated PWE are seen to be more conservative. The comparison between the analytical results and the Monte Carlo results is rough here because a much larger number of simulations are required to establish the intercept for the low PWE. Nevertheless, it is reasonable to infer that the two factors are significant for reducing variance based upon the analytical and Monte Carlo results.

Clearly variances should not be pooled, and Satterthwaite's approximate test as described in Chapter 9 should be used. The significance of the findings for the λ_{ij} taken from the Lambda Coefficients worksheet are shown in Table 11.9. The spreadsheet expressions used are also shown for completeness. Factors 11 and 31 are also seen to be highly

Table 11.6 Results of the individual test using two separate paired sets of df to arrive at an upper and lower limit on the single-tail significance of the factors on log variance.

ALPHAXI = 0.05

		XI	Gij	MIN(n) PWE	MIN(n) EWE	MAX(n) PWE	MAX(n) EWE	Interpolated PWE	Interpolated EWE	SIGXI			REDXI
0	**0**	5.26	0.91	0.11	0.11	0.033	0.033	0.042	0.042	significant	**0**	**0**	5.26
0	**11**	9.35	1.67	0.02	0.12	0.001	0.008	0.003	0.021	significant	**0**	**11**	9.3526
0	**12**	−0.74	−0.10	0.44	2.66	0.415	2.492	0.418	2.511	NOT	**0**	**12**	0.00
0	**21**	−2.18	−0.35	0.31	1.86	0.230	1.378	0.239	1.432	NOT	**0**	**21**	0.00
0	**22**	2.76	0.44	0.27	1.60	0.176	1.054	0.186	1.115	NOT	**0**	**22**	0.00
0	**31**	8.56	1.48	0.03	0.19	0.003	0.018	0.006	0.037	significant	**0**	**31**	8.5602
0	**32**	1.96	0.31	0.33	1.97	0.252	1.510	0.260	1.561	NOT	**0**	**32**	0.00
0	**0**	#N/A	#N/A	#N/A	#N/A	#N/A	#N/A	#N/A	#N/A	#N/A	**0**	**0**	#N/A
0	**0**	#N/A	#N/A	#N/A	#N/A	#N/A	#N/A	#N/A	#N/A	#N/A	**0**	**0**	#N/A

Left block formulas:

```
XI  =MMULT(XS,-10*LOG(SVAR))
Gij =XI/SQRT(50*COV)
PWE =FDIST(10^ABS(Gij),MIN(n)-1,MIN(n)-1)
EWE =PWE*(w-1)    Off baseline
```

Right block formulas:

```
PWE   =FDIST(10^ABS(Gij),MAX(n)-1,MAX(n)-1)
EWE   =L11   Drag
PWE   =IF(MAX(n)=MIN(n),L11,I11-(I11-L11)*(AVGn-MIN(n))/(MAX(n)-MIN(n)))   N11
EWE   =(w-1)*N12   Drag   O12
SIGXI =IF(O11<ALPHAXI,"significant","NOT")   Drag
REDXI =G11   S11
REDXI =G12*IF(P12="significant",1,0)   S12   Drag
```

Table 11.7 Monte Carlo simulation of the ξ_{ij} coefficients (name XIijSIM).

	D	E	F	G	H	I	J
38		Simulated					
39		population					
40	**Trial**	variance			**XIijSIM**		
41	**1**	0.112	**0.000**	**0**	5.98		
42	**2**	0.041		**0**	**11**	4.32	
43	**3**	0.019		**0**	**12**	-1.83	
44	**4**	0.004		**0**	**21**	-0.76	
45	**5**	0.047		**0**	**22**	4.33	
46	**6**	0.088		**0**	**31**	10.65	
47	**7**	0.613		**0**	**32**	2.23	
48	**8**	0.406					
49	**9**	0.014					
50		=(n-1)*SVAR/CHIINV(1-RAND(),n-1)					
51		**XIijSIM**	=MMULT(XS,-10*LOG(E41:E49))				
52							

Table 11.8 The column for XIijSIM in Table 11.7 is transformed into a row so that the repeats of the simulations are pushed down instead of across the spreadsheet.

	K	L	M	N	O	P	Q	R
42		**0**	**11**	**12**	**21**	**22**	**31**	**32**
43		5.98	4.32	-1.83	-0.76	4.33	10.65	2.23
44								
45								
46	**1**	6.67	6.80	-3.10	-6.88	6.49	7.17	-0.51
47	**2**	8.10	6.98	-2.77	-2.48	3.00	6.79	1.94
48	**3**	4.30	8.03	2.44	-5.82	-0.69	8.10	3.91
49	**4**	3.20	1.40	-7.72	6.27	8.19	7.62	2.95
50	**5**	3.44	14.16	-2.20	0.56	1.81	9.84	-2.07
51	**6**	5.99	9.29	-4.74	-3.96	5.96	9.63	4.45
52	**7**	3.64	12.16	4.55	-4.30	0.94	8.68	2.79
53	**8**	8.69	4.19	-2.76	-0.82	2.03	5.62	0.35
54	**9**	5.61	8.79	-4.56	-0.23	1.43	7.22	1.13
55	**10**	4.22	13.88	5.33	-4.60	1.91	2.73	-1.04

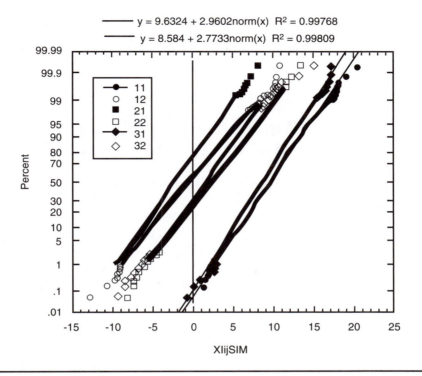

Figure 11.1 Results of 1000 simulations for XIijSIM plotted on normal probability paper.

Table 11.9 Steps in constructing the effective df and significance for the factors.

	E	F	G	H	I	J	K	L	M	N	O	P
7								**ALPHALAM**				
8								0.1				
9												
10			**LAM**	**SDij**	**DFij**	**t**	**PWE2**	**EWE**	**SIGLAM**			**REDLAM**
11	0	0	9.95	0.15	11.41	65.43	0.00	0.00	significant	0	0	9.95
12	0	11	4.98	0.09	16.71	52.92	0.00	0.00	significant	0	11	4.98
13	0	12	0.17	0.22	7.78	0.78	0.23	1.38	NOT	0	12	0.00
14	0	21	0.11	0.18	8.86	0.60	0.28	1.69	NOT	0	21	0.00
15	0	22	0.06	0.18	8.38	0.36	0.36	2.18	NOT	0	22	0.00
16	0	31	3.96	0.15	7.72	27.26	0.00	0.00	significant	0	31	3.96
17	0	32	0.09	0.18	8.99	0.49	0.32	1.91	NOT	0	32	0.00
18	0	0	#N/A	#N/A	#N/A	#N/A	#N/A	#N/A	#N/A	0	0	#N/A
19	0	0	#N/A	#N/A	#N/A	#N/A	#N/A	#N/A	#N/A	0	0	#N/A
20												
21	**LAM**	=MMULT(XS,Y)					**SIGLAM**	=IF(L11<ALPHALAM,"significant","NOT")				
22	**SDij**	=SQRT(MMULT(XS^2,SVAR/n))					**REDLAM**	=G11				
23	**DFij**	=SDij^4/MMULT(XS^4,(SVAR/n)^2/(n-1))					**REDLAM**	=G12*IF(M12="significant",1,0)				
24	**t**	=LAM/SDij										
25	**PWE2**	=TDIST(ABS(t),DFij,1)										
26	**EWE**	=PWE2*(w-1)										
27												

significant in increasing the mean relative to the baseline, trial 1. At this juncture, the analysis and tests for statistical significance have been completed. The strategic significance of the two factors could be checked at this juncture by looking at the change in value due to the improvements in the mean and variance. This process is described in Chapter 10 and need not be repeated here.

11.2 WHEN INTERACTIONS ARE PRESENT AND YOU IGNORE THEM, INITIALLY

Taguchi, based upon extensive experience, has recommended that, when you do not have knowledge that one or more interactions are important, you fill the available interaction columns in the design matrix with main effects. Most of the orthogonal arrays listed by Taguchi and Konishi[1] are, in fact, full factorial designs in which additional main effects have been inserted in the interaction columns. Taguchi also recommends that a confirmation experiment be performed using the factors found favorable to test the assumption that interactions were weak. The following example represents a situation in which three main effects at two levels each are evaluated using a progression of three different designs in Table 11.10 through Table 11.12.

The population was chosen such that only the 1121 interaction affected variance. Array 1 in Table 11.10 (a) is a $L_4(2^3)$ OA in which interactions are ignored. Its confounding matrix is shown as Table 11.10 (b) where it is seen that the 1121 interaction confounds with 11, 21, and 31. (Computation of a confounding matrix is described in Appendix C.) Array 2 in Table 11.11 adds one more trial to the $L_4(2^3)$ OA plus a column for the 1121 interaction. Array 3 in Table 11.12 is a special $L_8(2^3)$ design derived from a $L_8(2^3)$ FF design with the triplet interaction removed. The three designs are used in concert to illustrate the types of steps that might occur when the assumption that interactions are negligible was incorrect.

Table 11.10   (a) $L_4(2^3)$ Design Array 1 and (b) The confounding matrix for Array 1.

(a)

Trial	0	11	21	31
1	1	0	0	0
2	1	0	1	1
3	1	1	0	1
4	1	1	1	0

(b)

	0	11	21	31	1121	1131	2131
0	1	0	0	0	0	0	0
11	0	1	0	0	0.5	0.5	-0.5
21	0	0	1	0	0.5	-0.5	0.5
31	0	0	0	1	-0.5	0.5	0.5

Table 11.11 (a) Design Array 2 is formed by adding trial 8 to matrix 1. (b) The confounding matrix for Array 2.

(a)

Trial	0	11	21	31	1121
1	1	0	0	0	0
2	1	0	1	1	0
3	1	1	0	1	0
4	1	1	1	0	1
8	1	1	1	1	1

(b)

	0	11	21	31	1121	1131	2131
0	1.0	0.0	0.0	0.0	0.0	0.0	0.0
11	0.0	1.0	0.0	0.0	0.0	0.0	-1.0
21	0.0	0.0	1.0	0.0	0.0	-1.0	0.0
31	0.0	0.0	0.0	1.0	0.0	1.0	1.0
1121	0.0	0.0	0.0	0.0	1.0	1.0	1.0

Table 11.12 Design Array 3 represented by the $L_8(2^3)$ design less triplet interaction.

Trial	0	11	21	31	1121	1131	2131
1	1	0	0	0	0	0	0
2	1	0	1	1	0	0	1
3	1	1	0	1	0	1	0
4	1	1	1	0	1	0	0
5	1	0	0	1	0	0	0
6	1	0	1	0	0	0	0
7	1	1	0	0	0	0	0
8	1	1	1	1	1	1	1

Assume that the objective of the experiment was to reduce the baseline variance substantially. Thus, the lambda form of the OA was chosen over the phi form because of the need to measure the significance of the coefficients relative to the trial 1 baseline. The population statistics chosen for this problem are shown in Table 11.13 for all eight trials of the $L_8(2^3)$ design (Array 3), which includes the trials for Arrays 1 and 2. Table 11.14 lists the lambda coefficients for the population.

The results found using Array 1 (see Table 11.15 and Table 11.16) suggested that factor 21 was best for reducing variance and a confirmation trial was run with this factor in place and with factors 11 and 31 at their baseline levels. The outcomes (not shown) of the confirmation trial were disappointing in that the resulting variance was no better than the baseline, being the result expected for $L_4(2^3)$ experiment given the population statistics.

Table 11.13 The assumed population mean and variance for the problem.

Trial	Population Mean	Variance
1	10	3.1623
2	10	3.1623
3	10	3.1623
4	10	0.1995
5	10	3.1623
6	10	3.1623
7	10	3.1623
8	10	0.1995

Table 11.14 The population lambda coefficients for the mean and −10 log variance.

	Population coefficients λ_{ij}	ξ_{ij}
0	10	−5
11	0	0
21	0	0
31	0	0
1121	0	12
1131	0	0
2131	0	0

Table 11.15 The replications, sample variances, and means for the first experiment (Array 1).

	Replications						
Trial	1	2	3	4	5	SVAR	Y
1	9.715	13.916	9.349	10.346	10.260	3.363	10.717
2	6.897	8.148	8.508	8.282	10.908	2.132	8.549
3	11.841	9.881	9.440	9.705	6.779	3.268	9.529
4	9.804	10.099	10.298	10.554	10.546	0.101	10.260

Table 11.16 The independent analysis of the factors on −10 log variance for Arrays 1 through 3.

	XI ij			Gij		
	Array 1	Array 2	Array 3	Array 1	Array 2	Array 3
0	−5.267	−5.267	−5.889	−0.745	−0.745	−0.890
11	6.683	1.517	1.047	0.945	0.107	0.121
21	8.538	3.372	2.996	1.207	0.238	0.346
31	−6.558	−1.392	−1.791	−0.927	−0.139	−0.207
1121		10.332	11.178		0.517	1.118
1131			0.868			0.087
2131			0.774			0.077

	F			EWE		
	Array 1	Array 2	Array 3	Array 1	Array 2	Array 3
0	5.558	5.558	7.769			
11	8.812	1.280	1.321	0.087	1.633	2.382
21	16.124	1.732	2.218	0.029	1.216	1.378
31	8.462	1.378	1.610	0.093	1.527	1.968
1121		3.286	13.115		0.552	0.086
1131			1.221			2.553
2131			1.195			2.601

(Note that if factors 11 and 21 had been chosen, then the 1121 interaction would have been captured, unwittingly.)

With this setback, the outcomes of the original experiment using Array 1 were studied to see what might have gone wrong. The ξ_{ij} (XIij) coefficients are shown in Table 11.16 along with those obtained from the follow-on experiments using Arrays 2 and 3. (See Equations (9.3) through (9.5) for the descriptions of the terms used in the analysis.) A possible explanation of the discrepancy between the results for Array 1 and those of the confirmation trial is that a strong 1121 interaction existed. This is indicated by the fact that both factors 11 and 21 affected the −10 log variance in a positive manner and factor 31 affected it in a negative manner, this finding being consistent with the results for column 1121 for the confounding matrix in Table 11.10(b). In fact, if the 1121 interaction was assumed to be the only important contributor to the experiment, the confounding matrix and the results in Table 11.16 show that ξ_{1121} should equal 17.2, which is two times the sum of factors 11 and 21 minus factor 31. The true value of this coefficient for the population is 12.

Consequently, a fifth independent trial (trial 8 in Array 2) was run to check this possibility. The variance and mean outcomes of this trial are listed in Table 11.17. Although the resulting value of 10.3 for the ξ_{1121} coefficient in column XIij computed for Array 2 in Table 11.16 is relatively large, its EWE does not support its being taken as significant. Not giving up, we added three additional trials (Array 3) to see if the 1131 and 2131 pairwise interactions could be playing a role. The replications for all eight trials are shown in Table 11.18 and the resulting coefficients for the −10 log variances are listed under the columns for Array 3 in Table 11.16.

Table 11.17 The replications, sample variances, and means for the second experiment (Array 2 used).

| Trial | \multicolumn{5}{c}{Replications} | | |
	1	2	3	4	5	SVAR	Y
1	9.715	13.916	9.349	10.346	10.260	3.363	10.717
2	6.897	8.148	8.508	8.282	10.908	2.132	8.549
3	11.841	9.881	9.440	9.705	6.779	3.268	9.529
4	9.804	10.099	10.298	10.554	10.546	0.101	10.260
8	10.142	10.721	10.144	9.885	10.700	0.139	10.318

Table 11.18 The replications, sample variances, and means for the third experiment (Array 3 used).

| Trial | \multicolumn{5}{c}{Replications} | | |
	1	2	3	4	5	SVAR	Y
1	9.715	13.916	9.349	10.346	10.260	3.3630	10.7174
2	6.897	8.148	8.508	8.282	10.908	2.1317	8.5487
3	11.841	9.881	9.440	9.705	6.779	3.2680	9.5291
4	9.804	10.099	10.298	10.554	10.546	0.1011	10.2600
5	13.459	7.505	10.784	9.975	7.078	6.7637	9.7602
6	8.463	11.742	10.955	9.931	8.346	2.2464	9.8873
7	10.605	8.118	9.676	10.669	13.273	3.5193	10.4681
8	10.142	10.721	10.144	9.885	10.700	0.1393	10.3184

The three experiments were simultaneously simulated 500 times using the population statistics in Table 11.13. The results are summarized in Table 11.19. The criteria for detection of the 1121 interaction for Array 1 was that if factors 11 and 21 were both less than 10% Type I EWE, they would simultaneously be selected resulting in the 1121 interaction being captured by serendipity. The selection criteria for Arrays 2 and 3 was that the EWE for 1121 was less than 10%. It is seen that the use of the $L_8(2^3)$ design (Array 3) yielded a power of detection for the influence of factor 1121 on -10 log variance that was higher than that for Arrays 1 and 2. (Analysis of the factors on -10 log variance is only approximate for Array 2 because its solution matrix is not perfectly balanced.)

These findings are not surprising, on inspecting the matrices in Table 11.20 for the three designs. The square root of cov_{1121} for Array 2 is twice that for Array 3, making Array 2 inferior to Array 3. Although Array 1 was unable to solve for the 1121 coefficient in a direct manner, its COV column vector shows that it is more efficient than the other two for

Table 11.19 Criteria for significance used in analysis.

Design array	# Trials	% Detection	% Detection per trial
1	4	21	5.25
2	5	19	3.80
3	8	54	6.75

Table 11.20 The solution matrices and the diagonals of covariance matrices for the three design matrices.

	1	2	3	4	COV
0	1	0	0	0	1
11	-0.5	-0.5	0.5	0.5	1
21	-0.5	0.5	-0.5	0.5	1
31	-0.5	0.5	0.5	-0.5	1

	1	2	3	4	8	COV
0	1	0	0	0	0	1
11	-1	0	1	1	-1	4
21	-1	1	0	1	-1	4
31	0	0	0	-1	1	2
1121	1	-1	-1	-1	2	8

	1	2	3	4	5	6	7	8	COV
0	0.875	-0.125	-0.125	-0.125	0.125	0.125	0.125	0.125	0.875
11	-0.75	0.25	0.25	0.25	-0.25	-0.25	0.75	-0.25	1.5
21	-0.75	0.25	0.25	0.25	-0.25	0.75	-0.25	-0.25	1.5
31	-0.75	0.25	0.25	0.25	0.75	-0.25	-0.25	-0.25	1.5
1121	0.5	-0.5	-0.5	0.5	0.5	-0.5	-0.5	0.5	2
1131	0.5	-0.5	0.5	-0.5	-0.5	0.5	-0.5	0.5	2
2131	0.5	0.5	-0.5	-0.5	-0.5	-0.5	0.5	0.5	2

the case when there are no interactions. This supports Taguchi's paradigm of favoring main effect designs, at least for screening.

When Array 1 is used, the confounding of the 1121 interaction with 31 made the 31 coefficient significant roughly 41% of the time. However, the sign of the coefficient, in almost all cases, was negative and thus it would not be selected over the baseline 30, thereby avoiding a Type I error.

There is a simpler way to analyze this problem, which is to examine the outcomes without the use of the linear model. As the objective was to reduce the variance relative to trial 1, the set of factors used in trial 4 of Table 11.15 appears to have done this. The test of significance of this trial on variance is simply the standard F test result suitably corrected for experiment-wise error. As there are three off-baseline trials for Array 1, the EWE is computed by multiplying the pairwise error by 3. The F ratio is equal to 33.27, and the two df are each equal to 4. When substituted into the arguments for FDIST, the Type I EWE is given by

$$3 * \text{FDIST}(33.27,4,4) = 0.0075$$

Thus the solution to the problem with high confidence is to use the factors that were evaluated in trial 4. The relative power of the F test was explored using a total of 500 simulations for Array 1 with sample measurements taken randomly from the populations for the trials. The frequency for selecting trial 4 as significant at 10% EWE was 75% overall (19% per experimental trial), which represents substantial improvement over the full factorial experiment.

Why not solve all problems this way? Why use the linear model? The reason is that the model offers the possibility of arriving at a better solution than found for the best experimental trial with no further analysis. For example, Array 1 did not evaluate the possibility of all three factors being present at their off-baseline levels. When a full factorial experiment is used, in principle, you also do not need a model to find the best solution, as all possible solutions have been evaluated and the best solution given by the trial with the best outcome.

The linear model also provides insight into the relative importance of the factors and the nature of interactions if they are present. It may be that the trial having the best outcome has one or more factors that are costly to implement but do not influence the mean and variance. You would not know this without having the results given by the model. Nevertheless, the F test clearly shows that this was very helpful as part of the overall strategy in analyzing the outcomes for the sample variances and should be routinely used before making the more in-depth analysis. In similar fashion, the t-test can be used to evaluate the difference between the sample means for the trials.

11.3 NONREGULAR DESIGNS

11.3.1 $L_{12}(2^{11})$

A *regular* OA starts with a FF design and then fills interaction columns with main effects. Two-level regular designs, for example, go from L4, L8, L16, L32, and so forth, leaving gaps. Nonregular designs provide for a broader and more efficient range of options for experimental designs. The $L_{12}(2^{11})$ nonregular design in Table 11.21 is a "gap filler." However, each main effect is confounded with multiple two-factor interactions. The confounding matrix is shown in Table 11.22 for selected two-factor interactions.

The solution matrix for the $L_{12}(2^{11})$ design is shown in Table 11.23. Certain rows, for example those for factors 11, 21, and 31, are balanced in that for every positive element there is a negative element of the same absolute value. Other rows, for example 51, 61, and 71, do not have this property. Those factors having unbalanced rows will result in an approximate measure of Type I error when the F test for the influence of the factors on log variance is used.

11.3.2 $L_8(4^1,2^4)$

The development of a $L_8(4^1,2^4)$ design from a $L_8(2^7)$ design is shown in Table 11.24. The lambda form for the design matrix is also shown. This is just one example of how a regular design can be modified to efficiently mix factors with different levels. The solution matrix for this design in Table 11.25 shows that each positive element is balanced by a negative element of the same absolute value.

Table 11.21 The $L_{12}(2^{11})$ nonregular design matrix. Every factor is confounded with two-factor interactions.

	0	11	21	31	41	51	61	71	81	91	10,1	11,1
1	1	0	0	0	0	0	0	0	0	0	0	0
2	1	0	0	0	0	0	1	1	1	1	1	1
3	1	0	0	1	1	1	0	0	0	1	1	1
4	1	0	1	0	1	1	0	1	1	0	0	1
5	1	0	1	1	0	1	1	0	1	0	1	0
6	1	0	1	1	1	0	1	1	0	1	0	0
7	1	1	0	1	1	0	0	1	1	0	0	0
8	1	1	0	1	0	1	1	1	0	0	1	1
9	1	1	0	0	1	1	1	0	1	1	0	0
10	1	1	1	1	0	0	0	0	1	1	1	1
11	1	1	1	0	0	0	1	0	0	0	1	1
12	1	1	1	0	1	1	0	1	0	1	0	0

Table 11.22 The confounding matrix between the main effects and several selected pairwise interactions for the $L_{12}(2^{11})$ nonregular design.

	1121	1131	1141	1151	1161	1171
0	0.000	0.000	0.000	0.000	0.000	0.000
11	0.500	0.500	0.500	0.500	0.500	0.500
21	0.500	-0.167	-0.167	-0.167	-0.167	-0.167
31	-0.333	0.667	-0.333	0.000	0.000	0.000
41	0.000	-0.500	0.500	-0.500	0.000	0.000
51	-0.167	0.000	0.000	0.667	0.167	0.167
61	-0.333	-0.167	-0.167	0.167	0.667	-0.333
71	0.000	0.167	0.167	0.167	-0.333	0.667
81	-0.167	0.167	0.167	-0.167	-0.167	-0.167
91	0.167	0.000	0.000	0.333	-0.167	-0.167
10,1	0.500	-0.500	0.500	-0.500	-0.500	0.500
11,1	-0.167	0.333	-0.667	0.000	0.500	-0.500

Table 11.23 The solution matrix for the $L_{12}(2^{11})$ design.

	1	2	3	4	5	6	7	8	9	10	11	12
0	1.000	0.000	0.000	0.000	0.000	0.000	0.000	0.000	0.000	0.000	0.000	0.000
11	-0.167	-0.167	-0.167	-0.167	-0.167	-0.167	0.167	0.167	0.167	0.167	0.167	0.167
21	-0.167	-0.167	-0.167	0.167	0.167	0.167	-0.167	-0.167	-0.167	0.167	0.167	0.167
31	0.000	-0.333	0.000	0.000	0.000	0.333	0.000	0.333	0.000	0.333	-0.333	-0.333
41	-0.500	0.000	0.500	0.000	0.000	0.000	0.500	-0.500	0.000	-0.500	0.500	0.000
51	0.000	-0.167	0.000	0.167	0.167	-0.167	-0.333	0.333	0.167	0.000	-0.333	0.167
61	-0.167	0.000	-0.167	0.000	0.000	0.333	-0.167	0.167	0.333	-0.167	0.167	-0.333
71	-0.167	0.333	-0.167	0.000	0.000	0.000	0.167	0.167	-0.333	-0.167	-0.167	0.333
81	-0.167	0.167	-0.167	0.167	0.167	-0.167	0.167	-0.167	0.167	0.167	-0.167	-0.167
91	0.000	0.167	0.000	-0.167	-0.167	0.167	-0.333	0.000	0.167	0.333	-0.333	0.167
10,1	-0.500	0.500	0.500	-0.500	0.500	-0.500	0.500	-0.500	-0.500	-0.500	0.500	0.500
11,1	0.000	-0.167	0.000	0.500	-0.500	0.167	-0.333	0.333	0.167	0.333	0.000	-0.500

Table 11.24 The development of a $L_8(4^1,2^4)$ design from a $L_8(2^7)$ design. The resulting lambda form X matrix is also shown for completeness.

$L_8(2^7)$

	1	2	3	4	5	6	7
1	1	1	1	1	1	1	1
2	1	1	1	2	2	2	2
3	1	2	2	1	1	2	2
4	1	2	2	2	2	1	1
5	2	1	2	1	2	1	2
6	2	1	2	2	1	2	1
7	2	2	1	1	2	2	1
8	2	2	1	2	1	1	2

$L_8(4^1,2^4)$

	1	2	3	4	5
1	1	1	1	1	1
2	1	2	2	2	2
3	2	1	1	2	2
4	2	2	2	1	1
5	3	1	2	1	2
6	3	2	1	2	1
7	4	1	2	2	1
8	4	2	1	1	2

X

	0	11	12	13	21	31	41	51
1	1	0	0	0	0	0	0	0
2	1	0	0	0	1	1	1	1
3	1	1	0	0	0	0	1	1
4	1	1	0	0	1	1	0	0
5	1	0	1	0	0	1	0	1
6	1	0	1	0	1	0	1	0
7	1	0	0	1	0	1	1	0
8	1	0	0	1	1	0	0	1

Table 11.25 The solution matrix for the $L_8(4^1,2^4)$ design.

XS

	1	2	3	4	5	6	7	8
0	1	0	0	0	0	0	0	0
11	-0.5	-0.5	0.5	0.5	0	0	0	0
12	-0.5	-0.5	0	0	0.5	0.5	0	0
13	-0.5	-0.5	0	0	0	0	0.5	0.5
21	-0.25	0.25	-0.25	0.25	-0.25	0.25	-0.25	0.25
31	-0.25	0.25	-0.25	0.25	0.25	-0.25	0.25	-0.25
41	-0.25	0.25	0.25	-0.25	-0.25	0.25	0.25	-0.25
51	-0.25	0.25	0.25	-0.25	0.25	-0.25	-0.25	0.25

11.3.3 $L_9(2^1,3^3)$ and $L_9(2^2,3^3)$

The transformation of the $L_9(3^4)$ design into an $L_9(2^1,3^3)$ design is shown in Table 11.26 by changing level 3 in column 1 to level 1. The lambda form of the design matrix is shown in Table 11.27. The solution matrix for this design in Table 11.28 is balanced for all factors except for factor 11. There is a choice for trials 7 through 9 of whether to use level 1 or level

Table 11.26 The transformation of the $L^9(3_4)$ design into an $L^9(2^1,3^3)$ design.

$L_9(3^4)$

	1	2	3	4
1	1	1	1	1
2	1	2	2	2
3	1	3	3	3
4	2	1	2	3
5	2	2	3	1
6	2	3	1	2
7	3	1	3	2
8	3	2	1	3
9	3	3	2	1

$L_9(2^1, 3^3)$

	1	2	3	4
1	1	1	1	1
2	1	2	2	2
3	1	3	3	3
4	2	1	2	3
5	2	2	3	1
6	2	3	1	2
7	1	1	3	2
8	1	2	1	3
9	1	3	2	1

Table 11.27 The design matrix for $L_9(2^1,3^3)$ design.

	0	11	21	22	31	32	41	42
1	1	0	0	0	0	0	0	0
2	1	0	1	0	1	0	1	0
3	1	0	0	1	0	1	0	1
4	1	1	0	0	1	0	0	1
5	1	1	1	0	0	1	0	0
6	1	1	0	1	0	0	1	0
7	1	0	0	0	0	1	1	0
8	1	0	1	0	0	0	0	1
9	1	0	0	1	1	0	0	0

2 for factor 1. The transformation of an $L_9(3^4)$ design into an $L_9(2^2,3^3)$ design is shown in Table 11.29. The two-level factors, written initially as (a0,a1) and (b0,b1), become (10,11) and (20,21) in the transformed design matrix shown in Table 11.30. The solution matrix is

Table 11.28 The $L_9(2^1,3^3)$ solution matrix.

	1	2	3	4	5	6	7	8	9	COVij
0	0.8333	-0.167	-0.167	1E-16	1E-16	1E-16	0.1667	0.1667	0.1667	0.833
11	-0.167	-0.167	-0.167	0.3333	0.3333	0.3333	-0.167	-0.167	-0.167	0.500
21	-0.333	0.3333	0	-0.333	0.3333	0	-0.333	0.3333	0	0.667
22	-0.333	0	0.3333	-0.333	0	0.3333	-0.333	0	0.3333	0.667
31	-0.333	0.3333	0	0.3333	0	-0.333	0	-0.333	0.3333	0.667
32	-0.333	0	0.3333	0	0.3333	-0.333	0.3333	-0.333	0	0.667
41	-0.333	0.3333	0	0	-0.333	0.3333	0.3333	0	-0.333	0.667
42	-0.333	0	0.3333	0.3333	-0.333	0	0	0.3333	-0.333	0.667

Table 11.29 The transformation of the $L_9(3^4)$ design into an $L_9(2^2,3^3)$ design.

$L_9(3^4)$

	1	2	3	4
1	1	1	1	1
2	1	2	2	2
3	1	3	3	3
4	2	1	2	3
5	2	2	3	1
6	2	3	1	2
7	3	1	3	2
8	3	2	1	3
9	3	3	2	1

$L_9(2^2,3^3)$

	1, 2	3	4	5
1	a0,b0	1	1	1
2	a0,b0	2	2	2
3	a0,b0	3	3	3
4	a0,b1	1	2	3
5	a0,b1	2	3	1
6	a0,b1	3	1	2
7	a1,b0	1	3	2
8	a1,b0	2	1	3
9	a1,b0	3	2	1

shown in Table 11.31. The 11 coefficient measures the effect of changing a factor from its baseline level of a0 to level a1. The 21 coefficient measures the effect of changing factor b from its baseline level of b0 to b1.

Table 11.30   The lambda form of the $L_9(2^2,3^3)$ design matrix.

	0	11	21	31	32	41	42	51	52
1	1	0	0	0	0	0	0	0	0
2	1	0	0	1	0	1	0	1	0
3	1	0	0	0	1	0	1	0	1
4	1	0	1	0	0	1	0	0	1
5	1	0	1	1	0	0	1	0	0
6	1	0	1	0	1	0	0	1	0
7	1	1	0	0	0	0	1	1	0
8	1	1	0	1	0	0	0	0	1
9	1	1	0	0	1	1	0	0	0

Table 11.31   The lambda form of the $L_9(2^2,3^3)$ solution matrix.

	1	2	3	4	5	6	7	8	9
0	1.000	0.000	0.000	0.000	0.000	0.000	0.000	0.000	0.000
11	-0.333	-0.333	-0.333	0.000	0.000	0.000	0.333	0.333	0.333
21	-0.333	-0.333	-0.333	0.333	0.333	0.333	0.000	0.000	0.000
31	-0.333	0.333	0.000	-0.333	0.333	0.000	-0.333	0.333	0.000
32	-0.333	0.000	0.333	-0.333	0.000	0.333	-0.333	0.000	0.333
41	-0.333	0.333	0.000	0.333	0.000	-0.333	0.000	-0.333	0.333
42	-0.333	0.000	0.333	0.000	0.333	-0.333	0.333	-0.333	0.000
51	-0.333	0.333	0.000	0.000	-0.333	0.333	0.333	0.000	-0.333
52	-0.333	0.000	0.333	0.333	-0.333	0.000	0.000	0.333	-0.333

11.4 SUMMARY

Things will go wrong: No matter how carefully an experiment is planned, disruptions to the plan may occur. For example, specimens break or are lost and set points can be off.

Recovery: Often there are means for recovering from a disruption. For example, the variance for an experimental trial may turn out to be much larger than expected. If this issue is caught during the running of the experiment, then it may be possible to run additional samples for this trial. Computer simulation can be used to compute the significance of the coefficients on variance when the sample size is not constant.

Interactions ignored: When using designs that are saturated or nearly saturated with main effects, interactions may confound the results to the extent that the wrong factors and factor levels are selected for production. It is highly recommended to explore the nature of possible pairwise interactions before running the experiment by constructing the confounding matrix. A confirmation experiment also needs to be run with the main effects identified as promising to ensure that the projected outcomes are close to those of the confirmation experiment.

Cross-check analysis: The best outcome for the individual trials needs to be examined to see if it contains the factors at the levels projected as promising for production. This is useful because *the outcome for every trial expresses all of the interactions between the factors for that trial.* Major discrepancies between the two sets of factor levels should raise concern, and so should a major discrepancy in the size of the outcome.

Nonregular designs: Nonregular designs are useful in bridging gaps in the design space between regular designs and in mixing factors conveniently having different levels.

REFERENCE

1. G. Taguchi and S. Konishi. 1987. *Taguchi Methods Orthogonal Arrays and Linear Graphs.* Livonia, MI: ASI Press, Livonia, MI.

12

Applications of Lognormal, Binomial, and Poisson Distributions

> *Insight: The statistics for CTV attributes having non-negative character cannot be modeled rigorously using the normal distribution.*

Key Topics

Lognormal, binomial, and Poisson distributions	mirror defects
	windshield molding defects
bottom-line metrics analysis	solder-joint defects

12.1 ATTRIBUTES WITH NON-NEGATIVE CHARACTER

In Chapter 5, three basic CTV attribute types were introduced: SIB, LIB, and NIB. The NIB was separated into NIB1 and NIB2. NIB1 examples are less demanding to model because each has a scaling factor for placing the mean at the target specification. An important feature of the CTV attributes considered in this chapter is that they can never be less than zero. Vibration intensity, surface roughness, degree of illumination, and noise are examples of physical attributes that cannot have negative values. These are not always associated with SIB value functions having a maximum at an ideal specification $g_I = 0$. Interior noise in a room or a car, for example, may be optimum at 40 dBA.[1] The surface of the bore of an internal combustion engine has an optimum level of roughness. It follows that non-negative, random, physical variables cannot follow a normal distribution, which ranges from minus to plus infinity. They are likely instead to follow, at least approximately, distributions such as the lognormal, binomial, Poisson, or Weibull.

195

12.2 APPLICATION OF THE LOGNORMAL DISTRIBUTION TO A SIB PROBLEM

A hypothetical SIB value curve for a reflecting telescope is shown in Figure 12.1 versus the number of defects g in the mirror. The telescope, designed for the consumer market, has a maximum value of \$690 at $g_I = 0$, but when the number of defects per unit area is 70 or more, the contrast is so poor that the telescope has no value. Methods for constructing value curves are discussed in Chapter 5.

   Assume that the baseline level of defects in the current telescope is g_0, and the baseline value of the telescope is V_0. The vertical and horizontal lines show these levels, respectively, in Figure 12.1. The major financial parameters for the problem are listed in Table 12.1 along with the names given to them for the spreadsheet computations. The goal is to reduce, cost effectively, the number of defects in the coating formed using a sputtering technique. Four processing factors represented by substrate temperature, vacuum pressure, settling time before deposition begins, and cleaning methods are to be evaluated at three levels each. Interactions between the factors are believed to be negligible. Thus, the analysis provided by the L9(3^4) SDW is appropriate for this problem, the $L_9(3^4)$ OA being shown in Table 12.2. Five defect replications per trial were taken at random from simulated lognormal populations. The natural logarithms of the replications are also shown in Table 12.2.

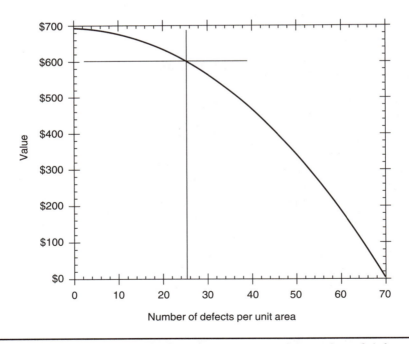

Figure 12.1   Hypothetical value curve for telescope versus the number of defects in mirror.

Table 12.1 Financial parameters for problem.

Critical attribute	gC=	70	Baseline demand	D0=	200000
Ideal attribute	gl=	0	Total demand	DT=	500000
Baseline attribute	g0=	25.4	Number of competitors	NC=	3
Exponential weighting	GAMMA=	1	Average price	PAVG=	$280
Baseline value	V0=	$600	E2	ELAS2=	0.8
Negative slope of demand	K=	1429	k_T^*	KTSTAR=	0.141
Baseline price	P0=	$300	Baseline cost	C0=	$75

Table 12.2 $L_9(3^4)$ OA used for the experimental design and the natural logs of the five defect replications per trial.

	Base	Temp	Temp	Press	Press	Time	Time	Clean	Clean							
Trial	0	11	12	21	22	31	32	41	42		1	2	3	4	5
1	1	0	0	0	0	0	0	0	0	1	3.11	2.83	2.96	3.71	3.31
2	1	0	0	1	0	1	0	1	0	2	3.40	4.45	3.23	3.25	3.26
3	1	0	0	0	1	0	1	0	1	3	0.59	0.61	0.33	0.37	-0.2
4	1	1	0	0	0	1	0	0	1	4	3.78	3.37	3.43	3.30	3.84
5	1	1	0	1	0	0	1	0	0	5	1.53	1.72	2.07	2.10	1.65
6	1	1	0	0	1	0	0	1	0	6	2.05	1.36	2.06	2.11	0.94
7	1	0	1	0	0	0	1	1	0	7	1.63	1.50	2.10	1.79	2.01
8	1	0	1	1	0	0	0	0	1	8	2.30	3.30	2.91	2.25	3.96
9	1	0	1	0	1	1	0	0	0	9	1.72	1.82	2.17	1.27	1.75

Table 12.3 Solution matrix for the design in Table 12.2.

		1	2	3	4	5	6	7	8	9	COV
Base	0	1	1E-16	1E-16	1E-16	1E-16	1E-16	1E-16	1E-16	1E-16	1
Temp	11	-0.333	-0.333	-0.333	0.3333	0.3333	0.3333	0	0	0	0.67
Temp	12	-0.333	-0.333	-0.333	0	0	0	0.3333	0.3333	0.3333	0.67
Press	21	-0.333	0.3333	0	-0.333	0.3333	0	-0.333	0.3333	0	0.67
Press	22	-0.333	0	0.3333	-0.333	0	0.3333	-0.333	0	0.3333	0.67
Time	31	-0.333	0.3333	0	0.3333	0	-0.333	0	-0.333	0.3333	0.67
Time	32	-0.333	0	0.3333	0	0.3333	-0.333	0.3333	-0.333	0	0.67
Clean	41	-0.333	0.3333	0	0	-0.333	0.3333	0.3333	0	-0.333	0.67
Clean	42	-0.333	0	0.3333	0.3333	-0.333	0	0	0.3333	-0.333	0.67

The solution matrix represented by array variable XS and the diagonal elements of the covariance matrix are shown in Table 12.3. The lambda form is used because the objective is to make a significant improvement relative to the baseline, trial 1. Note, the solution matrix is fully balanced in that there is an element of opposite sign and identical absolute value for each off-baseline element in each row.

The population means and variances for the defect concentrations, g, for each trial are shown in Table 12.4 in columns μ and σ^2, respectively. The array variables LPOPMEAN and LPOPVAR are the means and variances for the normally distributed populations representing the natural logs of the defect, $Ln(g)$. The array named

$$\text{LAMLPOP} = \text{MMULT}(\text{XS,LPOPMEAN}) \tag{12.1}$$

displays the values for the λ_{ij} coefficient for the $Ln(g)$ populations, and

$$\text{XIijLPOP} = \text{MMULT}(\text{XS,-10*LOG(LPOPVAR)}) \tag{12.2}$$

displays values of the ξ_{ij} coefficients for the $Ln(g)$ populations. Of course, in any real problem, none of the information in Table 12.4 would be known.

The population statistics were chosen such that factors 22 and 32 favorably influence the defect populations in that they moved the mean toward zero and reduced variance. Also note that factors 11, 12, and 42 make nonzero contributions to the log variance in the XIijPOP column.

The results for the defect concentrations generated by the simulated experiments are shown in Table 12.5. The normally distributed Ln transformed replications shown in Table 12.2 were actually simulated first using the NORMINV function

$$\text{NORMINV(RAND(),LPOPMEAN,SQRT(LPOPVAR))} \tag{12.3}$$

and the defect concentrations, g, in Table 12.5 were computed from them. The sample means, Y, and sample variances, SVAR, shown in Table 12.6 are for the $Ln(g)$ variable. In an actual experiment $Ln(g)$ would need to be graphed on normal probability paper to support the assumption, based upon a linear outcome for the plot, that the transformed replications

Table 12.4 Population statistics for the hypothetical problem.

Trial	Lognormal population		Regular population		ij	Lognormal population	
	LPOPMEAN	**LPOPVAR**	μ	σ^2		**LAMLPOP**	**XI ijLPOP**
1	3.2	0.2	27.11	163	0	3.2	6.99
2	3.2	0.2	27.11	163	11	0	-0.65
3	0.2	0.05	1.25	0.08	12	0	-0.65
4	3.2	0.2	27.11	163	21	0	0.00
5	1.7	0.125	5.83	4.5	22	-1.5	2.69
6	1.7	0.125	5.83	4.5	31	0	0.00
7	1.7	0.125	5.83	4.5	32	-1.5	2.69
8	3.2	0.2	27.11	163	41	0	0.00
9	1.7	0.125	5.83	4.5	42	0	0.65

Table 12.5   Simulated experimental outcomes for defect concentrations.

Trial	1	2	3	4	5
1	22.50	17.03	19.35	40.68	27.50
2	29.96	85.53	25.40	25.83	25.93
3	1.80	1.85	1.39	1.44	0.82
4	43.77	29.10	31.00	27.10	46.70
5	4.63	5.60	7.93	8.18	5.23
6	7.75	3.89	7.81	8.21	2.57
7	5.09	4.50	8.19	6.02	7.50
8	9.96	27.22	18.42	9.48	52.50
9	5.58	6.20	8.78	3.56	5.73

Table 12.6   Sample means (name Y) and sample variance (name SVAR) for $Ln(g)$ as taken from the L9(3^4) SDW. The results for the models for the sample means and variances are also shown for their default reduced models.

z	w
9	9

n	Trial	Y	YMODEL	Trial	SVAR	Model SVARMODEL
5	1	3.186	3.186	1	0.116	0.116
5	2	3.518	3.186	2	0.275	0.116
5	3	0.339	0.312	3	0.107	0.116
5	4	3.545	3.186	4	0.062	0.116
5	5	1.816	1.896	5	0.066	0.116
5	6	1.702	1.602	6	0.275	0.116
5	7	1.809	1.896	7	0.064	0.116
5	8	2.945	3.186	8	0.516	0.116
5	9	1.746	1.602	9	0.103	0.116

were normally distributed. When some tests have been suspended, the maximum likelihood technique can be used, as described in Appendix H, to estimate the means and variances.

The results for the F test method for evaluating the significance of the individual factors on -10 log variance are shown in Table 12.7, which was generated by the XI Coefficients worksheet of the SDW. This test, as described in Chapter 9, requires that the replications be taken from a normally distributed population, which was the case on making the log transformation of the defect concentrations. The EWE for the log variance of the off-baseline coefficients are seen to be large and none is taken as being significant using 5% for alpha. This may be surprising, as the factors 22 and 32 were chosen to affect variance

Table 12.7 Independent test of factors on homogeneity of variance.

E	F	G	H	MIN(n)		K	MAX(n)		Interpolated		P	Q	R	S
						ALPHAXI								Reduced XI
														Model
		XI	**Gij**	**PWE**	**EWE**	0.05	**PWE**	**EWE**	**PWE**	**EWE**	**SIGXI**			**REDXI**
Base	0	9.35	1.32	0.006	0.006		0.006	0.006	0.006	0.006	significant	**Base**	0	9.35
Temp	11	1.62	0.28	0.273	2.186		0.273	2.186	0.273	2.186	NOT	**Temp**	11	0
Temp	12	0.010	0.002	0.499	3.988		0.499	3.988	0.499	3.988	NOT	**Temp**	12	0
Press	21	-4.366	-0.756	0.060	0.481		0.060	0.481	0.060	0.481	NOT	**Press**	21	0
Press	22	-2.746	-0.476	0.157	1.256		0.157	1.256	0.157	1.256	NOT	**Press**	22	0
Time	31	3.243	0.562	0.119	0.953		0.119	0.953	0.119	0.953	NOT	**Time**	31	0
Time	32	5.228	0.906	0.034	0.272		0.034	0.272	0.034	0.272	NOT	**Time**	32	0
Clean	41	-2.618	-0.454	0.168	1.344		0.168	1.344	0.168	1.344	NOT	**Clean**	41	0
Clean	42	-2.114	-0.366	0.217	1.737		0.217	1.737	0.217	1.737	NOT	**Clean**	42	0

XI =MMULT(XS,-10*LOG(SVAR))

Gij =XI/SQRT(50*COV)

PWE =FDIST(10^ABS(Gij),MIN(n)-1,MIN(n)-1)   *Off baseline*

EWE =PWE*(w-1)

Drag N11

PWE =FDIST(10^ABS(Gij),MAX(n)-1,MAX(n)-1)

EWE =(w-1)*L12

PWE =IF(MAX(n)=MIN(n),L11,l11-(l11-L11)*(AVGn-MIN(n))/(MAX(n)-MIN(n)))

EWE =(w-1)*N12

SIGXI =IF(O11<ALPHAXI,"significant","NOT")

S11 **REDXI** =G11

S12 **REDXI** =G12*IF(P12="significant",1,0)

in setting up the simulated problem. But the analysis of the influence of the factors on variance is still incomplete at this juncture, as the defect concentrations need to be evaluated in regular units. The default model (REDXI) has only one term, which leads to the constant value for the variance model in Table 12.6.

The results for Satterthwaite's approximate t-test of the significance of the factors on the means are shown in Table 12.8, as generated by the Lambda Coefficients worksheet. The df for the factors in Table 12.8 for the off-baseline coefficients are between 12 and 17, in contrast to the pooled df of 36. None of the df are small except for trial 1, where the df is 4, which is equal to that for a single trial. This is as it should be because only trial 1 with 4 df contributed to the computation of λ_0 in the solution matrix in Table 12.3. The df for off-baseline coefficients are higher because each was computed from the outcomes of six trials. Two off-baseline coefficients, 22 and 32, were found significant leading to the default model REDXI having nonzero values for factors 0, 22, and 32. The model for Y in Table 12.6 (YMODEL) was constructed using this default model.

At this juncture, the statistical significance of the factors on the $Ln(g)$ transformed replications has been determined. The distribution for g should follow a lognormal distribution, at least approximately, because of their non-negative character. This provided insight into how the factors individually affected the mean and variance of $Ln(g)$. Next the statistical significance of the factors on the *untransformed* attributes, g, needs to be evaluated. This step is critical, as the ultimate goal is to understand the strategic significance of the factors on value, which is a function of g, not $Ln(g)$. The fundamental metrics of value and variable cost can then be used to project bottom-line metrics such as cash flow and market share.

Table 12.8   Determination of the standard deviation, SDij, df, and DFij for Satterthwaite's test.

| | | | | | | ALPHALAM | | | | | |
| | | | | | | 0.05 | | | | | |
		LAM	SDij	DFij	t	PWE2	EWE	SIGLAM			REDLAM
Base	0	3.186	0.152	4.0	20.90	0.000		significant	**Base**	0	3.186
Temp	11	0.007	0.141	17.6	0.05	0.481	3.85	NOT	**Temp**	11	0.000
Temp	12	-0.181	0.162	14.6	-1.12	0.141	1.13	NOT	**Temp**	12	0.000
Press	21	-0.087	0.156	13.1	-0.56	0.294	2.35	NOT	**Press**	21	0.000
Press	22	-1.584	0.127	17.7	-12.46	0.000	0.00	significant	**Press**	22	-1.584
Time	31	0.325	0.173	16.3	1.88	0.039	0.31	NOT	**Time**	31	0.000
Time	32	-1.290	0.159	13.9	-8.09	0.000	0.00	significant	**Time**	32	-1.290
Clean	41	0.093	0.141	17.6	0.66	0.259	2.07	NOT	**Clean**	41	0.000
Clean	42	0.027	0.147	12.1	0.18	0.428	3.43	NOT	**Clean**	42	0.000

LAM =MMULT(XS,Y)
SDij =SQRT(MMULT(XS^2,SVAR/n))
DFij =SDij^4/MMULT(XS^4,(SVAR/n)^2/(n-1))
t =LAM/SDij
PWE2 =TDIST(ABS(t),DFij,1)
EWE =PWE*(w-1)   *off-baseline*

12.1.1 Bottom-line Metrics Analysis

The first step in the Monte Carlo analysis of the bottom-line metrics for a lognormal problem is to simulate the ranges of possible population means, μ_{Ln}, and variances, σ^2_{Ln}, for the normally distributed $Ln(g)$ variable. These results are transformed into the ranges expected for the population mean, μ, and variance, σ^2, of the lognormally distributed variables g. The transformations from μ_{Ln} and σ^2_{Ln} to μ and σ^2 are made using the standard expressions

$$\mu = \exp\left(\mu_{Ln} + \frac{\sigma^2_{Ln}}{2}\right) \tag{12.4}$$

$$\sigma^2 = \exp\left(2\mu_{Ln}\right)\left\{\exp\left(2\sigma^2_{Ln}\right) - \exp\left(\sigma^2_{Ln}\right)\right\} \tag{12.5}$$

Note that μ and σ^2 are each a function of μ_{Ln} and σ^2_{Ln}. It follows that, if a factor reduces μ_{Ln}, it also reduces both the mean μ and the variance σ^2. A single set of Monte Carlo simulations for the population means and variances for the $Ln(g)$ variable is shown in Table 12.9, along with the transformation to the population means and variances for the g variable. These results were taken from the Variance Mean & CIQ worksheet of the SDW. The expressions for the array names are listed at the bottom of the table. The array names LPOPVARSIM and LPOPYSIM represent simulations of possible population variances and means, respectively, of the $Ln(g)$ variable. POPVARSIM and POPYSIM represent their conversions to the space of the g variable using Equations (12.4) and (12.5).

Table 12.9 Typical Monte Carlo simulation of possible population variances and means for the normally distributed $Ln(g)$ variable and conversion to the lognormally distributed g variable.

Trial	RN1	LPOPVARSIM	RN2	tSIM	LPOPYSIM	POPVARSIM	POPYSIM
1	0.552	0.126	0.383	-0.318	3.138	81	24.5
2	0.416	0.387	0.718	0.629	3.666	1063	47.4
3	0.925	0.050	0.461	-0.104	0.324	0	1.4
4	0.856	0.036	0.777	0.846	3.639	55	38.8
5	0.582	0.067	0.030	-2.591	1.519	2	4.7
6	0.438	0.370	0.954	2.198	2.218	55	11.1
7	0.366	0.099	0.178	-1.043	1.691	3	5.7
8	0.384	0.775	0.763	0.789	3.198	1526	36.1
9	0.297	0.190	0.182	-1.023	1.599	6	5.4

RN1	=RAND()
LPOPVARSIM	=(n-1)*SVAR/CHIINV(1-RN1,n-1)
RN2	=RAND()
tSIM	=IF(RN2>0.5,1,-1)*TINV(IF(RN2>0.5,2*(1-RN2),2*RN2),n-1)
LPOPYSIM	=Y+tSIM*SQRT(SVAR/n)
POPVARSIM	=EXP(2*LPOPYSIM)*(EXP(2*LPOPVARSIM)-EXP(LPOPVARSIM))
POPYSIM	=EXP(LPOPYSIM+LPOPVARSIM/2)

Next, for additional insight, the coefficients $\xi_{ij}(-10Log(\sigma^2(q))$ and $\lambda_{ij}(10Log(\mu(q))$ for the functions given by the terms in parenthesis are computed. The taking of logarithms is done here to improve additivity and is particularly important because it prevents predicting a physically impossible negative variance or negative mean when factors are combined. Typical simulated outcomes for these coefficients are shown in Table 12.10. A total of 1000 simulations were run and the outcomes are plotted on normal probability paper in Figure 12.2 and Figure 12.3.

Table 12.10 Simulation outcomes for the coefficients of −10 log base 10 of the simulated population variances and 10 log base 10 of the simulated population means.

=TRANSPOSE(MMULT(XS,-10*LOG(POPVARSIM)))
Regular space variance coefficients

	Base 0	Temp 11	Temp 12	Press 21	Press 22	Time 31	Time 32	Clean 41	Clean 42
	-18.04	1.18	-15.58	-20.61	12.85	11.29	31.53	-7.79	-14.33
1	-17.55	-4.06	-7.38	-6.96	10.23	0.75	11.55	2.50	1.74
2	-19.96	4.37	-6.99	-2.58	18.40	5.49	14.35	-6.92	-10.43
3	-16.59	-6.54	-2.39	-3.53	14.17	0.69	16.92	-6.92	-6.93
4	-22.31	7.94	9.79	-5.35	12.95	-11.34	16.68	-6.00	-3.55
5	-28.08	15.98	-4.36	-23.49	14.17	9.09	34.70	-11.42	-14.93
6	-17.82	-9.26	-4.98	-10.00	0.75	14.98	32.37	-8.67	-8.97
7	-17.68	0.77	0.85	-6.51	10.43	2.17	18.74	-7.17	-5.19
8	-21.78	2.11	0.11	0.12	9.80	4.28	12.23	0.00	-3.94
9	-22.60	3.63	-1.78	-2.94	13.08	2.00	17.44	0.20	0.18
10	-21.49	4.04	-2.99	-5.88	12.17	0.31	14.82	-3.15	-0.96

=TRANSPOSE(MMULT(XS,10*LOG(POPYSIM)))
Regular space mean coefficients

	Base 0	Temp 11	Temp 12	Press 21	Press 22	Time 31	Time 32	Clean 41	Clean 42
	14.57	0.07	3.02	3.90	-7.00	-2.29	-10.16	1.04	2.58
1	13.15	0.67	0.29	0.59	-6.48	1.68	-4.94	-0.07	0.13
2	15.56	-1.27	1.55	0.44	-7.69	-1.53	-7.44	0.25	2.41
3	14.05	-0.18	-1.08	-0.38	-6.92	1.86	-5.81	1.35	0.90
4	15.25	-1.99	-2.63	0.09	-6.68	3.30	-5.79	0.73	-0.38
5	14.89	-1.39	1.54	3.77	-7.41	-1.10	-9.41	2.86	3.44
6	13.65	1.39	0.35	-0.14	-5.17	-1.75	-8.71	2.53	2.45
7	13.00	0.07	-0.66	0.53	-6.44	1.42	-6.35	1.85	1.32
8	14.23	-0.02	-0.51	-1.81	-6.52	0.81	-4.77	0.11	0.29
9	14.80	-0.04	-0.55	-0.25	-7.44	1.53	-6.34	-0.50	-0.41
10	14.94	-0.61	-0.65	-0.21	-6.70	0.90	-6.14	0.37	0.10

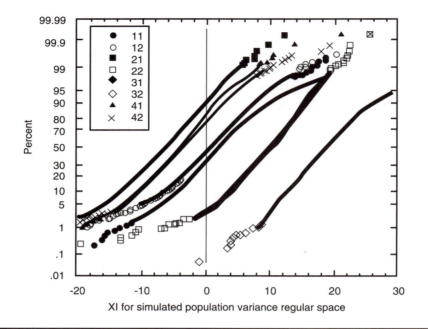

Figure 12.2 Results of the Monte Carlo simulation for the $\xi_{ij}(-10Log(\sigma^2(q))$ coefficients.

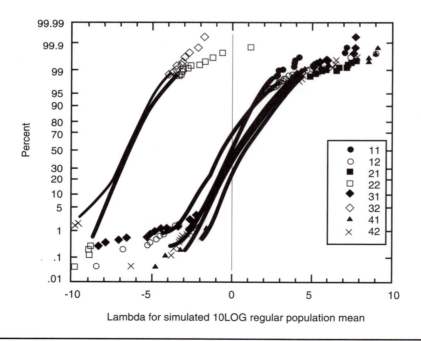

Figure 12.3 Results of the Monte Carlo simulation for the $\lambda_{ij}(10Log(\mu(q))$ coefficients.

These simulations, generated as part of the Variance Mean & CIQ worksheet, show that factor 32 is significant for reducing variance but factor 22 at 3% PWE and 21% EWE is not, generating a Type II error for factor 22. It is clear from the plots that the distributions are not normal. As expected, factors 22 and 32 are highly effective at reducing the number of defects, Figure 12.3.

One set of simulated outcomes for the CIQ and the resulting lambda SN coefficients $\lambda_{ij}(\Omega)$ named LAMSN1 = MMULT(XS,−10*LOG(CIQSIM1) is shown in Table 12.11 as taken from the Variance Mean & CIQ worksheet. The expressions for the macros used for ktSIM1 and VALUESIM1 are given in the SDW. The normal probability plot of the value differences for implementing the 22 and 32 coefficients relative to the baseline condition is shown in Figure 12.4. These were computed from 1000 simulations of the type shown in Table 12.11 using the expression

$$\Delta V = -\left[10^{-(\lambda_0(\Omega)+\lambda_{22}(\Omega)+\lambda_{32}(\Omega))/10} - 10^{-\lambda_0(\Omega)/10} \right] \tag{12.6}$$

A horizontal line is drawn at 1% PWE. (The EWE correction is not made, as the null hypothesis for factors 22 and 32 has already been rejected.) From Figure 12.4, the combined variable cost for implementing factors 22 and 32 should be less than $30 to have 99% confidence that the value added would be greater than the added cost.

On seeing that factors 22 and 32 significantly improved value, their variable cost implications were analyzed. For this hypothetical problem, factor 22 was found to increase variable cost by $4 per unit and factor 32 was found to increase it by $6 per unit. Although the two favorable factors have been combined and their combined significance has been evaluated, it would have been prudent to have first evaluated each independently to see if each would provide an added value greater than the variable cost for the attribute.

Table 12.11 Simulation of the CIQ and its lambda coefficients.

Trial	fvSIM1	ktSIM1	VIDEAL	VALUESIM1	CIQSIM1			LAMSN1
1	1.010	0.141	691	595	96.32	Base	0	-19.84
2	0.623	0.141	691	224	467.05	Temp	11	-0.46
3	1.151	0.141	691	691	0.30	Temp	12	0.40
4	0.798	0.141	691	471	219.66	Press	21	-2.56
5	1.146	0.141	691	688	3.37	Press	22	11.52
6	1.123	0.141	691	666	24.95	Time	31	0.89
7	1.144	0.141	691	686	5.06	Time	32	17.58
8	0.845	0.141	691	292	398.90	Clean	41	-5.19
9	1.145	0.141	691	686	5.05	Clean	42	-4.01

  fvSIM1 =((gl-gC)^2-(gl-(1-SF)*POPYSIM-SF*gT)^2)/((gl-gC)^2-(gl-g0)^2)
  ktSIM1 *Macro*
  VIDEAL =V0*(((gl-gC)^2-(gl-gl)^2)/((gl-gC)^2-(gl-g0)^2))^GAMMA
 VALUESIM1 *Macro*
  CIQSIM1 =VIDEAL-VALUESIM1
  LAMSN1 =-MMULT(XS,10*LOG(CIQSIM1))

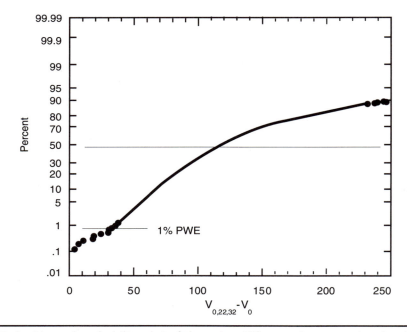

Figure 12.4 Normal probability plot of the value difference between that for the combination 0, 22, 32 and that for the baseline.

The change in demand, assuming competitors do not change the value and price of their product, is given by

$$\delta D = K(\delta V - \delta P)$$
$$= K(\delta V - \delta C)/2$$

on using the rule of thumb that the price change is equal to one-half the sum of the value plus cost changes. Assuming that the added investment is negligible and that there is no change in fixed cost, the projected change in annual cash flow is given by

$$\delta A = D_0 \left[\delta P - \delta C\right] + \delta D \left[P_0 - C_0\right]$$
$$= \left[\frac{\delta V - \delta C}{2}\right]\left\{D_0 + K\left[P_0 - C_0\right]\right\} \qquad (12.7)$$

Apart from a shift and multiplication by a constant, the distribution for the change in cash flow is identical to the distribution for value.

12.3 APPLICATION OF THE BINOMIAL DISTRIBUTION TO A SIB PROBLEM

An oft-used measure of the lack of quality of a batch of manufactured parts is the fraction of parts p deemed as being unacceptable in a random sample of n parts, the fraction of good parts in the sample being $1 - p$. The expected outcome for a single randomly selected part is analogous to that for the toss of a weighted (unfair) coin, a so-called Bernoulli trial (see Section 4.1.7). The symbol B is used to represent the number of bad parts in a random sample of size n given the probability κ of finding a bad part in the population. The values that B can take on for a single sample, $n = 1$, are 0 and 1, the frequency distribution being given by $f(B, n = 1, \kappa) = \kappa^B (1 - \kappa)^{1-B}$. The discrete frequency distribution for Y for n Bernoulli trials (n replications) is that for a binomial distribution (see Equation 4.23)

$$f(B, n, \kappa) = \left[\frac{n!}{[n-B]! B!} \right] \kappa^B (1-\kappa)^{n-B} \qquad (12.8)$$

the possible values for B now ranging in integer steps from 0 to n.

In a production experiment, the sample fraction of bad parts in trial q is given by $p = p(q) = B(q)/n(q)$. The problem, in a nutshell, is "Given $p(q)$ and $n(q)$, what is the distribution for the possible κ for the population?" Because the distribution is discrete, the range of the fractional values for κ is taken conveniently as B_p / N_p, in which B_p is a possible integer number of bad parts in the population and N_p is the size of the population. If the population is arbitrarily large, then the possible κ are arbitrarily dense.

12.3.1 Windshield Molding Problem

The problem of dents in windshield moldings caused by debris in the die described by Wu and Hamada[2] represents an excellent case study for exploring the application of the binomial distribution to this class of quality problems. Visual inspection was used to identify whether a molding was good (acceptable) or bad (unacceptable). Four factors at two levels each were investigated for improving the acceptability of the stampings:

1. Poly-film thickness

2. Oil mixture

3. Cotton versus nylon glove

4. Dry versus oily metal blanks

Trial 1 is taken as the baseline condition, and the lambda form for the $L_8(2^4)$ OA, Table 12.12, is used to evaluate the influence of these factors. A total of $n = 1000$ parts were evaluated at each level. This design was constructed by eliminating and rearranging columns in the L8(2^7) SDW for the binomial distribution. The column vector representing the sample measurement $B(q)$ of the number of bad parts for trials 1 through q is named BP in Table 12.12. The sample fraction of bad parts is defined as the variable $p(q) = B(q) / n$. The lambda coefficients computed for the function $Ln(p)$ are assumed to follow a t-statistic, and the uncertainty in the population mean for a given lambda coefficient is given by

$$\mu_{ij} = \lambda_{ij} + t\sqrt{s_{ij}^2}$$ (12.9)

The outcomes vector, Y, in Table 12.13 is equal to $Ln(p)$, the natural log of the fraction of bad parts for each of the eight trials. The second column, YMODEL, is the default model for Y, and the third column, pMODEL, is the default model for p. The variance of the fraction of bad parts is $p(1 - p) / 1000$. This parabolic form is shown in Figure 12.5 as a function of p. The computation of R^2 is for pMODEL.

Table 12.12 The $L_8(2^4)$ design and solution matrices used to explore the influence of the factors on reducing the number of bad parts exhibiting dimples. The outcomes BP of bad parts based upon a sample size of 1000 are also shown. Computations were taken from the Design and Outcomes worksheet of the modified L8(2^7) SDW.

Trial	Base 0	A 11	B 21	C 31	D 41	Trial	BP	n	p
1	1	0	0	0	0	1	659	1000	0.659
2	1	0	0	1	1	2	172	1000	0.172
3	1	0	1	0	0	3	655	1000	0.655
4	1	0	1	1	1	4	358	1000	0.358
5	1	1	0	0	1	5	92	1000	0.092
6	1	1	0	1	0	6	30	1000	0.030
7	1	1	1	0	1	7	39	1000	0.039
8	1	1	1	1	0	8	31	1000	0.031

		1	2	3	4	5	6	7	8	COV
Base	0	0.625	0.125	0.375	-0.125	0.125	0.125	-0	-0.13	0.625
A	11	-0.25	-0.25	-0.25	-0.25	0.25	0.25	0.3	0.25	0.500
B	21	-0.25	-0.25	0.25	0.25	-0.25	-0.25	0.3	0.25	0.500
C	31	-0.25	0.25	-0.25	0.25	-0.25	0.25	-0	0.25	0.500
D	41	-0.25	0.25	-0.25	0.25	0.25	-0.25	0.3	-0.25	0.500

Table 12.13 The outcomes Y expressed as the natural log of the fraction of bad parts *p*. The default models for Y and *p* are also shown along with R2 for the model for *p*.

	z	w			
	8	5			
				0.020	0.515
Trials	**Y**	**YMODEL**	**pMODEL**	**SSE**	**SSY**
1	-0.42	-0.41	0.665		
2	-1.76	-1.23	0.292	**R^2** 0.96	
3	-0.42	-0.41	0.665		
4	-1.03	-1.23	0.292		
5	-2.39	-2.65	0.070		
6	-3.51	-3.48	0.031		
7	-3.24	-2.65	0.070		
8	-3.47	-3.48	0.031		
Y	=LN(p)				

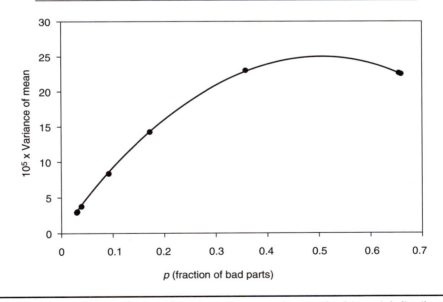

Figure 12.5 The variance of *p* as a function of *p* according to the binomial distribution.

It is imperative for this problem to use the linear model for *Ln(p)* rather than *p* for additivity purposes, avoiding the chance of predicting that certain combinations of factors would result in a negative value for *p*. The variance of *Ln(p)* computed from the first order Taylor expansion approximation of $\delta p / p \cong \delta(Ln(p))$ is given by

$$VAR(Ln(p(q))) \cong \left[\frac{1}{p^2(q)}\right] VAR(p(q)) = \frac{1 - p(q)}{p(q)n(q)} \qquad (12.10)$$

Because of the large sample size, Equation (12.10) is expected to be a very good approximation for this problem. This conclusion is verified by the Monte Carlo process used to re-examine this problem in Appendix D, representing an approach that can be used when Equation (12.10) is not a good approximation.

The lambda coefficients, LAM, computed for *Ln(p)* are shown in Table 12.14 along with their EWE computed from the variances for *Ln(p)* given by Equation (12.8). The factor standard deviations, s_{ij}, are listed as the column vector named SDij. Factors A and C are each seen to be significant in reducing *p* on changing from level 0 to level 1. The fact that one or more coefficients were found to be highly significant is not surprising as there were marked differences in the outcomes from the experimental trials. Figure 12.6 compares the cumulative distributions for trials 1 and 6, showing virtually no overlap in the two distributions.

Table 12.14 Computation of the lambda coefficients for *Ln(p)* and their EWE using the estimated values for the variance of *Ln(p)* from Equation (12.8). Results were taken from the Lambda Coefficients worksheet of the modified L8(2^7) SDW for the binomial distribution.

ALPHALAM

0.05

		LAM	SDij	DFij	t	PWE2	EWE	SIGLAM			REDLAM
Base	0	-0.408	0.044	5084	-9.3	0.00	0.00	significant	Base	0	-0.41
A	11	-2.246	0.081	4057	-27.6	0.00	0.00	significant	A	11	-2.25
B	21	-0.025	0.081	4057	-0.3	0.38	1.52	NOT	B	21	0.00
C	31	-0.824	0.081	4057	-10.1	0.00	0.00	significant	C	31	-0.82
D	41	-0.149	0.081	4057	-1.8	0.03	0.13	NOT	D	41	0.00
		#N/A	#N/A	#N/A	#N/A	#N/A	#N/A	#N/A	####	###	#N/A
		#N/A	#N/A	#N/A	#N/A	#N/A	#N/A	#N/A	####	###	#N/A
		#N/A	#N/A	#N/A	#N/A	#N/A	#N/A	#N/A	####	###	#N/A

LAM	=MMULT(XS,Y)
SDij	=SQRT(MMULT(XS^2,(1/p^2)*p*(1-p)/n))
DFij	=SDij^4/MMULT(XS^4,((1/p^2)*p*(1-p)/n)^2/(n-1))
t	=LAM/SDij
PWE2	=TDIST(ABS(t),DFij,1)
EWE	=(w-1)*PWE2

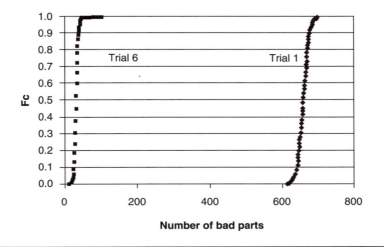

Figure 12.6   Comparison of computed cumulative distributions for trials 1 and 6.

12.4 APPLICATION OF THE POISSON DISTRIBUTION TO A SIB PROBLEM

Another important quality measure is the number of defects that occur in a given region of a part or the number of defective parts produced over a given period of time. The Poisson distribution is often applicable to this class of problems. The frequency distribution for a statistic Y that follows the Poisson distribution over a general interval $\tilde{t}$ (time or space) is given by (see Section 4.1.7)

$$f(Y,\lambda\tilde{t}) = \frac{\left[\lambda\tilde{t}\right]^{Y}\exp(-\lambda\tilde{t})}{Y!} \tag{12.11}$$

Both the mean μ and the variance σ^2 of the Poisson distribution are equal to $\lambda\tilde{t}$. When the general interval $\tilde{t}$ is fixed for a series of experiments, Equation (12.11) can be written in the same form as Equation (4.22)

$$f(Y,\mu) = \frac{\mu^{Y}\exp(-\mu)}{Y!} \tag{12.12}$$

The key assumption leading to the Poisson distribution for quality studies is that the number of defects over an interval is independent of the number found in another area or time period. When the interval is small, the probability of finding one defect is assumed to increase linearly with the size of the interval. Also when the time and area are made very small, the probability of finding two or more defects in the interval is assumed to be zero.

12.4.1 Solder-joint Defect Problem

Consider the following simulated experiment patterned after the wave-soldering problem re-examined by Wu and Hamada[3]. The following seven factors were evaluated for reducing the number of defects:

A. Prebake temperature	E. Cooling time
B. Flux density	F. Ultrasonic agitator
C. Conveyer speed	G. Solder temperature
D. Preheat condition	

The design matrix (X), Table 12.15, included the seven main effects plus eight selected interactions. The solution matrix (XS) and the diagonal elements of the covariance matrix are shown in Table 12.16.

Table 12.15   Design matrix, X.

	0	A 11	B 21	C 31	D 41	E 51	F 61	G 71	AB 1121	AC 1131	AD 1141	BC 2131	BD 2141	CD 3141	CE 3151	ABC 112131
1	1	-1	-1	-1	-1	-1	-1	-1	1	1	1	1	1	1	1	-1
2	1	-1	-1	-1	1	1	1	1	1	1	-1	1	-1	-1	-1	-1
3	1	-1	-1	1	-1	-1	1	1	1	-1	1	-1	1	-1	-1	1
4	1	-1	-1	1	1	1	-1	-1	1	-1	-1	-1	-1	1	1	1
5	1	-1	1	-1	-1	1	-1	1	-1	1	1	-1	-1	1	-1	1
6	1	-1	1	-1	1	-1	1	-1	-1	1	-1	-1	1	-1	1	1
7	1	-1	1	1	-1	1	1	-1	-1	-1	1	1	-1	-1	1	-1
8	1	-1	1	1	1	-1	-1	1	-1	-1	-1	1	1	1	-1	-1
9	1	1	-1	-1	-1	1	1	-1	-1	-1	-1	1	1	1	-1	1
10	1	1	-1	-1	1	-1	-1	1	-1	-1	1	1	-1	-1	1	1
11	1	1	-1	1	-1	1	-1	1	-1	1	-1	-1	1	-1	1	-1
12	1	1	-1	1	1	-1	1	-1	-1	1	1	-1	-1	1	-1	-1
13	1	1	1	-1	-1	-1	1	1	1	-1	-1	-1	-1	1	1	-1
14	1	1	1	-1	1	1	-1	-1	1	-1	1	-1	1	-1	-1	-1
15	1	1	1	1	-1	-1	-1	-1	1	1	-1	1	-1	-1	-1	1
16	1	1	1	1	1	1	1	1	1	1	1	1	1	1	1	1

Table 12.16   Solution matrix, XS, having elements equal to ± 1/6.

	1	2	3	4	5	6	7	8	9	10	11	12	13	14	15	16	COV
0	0.063	0.063	0.063	0.063	0.063	0.063	0.063	0.063	0.063	0.063	0.063	0.063	0.063	0.063	0.063	0.0625	0.063
11	-0.06	-0.06	-0.06	-0.06	-0.06	-0.06	-0.06	-0.06	0.063	0.063	0.063	0.063	0.063	0.063	0.063	0.0625	0.063
21	-0.06	-0.06	-0.06	-0.06	0.063	0.063	0.063	0.063	-0.06	-0.06	-0.06	-0.06	0.063	0.063	0.063	0.0625	0.063
31	-0.06	-0.06	0.063	0.063	-0.06	-0.06	0.063	0.063	-0.06	-0.06	0.063	0.063	-0.06	-0.06	0.063	0.0625	0.063
41	-0.06	0.063	-0.06	0.063	-0.06	0.063	-0.06	0.063	-0.06	0.063	-0.06	0.063	-0.06	0.063	-0.06	0.0625	0.063
51	-0.06	0.063	-0.06	0.063	0.063	-0.06	0.063	-0.06	0.063	-0.06	0.063	-0.06	-0.06	0.063	-0.06	0.0625	0.063
61	-0.06	0.063	0.063	-0.06	-0.06	0.063	0.063	-0.06	0.063	-0.06	-0.06	0.063	0.063	-0.06	-0.06	0.0625	0.063
71	-0.06	0.063	0.063	-0.06	0.063	-0.06	-0.06	0.063	-0.06	0.063	0.063	-0.06	0.063	-0.06	-0.06	0.0625	0.063
1121	0.063	0.063	0.063	0.063	-0.06	-0.06	-0.06	-0.06	-0.06	-0.06	-0.06	-0.06	0.063	0.063	0.063	0.0625	0.063
1131	0.063	0.063	-0.06	-0.06	0.063	0.063	-0.06	-0.06	-0.06	-0.06	0.063	0.063	-0.06	-0.06	0.063	0.0625	0.063
1141	0.063	-0.06	0.063	-0.06	0.063	-0.06	0.063	-0.06	-0.06	0.063	-0.06	0.063	-0.06	0.063	-0.06	0.0625	0.063
2131	0.063	0.063	-0.06	-0.06	-0.06	-0.06	0.063	0.063	0.063	0.063	-0.06	-0.06	-0.06	-0.06	0.063	0.0625	0.063
2141	0.063	-0.06	0.063	-0.06	-0.06	0.063	-0.06	0.063	0.063	-0.06	0.063	-0.06	-0.06	0.063	-0.06	0.0625	0.063
3141	0.063	-0.06	-0.06	0.063	0.063	-0.06	-0.06	0.063	0.063	-0.06	-0.06	0.063	0.063	-0.06	-0.06	0.0625	0.063
3151	0.063	-0.06	-0.06	0.063	-0.06	0.063	0.063	-0.06	-0.06	0.063	0.063	-0.06	0.063	-0.06	-0.06	0.0625	0.063
112131	-0.06	-0.06	0.063	0.063	0.063	0.063	-0.06	-0.06	0.063	0.063	-0.06	-0.06	-0.06	-0.06	0.063	0.0625	0.063

The analysis here does not use the original data. Instead, to ensure that Poisson distributions were being sampled, three replications per trial were selected from Poisson distributions whose means are shown in column YPOP of Table 12.17, the population variances being equal to the population means. The sequence of computations leading to an assessment of the significance of the phi coefficients of $-Ln(Y)$ are shown in Table 12.18, the logarithms of the average outcomes Y being taken to improve additivity. (Note that a SDW was not used for the analysis.) The t statistics vector (t) was determined using the sample variances for $-Ln(Y)$ equal to $1 / Y$ (YRECIP) as given by the first order Taylor expansion approximation for the variance of $-Ln(Y)$. The coefficients found can be compared to those for the population in column PHIPOP of Table 12.18. Results for 31, 71, 1131, and 2141 are seen to be in agreement. Coefficients for factors 11, 51, and 3151 are relatively small for the population and were not found significant making them Type II errors. At 5% EWE, factor 3141 represents a Type I error. The Monte Carlo analysis of this problem in Appendix E is in good agreement.

Table 12.17 Outcomes for the 16 trials. The name array YPOP lists the population means for the defects from which the samples were randomly selected.

	Replications			SVAR	Y	YPOP
1	14	19	16	6.33	16.33	15
2	9	8	9	0.33	8.67	12
3	11	8	6	6.33	8.33	11
4	52	45	42	26.33	46.33	54
5	13	9	14	7.00	12.00	12
6	13	22	13	27.00	16.00	15
7	37	46	60	134.33	47.67	54
8	13	20	16	12.33	16.33	11
9	12	20	5	56.33	12.33	10
10	8	8	10	1.33	8.67	9
11	18	8	13	25.00	13.00	16
12	73	88	68	108.33	76.33	68
13	11	16	12	7.00	13.00	9
14	12	10	10	1.33	10.67	10
15	102	75	71	284.33	82.67	68
16	21	13	18	16.33	17.33	16

Table 12.18 Computation of the phi coefficients and their EWE using the Taylor expansion approximation of $1/Y$ for the sample variances for $Ln(Y)$. The coefficients for the population statistics are shown in the last column, PHIPOP for comparison with PHI.

Trial	YRECIP	ij	VARij	SDij	Dij	DFij	PHI	t	PWE	EWE	PHIPOP
1	0.0612	0	0.0014	0.037	7.7E-08	25.3	-2.912	-77.905	0		-2.884
2	0.1154	11	0.0014	0.037	7.7E-08	25.3	-0.059	-1.584	0.063	0.94	0.011
3	0.1200	21	0.0014	0.037	7.7E-08	25.3	-0.102	-2.732	0.006	0.09	0.000
4	0.0216	31	0.0014	0.037	7.7E-08	25.3	-0.435	-11.649	0.000	0.00	-0.461
5	0.0833	41	0.0014	0.037	7.7E-08	25.3	0.003	0.074	0.471	7.06	0.000
6	0.0625	51	0.0014	0.037	7.7E-08	25.3	0.082	2.194	0.019	0.28	-0.003
7	0.0210	61	0.0014	0.037	7.7E-08	25.3	0.014	0.388	0.351	5.26	0.000
8	0.0612	71	0.0014	0.037	7.7E-08	25.3	0.450	12.030	0.000	0.00	0.421
9	0.0811	1121	0.0014	0.037	7.7E-08	25.3	0.024	0.633	0.266	3.99	0.000
10	0.1154	1131	0.0014	0.037	7.7E-08	25.3	-0.135	-3.612	0.001	0.01	-0.162
11	0.0769	1141	0.0014	0.037	7.7E-08	25.3	0.040	1.072	0.147	2.20	0.000
12	0.0131	2131	0.0014	0.037	7.7E-08	25.3	-0.031	-0.842	0.204	3.06	0.000
13	0.0769	2141	0.0014	0.037	7.7E-08	25.3	0.315	8.431	0.000	0.00	0.339
14	0.0938	3141	0.0014	0.037	7.7E-08	25.3	-0.109	-2.925	0.004	0.05	0.000
15	0.0121	3151	0.0014	0.037	7.7E-08	25.3	-0.014	-0.369	0.358	5.36	-0.033
16	0.0577	112131	0.0014	0.037	7.7E-08	25.3	0.018	0.484	0.316	4.75	0.000

YRECIP =1/Y	**PHI** =MMULT(XS,-LN(Y))
VARij =MMULT(XS^2,YRECIP/3)	**t** =PHI/SDij
SDij =SQRT(VARij)	**PWE** =TDIST(ABS(t),DFij,1)
Dij =MMULT(XS^4,(YRECIP/3)^2*(1/2))	**EWE** =15*PWE
DFij =(VARij)^2/Dij	**PHIPOP** =MMULT(XS,-LN(YPOP))

12.5 SUMMARY

Attributes with non-negative character: An important class of attributes has non-negative character. This includes surface roughness, degree of illumination, noise level, vibration level, fatigue life, and the coefficient of friction. When using regression models to discover control factors for improving these attributes, sample outcomes should be modeled with the appropriate distribution having non-negative character, such as the lognormal, binomial, Poisson, or Weibull distribution.

Lognormal distribution: A random variable, *g,* is lognormally distributed if the logarithm of *g* follows a normal distribution. When the variable of strategic importance is *g* and not log(*g*), the analysis of the lognormal problem can proceed, as done here, by first log transforming the replications. These should then be plotted on normal probability paper to verify their lognormal character. Next regression analysis is performed simply to gain insight as to which control factors significantly influence the mean and variance of the log(*g*) transformed data. The insight gained must be used with caution because the significance test of importance is that for the control factors on the CIQ, value, and cash flow, which are a function of the statistics for *g*. Monte Carlo simulations are performed using the normally distributed log(*g*) and the outcomes are transformed to simulate the ranges for the population variance and mean of *g*. The CIQ or values are computed for each trial for each simulation. These are then log transformed for additivity purposes, and the significance of the control factors are then determined from the intercepts of their distributions with the vertical line at zero.

Binomial distribution: The probability distribution for the number *p* of defective parts may often follow a binomial distribution. The number of defects *p* is transformed $Ln(p)$ for improving additivity and normality, having a variance given by Equation (12.10).

Poisson distribution: The number of random defects per unit area is likely to follow a Poisson distribution. The average outcomes for each trial (*Y*) were log transformed here for improving additivity and normality. The Taylor expansion for the variance of $Ln(Y)$ equal to $1 / (nY)$ was used with Satterthwaite's df to compute the significance of the factors.

REFERENCES

1. W. E. Woodson, B. Tillman, and P. Tillman. 1992. *Human Factors Design Handbook.* New York: McGraw-Hill, p. 685.
2. C. F. J. Wu and M. Hamada. 2000. *Experiments Planning, Analysis, and Parameter Design Optimization.* New York: John Wiley & Sons, pp. 585–586, table 13.8.
3. Ibid., pp. 563–564 and 572–573.

13

LIB and the Weibull Distribution

Insight: The times to failure often follow the Weibull distribution.

Key Topics

The larger-is-better problem   Monte Carlo simulation

drill bit breakage   maximum likelihood estimates

Weibull distribution

13.1 LOGNORMAL VERSUS WEIBULL

The lifetimes of parts and tools subject to fatigue, wear, and corrosion often follow the Weibull distribution. The first step in examining this important class of problems is to compute the location and shape parameters for the Weibull distribution from sample measurements. This is can be done in two ways. The first, which is more transparent, uses linear regression analysis. The second uses the maximum likelihood (ML) method,[1,2,3] which is more fundamental and provides a distinct advantage when some tests have been suspended (a form of lifetime censoring). These parameters are then used in Monte Carlo simulations to arrive at the distributions for the strategic outcomes. When dedicated software is not available, maximization of the log likelihood function can be programmed for the Weibull and other distributions using the spreadsheet's Solver function. A comparison of the outcomes from the two approaches is made at the end of this chapter. Computer simulations have shown that both result in biased estimates of the location and shape parameters, which becomes more pronounced as the sample size is reduced.[3]

13.2 COST OF DRILL BIT BREAKAGE

Consider, for illustration, the following *hypothetical* drill bit (bit) problem. It is patterned, somewhat, after the study by Montmarquet[4] of high-speed drill bits (bits) that were relatively inexpensive to purchase but were costly in production due to their propensity for breakage. (Montmarquet's experiment is re-examined here in Appendix H.) It follows that the incremental variable cost of the part being manufactured, $C(x)$, is equal to the fully accounted cost, C_D, for the use and breakage of a bit in production times the number of holes drilled per part, N_H, divided by the number of times, x, that a bit survives the drilling of a hole before failure:

$$C(x) = N_H C_D / x \tag{13.1}$$

The fully accounted cost C_D includes the cost of the bit, the cost associated with the time lost in replacing the broken bit, and the cost associated with any damage to the part as a result of breakage. The expected value of the cost per unit for a distribution of bit lifetimes is equal to the integral over the lifetime of the bits of the frequency distribution multiplied by the incremental variable cost:

$$E[C(x)] \equiv \int_0^\infty f(x)C(x)dx$$

$$= N_H C_D E(1/x) \tag{13.2}$$

$$= N_H C_D \left[\overline{\frac{1}{x}} \right]$$

The expected value for the cost per unit can also be expressed by expanding $C(x)$ in a Taylor series about the mean, μ. When terms through only the second order are included, the cost per unit is

$$C(\mu, \sigma^2) = \int_0^\infty f(x)C(x)dx$$

$$= C(x)\Big|_{x=\mu} + \frac{1}{2} \frac{\partial^2 C(x)}{\partial x^2}\Big|_{x=\mu} \sigma^2 \tag{13.3}$$

$$= \frac{N_H C_D}{\mu} + \frac{N_H C_D \sigma^2}{\mu^3}$$

It was assumed implicitly in writing Equations (13.2) and (13.3) that the number of parts made before breakage was much greater than N_H. The form of Equation (13.2) is simpler to work with than Equation (13.3) and will be used in what follows.

Cobalt, nickel, and molybdenum concentrations were evaluated at two levels each to see if bit durability could be improved on a cost-effective basis versus the baseline level. For this part $N_H = 1$. The $L_4(2^3)$ OA shown in Table 13.1 was chosen for the experimental design. Its solution matrix is shown in Table 13.2. The fully accounted cost of each bit is given in the last column of Table 13.1. Factors 11, 21, and 31 are for the alternate cobalt, nickel, and tungsten concentrations, respectively. The added variable cost per unit of the four different bits for trials 1 through 4 are shown in Figure 13.1 as a function of bit life based upon Equation (13.1). At a fixed bit life, the baseline bit is seen to be the most cost effective but its lifetime in production is short. The positive curvature in Figure 13.1 is such that variation about the mean will also increase variable cost, per Equation (13.3).

Table 13.1 The $L_4(2^3)$ design matrix and cost per bit.

Trial	0	11	21	31	COST
1	1	0	0	0	10
2	1	0	1	1	29
3	1	1	0	1	27
4	1	1	1	0	22

Table 13.2 The $L_4(2^3)$ solution matrix.

ij	1	2	3	4
0	1	0	0	0
11	-1/2	-1/2	1/2	1/2
21	-1/2	1/2	-1/2	1/2
31	-1/2	1/2	1/2	-1/2

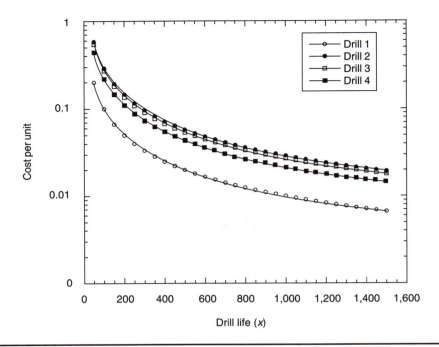

Figure 13.1   Cost per unit versus bit life for each of the four bits tested.

13.3 WEIBULL DISTRIBUTION

The outcomes for bit life found for each trial are shown in Table 13.3, which were taken from Weibull population statistics shown in Table 13.4. From prior knowledge, the outcomes are expected to follow the Weibull distribution, which has a cumulative distribution function as of the lifetime x given by

$$F_C(x) = 1 - \exp(-(x / \beta_W)^{\alpha_w})$$

(13.4)

where α_W and β_W are empirical parameters (see Chapter 4) related to the shape and location of the Weibull distribution, respectively.

Table 13.3   Simulated replications of the bit lifetimes for each trial. SVAR is the list of sample variance and Y is the list of sample means. Neither SVAR nor Y is used in the subsequent computations.

					Replications							
Trial	1	2	3	4	5	6	7	8	9	10	SVAR	Y
1	156	623	415	470	189	378	286	626	291	103	33569	354
2	478	443	464	152	267	245	405	199	86	661	31821	340
3	2021	1118	1224	1738	1207	1374	1888	1391	1708	1137	109512	1481
4	1140	1187	1853	1104	2329	776	1195	1747	1721	1324	212814	1438

Table 13.4 Population statistics for the Weibull distributions.

	Population Statistics				
Trial	Mean	Var	SD	ALPHA	BETA
1	310	26289	162	2	350
2	310	26289	162	2	350
3	1405	155349	394	4	1550
4	1405	155349	394	4	1550

The least square error process for arriving at sample estimates, noted as $\hat{\alpha}_w$ and $\hat{\beta}_w$ for the Weibull distribution is obtained by transforming Equation (13.4) into a linear form. When the natural log of Equation (13.4) is taken and the population statistics are replaced with sample estimates, the expression for the lifetime is given by

$$x = \hat{\beta}_w \left[-Ln(1 - F_C(x)) \right]^{1/\hat{\alpha}_w} \tag{13.5}$$

After the natural log is taken one more time, a linear relationship is found between $Ln(-Ln(1 - F_C))$ and the natural log of the lifetimes:

$$Ln\left(-Ln(1 - F_C(x))\right) = b + \hat{\alpha}_w Ln(x) \tag{13.6}$$

The slope of the relationship provides the estimates of the shape parameter, and the intercept b is related to the shape and location parameters by the expression

$$b = -\hat{\alpha}_w Ln\left(\hat{\beta}_w\right) \tag{13.7}$$

It follows that $\hat{\beta}_w$ can be computed as

$$\hat{\beta}_w = \exp\left(-b / \hat{\alpha}_w\right) \tag{13.8}$$

The analysis is intended to answer several related questions:

1. Do any of the control factors offer cost effective improvements in bit durability?

2. What is the Type I error for assuming that a given control factor (representing an alloy composition change) will reduce the overall cost per part?

3. Do the 90% confidence level variable cost savings exceed the six months breakeven time requirement vis-à-vis the investment level of $2,000 needed to tool the new bit for production?

13.3.1 Monte Carlo Simulation

The replications in Table 13.3 are rearranged in rank order in columns in Table 13.5. Replications (REP1, REP2, etc.) for each of the trials are listed as columns REP1 through REP4. Named variable FC is the estimated cumulative distributions and LLONEmFC represents the computation for $Ln\left(-Ln(1-F_c(x))\right)$. The spreadsheet expressions for FC and LLONEmFC are given at the bottom of Table 13.5. Also shown at the bottom of Table 13.5 are the least square estimated slopes for the shape variables $\hat{\alpha}_w$ (EALPHA), the intercepts (INTERCEPT), and the location parameters $\hat{\beta}_w$ (EBETA). The specific spreadsheet expressions in Table 13.5 refer to computations for trial 1 (cells I66 through I68). The plots of these data are shown in Figure 13.2 through Figure 13.5. The slopes and intercepts in Table 13.5 are in agreement with the slopes and intercepts from the plots. It is mandatory in plotting Weibull data for arriving at measurements of $\hat{\alpha}_w$ and $\hat{\beta}_w$ that the same failure mode is involved for all samples. The lifetimes for samples that failed by another mode should be treated as suspended data points.

Table 13.5 Computation of slopes and intercepts for the inverse plots.

	F	G	H	I	J	K	L
52					Trial		
53	**Replication**			**1**	**2**	**3**	**4**
54	**Rank**	**FC**	**LLONEmFC**	**REP1**	**REP2**	**REP3**	**REP4**
55	1	0.05	-2.970	103	86	1118	776
56	2	0.15	-1.817	156	152	1137	1104
57	3	0.25	-1.246	189	199	1207	1140
58	4	0.35	-0.842	286	245	1224	1187
59	5	0.45	-0.514	291	267	1374	1195
60	6	0.55	-0.225	378	405	1391	1324
61	7	0.65	0.049	415	443	1708	1721
62	8	0.75	0.327	470	464	1738	1747
63	9	0.85	0.640	623	478	1888	1853
64	10	0.95	1.097	626	661	2021	2329
65							
66			**EALPHA**	2.02	1.93	5.12	3.65
67			**INTERCEPT**	-12.10	-11.53	-37.79	-26.92
68			**EBETA**	402	388	1613	1596
69							
70			I66 =SLOPE(LLONEmFC,LN(REP1))				
71			I67 =INTERCEPT(LLONEmFC,LN(REP1))				
72			I68 =EXP(-(INTERCEPT)/EALPHA)				
73							
74			**FC** =(F55-0.5)/10				
75			**LLONEmFC** =LN(-LN(1-FC))				

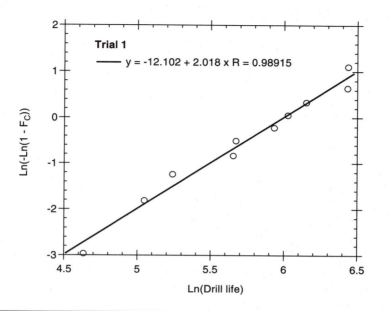

Figure 13.2   Weibull plot for trial 1.

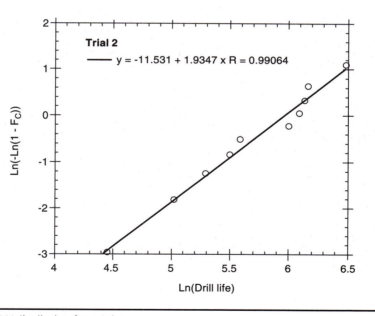

Figure 13.3   Weibull plot for trial 2.

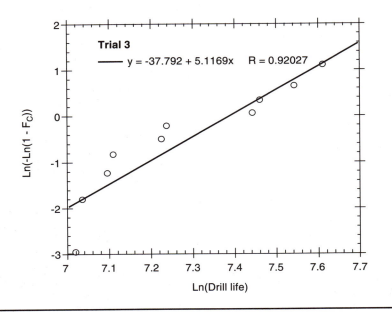

Figure 13.4 Weibull plot for trial 3.

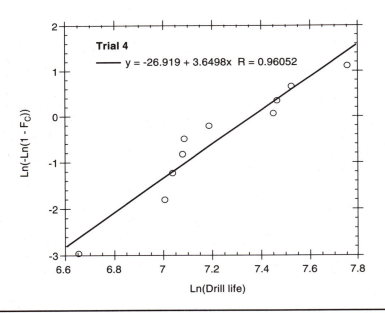

Figure 13.5 Weibull plot for trial 4.

The outcomes of the Monte Carlo simulations developed in Table 13.6 through Table 13.8 are shown in Figure 13.6. Table 13.6 shows the simulated results for the lifetimes computed from Equation (13.5) and the reciprocal of these lifetimes. The costs for the bits for each trial are multiplied by the reciprocal lifetime in Table 13.7 to compute the cost per part due to breakage for this particular simulation. These costs are then trans-

Table 13.6 Simulation of lifetimes and reciprocal lifetimes.

	F	G	H	I	J	K	L	M	N	O	P	Q
84				Simulated lifetimes					Reciprocal of simulated lifetimes			
85				**1**	**2**	**3**	**4**		**1**	**2**	**3**	**4**
85				0.59	0.11	0.30	0.04					
86			**RN=RAND()**						=1/I87			
87			=EBETA*(-LN(1-RN))^(1/EALPHA)	382	130	1313	643		0.00262	0.00769	0.00076	0.00156
88												
89												
90				271	579	1320	1942		0.0037	0.0017	0.0008	0.0005
91				552	365	1588	661		0.0018	0.0027	0.0006	0.0015
92				137	603	1860	1753		0.0073	0.0017	0.0005	0.0006
93				270	278	1235	1942		0.0037	0.0036	0.0008	0.0005
94				639	224	1234	1191		0.0016	0.0045	0.0008	0.0008
95				285	409	1661	793		0.0035	0.0024	0.0006	0.0013
96				482	330	1163	2002		0.0021	0.0030	0.0009	0.0005
97				357	172	1926	1224		0.0028	0.0058	0.0005	0.0008
98				151	36	1440	1687		0.0066	0.0279	0.0007	0.0006
99				320	194	1182	1719		0.0031	0.0052	0.0008	0.0006

formed using a rolling average over 10 rows for each of the four trials (columns X through AA) in Table 13.7. Finally in Table 13.8, the lambda coefficients for −10 log of the costs are computed. In column AK the distribution of the average cost savings per part is computed on replacing the baseline bit with the bit for factor 11.

Table 13.7 Computed bit costs and average costs over 10 bits.

	R	S	T	U	V	W	X	Y	Z	AA
84										
84		Drill cost divide by simulated lifetime					Cost averaged over ten drills			
85		1	2	3	4		1	2	3	4
86		=N90:Q90*TRANSPOSE(COST)					=AVERAGE(S90:S99)			
87										
88										
89										
90		0.037	0.050	0.020	0.011		0.036	0.170	0.019	0.017
91		0.018	0.080	0.017	0.033		0.035	0.170	0.018	0.018
92		0.073	0.048	0.015	0.013		0.035	0.174	0.019	0.021
93		0.037	0.104	0.022	0.011		0.031	0.195	0.019	0.021
94		0.016	0.130	0.022	0.018		0.030	0.195	0.019	0.022
95		0.035	0.071	0.016	0.028		0.032	0.186	0.019	0.021
96		0.021	0.088	0.023	0.011		0.032	0.190	0.019	0.020
97		0.028	0.169	0.014	0.018		0.033	0.194	0.019	0.021
98		0.066	0.810	0.019	0.013		0.035	0.186	0.019	0.020
99		0.031	0.150	0.023	0.013		0.032	0.134	0.019	0.020

Table 13.8 Lambda coefficients for the −10 log average of 10 bit costs and a computation of the overall cost savings in replacing the baseline bit with factor 11.

	AC	AD	AE	AF	AG	AH	AI	AJ	AK
84	Lambda coefficients for average drill costs per part								
85	0	11	21	31		=10^(-AC90/10)			
86	=TRANSPOSE(MMULT(XS,TRANSPOSE(-10*LOG(X90:AA90))))							=10^(-(AC90+AD90)/10)	
87									=AH90-AJ90
88						**Base**		**Base plus 11**	**Difference**
89									
90	14.42	6.39	-3.10	-3.62		0.036		0.008	0.028
91	14.58	6.24	-3.38	-3.49		0.035		0.008	0.027
92	14.51	5.94	-3.76	-3.15		0.035		0.009	0.026
93	15.05	5.87	-4.25	-3.71		0.031		0.008	0.023
94	15.18	5.78	-4.36	-3.73		0.030		0.008	0.022
95	14.98	5.81	-4.09	-3.58		0.032		0.008	0.023
96	14.93	5.99	-3.96	-3.75		0.032		0.008	0.024
97	14.85	6.04	-4.13	-3.59		0.033		0.008	0.025
98	14.59	6.05	-3.75	-3.53		0.035		0.009	0.026
99	14.99	5.22	-3.28	-2.99		0.032		0.010	0.022

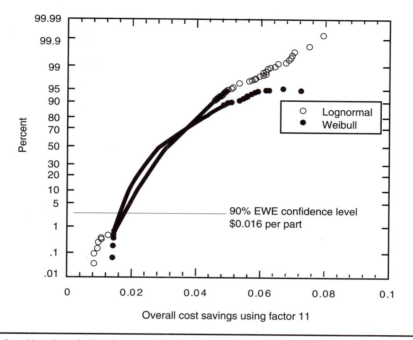

Figure 13.6 Simulated distributions for the overall cost savings as computed by the Weibull simulation method and by the lognormal approximation.

When analyzing the Weibull regression problem, it is always a good idea to check the results using the lognormal approximation to the replications. The results for the lognormal approximation are also shown in Figure 13.6. The two are seen to be similar in the high confidence region of interest.

13.4 ML ESTIMATES OF THE SHAPE AND LOCATION PARAMETERS

The ML process, as discussed earlier, is the preferred method for estimating the parameters governing the population statistics from sample measurements. This is especially true when some of the tests have been censored. ML estimates are generated by maximizing the likelihood function, L, given by

$$L = C_{ML} \prod_i f_i \prod_j \left[1 - F_{C,j} \right]$$

(13.9)

with respect to the unknown parameters. The terms in the argument of the first product in Equation (13.9) are the frequency distributions, f_i, computed for the lifetimes x_i associated with the failure mode under investigation. The terms of the arguments in the second product are one minus the cumulative distributions, F_{Cj}, computed for the lifetimes x_j associated with right censored tests (tests that have been suspended). The parameter, C_{ML}, is a normalization constant, which ensures that the integral of the likelihood function over its domain is unity. However, it is the log of the likelihood function that is actually maximized because it is numerically efficient to do so, which means that the value of the normalization constant can be ignored in searching for the maximum. Three types of censoring regions are shown as shaded on the Weibull distribution in Figure 13.7.

The time span (or number of test cycles) from zero to t_1 is the left censoring region in that the part was known to have failed during this time span, the exact time being unknown. The probability of failure for left censoring is the integral of the frequency function, $f(t)$, from zero to t_1, which is equal to $F_C(t_1)$. The time span from t_2 to t_3 is an interval censored region, the part having failed somewhere between these two times. The interval from t_4 to infinity is right censored, the test being suspended at time t_4 before failure. The uncensored condition arises when the time of failure or the number of cycles to failure is known. This situation is described by Figure 13.7 when the interval $t_3 - t_2$ goes to an arbitrarily small value, Δt, in which case the probability of failure becomes $f(t_2)\Delta t$. Uncensored failures in Equation (13.9) are included in the first set of products, the time interval Δt being included in the constant. The second set of products are for suspended (right censored) tests. The products for left and interval censored tests can be added to the expression as needed.

The ML estimates for the shape, EALPHA, and location, EBETA, parameters for this problem are compared to the values obtained from the regression analysis in Table 13.9.

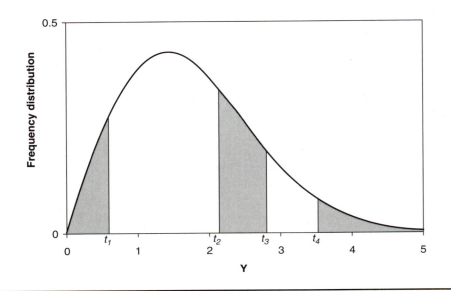

Figure 13.7 Three types of regions for censoring: left, interval, and right.

Table 13.9 Comparison of regression and ML estimates for the shape (EALPHA) and location (EBETA) parameters for the four trials. The population values are also shown for reference.

		TRIAL			
		1	**2**	**3**	**4**
Regression	**EALPHA**	2.02	1.93	5.12	3.65
	EBETA	402	388	1613	1596
ML	**EALPHA**	2.18	2.14	5.13	3.52
	EBETA	401	385	1610	1598
Population	**ALPHA**	2	2	4	4
	BETA	350	350	1550	1550

They are seen to be in good agreement due to the fact that the sample size of 10 is not small and no tests were suspended. The values of these parameters for the population are shown for reference. The ML estimates were made using Solver. Outputs from the spreadsheet template used for the computations are shown in Table 13.10. The 10 replications shown are those for trial 4 divided by 1000. The size reduction was necessary to keep the computations within the numerical bounds required by Solver. This conditioning and input of reasonable initial estimates of the parameters of interest are critical to use Solver outcomes with confidence. The user needs to have an idea of at least the order of magnitude of the answer and needs to use it as a cross check against the possibility that Solver will arrive at an answer far off the mark.

The template was programmed so that any mix of failed and right censored tests could be analyzed within the (arbitrary) limitation of 10 replications. Below each entry an F or an S is entered, respectively, for the lifetime associated with a failure or suspension. When an F is entered, a one is automatically entered in the cell below it; otherwise a zero is automatically entered. In cell AC37, the value for the Weibull frequency distribution is computed for the lifetime in cell AC32. In cell AC38, one minus the Weibull cumulative distribution is computed. The proper expressions (f_i or $1 - F_{c,j}$) associated with the lifetimes are sorted out by the algorithm in cells AC40 through cell AL40.

Cells AC43, AC44, AC45, and so on compute the log likelihood functions for a sample size of three, four, five, and so forth respectively. Initial estimates for the shape parameter, named a, and the location parameter, named b, are entered in cells AF43 and AF44, respectively. The values in these cells are changed by Solver and become the solutions for EALPHA and EBETA/1000, respectively, after it has completed its search and found the two values that maximize the log likelihood. When using the template, the target for Solver is selected from the cell in the column AC43 to AC50 that corresponds to the sample size of interest, which was cell AC50 for this problem. The spreadsheet expressions for selected cells are shown at the bottom of Table 13.10.

Table 13.10 Computations for ML estimates for the shape and location parameters using Solver. The lifetimes shown are for trial 4, divided by 1000. The suspended test expression shown at the bottom of the page for cell AC38 is for right censored lifetimes.

	AA	AB	AC	AD	AE	AF	AG	AH	AI	AJ	AK	AL
30								Replication				
31			**1**	**2**	**3**	**4**	**5**	**6**	**7**	**8**	**9**	**10**
32		**Lifetime**	0.776	1.104	1.14	1.187	1.195	1.324	1.721	1.747	1.853	2.329
33	**Fail="F" ıspended="S"**		F	F	F	F	F	F	F	F	F	F
34			1	1	1	1	1	1	1	1	1	1
35												
36												
37		**Fail**	0.3295	0.6608	0.6936	0.7330	0.7393	0.8190	0.7253	0.7021	0.5941	0.1316
38		**Suspended**	0.9245	0.7620	0.7376	0.7041	0.6982	0.5972	0.2730	0.2544	0.1856	0.0231
39												
40			0.3295	0.6608	0.6936	0.7330	0.7393	0.8190	0.7253	0.7021	0.5941	0.1316
41												
42			**n**	**LN(Likelihood)**		**Name**	**ML est.**					
43			3	-1.890		a	3.522	**EALPHA**				
44			4	-2.201		b	1.598	**EBETA/1000**				
45			5	-2.503								
46			6	-2.703								
47			7	-3.024								
48			8	-3.377								
49			9	-3.898								
50			10	-5.926								

AC37 =((a/b)*(AC$32/b)^(a-1))*EXP(-((AC$32/b)^a))

AC38 =EXP(-((AC32/b)^a))

AC40 =AC34*AC37+(1-AC34)*AC38

AC43 =LN(PRODUCT(AC40:AE40))

AC44 =LN(PRODUCT(AC40:AF40))

13.5 SUMMARY

Lognormal versus Weibull: Most SIB problems can be modeled using a lognormal distribution as an approximation. This also applies to LIB problems, as they usually can be transformed into a SIB problem by converting the attribute *x* to *g* = 1/*x*. Nevertheless, certain LIB problems are better described by a Weibull distribution; when this is the case, it is more accurate to solve the problem using that distribution. Nevertheless, it is good practice to perform the lognormal analysis as a check against the more involved Weibull analysis.

Fundamental metrics: The fundamental metrics for the LIB problem should be carefully examined before setting up and analyzing the strategic experiment as it influences the form of the variable that needs to be measured and simulated. Increased manufacturing costs increase variable cost per unit, whereas increased operating costs reduce value to the customer.

Regression versus ML estimates: Regression and ML techniques were used here to estimate the Weibull shape and location parameters. The ML estimates will usually be more accurate for small sample sizes and for problems involving suspended tests (see Appendix H). As shown here, Solver can be used to generate the ML estimates if dedicated software is not available. When using ML estimates, Weibull plots and regression estimates should still be made to provide a cross-check.

Monte Carlo simulation solution for strategic distribution: The simulation approach to the Weibull problem considered here was divided into five steps: (1) Plots of the data to examine the fitness of the Weibull distribution for the data, followed by an estimate of the location and shape parameters. (2) Computer simulation of lifetimes, Table 13.6, using the RAND() function to represent the cumulative distribution, Equation (13.5). (3) Conversion of simulated bit lifetimes to cost per unit manufactured and average cost, Table 13.7. (4) Computation of the lambda coefficients of –10 times the log to the base 10 of the average costs. (5) Plots on normal probability paper to determine the distribution for the overall cost savings and confidence level, Figure 13.7.

REFERENCES

1. W. O. Meeker and L. A. Escobar. 1998. *Statistical Methods for Reliability Data.* New York: John Wiley & Sons, pp. 427–460.
2. C. F. J. Wu and M. Hamada. 2000. *Experiments Planning, Analysis, and Parameter Design Optimization.* New York: John Wiley & Sons, pp. 533–539.
3. D. R. Abernethy, J. E. Breneman, C. H. Medlin, and G. L. Reinman. November 1983. *Weibull Analysis Handbook,* Report # AFWAL-TR-83-2070, U.S. Department of Commerce, NTIS.
4. F. Montmarquet. November 1988. *Printed Circuit Drill Bit Design Optimization Using Taguchi Methods, 0.013 Diameter Bits.* Sixth Symposium on Taguchi Methods, Dearborn, MI: American Supplies Institute, pp. 207–216.

14

Signal-Response (Dynamic or Multiple Target) Problems

> *Insight: Two nested experiments are used to analyze signal-response problems. One examines the nature of the response over the range of the signal factor, and the other examines the nature of the response over the set of control factors.*

Key Topics

Signal-response experiments	strategic analysis of control factors
orthogonal polynomials	Special Vectors
injection molding	

14.1 INTRODUCTION

Before the development of the automotive disc brake and its widespread application, the duo-servo drum brake was used extensively because it generated a relatively large braking torque for a nominal amount of pedal effort. However, the torque was a nonlinear and often erratic function of pedal effort due to the high sensitivity of the brake to the coefficient of friction of the lining, which varied with humidity and lining temperature. As a result, pulls to one side or the other were not uncommon and the driver also had to carefully modulate pedal force to avoid rear wheel lock-up and loss of stability on hard stops. Disc brakes, because they have a more linear signal-response relationship and greater fade resistance, have replaced drum brakes on many automobiles even though they are more costly to manufacture.

A smooth, linear response to an input signal is a desirable feature for most controls. Moreover, when the signal is returned to its former position, the response is expected to return to its former level. Control factors can be evaluated for improving the signal-response relationship using design of experiments methods. The experiments, however, are

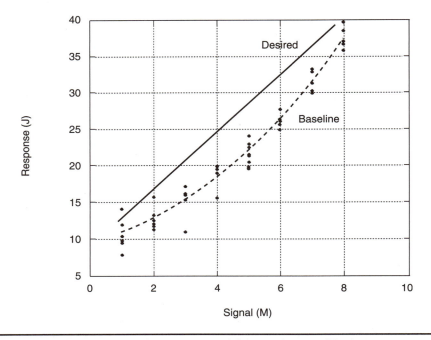

Figure 14.1 The objective is to discover control factors that modify the response so that it becomes linear with the signal having minimal variance.

more complex in that they need to evaluate how the control factors simultaneously affect multiple targets rather than a single target. This problem is referred to here as "signal-response." Taguchi, one of the first to explore this type of problem, referred to it as "dynamic." Others have termed it "multiple response."

Signal-response problems involve two nested experiments, noted here as the *signal factor experiment* and the *control factor experiment*.[1] The objective is to find a set of control factors that change the nonlinear baseline response, *J*, having troublesome variability to a linear response with little or no variability (see Figure 14.1). The signal factor, noted as *M*, is stepped across its useful range in equal amounts, and the mean and the variance of the response are measured at each step.

14.2 ORTHOGONAL POLYNOMIALS

Signal factor experiments use discrete orthogonal polynomial (OP) expansions to model the response of interest as a function of the signal factor *M*. The design matrix for signal factors is named XOP#, where # is the number of discrete steps, N_M, chosen for the signal variable. The number of rows in XOP# is equal to N_M. The number of columns in XOP# is three, which are labeled 0, 1, and 2, representing the base, linear, and quadratic OP coefficients, respectively. Only these three coefficients are used here, as they are sufficient for most problems.

The signal factor experiment is repeated for each trial in the control factor design matrix, which results in three OP expansion coefficients and their variances being computed for each trial of the control factor experiment. Five SDW templates have been generated covering the signal factor levels from four to eight. They have file names OP#SDW, the symbol # being as defined previously.

The OP of order i is written as $P_i(M)/\sqrt{C_i}$ where C_i is a weighting factor, which satisfies the orthogonality conditions (for $i, k \neq 0$):

$$\sum_{j}^{N_M} \frac{P_i(M_j)P_k(M_j)}{\sqrt{C_iC_k}} = \begin{cases} 0 & i \neq k \\ 1 & i = k \end{cases} \tag{14.1}$$

The M_j represent the discrete levels of the signal factor from $j = 1$ to N_M. For the OP of order $i = 0$, $C_0 = 1$, and $P_0(M_j) = 1$. The general OP expansion for trial q is of the form

$$J(q,M) = a_0(q) + a_1(q)P_1(M)/\sqrt{C_1} +$$
$$a_2(q)P_2(M)/\sqrt{C_2} + ... \tag{14.2}$$

OPs are used because (1) they provide a better relative comparison of the strengths of the coefficients than a Taylor series of the form $M^0, M^1, M^2, ...$ and (2) the resulting values for the OP coefficients $a_i(q)$ for i equal to 0, 1, 2, and so on are independent of one another, which is not true for the Taylor expansion.

When both sides of Equation (14.2) are multiplied by $P_i(M)/\sqrt{C_i}$ and summed over the discrete values for M, the following expressions are found for the OP coefficients

$$a_0(q) = \sum_{j=1}^{N_M} J(q,M_j)/N_M$$

$$a_1(q) = \sum_{j=1}^{N_M} J(q,M_j)P_1(M_j)/\sqrt{C_1} \tag{14.3}$$

$$a_2(q) = \sum_{j=1}^{N_M} J(q,M_j)P_2(M_j)/\sqrt{C_2}$$

The individual, unweighted OPs of the forms

$$P_0(M_j) = 1$$

$$P_1(M_j) = M_j \tag{14.4}$$

$$P_2(M_j) = c_0 + c_2 M_j^2$$

can be used in place of the weighted OPs. When N_M is odd, the range of levels includes level 0, the next levels above and below 0 being 1 and -1, respectively, for a step size of 1. When N_M is even, level 0 is not included, and the two central levels are at -1 and 1 for a step size of two. For example, if there are three levels for the signal factor, the logical choice is to take the allowable values for the signal factor M_j to be -1, 0, and $+1$. The three levels $(-1, 0, 1)$ could correspond to three equally spaced physical settings such as (15, 20, 25), (100, 125, 150), and so on.

The parameters c_0 and c_2 depend upon the number of uniform, discrete steps being considered for the signal factor. Because the sum of the quadratic coefficients over the domain is equal to zero, it follows on summing the expression for $P_2(M_j)$ in Equation (14.4) over the N_M levels that c_0 and c_2 are related by the expression

$$c_0 = \frac{-c_2}{N_M} \sum_{j=1}^{N_M} M_j^2 \qquad (14.5)$$

When this result for c_0 is substituted into the expression for $P_2(M_j)$, the relation becomes

$$P_2(M_j) = c_2 \left[\frac{-1}{N_M} \sum_{k=1}^{N_M} M_k^2 + M_j^2 \right] \qquad (14.6)$$

The parameter c_2 is chosen so that the absolute value of the minimum in $P_2(M_j)$ is equal to one or zero. This results in c_2 being expressed as

$$c_2 = \begin{cases} = 1, \text{ if } ABS\left(MIN\left[\frac{-1}{N_M} \sum_{k=1}^{N_M} M_k^2 + M_j^2 \right] \right) = 0. \\[4mm] = 1 \bigg/ ABS\left(MIN\left[\frac{-1}{N_M} \sum_{k=1}^{N_M} M_k^2 + M_j^2 \right] \right) \text{ otherwise} \end{cases} \qquad (14.7)$$

The expression for $P_2(M_j)$ in Equation (14.6) with c_2 given by Equation (14.7) is readily computed over the various ranges N_M of interest using the spreadsheet. Outcomes computed in this manner for the $P_1(M_j)$ (linear) and $P_2(M_j)$ (quadratic) OPs for levels 3 to 8 are given in Table 14.1.

Table 14.1 Linear and quadratic OPs for levels 3 to 8.

N_M		j=1	2	3	4	5	6	7	8
3	Linear	-1	0	1					
	Quadratic	1	-2	1					
4	Linear	-3	-1	1	3				
	Quadratic	1	-1	-1	1				
5	Linear	-2	-1	0	1	2			
	Quadratic	2	-1	-2	-1	2			
6	Linear	-5	-3	-1	1	3	5		
	Quadratic	5	-1	-4	-4	-1	5		
7	Linear	-3	-2	-1	0	1	2	3	
	Quadratic	5	0	-3	-4	-3	0	5	
8	Linear	-7	-5	-3	-1	1	3	5	7
	Quadratic	7	1	-3	-5	-5	-3	1	7

If the signal factor range begins at an origin where the output is zero, the ideal form of the relationship between the signal factor and the response, will be of the form

$$\tau(M) = b_1 P_1(M) / \sqrt{C_1} \tag{14.8}$$

If the range of the signal factor is about a nonzero origin, then the ideal form would be

$$\tau(M) = b_0 + b_1 P_1(M) / \sqrt{C_1} \tag{14.9}$$

For example, if Equation (14.8) were the appropriate ideal form, then the objective of the experiment would be realized by finding a set of control and adjustment factors that reduce a_0 and a_2 to zero, transform a_1 to b_1, and eliminate variation.

The adjustment factor, when it exists, acts as a multiplier $h (= b_1/a^*_1)$ in changing the linear coefficient to the desired level b_1 after the linear coefficient has first been improved upon in going from a_1 to a^*_1. The transformation to a^*_1 is made by evaluating the control factors and choosing the set that best meets the objective of the experiment. Use of the adjustment factor also changes the variance of the slope by a multiple equal to h_2. However, the ratio of the slope squared to its variance remains constant.

In a mechanical system, the adjustment factor could be the ratio between two gears. In an electric circuit, the adjustment factor could be the gain in an amplifier. When an adjustment factor is available, it is usually desirable to choose first the control factors that make a^*_1 as large as possible as this renders the adjustment factor as small as possible, thereby either not increasing variance as much or even reducing variance if $h < 1$. The improved response function J^* is changed to $\tau^* = hJ^* + \text{const.}$ on applying the adjustment factor. The relationship between the adjusted and unadjusted variances is $Var(\tau^*) = h^2 Var(J^*)$.

The OP coefficients will not be solved for formally using Equation (14.3). Instead the regular least square solution given by $\hat{a} = X_{S,OP}J$ will be used. If the elements of the solution matrix $X_{S,OP}$(XSOP) for the OP coefficient $i (= 0,1,2)$ at level j of the signal factor for trial q are written as $\omega_i(q,j)$, then it follows that the OP coefficients are given by

$$\hat{a}_i(q) = \sum_j \omega_i(q,j) J(q,j)$$

The baseline OP coefficients for each of the trials act as the column vector Y in a SDW dedicated to the baseline OPs. The SDW also calls for the column vector SVAR of sample variances $s_i^2(q)$ associated with each OP coefficient i for each trial q. The sample variances are computed by multiplying the variances of the means of the OP coefficients by n to convert them to sample variances. Thus, from Equation (7.9), the $s_i^2(q)$ are given by

$$s_i^2(q) = n \sum_j \omega_i^2(q,j) \frac{s^2(q,j)}{n} = \sum_j \omega_i^2(q,j) s^2(q,j)$$

where $s^2(q, j)$ is the sample variance for trial q at level j of the signal factor. The sample variances $s_0^2(q)$ for the baseline OP coefficients are copied and pasted into the same baseline SDW as the column vector SVAR. The linear and quadratic OP coefficients along with their respective sample variances $s_1^2(q)$ and $s_2^2(q)$, respectively, are similarly copied and pasted into their own SDWs. On making these entries, the lambda or phi coefficients for Y and the Xi coefficients for −10log(SVAR) are then automatically computed for the base, linear, and quadratic OP coefficients in their respective SDWs.

14.3 PROCESS FOR STRATEGIC SIGNAL-RESPONSE ANALYSIS

After the signal factor range and the experimental design for the control factors have been selected and the experiments run, the results need to be analyzed to determine which of the factors are important in reducing the CIQ (improving value). The overall analysis process is divided into four basic operations:

1. *Select the OP#SDW template*. Choose the template that supports the number of levels chosen for the signal factor. For example, if the signal factor range for each trial in the control factor experiment were six, then the OP6SDW should be used. The averages (ActualAvg) and variances (ActualVar) are entered into the Data worksheet in this template. The coefficients for the three OPs and their sample variances are then computed automatically in the OP worksheet. The number of replications for each trail *(q)* for signal factor setting *(j)* given by $n(q, j)$ should be kept constant and equal to *n*.

2. *Compute the lambda (or phi) and Xi coefficients*. Copy the base OP coefficients $a_0(q)$ for the mean from the OP#SDW and paste them into the column for Y in the base factor SDW using the paste>special>value command. Similarly, copy the sample variances $s_0^2(q)$ for the base coefficients and paste them into the column for SVAR in the base factor SDW. This is repeated for the linear and quadratic OPs using a new SDW for each. The lambda and Xi coefficients for the control factors are then computed automatically.

3. *Select the Special Vectors*. Examine the sign and significance of the lambda and Xi coefficients to infer which factors and which of their levels appear best for reducing the CIQ and improving value. Identify several "Special Vectors" of factor combinations that look most promising for meeting the objectives of the experiment. For example, one Special Vector could be the combination of factor levels that looks most promising for reducing variance. Another could be the combination that is expected to increase the slope the most. A third could be the combination that best reduced the second order coefficient. Of course, every combination of main effects could be evaluated in a systematic manner using the full factorial array of main effects. However, a combinatorial explosion results as the number of main effects increase, an $L_8(2^7)$ design generating 128 different combinations.

4. *Analyze the Special Vectors*. Transfer the special vectors to the OP#SDW. Determine which Special Vector generates the smallest CIQ.

14.4 CASE STUDY

DeMates' signal-response problem involving the weight of injection molded parts provides an excellent case study for this class of problems.[2] The signal was the injection molding pressure varied over the range from 650 to 1000 psi in equal increments of 50 psi, resulting in eight signal factor levels. A total of eight replications (four at each of two compound noise factor levels) were made for each setting of the signal factor for each experimental trial. A total of seven control factors, A through G (11 through 71) in Table 14.2, were evaluated at two levels each using an $L_8(2^7)$ OA. The approach taken here is similar but not identical to that used by Miller and Wu in their re-analysis.[3] The major differences are that the noise factors are not folded into the design matrix here and that value assessments are made for selected combinations of control factors as represented by the special vectors. DeMates used Taguchi's process for dynamic problems, which selects the control factors that maximized the log of the ratio of the slope of the response squared divided by the variance[1].

14.4.1 Evaluating the OP expansion coefficients

The injection pressures and the $j = 1$ to 8 levels chosen for M_j are shown in the first two columns of Table 14.3. The even choice of 8 levels of the signal factor places four levels on either side of the center. The response was modeled to second order in the OP. The solution for $P_1(M_j)$ is

$$P_1(M_j) = M_j \qquad (14.10)$$

From Equations (14.6) and (14.7), $P_2(M_j)$ is given by

$$P_2(M_j) = \frac{1}{4}\left[-21 + M_j^2\right] \qquad (14.11)$$

The specific values for the two OPs are listed for $N_M = 8$ in Table 14.1. The discrete functions $P_1(M_j)$ and $P_2(M_j)$ shown in Figure 14.2 display linear and quadratic behavior, respectively, as a function of the range of injection pressures studied.

Table 14.2 Seven control factors considered by DeMates in his injection molding case study.

A. 11 injection speed
B. 21 clamp time
C. 31 high injection time
D. 41 low injection time
E. 51 clamp pressure
F. 61 water cooling
G. 71 low injection pressure

Table 14.3 The values for $P_i(M_j)$ for i equal to 0, 1, and 2 versus the levels of the signal factor taken from the OP8SDW. The 8×3 array named XOP8 is used in the computations that follow.

		XOP8		
		i		
Pressure	**j**	**0**	**1**	**2**
650	1	1	-7	7
700	2	1	-5	1
750	3	1	-3	-3
800	4	1	-1	-5
850	5	1	1	-5
900	6	1	3	-3
950	7	1	5	1
1000	8	1	7	7
			C1	**C2**
			168	168

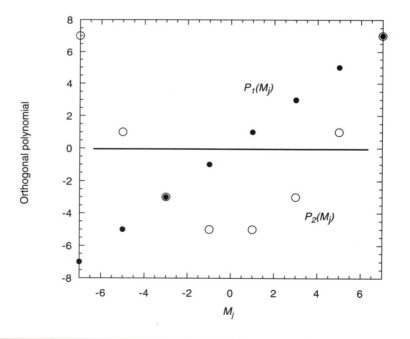

Figure 14.2 The functions $P_1(M_j)$ and $P_2(M_j)$ as a function of the eight discrete levels of the signal factor, M_j.

The three columns for $P_i(M_j)$ in Table 14.3 are for the base, linear, and quadratic levels. The elements in the three columns by eight rows for the $P_i(M_j)$ represent the signal factor design matrix $\mathbf{X}_{OP}$ (XOP8) in the expression $\mathbf{J} = \mathbf{X}_{OP}\mathbf{a} + \mathbf{e}$ coupling the part weights to the signal factor, M_j. The $P_i(M_j)$ are used to compute the OP expansion coefficients represented by the vector $\mathbf{a}(q)$, which is a function of each trial (q). The two weighting factors C_1 and C_2 were not used because solutions for the coefficients are being generated using regression. The expression relating the outcomes for trial (q) to the OP coefficients is given by

$$
\begin{vmatrix} J(q,1) \\ J(q,2) \\ J(q,3) \\ J(q,4) \\ J(q,5) \\ J(q,6) \\ J(q,7) \\ J(q,8) \end{vmatrix} = \begin{vmatrix} 1 & -7 & 7 \\ 1 & -5 & 1 \\ 1 & -3 & -3 \\ 1 & -1 & -5 \\ 1 & 1 & -5 \\ 1 & 3 & -3 \\ 1 & 5 & 1 \\ 1 & 7 & 7 \end{vmatrix} \begin{vmatrix} a_0(q) \\ a_1(q) \\ a_2(q) \end{vmatrix} + \mathbf{e}
\tag{14.12}
$$

The solution matrix $\mathbf{X}_{S,OP}$ (XSOP8) for the signal factor experiment is shown in Table 14.4. The average part weights (ActualAvg) and their variances (ActualVar) are shown in Table 14.5 and Table 14.6, respectively[3]. The plot of the response for trial 1 versus the signal factor is shown in Figure 14.3.

Table 14.4 The solution matrix $X_{S,OP}$ (XSOP8) for computing the OP coefficients for fitting the part weights to the signal factor taken from the OP8SDW.

	650	700	750	800	850	900	950	1000
OP	1	2	3	4	5	6	7	8
0	0.125	0.125	0.125	0.125	0.125	0.125	0.125	0.125
1	-0.042	-0.030	-0.018	-0.006	0.006	0.018	0.030	0.042
2	0.042	0.006	-0.018	-0.030	-0.030	-0.018	0.006	0.042

Table 14.5 Average part weights versus the signal factor for each experimental trial of the $L_8(2^7)$ OA taken from the Data worksheet in the OP8SDW.

				Averages (ActualAvg)				
j=	1	2	3	4	5	6	7	8
				Mj				
Trial	-7	-5	-3	-1	1	3	5	7
1	638.3	643.6	646.2	655.6	667.1	673.1	691.4	711.2
2	635.5	641.6	642.8	652.9	661.7	666.8	685.8	710.2
3	639.9	644.8	647.6	656.4	667.8	674.2	692.0	711.4
4	642.3	645.9	647.9	655.9	665.4	673.1	690.0	710.4
5	641.7	645.3	647.6	654.2	663.8	673.6	687.4	708.7
6	650.7	655.4	659.7	666.5	671.2	678.4	695.0	717.7
7	639.9	644.4	647.8	656.1	664.9	675.0	692.2	711.0
8	637.1	641.9	646.3	654.0	663.6	672.4	689.7	709.5

Table 14.6 Sample variances $s^2(j, q)$ of part weight versus the signal factor for each experimental trial of the $L_8(2^7)$ OA taken from the Data worksheet in the OP8SDW.

				Variances (ActualVar)				
j=	1	2	3	4	5	6	7	8
				Mj				
Trial	-7	-5	-3	-1	1	3	5	7
1	6.59	1.94	1.66	2.19	3.25	4.60	4.18	13.24
2	4.29	2.91	2.46	3.27	7.68	31.97	25.86	7.02
3	3.00	4.67	3.59	7.42	5.08	5.81	14.41	6.12
4	0.89	5.01	4.53	10.82	18.21	10.40	11.22	6.03
5	0.38	0.27	0.20	0.86	12.92	1.11	1.97	4.21
6	0.19	0.31	0.25	0.42	0.23	0.47	2.85	1.53
7	0.09	0.15	0.14	0.15	0.28	0.05	0.34	0.66
8	1.20	1.67	0.90	2.00	1.63	0.60	0.27	0.44

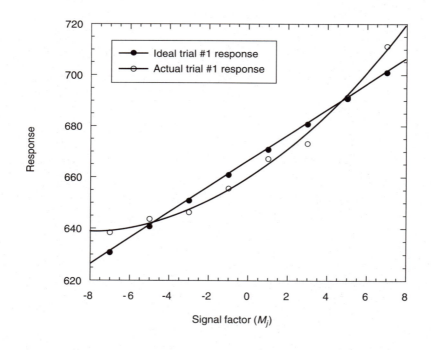

Figure 14.3 Plot of the ideal and the actual responses for trial 1 before applying the adjustment factor.

The OP expansion coefficients for the means (Y) and their variances (SVAR) are shown in Table 14.7 as computed, respectively, from the spreadsheet expressions

$$Y = TRANSPOSE(MMULT(XSOP8,TRANSPOSE(ActualAvg)))$$

and

$$SVAR = TRANSPOSE(MMULT(XSOP8\char`\^2,TRANSPOSE(ActualVar)))$$

The expressions were written first for trial 1 and the remaining rows were generated by dragging down the two expressions listed for the first trial.

14.4.2 Influence of the Control Factors on the OP Expansion Coefficients

The next step in the analysis is to enter the results for the three OP coefficients in Table 14.7 into a separate L8(2^7) SDW for each to determine how they are influenced by the control factors. The $L_8(2^7)$ design matrix (X) is shown for completeness in Table 14.8 and the solution matrix (XS) is shown in Table 14.9.

Table 14.7 Computation of the OP expansion coefficients for the means and the sample variances for the OP coefficients taken from the OP8 SDW. The base, linear, and quadratic OP coefficients and the sample variances become, respectively, the name variables Y and SVAR for the base, linear, and quadratic L8(2^7) SDWs.

	OP Coefficients				Sample variances for the OP coefficients		
	0	1	2		0	1	2
1	665.82	5.008	1.252	1	0.588	0.042	0.041
2	662.15	4.908	1.464	2	1.335	0.056	0.041
3	666.76	4.926	1.245	3	0.783	0.036	0.031
4	666.35	4.659	1.401	4	1.049	0.032	0.043
5	665.29	4.564	1.377	5	0.343	0.011	0.021
6	674.31	4.332	1.347	6	0.098	0.006	0.004
7	666.40	4.924	1.309	7	0.029	0.002	0.002
8	664.32	4.962	1.275	8	0.136	0.005	0.007

Table 14.8 The phi L8(2^7) design matrix X coupling the control factors to the outcomes in the experiment.

Trial	Base 0	A 11	B 21	C 31	D 41	E 51	F 61	G 71
1	1	−1	−1	−1	−1	−1	−1	−1
2	1	−1	−1	−1	1	1	1	1
3	1	−1	1	1	−1	−1	1	1
4	1	−1	1	1	1	1	−1	−1
5	1	1	−1	1	−1	1	−1	1
6	1	1	−1	1	1	−1	1	−1
7	1	1	1	−1	−1	1	1	−1
8	1	1	1	−1	1	−1	−1	1

Table 14.9 The solution matrix, XS, for the $L_8(2^7)$ design matrix.

		1	2	3	4	5	6	7	8	COV
Base	0	0.125	0.125	0.125	0.125	0.125	0.125	0.125	0.125	0.125
A	11	−0.125	−0.125	−0.125	−0.125	0.125	0.125	0.125	0.125	0.125
B	21	−0.125	−0.125	0.125	0.125	−0.125	−0.125	0.125	0.125	0.125
C	31	−0.125	−0.125	0.125	0.125	0.125	0.125	−0.125	−0.125	0.125
D	41	−0.125	0.125	−0.125	0.125	−0.125	0.125	−0.125	0.125	0.125
E	51	−0.125	0.125	−0.125	0.125	0.125	−0.125	0.125	−0.125	0.125
F	61	−0.125	0.125	0.125	−0.125	−0.125	0.125	0.125	−0.125	0.125
G	71	−0.125	0.125	0.125	−0.125	0.125	−0.125	−0.125	0.125	0.125

Shown in Table 14.10 through Table 14.12 are the ξ_{ij} (XI) coefficients for the influence of the control factors on -10 times the log variance for the base, linear, and quadratic levels of the OP, respectively. The spreadsheet expressions are shown at the bottom of Table 14.10. Coefficient ξ_{11} for factor A is seen to be large positive for each of the OPs, which is favorable in reducing the variance of each. It is also interesting to note that the sign of a given factor is the same across the three levels except for the two weakest coefficients. If the desire were simply to identify the Special Vector that best reduced variation, the results in Table 14.10 show that this is level 1 for A, B, and F and level −1 for C, D, E, and G.

Table 14.10 Computation of the ξ_{ij} and their significance as taken from the L8(2^7) SDW for the base OP.

		XI	Gij	PWE	EWE	ALPHAXI
				MIN(n)		0.05
Base	0	5.086	2.034	0.000	0.00	
A	11	4.609	1.844	0.000	0.00	
B	21	1.134	0.454	0.096	0.67	
C	31	-1.182	-0.473	0.087	0.61	
D	41	-0.760	-0.304	0.188	1.32	
E	51	-0.447	-0.179	0.300	2.10	
F	61	1.234	0.494	0.078	0.55	
G	71	-1.806	-0.722	0.022	0.15	

XI	=MMULT(XS,-10*LOG(SVAR))
Gij	=XI/SQRT(50*COV)
PWE	=FDIST(10^ABS(Gij),MIN(n)-1,MIN(n)-1)
EWE	=PWE*(w-1) Off baseline

Table 14.11 Computation of the ξ_{ij} and their significance as taken from the L8(2^7) SDW for the linear OP.

		XI	Gij	MIN(n) PWE	EWE	ALPHAXI 0.05
Base	0	18.460	7.384	0.000	0.00	
A	11	4.564	1.826	0.000	0.00	
B	21	1.442	0.577	0.050	0.35	
C	31	-0.667	-0.267	0.218	1.53	
D	41	-0.346	-0.138	0.343	2.40	
E	51	0.152	0.061	0.429	3.00	
F	61	0.664	0.266	0.219	1.53	
G	71	-1.112	-0.445	0.100	0.70	

Table 14.12 Computation of the ξ_{ij} and their significance as taken from the L8(2^7) SDW for the quadratic OP.

		XI	Gij	MIN(n) PWE	EWE	ALPHAXI 0.05
Base	0	18.339	7.336	0.000	0.00	
A	11	4.223	1.689	0.000	0.00	
B	21	1.194	0.478	0.085	0.59	
C	31	-0.908	-0.363	0.146	1.02	
D	41	0.003	0.001	0.499	3.49	
E	51	-0.371	-0.149	0.332	2.32	
F	61	1.809	0.724	0.021	0.15	
G	71	-1.434	-0.574	0.051	0.36	

Next, the influence of the control factors on the three OP coefficients for the means needs to be examined. This is done by computing three φ_{ij} coefficients, as shown in Table 14.13 through Table 14.15. For simplicity in using the SDW, the title of the column was changed from LAM to PHI but the array name for the column was left unchanged as LAM.

Table 14.13 Computation of the control factor coefficients ϕ_{ij} and their significance, as taken from the L8(2^7) SDW for the base OP.

						ALPHALAM	
							0.05

		PHI	SDij	DFij	t	PWE2	EWE
Base	0	666.43	0.09	33.38	7221.33	0.00	0.00
A	11	1.15	0.09	33.38	12.50	0.00	0.00
B	21	-0.47	0.09	33.38	-5.08	0.00	0.00
C	31	1.75	0.09	33.38	18.99	0.00	0.00
D	41	0.36	0.09	33.38	3.88	0.00	0.00
E	51	-1.38	0.09	33.38	-14.91	0.00	0.00
F	61	0.98	0.09	33.38	10.62	0.00	0.00
G	71	-1.80	0.09	33.38	-19.47	0.00	0.00

PHI	=MMULT(XS,Y)
SDij	=SQRT(MMULT(XS^2,SVAR/n))
DFij	=SDij^4/MMULT(XS^4,(SVAR/n)^2/(n-1))
t	=LAM/SDij
PWE2	=TDIST(ABS(t),DFij,1)
EWE	=PWE2*(w-1) *Off baseline*

Table 14.14 Computation of the control factor coefficients ϕ_{ij} and their significance, as taken from the L8(2^7) SDW for the linear OP.

						ALPHALAM	
							0.05

		PHI	SDij	DFij	t	PWE2	EWE
Base	0	4.79	0.02	34.03	247.90	0.00	0.00
A	11	-0.09	0.02	34.03	-4.66	0.00	0.00
B	21	0.08	0.02	34.03	4.26	0.00	0.00
C	31	-0.17	0.02	34.03	-8.56	0.00	0.00
D	41	-0.07	0.02	34.03	-3.62	0.00	0.00
E	51	-0.02	0.02	34.03	-1.12	0.14	0.95
F	61	-0.01	0.02	34.03	-0.67	0.25	1.78
G	71	0.05	0.02	34.03	2.83	0.00	0.03

Table 14.15 Computation of the control factor coefficients ϕ_{ij} and their significance, as taken from the L8(2^7) SDW for the quadratic OP.

ALPHALAM

						0.05

		PHI	SDij	DFij	t	PWE2	EWE
Base	0	1.33	0.02	37.44	69.34	0.00	0.00
A	11	-0.01	0.02	37.44	-0.35	0.36	2.54
B	21	-0.03	0.02	37.44	-1.37	0.09	0.63
C	31	0.01	0.02	37.44	0.46	0.33	2.28
D	41	0.04	0.02	37.44	1.97	0.03	0.20
E	51	0.05	0.02	37.44	2.80	0.00	0.03
F	61	0.01	0.02	37.44	0.39	0.35	2.45
G	71	0.01	0.02	37.44	0.34	0.37	2.58

Satterthwaite's approximate t-test was used to evaluate the significance of the φ_{ij}. The specific spreadsheet expression for computing a given array is shown at the bottom of Table 14.13. Based upon the EWE, all of the off-baseline control factors have significant influence on the base level OP coefficients. All but factors E and F are significant for the linear OP coefficients. However, their impact on the OP coefficients for the means is not large. Although factor A, for example, is seen to reduce variance in going from level −1 to 1 in Table 14.10, it reduces the slope (which is unfavorable) by only by a small amount (see Table 14.14). Thus, it is favorable to set factor A at level 1 because its reduction in variance offsets the minor reduction in slope. Only off-baseline factor E has a significant influence on the quadratic coefficients (see Table 14.15).

Thus, at this juncture, the quadratic contribution of the signal factor to the response cannot be eliminated using the control factors studied in the experiment. Nor can the coefficient of the linear OP be increased by a large amount. However, control factor A was found to generate a significant reduction in variance, and control factor E, when set at −1, was found to generate a significant reduction in the coefficient for the second order OP.

14.4.3 Strategic Analysis of the Control Factors

The next step in the analysis is to consider how the factors influence the strategic metrics of value and variable cost. The factors in Table 14.2 that affect processing time will likely influence variable cost, which would need to be assessed in relation to the value added. Apart from a multiplication constant, the loss in value associated with a given set of control factors is computed by summing the difference squared between the ideal response τ and the projected actual response τ^* over each level of the signal factor. The value loss represents the CIQ for the combination of factors relative to the ideal value. Based on Equation (2.8), the formal relationship between the value loss and the CIQ after applying the adjustment factor can be written as

$$\Omega \equiv \frac{1}{N_M} \sum_{j=1}^{N_M} \left[V\left(\tau(M_j)\right) - V\left(\tau^*(M_j)\right) \right] \tag{14.13}$$

The CIQ (loss in value from ideal) at a given signal factor level in Equation (14.12) can be expressed in terms of the square of the deviation between the mean and its ideal position plus the variance:

$$\Omega = \frac{k_S}{N_M} \sum_{j=1}^{N_M} \left[\left[\tau_j^* - \tau_j \right]^2 + h^2 \sigma_j^2 \right] \tag{14.14}$$

Except for the summation over all levels of the signal factor, Equation (14.13) is similar in form to Equation (5.7). The specific form of the adjusted response is given by

$$\tau_j^* = hJ_j^* + c_F \tag{14.15}$$

The term c_F is a constant that ensures that the average of the τ_j^* responses having the adjusted slope is the same as the average of the ideal response, which yields

$$c_F = \frac{1}{N_M} \left[\sum_{j=1}^{N_M} \tau_j - h \sum_{j=1}^{N_M} J_j^* \right] \tag{14.16}$$

$$= \left[1 - h \right] \bar{\tau}_j = \left[1 - h \right] \bar{J}_j = \left[1 - h \right] a_0$$

This term is needed in order to make meaningful, relative comparisons between the CIQs for different choices of control factors.

14.4.3.1 Special Vectors for Control Factors

Combinations of control factors (Special Vectors) already identified as most promising need to be evaluated to determine the set that yields the minimum CIQ. As the control factors for this problem have only two levels, the vector for an arbitrary set consists of ones and minus ones using the phi array. The special vectors are shown in Table 14.16. The first vector represents the control factors for trial 7. This vector was chosen because trial 7 had the minimum average variance of all of the trials, (Table 14.6). The second vector was chosen because it minimized the second order contribution. The third represents the vector chosen by DeMates as best on the basis of his analysis of the experimental outcomes. The next two are used to contrast the outcomes and factors that minimize and maximize variance, respectively. The final vector is for the set of control factors actually used by DeMates in his confirmation experiment and in production. The steps taken in computing the CIQs for the special vectors are described in Table 14.17 through Table 14.24. The spreadsheet expressions used in the computations are shown at the bottom of each table.

Table 14.16 Special control factor vectors (SPVEC) chosen for evaluation of their strategic impact.

	Base	A	B	C	D	E	F	G
NameSpecVec	**0**	**11**	**21**	**31**	**41**	**51**	**61**	**71**
Trial 7	1	1	1	−1	−1	1	1	−1
Minimize 2nd order	1	1	1	−1	−1	−1	−1	−1
DeMates' choice	1	1	−1	1	−1	1	−1	−1
Minimize variance	1	1	1	−1	−1	−1	1	−1
Maximize variance	1	−1	−1	1	1	1	−1	1
Conf Exp.	1	1	−1	1	−1	−1	−1	−1

Table 14.17 Control factor coefficients (MEANijMj) for means as a function of the level of the signal factor.

		\multicolumn{8}{c}{Mj}

		−7	**−5**	**−3**	**−1**	**1**	**3**	**5**	**7**
Base	0	640.675	645.366	648.228	656.448	665.689	673.308	690.434	711.263
A	11	1.669	1.394	2.119	1.252	0.173	1.530	0.634	0.459
B	21	−0.878	−1.119	−0.847	−0.842	−0.273	0.355	0.531	−0.678
C	31	2.947	2.497	2.481	1.789	1.377	1.498	0.650	0.781
D	41	0.722	0.831	0.922	0.880	−0.208	−0.670	−0.312	0.700
E	51	−0.822	−1.078	−1.725	−1.664	−1.739	−1.202	−1.587	−1.191
F	61	0.825	1.178	1.234	1.505	0.708	0.286	0.803	1.303
G	71	−2.125	−1.950	−2.156	−2.070	−1.461	−1.589	−1.697	−1.325

=MMULT(XS,ActualAvg)

Table 14.18 Predicted sample means for Special Vectors (MeanSpecVec) as a function of signal factor setting.

	\multicolumn{8}{c}{Mj}

	−7	**−5**	**−3**	**−1**	**1**	**3**	**5**	**7**
Trial 7	639.9	644.4	647.8	656.1	664.9	675.0	692.2	711.0
Minimize 2nd order	639.9	644.2	648.7	656.4	666.9	676.9	693.7	710.8
DeMates' choice	645.9	649.2	652.0	658.4	666.7	676.8	690.8	711.3
Minimize variance	641.6	646.5	651.2	659.4	668.3	677.4	695.4	713.4
Maximize variance	639.8	644.2	645.2	653.5	663.1	669.2	685.5	709.1
Conf Exp.	647.6	651.4	655.4	661.7	670.2	679.2	694.0	713.7

=MMULT(SPVEC,MEANijMj)

Table 14.19 Control factor coefficients (XIijMj) for –10xlog variances as a function of the level of the signal factor.

		-7	-5	-3	-1	1	3	5	7
					Mj				
Base	0	0.279	-0.559	0.472	-2.242	-4.371	-2.694	-4.943	-4.766
A	11	4.979	4.742	5.024	4.661	4.037	7.178	5.663	4.072
B	21	1.060	-1.368	-1.274	-1.201	0.315	2.017	2.011	2.182
C	31	1.499	-0.176	-0.230	-1.420	-1.740	-1.050	-2.449	-1.177
D	41	-0.123	-1.622	-1.471	-1.441	0.058	-2.241	-0.942	1.121
E	51	1.904	1.107	0.790	0.597	-2.377	-0.496	-0.765	-0.416
F	61	1.365	1.061	0.785	1.790	3.369	1.068	-1.437	0.664
G	71	-2.213	-1.423	-0.959	-1.815	-2.918	-2.539	-0.812	0.007

=MMULT(XS,–10*LOG(ActualVar))

Table 14.20 Predicted sample variances for Special Vectors (VarSpecVec) as a function of signal factor settings.

	-7	-5	-3	-1	1	3	5	7
				Mj				
Trial 7	0.09	0.15	0.14	0.15	0.28	0.05	0.34	0.66
Minimize 2nd order	0.41	0.41	0.29	0.45	0.44	0.07	0.12	0.74
DeMates' choice	0.14	0.14	0.13	0.37	3.37	0.34	1.35	4.23
Minimize variance	0.22	0.25	0.21	0.20	0.09	0.04	0.24	0.55
Maximize variance	4.03	5.14	3.92	14.36	80.71	84.78	41.19	16.40
Conf Exp.	0.33	0.24	0.18	0.49	1.13	0.27	0.95	3.49

=10^(–MMULT(SPVEC,XIijMj)/10)

Table 14.21 Ideal intercepts, slopes, h and c_F for Special Vectors.

DesiredSlope
1

	REDINT	REDSLOPE	h	c_F
Trial 7	666.4	4.92	0.203	531.05
Minimize 2nd order	667.2	4.99	0.200	533.56
DeMates' choice	668.9	4.45	0.224	518.72
Minimize variance	669.2	4.97	0.201	534.43
Maximize variance	663.7	4.60	0.217	519.54
Conf Exp.	671.6	4.50	0.222	522.31

REDINT	=MMULT(SPVEC,REDMODEL)
REDSLOPE	*above expression for two columns*
h	=DesiredSlope/REDSLOPE
c_F	=(1-h)*REDINT

Table 14.22 Ideal average weights (IdealWeight) for Special Vectors as a function of signal factor setting.

				Mj				
	-7	-5	-3	-1	1	3	5	7
Trial 7	659.4	661.4	663.4	665.4	667.4	669.4	671.4	673.4
Minimize 2nd order	660.2	662.2	664.2	666.2	668.2	670.2	672.2	674.2
DeMates' choice	661.9	663.9	665.9	667.9	669.9	671.9	673.9	675.9
Minimize variance	662.2	664.2	666.2	668.2	670.2	672.2	674.2	676.2
Maximize variance	656.7	658.7	660.7	662.7	664.7	666.7	668.7	670.7
Conf Exp.	664.6	666.6	668.6	670.6	672.6	674.6	676.6	678.6
	=REDINT+REDSLOPE*Mj*h							

Table 14.23 Projected average weights (ProjWeight) for Special Vectors as a function of signal factor setting after introducing the adjustment factor.

				Mj				
	-7	-5	-3	-1	1	3	5	7
Trial 7	661.0	661.9	662.6	664.3	666.1	668.2	671.6	675.5
Minimize 2nd order	661.7	662.6	663.5	665.0	667.1	669.1	672.5	675.9
DeMates' choice	663.7	664.5	665.1	666.5	668.4	670.7	673.8	678.4
Minimize variance	663.6	664.6	665.5	667.2	669.0	670.8	674.4	678.1
Maximize variance	658.5	659.5	659.7	661.5	663.6	664.9	668.4	673.6
Conf Exp.	666.3	667.1	668.0	669.4	671.3	673.3	676.6	681.0
	=h*MeanSpecVec+CorFac							

Table 14.24 Projected CIQ for Special Vectors as a function of signal factor setting.

				Mj					Sum of
	-7	-5	-3	-1	1	3	5	7	losses
Trial 7	2.64	0.28	0.62	1.20	1.74	1.55	0.07	4.26	12.4
Minimize 2nd order	2.38	0.17	0.50	1.36	1.13	1.13	0.11	3.02	9.8
DeMates' choice	3.41	0.35	0.65	1.88	2.37	1.54	0.07	6.59	16.9
Minimize variance	2.10	0.21	0.38	0.93	1.36	1.77	0.08	3.65	10.5
Maximize variance	3.45	0.83	1.20	2.17	5.11	7.28	2.01	9.02	31.1
Conf Exp.	2.74	0.26	0.38	1.50	1.79	1.78	0.05	5.70	14.2
	=(IdealWeight–ProjWeight)^2+VarSpecVec*h^2								

14.4.4 CIQs for Special Vectors

The CIQs for the Special Vectors are determined by first computing two sets of coefficients for the control factors. One is the set of coefficients (MEANijMj) that measures the influence of the control factors on the means as measured across the range of the signal factor. The results are shown in Table 14.17. The predicted means for the Special Vectors

(MeanSpecVec) as a function of the signal factor are shown in Table 14.18. The spreadsheet expression for MeanSpecVec is shown at the bottom of Table 14.18.

The other is the set of coefficients (XIijMj) that measure the influence of the control factors on -10 times the log variances across the range of the signal factor. These results are shown in Table 14.19. The predicted variances (VarSpecVec) for the special vectors as a function of the signal factor are shown in Table 14.20. The expression for VarSpecVec is shown at the bottom of Table 14.20.

14.4.4.1 Ideal Response Behavior

The ideal response behavior for each Special Vector described by Equation (14.9), which has no quadratic or variance contributions, was computed using a reduced model having only the base and linear OP coefficients in Table 14.13 and Table 14.14, forming an 8×2 array named REDMODEL. The resulting intercepts and slopes, named REDINT and REDSLOPE, respectively, are shown in Table 14.21 along with the values computed for h and c_F. The equations used in the spreadsheet computations are shown at the bottom of Table 14.21. The desired slope, (DesiredSlope) shown at the top left of Table 14.21, was taken as unity, which means that a change of δM in adjustment factor should yield the same nominal change in weight, $\delta W = \delta M$. The resulting ideal average weights (IdealWeight) computed according to Equation (14.9) are shown in Table 14.22, the spreadsheet expression being listed at the bottom of Table 14.22.

14.4.4.2 Actual Response Behavior

The projected weights (ProjWeight) for the special vectors after the introduction of the adjustment factor are shown in Table 14.23 as a function of the signal factor. These weights were computed according to Equation (14.14). The spreadsheet expression is shown at the bottom of Table 14.23. Table 14.24 and Figure 14.4 show that the CIQ is least for the vector that minimized the second order coefficient but only slightly better than the vector that minimized variance, the two vectors differing only in the level of one factor, F(61). The major movements in the CIQ for the control factor settings in Figure 14.4 arise from the differences between the means, only a small amount coming from differences in variance. A monetary computation of the CIQ (value loss) requires that the coefficient k_S in Equation (14.13) be determined from a DV method survey in which the value of an imperfect control is evaluated against a perfect baseline. The predicted outcomes for means and variances are shown in Figure 14.5 and Figure 14.6, respectively, for the control factors that minimize second order and DeMates' choice. As the population statistics are unknown, it cannot be determined which of the two analyses give the better selection of the control factor levels for minimizing the CIQ. The EWE significance levels here were computed for the Xi coefficients in the respective SDWs; whereas, Miller and Wu used half-normal plots[3]. The trends found for the significance of the factors using the two approaches were very similar, but the analytical approach used here identified more factors as being significant.

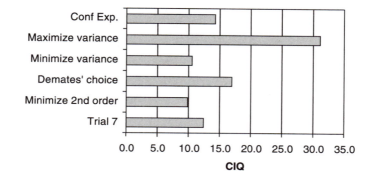

Figure 14.4 CIQ for special vectors from Table 14.24.

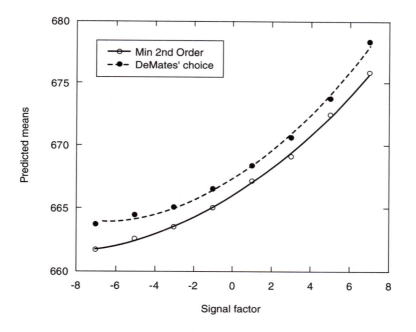

Figure 14.5 Predicted means as a function of the signal factor for two different choices of control factors.

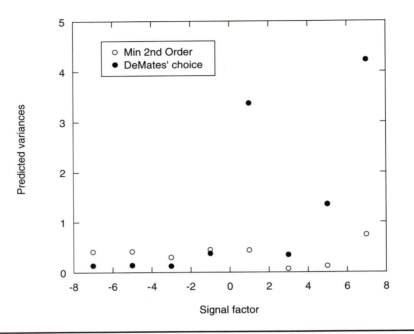

Figure 14.6 Predicted variances as a function of the signal factor for two different choices of control factors.

14.4.5 Strategic Significance

Monte Carlo simulation can be used to assess the strategic significance of the special vectors. The first step is to replace the mean values in Table 14.5 and the variances in Table 14.6 with Equations (4.12) and (5.17). The t and chi-square statistics are simulated over their ranges in standard fashion by using the RAND() function to select points off the respective cumulative distributions. Repeated simulations provide the distributions for the uncertainties in the population means and variances. The remaining computations from Table 14.17 through Table 14.24 are simply repeated for each of the simulations. The outcomes for 500 simulations are shown in Figure 14.7. The distributions are for the value improvement of the special vector that minimizes second order relative to three other special vectors as baselines. The difference, not surprisingly, between minimize second order and minimize variance is not significant. The other two are. The median values for the distributions are in agreement with the differences in the sum of losses shown in Table 14.24.

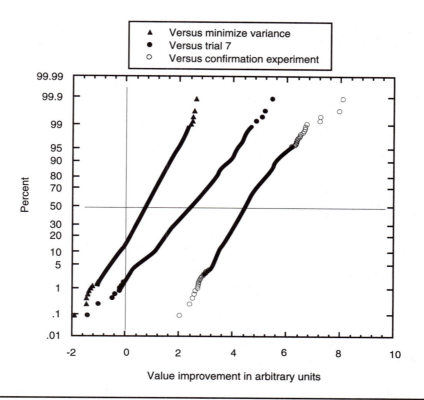

Figure 14.7   The relative value improvement forecast for the factors that minimize the second order contribution relative to three other special vectors.

14.5 SUMMARY

The 10 key steps in the Signal/Response analysis are summarized below:

Description
1. Choose signal factor and range for signal factor.
2. Select or generate the appropriate OP#SDW.
3. Select control factors and appropriate experimental design and SDW.
4. Run the experiment and compute the mean and variances for the response for each trial. Enter the results into the OP worksheet in the OP#SDW.
5. Copy the base OP coefficients and their respective sample variances and paste these values into Y and SVAR, respectively, in the SDW. Manually enter the number of replications for each trial.
6. Using new SDW files, repeat the above process for the linear and quadratic OP coefficients. This results in three separate SDWs. One for the base OP coefficients, one for the linear, and one for the quadratic.
7. Examine the outcomes for the lambda (or phi) coefficients and the Xi coefficients to discover which OP coefficients are most influential in a favorable manner for increasing the slope, reducing curvature, and reducing variance.
8. From the insight gained in Step 7, return to the OP#SDW and generate three sets of special vectors: the baseline set for trial 1, the set that minimizes variance, the set that minimizes curvature.
9. Compute the sum of losses for each. Examine the possibility of improving an outcome by considering changes in the factors where there is a difference between the special vector that minimizes second order and the one that minimizes variance.
10. With the best set of factor levels, perform a sensitivity analysis for those factors that affect cost to see if the benefit for changing the factor from baseline is greater than cost. Before this can be done, the losses need to be converted into dollar losses.

REFERENCES

1. M. S. Phadke. 1989. *Quality Engineering Using Robust Design.* New York: Prentice Hall, pp. 214–229.
2. J. DeMates. 1990. *Injection Molding Case Study.* Eighth Symposium on Taguchi Methods. Dearborn, MI: American Supplier Institute, pp. 313–331.
3. A. Miller and C. F. J. Wu. 1996. "Parameter Design for Signal-Response Systems: A Different Look at Taguchi's Dynamic Parameter Design," *Statistical Science* 11(2), pages 122–136.

15

Strategic Response Surface Maps

> *Insight: Response surfaces for the strategic financial metrics can be generated for continuous CTV attributes using a set of linked experiments.*

Key Topics

Central composite design	handling of noise factors
Box-Behnken design	propagation of variance
two-factor response surface	robust design using response surface methods

15.1 INTRODUCTION

The search for the best design is aided by the development of a response surface map (RSM) showing how the CTV attributes of the product at the system level vary as a function of several continuous subsystem or component variables. For strategic experimentation, the CTV attribute RSM needs to be transformed into strategic financial maps of value to the customer and projected cash flow to arrive at the best design solution from a business perspective.

A series of linked experiments are used to explore the RSM design space.[1] After each experiment, the results are analyzed to see which location appears most promising for centering the next experiment. The methodology has been highly developed for classical, physical experiments. Moreover, computational models are now being used in select industries to analyze the performance of complex products. This is now possible because the fidelity of transfer functions determined from computer models are capable of predicting accurately many aspects of the performance of automobiles, jet engines, and aircraft. As a result, more design iterations can be studied at less cost. This allows a wider range of design parameters to be evaluated and improves speed to market.

15.2 SPECIAL DESIGNS FOR RSM

The central composite design (CCD), shown graphically in Figure 15.1 for the case in which three control factors are being evaluated, is widely used for response surface maps. The open circle is the *central point* or baseline position for the start of the search. Surrounding the central point are eight *cube points* (filled circles), and six *star points,* on either side of the central point along each axis. All points have inverse symmetry through the origin. Of course, many other designs can and have been used to develop response surfaces. The Box-Behnken design (BBD) shown in Figure 15.2 is also popular.[2] It requires three or more main effects and is most helpful when a tighter space about the origin is to be explored. It has a central point surrounded by points on the edges of the cube or, for larger number of main effects, a hypercube. Three level OAs can also be used. Designs that fill space well, for example, Latin hypercube models are important to large computer-based design simulation experiments.[3]

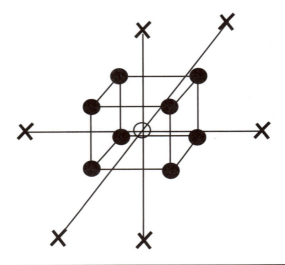

Figure 15.1   Graphical representation of a central composite design (CCD) for three control factors.

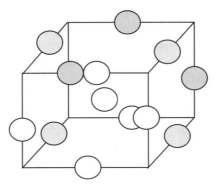

Figure 15.2   Box-Behnken design (BBD) for three main effects.

15.3 DEVELOPMENT OF A TWO-FACTOR RESPONSE SURFACE

The effort needed to develop a response surface increases as the number of control factors being investigated increases, but the process can be understood fully by considering only two control factors, A and B, which are taken to be component or subsystem attributes. The initial choices of units for the control factors are the standard ones such as horsepower, temperature, diameter, and so on. The range of numerical values chosen for A and B are shown in Table 15.1 for the initial screening experiment, which did not use the star points. For simplicity, the same range and values for the points were used for A and B. Once the points were specified in terms of their regular units, they were transformed into dimensionless, coded units. This provides a direct basis for comparing the relative importance of the factors.

The transformation of the regular units into coded units was made as follows: The coordinates for the central point given by $x_i(0) = 3$ in regular units for the first experiment were set equal to $X_i = 0$ in the coded units for each factor ($i = 1, 2$ for A and B, respectively). Next the cube points in regular units $x_i(1)$ were transformed to $X_i(1) = \pm 1$ in coded units, $X_i(1) = \left(x_i(1) - \mu_i(0)\right) / \left|\left(\mu_i(1) - \mu_i(0)\right)\right|$, where μ_i is the mean value for x_i. The individual parameters $x_i(q)$ can be noisy from process variation but are viewed, initially, as deterministic and equal to $\mu_i(q)$.

The design matrix shown inside the rectangular box in Table 15.2 for the initial screening experiment displays the coded units for the main effects represented by $X_1(q)$ and $X_2(q)$. The

Table 15.1   Regular and coded units for the two control factors being considered in the first experiment used for screening.

Regular units			
A	1.5	3	4.5
B	1.5	3	4.5
Coded units			
1	1	0	1
2	1	0	1

Table 15.2   Design matrix X and outcome vector Y for the initial screening experiment using only center and cube points.

Point type	A	B	Trial	0	A 1	B 2	AB 12	A^2 11	Y
cube	1.5	1.5	1	1	-1	-1	1	1	0.6656
cube	1.5	4.5	2	1	-1	1	-1	1	0.7969
cube	4.5	1.5	3	1	1	-1	-1	1	0.7969
cube	4.5	4.5	4	1	1	1	1	1	1.4906
center	3.0	3.0	5	1	0	0	0	0	1.1625
center	3.0	3.0	6	1	0	0	0	0	1.1625

regular units are shown under the columns labeled A and B on the left side of Table 15.2. The baseline row of a one followed by zeros indicates that it is a lambda design. Typically the central point is repeated several times to reduce the size of the element on the diagonal of the covariance matrix for the baseline coefficient. In the design, this trial is listed twice to generate the two replications, which is typical formatting for Level 1 problems.

Note that the double subscript index *ij* for main effects is not being used here to denote the coded, main effect variables as the problem involves continuous, differentiable variables. The interaction between the two design variables is represented by $X_{12}(q) = X_1(q)X_2(q)$ and the quadratic effect is represented by $X_{11}(q) = X_1(q)X_1(q)$. The only quadratic term taken is $X_{11}(q)$ because a separate column for $X_{22}(q) = X_2(q)X_2(q)$ would be identical for the screening experiment. The last column *Y* lists the outcomes. The outcome vector *Y* is taken to be a LIB system level attribute. It is a function of two lower-level design attributes (control factors), A and B.

The model for the system level outcomes Y in the initial screening experiment is written in terms of the coupling coefficients λ_i and λ_{ij}:

$$\hat{Y}(q) = \lambda_0 + \lambda_1 X_1(q) + \lambda_2 X_2(q) + \lambda_{12} X_{12}(q) + \lambda_{11} X_{11}(q) \tag{15.1}$$

The coefficients for the initial experiments listed in Table 15.3 were computed using the spreadsheet expression given by

$$LAM = MMULT(XS,Y)$$

The named array XS (not shown) is the solution matrix constructed from the design matrix in Table 15.2.

A simple graphical method, which consisted of plotting the outcomes *Y* versus the values for B as shown in Figure 15.3, was used to inspect the outcomes of the initial experiment. The values for both A and B are listed beside each point. The choice A = B = 4.5 is seen to be preferred to the other points for the LIB attribute. This choice is also supported by the fact that the coefficients for λ_1 and λ_2 are both positive and of the same size. However, by considering the outcomes directly as in Figure 15.3, the contributions from the 12 interaction and the quadratic term, 11, were automatically included.

Table 15.3 The λ coefficients (name array LAM) for the initial experiment.

ij	LAM
0	1.163
1	0.206
2	0.206
12	0.141
11	-0.225

Based upon the results shown in Figure 15.3, the follow-up experiment was centered on A = B = 4.5. As in the first experiment, the design matrix, solution matrix, outcomes, and diagonal of the covariance matrix were named X, XS, Y, and COV, respectively. Conversion of the added star points for the follow-up experiment from regular units $x_i(2)$ to the coded units is shown in Table 15.4 using the relationship

$$X_i(2) = (x_i(2) - \mu_i(0)) / |(\mu_i(1) - \mu_i(0))|$$

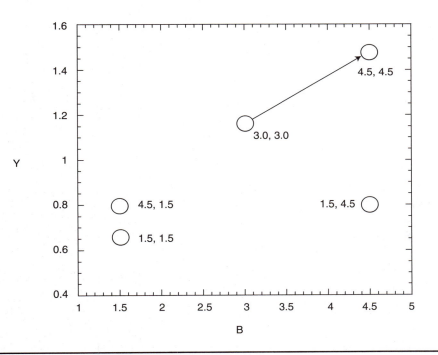

Figure 15.3 Plot of the LIB outcomes computed from the initial experiment.

Table 15.4 Regular and coded units for the two control factors being considered in the second experiment using the full set of points for the central composite design. Name wM is the number of main effects being considered.

		Regular units		Coded units	
		A	**B**	**A**	**B**
wM					
2	Center point	4.50	4.50	0.000	0.000
# Main Effects	Cube point	4.00	4.00	1.000	1.000
	Cube point	4.00	5.00	1.000	-1.000
	Cube point	5.00	4.00	-1.000	1.000
	Cube point	5.00	5.00	-1.000	-1.000
	Star point	3.79	4.50	1.414	0.000
	Star point	4.50	3.79	0.000	1.414
	Star point	5.21	4.50	-1.414	0.000
	Star point	4.50	5.21	0.000	-1.414

The rule of thumb is to place the star points in coded units on a hypersphere of radius $\alpha = \sqrt{w_M}$, where w_M is the number of main effects. As $w_M = 2$ for this problem, the star points are located at $\pm\sqrt{2}$. The second experiment was analyzed using a CCD SDW, and the results for the Design and Outcomes worksheet are shown in Table 15.5. The addition of the star points allows the lambda coefficients for the quadratic terms 11 and 22 to be independently estimated using the model

$$\hat{Y}(q) = \lambda_0 + \lambda_1 X_1(q) + \lambda_2 X_2(q) + \lambda_{12} X_{12}(q) + \lambda_{11} X_{11}(q) + \lambda_{22} X_{22}(q) \tag{15.2}$$

The coefficients in Table 15.6 were solved for in the standard manner using the spreadsheet expression

$$LAM = MMULT(XS, Y)$$

Table 15.5 Design matrix (X) and replications for second experiment using center, cube, and star points. The solution matrix (XS) and the diagonal of the covariance matrix (COV) are also shown.

Trial	Base 0	A 1	B 2	AB 12	A^2 11	B^2 22		REPLICATIONS 1	2	3	4
1	1	0.0000	0.0000	0	0	0		1.491	1.491	1.491	1.491
2	1	1.0000	1.0000	1	1	1		1.563			
3	1	1.0000	-1.0000	-1	1	1		1.450			
4	1	-1.0000	1.0000	-1	1	1		1.450			
5	1	-1.0000	-1.0000	1	1	1		1.400			
6	1	1.4142	0.0000	0	2	0		1.523			
7	1	0.0000	1.4142	0	0	2		1.523			
8	1	-1.4142	0.0000	0	2	0		1.408			
9	1	0.0000	-1.4142	0	0	2		1.408			

		1	2	3	4	5	6	7	8	9	COV
Base	0	1.000	0.000	0.000	0.000	0.000	0.000	0.000	0.000	0.000	1.000
A	1	0.000	0.125	0.125	-0.125	-0.125	0.177	0.000	-0.177	0.000	0.125
B	2	0.000	0.125	-0.125	0.125	-0.125	0.000	0.177	0.000	-0.177	0.125
AB	12	0.000	0.250	-0.250	-0.250	0.250	0.000	0.000	0.000	0.000	0.250
A^2	11	-0.500	0.062	0.062	0.062	0.062	0.188	-0.062	0.188	-0.062	0.344
B^2	22	-0.500	0.062	0.062	0.062	0.062	-0.063	0.188	-0.063	0.188	0.344

Table 15.6 The new λ coefficients (LAM) computed from the second experiment.

		LAM
Base	0	1.4906
A	1	0.0406
B	2	0.0406
AB	12	0.0156
A^2	11	-0.0125
B^2	22	-0.0125

The solution matrix in Table 15.5 does not exhibit the balanced property of having a negative element of the same absolute value for every positive element, which means that the *F* test for the significance of the individual factors on variance would be approximate, if used. Of course for this problem, there is only one replication per trial beyond trial 1, which means that the influence of the factors on variance cannot be determined. The response for the system level attribute *Y* was plotted as a function of A and B, as a surface in Figure 15.4 and as a contour plot in Figure 15.5, using the spreadsheet's charting capabilities.

The response surface shows that a maximum in *Y* exists near but above A = B = 5.21. In other words, a limit exists on *Y* with the present technology. At this stage, a third experiment using a central composite design centered about A = B = 5.5 could be run to better identify the location of the maximum point. Once located, the flatness of the response surface makes *Y* insensitive to minor production variations in A and B. If A and B were set to yield the maximum in *Y*, advantage could be taken of the nonlinear response to reduce variation similar to what was discussed for the dependence of the strength of the shear pin on heat treat temperature in Chapter 5.

However, the strategic target for A and B is the location where value *V*(*Y*) minus variable cost *C*(*Y*) is at a maximum, assuming that the investment level is independent of the values for A and B over the ranges shown and ignoring variation for the moment. The search for the target for this problem is shown in Figure 15.6, where it is seen to be well off the point where *Y* is a maximum. The expressions and coefficients used for value and cost were

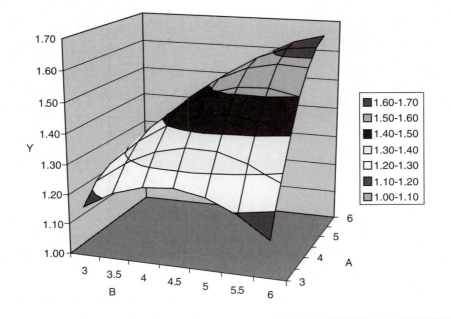

Figure 15.4 Three dimensional representation of the response surface as determined from the second experiment.

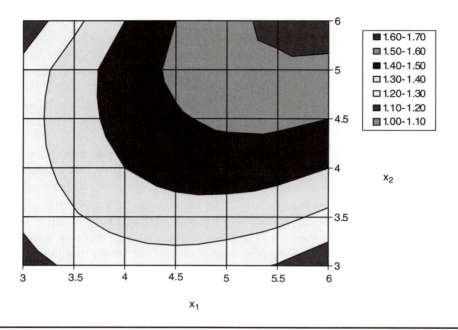

Figure 15.5 Contour representation of the response surface for the second experiment.

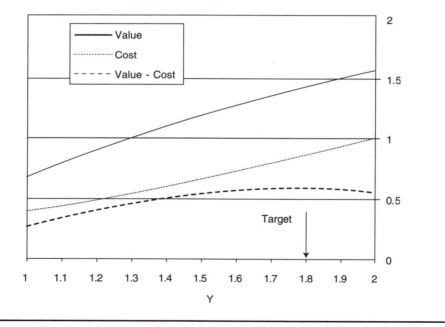

Figure 15.6 Value, variable cost, and value minus cost as a function of the system level attribute, Y.

$$\text{Value} = ((gI–gC)^2–(Y\_2–gI)^2)/((gI–gC)^2–(gI–g0)^2)$$

$$\text{Cost} = c0+cc*Y\_2^2$$

$$g0 = 1.3 \qquad c0 = 0.2$$

$$gI = 3.0 \qquad cc = 0.2$$

$$gC = 0.5$$

Manufacturing variations leading to control factor variance will reduce value and move the position for the target toward the point where *Y* is a maximum. The procedure for finding the target when variation is present is described in what follows.

15.4 HANDLING OF NOISE FACTORS IN RSM

Two different views exist for how to best assess the effects of noise.[4,5,6] As discussed in Section 5.5.3, one is Taguchi's innovative and very practical idea of introducing noise into the experiments in a controlled manner using a second orthogonal array (the so-called outer array or crossed array) to set the sequence of noise levels to be evaluated for each trial. However, the noise factors can also be treated as an additional set of control factors and folded into the design matrix. When this is done, the influence of the control factors on noise is determined from the coefficients for the interactions between the control and noise factors. When the noise factors are not folded into the design array, the influence of the control factors *ij* on noise is expressed by the ξ_{ij} coefficients, as discussed in Chapter 9.

The overarching question on completing a strategic experiment is "Should a recommendation be made to replace the current baseline product with an alternative design that may require a sizeable investment and an increase in variable cost?" In answering this question, the degree of confidence that the proposed design change has in meeting the desired strategic objective needs to be assessed. Simply put, the computed confidence level for obtaining a specific level of cash flow will be overly optimistic for the noisy production environment if the noise factors have been folded into the design as additional main effects.

15.5 MODELING THE MEAN AND VARIANCE IN RSM

15.5.1 Propagation of Variance

Consider the following problem: You have two variables, A and B, and wish to perform a strategic experiment to determine their targets. An excellent computer model exists that links the two variables to the system level attribute, Y, of interest to the customer. The plan is to develop a RSM for *Y* and convert it to a strategic RSM for $V(\mu, \sigma^2)$ in the form given by Equation (5.2) where μ and σ^2, are the population mean and variance of the system-level attribute, *Y*, respectively. This represents a *propagation of variance* (POV) method, in that it expands *Y* and its variance about the central point as a Taylor series expressed in terms of the differentials δx_i of the continuous, uncoded variables x_i. The RSM for variance is analogous to the *propagation of error* (POE) approach, in which the standard deviation is considered instead of variance. The variance plot is chosen here because it is the fundamental property related to value in strategic experimentation.

When the factors are statistically independent, the variance for two noisy main effects noted as $i = 1,2$ for A and B, respectively, is given by the approximation

$$\sigma^2(x_1, x_2) \cong \left[\frac{\lambda_1}{|\mu_1(1) - \mu_1(0)|} + \frac{[x_2 - \mu_2(0)]\lambda_{12}}{|\mu_2(1) - \mu_2(0)||\mu_1(1) - \mu_1(0)|} + \frac{2[x_1 - \mu_1(0)]\lambda_{11}}{|\mu_1(1) - \mu_1(0)|^2} \right]^2 \sigma_1^2 +$$

$$\left[\frac{\lambda_2}{|\mu_2(1) - \mu_2(0)|} + \frac{[x_1 - \mu_1(0)]\lambda_{12}}{|\mu_2(1) - \mu_2(0)||\mu_1(1) - \mu_1(0)|} + \frac{2[x_2 - \mu_2(0)]\lambda_{22}}{|\mu_2(1) - \mu_2(0)|^2} \right]^2 \sigma_2^2 + \sigma_0^2$$

(15.3)

where σ_1^2 and σ_2^2 are the population variances of A and B, respectively. The core variance is given by σ_0^2, which includes random noise from other sources and model error. Generalization of Equation (15.3) to more factors can be done by inspection. The three population variances are assumed known from prior studies of the capability of the manufacturing processes. When the expected value of Equation (15.2) is taken to compute the population mean, it is given by

$$\mu(x_1, x_2) = \lambda_0 + \lambda_1 \left[\frac{x_1 - \mu_1(0)}{|\mu_1(1) - \mu_1(0)|} \right] + \lambda_2 \left[\frac{x_2 - \mu_2(0)}{|\mu_2(1) - \mu_2(0)|} \right]$$

$$+ \lambda_{12} \left[\frac{x_1 - \mu_1(0)}{|\mu_1(1) - \mu_1(0)|} \right] \left[\frac{x_2 - \mu_2(0)}{|\mu_2(1) - \mu_2(0)|} \right]$$

(15.4)

$$+ \lambda_{11} \left[\frac{[x_1 - \mu_1(0)]^2 + \sigma_1^2}{|\mu_1(1) - \mu_1(0)|^2} \right] + \lambda_{22} \left[\frac{[x_2 - \mu_2(0)]^2 + \sigma_2^2}{|\mu_2(1) - \mu_2(0)|^2} \right]$$

Note, because of the quadratic terms $X_{ii}(q)$ in Equation (15.2), the variances of the two control factors also contribute uniformly to the mean across the domain and cause an increase or decrease, depending upon the signs of the λ coefficients.

The results for variance in Equation (15.3) and for the mean in Equation (15.4) are then substituted into the expression for $V(\mu, \sigma^2)$, which can be plotted across the domain to examine the dependence of value on the attributes. The λ coefficients deemed not significant can be eliminated from the model before generating the plot of the $V(\mu, \sigma^2)$ response surface. A variable cost response surface also exists, and it should be subtracted from the value curve to determine the target specifications for the factors.

The CCD used is described in Table 15.7. The problem is assumed to be of the NIB2 type having no scaling factor to move the attribute to the ideal position. The lambda coefficients are shown to the right of the design matrix, the model being exact in that there is no lack of

Table 15.7 CCD design matrix, replications, solution matrix, diagonal of covariance matrix, and lambda coefficients.

Trial	Base 0	A 1	B 2	AB 12	A^2 11	B^2 22	REPLICATIONS 1	2	3	4
1	1	0.0000	0.0000	0	0	0	20.00	20	20	20
2	1	1.0000	1.0000	1	1	1	22.20			
3	1	1.0000	-1.0000	-1	1	1	19.80			
4	1	-1.0000	1.0000	-1	1	1	19.80			
5	1	-1.0000	-1.0000	1	1	1	14.20			
6	1	1.4142	0.0000	0	2	0	21.83			
7	1	0.0000	1.4142	0	0	2	21.83			
8	1	-1.4142	0.0000	0	2	0	16.17			
9	1	0.0000	-1.4142	0	0	2	16.17			

		1	2	3	4	5	6	7	8	9	COV	LAM
Base	0	1.000	0.000	0.000	0.000	0.000	0.000	0.000	0.000	0.000	1.000	20.0
A	1	0.000	0.125	0.125	-0.125	-0.125	0.177	0.000	-0.177	0.000	0.125	2.0
B	2	0.000	0.125	-0.125	0.125	-0.125	0.000	0.177	0.000	-0.177	0.125	2.0
AB	12	0.000	0.250	-0.250	-0.250	0.250	0.000	0.000	0.000	0.000	0.250	-0.8
A^2	11	-0.500	0.062	0.062	0.062	0.062	0.188	-0.062	0.188	-0.062	0.344	-0.5
B^2	22	-0.500	0.062	0.062	0.062	0.062	-0.063	0.188	-0.063	0.188	0.344	-0.5

Table 15.8 Variances and value curve parameters.

VAR0	VAR1	VAR2		
0	0.3	0.2		
V0	gl	gC	g0	K
100	20	10	18	1.042
	K	$=V0/((gl-gC)^2-(gl-g0)^2)$		

fit error making the base variance $\sigma_0^2 = 0$. Replications are shown as equal to emphasize this fact but only one computation needs to be run. The variances used for σ_0^2, σ_1^2, and σ_2^2 are shown in Table 15.8 (names VAR0, VAR1, and VAR2) along with the parameters defining the value curve for this simulated problem. The exponential weighting coefficient was taken to be unity for simplicity.

The means computed across the domain for the system-level attribute, Y, are shown in Table 15.9. The row headings are in regular units for x_2 with the coded units listed in bold below them. The column index to the left lists the regular units for x_1 with its coded units in bold to the right. The expression used for the computation in cell AL23, shown at the bottom of the table, was dragged down and across to generate the array. The lambda coefficients λ_0, λ_1, and so on were normalized by the length and the length squared metrics to form the coefficients B_0, B_1, and so on for ease in computing the variance and mean, Equations (15.3) and (15.4) respectively, across the domain. The variances computed from Equation (15.3) are shown in Table 15.10 and the values to the customer computed from Equation (5.5) are shown in Table 15.11. The expressions used are shown at the bottom of the two tables. The structure of the computations in Table 15.9 can be copied directly into the contour and surface plotting routines in the spreadsheet.

Table 15.9 The means computed across the domain of interest for the system level attribute *Y*.

	AJ	AK	AL	AM	AN	AO	AP	AQ	AR	AS	AT
21			*3.5*	*3.75*	*4*	*4.25*	*4.5*	*4.75*	*5*	*5.25*	*5.5*
22		**CODED**	**-1**	**-0.75**	**-0.5**	**-0.25**	**0**	**0.25**	**0.5**	**0.75**	**1**
23	*3.5*	**-1**	3.80	6.48	8.90	11.08	13.00	14.68	16.10	17.28	18.20
24	*3.6*	**-0.9**	4.90	7.50	9.84	11.94	13.78	15.38	16.72	17.82	18.66
25	*3.7*	**-0.8**	5.96	8.48	10.74	12.76	14.52	16.04	17.30	18.32	19.08
26	*3.8*	**-0.7**	6.98	9.42	11.60	13.54	15.22	16.66	17.84	18.78	19.46
27	*3.9*	**-0.6**	7.96	10.32	12.42	14.28	15.88	17.24	18.34	19.20	19.80
28	*4*	**-0.5**	8.90	11.18	13.20	14.98	16.50	17.78	18.80	19.58	20.10
29	*4.1*	**-0.4**	9.80	12.00	13.94	15.64	17.08	18.28	19.22	19.92	20.36
30	*4.2*	**-0.3**	10.66	12.78	14.64	16.26	17.62	18.74	19.60	20.22	20.58
31	*4.3*	**-0.2**	11.48	13.52	15.30	16.84	18.12	19.16	19.94	20.48	20.76
32	*4.4*	**-0.1**	12.26	14.22	15.92	17.38	18.58	19.54	20.24	20.70	20.90
33	*4.5*	**0**	13.00	14.88	16.50	17.88	19.00	19.88	20.50	20.88	21.00
34	*4.6*	**0.1**	13.70	15.50	17.04	18.34	19.38	20.18	20.72	21.02	21.06
35	*4.7*	**0.2**	14.36	16.08	17.54	18.76	19.72	20.44	20.90	21.12	21.08
36	*4.8*	**0.3**	14.98	16.62	18.00	19.14	20.02	20.66	21.04	21.18	21.06
37	*4.9*	**0.4**	15.56	17.12	18.42	19.48	20.28	20.84	21.14	21.20	21.00
38	*5*	**0.5**	16.10	17.58	18.80	19.78	20.50	20.98	21.20	21.18	20.90
39	*5.1*	**0.6**	16.60	18.00	19.14	20.04	20.68	21.08	21.22	21.12	20.76
40	*5.2*	**0.7**	17.06	18.38	19.44	20.26	20.82	21.14	21.20	21.02	20.58
41	*5.3*	**0.8**	17.48	18.72	19.70	20.44	20.92	21.16	21.14	20.88	20.36
42	*5.4*	**0.9**	17.86	19.02	19.92	20.58	20.98	21.14	21.04	20.70	20.10
43	*5.5*	**1**	18.20	19.28	20.10	20.68	21.00	21.08	20.90	20.48	19.80
44		Cell AL23	=B_0+$AK23*B_1+AL$22*B_2+$AK23*AL$22*B_12+								
45			($AK23^2+VAR1)*B_11+(AL$22^2+VAR2)*B_22								

Table 15.10 Variance computed across the domain of interest for the system level attribute.

	AJ	AK	AL	AM	AN	AO	AP	AQ	AR	AS	AT
47											
48		CODED	3.5	3.75	4	4.25	4.5	4.75	5	5.25	5.5
			-1	-0.75	-0.5	-0.25	0	0.25	0.5	0.75	1
49	3.5	-1	62.72	53.26	44.58	36.68	29.57	23.24	17.7	12.94	8.96
50	3.6	-0.9	58.667	49.52	41.16	33.59	26.79	20.79	15.56	11.12	7.467
51	3.7	-0.8	54.751	45.93	37.89	30.63	24.16	18.47	13.57	9.447	6.111
52	3.8	-0.7	50.972	42.47	34.75	27.81	21.66	16.29	11.71	7.908	4.892
53	3.9	-0.6	47.329	39.15	31.75	25.13	19.30	14.25	9.985	6.505	3.809
54	4	-0.5	43.824	35.96	28.88	22.58	17.07	12.34	8.4	5.24	2.864
55	4.1	-0.4	40.456	32.91	26.15	20.18	14.98	10.58	6.952	4.112	2.056
56	4.2	-0.3	37.224	30	23.56	17.9	13.03	8.944	5.64	3.12	1.384
57	4.3	-0.2	34.13	27.23	21.11	15.77	11.22	7.45	4.466	2.266	0.85
58	4.4	-0.1	31.172	24.59	18.79	13.77	9.54	6.092	3.428	1.548	0.452
59	4.5	0	28.352	22.09	16.61	11.91	8	4.872	2.528	0.968	0.192
60	4.6	0.1	25.668	19.72	14.56	10.19	6.596	3.788	1.764	0.524	0.068
61	4.7	0.2	23.122	17.5	12.66	8.602	5.33	2.842	1.138	0.218	0.082
62	4.8	0.3	20.712	15.41	10.89	7.152	4.2	2.032	0.648	0.048	0.232
63	4.9	0.4	18.44	13.46	9.256	5.84	3.208	1.36	0.296	0.016	0.52
64	5	0.5	16.304	11.64	7.76	4.664	2.352	0.824	0.08	0.12	0.944
65	5.1	0.6	14.305	9.961	6.401	3.625	1.633	0.425	0.001	0.361	1.505
66	5.2	0.7	12.444	8.42	5.18	2.724	1.052	0.164	0.06	0.74	2.204
67	5.3	0.8	10.719	7.0147	4.095	1.959	0.607	0.039	0.255	1.255	3.039
68	5.4	0.9	9.1309	5.75	3.147	1.331	0.299	0.051	0.587	1.907	4.011
69	5.5	1	7.68	4.616	2.336	0.84	0.128	0.2	1.056	2.696	5.12
70		Cell AL49	=((B_1+AL\$48*B_12+2*\$AK49*B_11)^2)*VAR1+								
71			((B_2+\$AK49*B_12+2*AL\$48*B_22)^2)*VAR2+VAR0								

Table 15.11 Value to the customer across the domain of interest.

	AX	AY	AZ	BA	BB	BC	BD	BE	BF	BG	BH
47			3.5	3.75	4	4.25	4.5	4.75	5	5.25	5.5
48		CODED	-1	-0.75	-0.5	-0.25	0	0.25	0.5	0.75	1
49	3.5	-1	-234.5	-141.9	-70.6	-17.02	22.33	50.42	69.89	82.96	91.46
50	3.6	-0.9	-194.5	-110.3	-46.24	1.43	35.95	60.23	76.75	87.61	94.52
51	3.7	-0.8	-158.2	-82.0	-24.62	17.58	47.72	68.55	82.44	91.37	96.92
52	3.8	-0.7	-125.5	-56.78	-5.53	31.66	57.80	75.54	87.11	94.37	98.77
53	3.9	-0.6	-96.1	-34.32	11.25	43.85	66.38	81.36	90.89	96.72	100.16
54	4	-0.5	-69.8	-14.42	25.92	54.34	73.62	86.15	93.92	98.52	101.17
55	4.1	-0.4	-46.35	3.13	38.67	63.30	79.68	90.05	96.29	99.88	101.89
56	4.2	-0.3	-25.48	18.54	49.70	70.91	84.69	93.18	98.12	100.87	102.37
57	4.3	-0.2	-7.00	32.00	59.17	77.31	88.80	95.66	99.51	101.57	102.68
58	4.4	-0.1	9.29	43.69	67.26	82.64	92.13	97.60	100.54	102.05	102.85
59	4.5	0	23.59	53.80	74.11	87.05	94.79	99.08	101.27	102.36	102.93
60	4.6	0.1	36.08	62.48	79.87	90.67	96.89	100.19	101.79	102.55	102.92
61	4.7	0.2	46.95	69.89	84.68	93.59	98.53	101.01	102.14	102.64	102.87
62	4.8	0.3	56.34	76.18	88.66	95.94	99.79	101.60	102.36	102.68	102.75
63	4.9	0.4	64.42	81.48	91.92	97.80	100.74	102.02	102.50	102.66	102.58
64	5	0.5	71.34	85.92	94.58	99.26	101.46	102.32	102.58	102.60	102.34
65	5.1	0.6	77.22	89.60	96.73	100.39	101.98	102.52	102.61	102.50	102.00
66	5.2	0.7	82.20	92.65	98.44	101.26	102.37	102.65	102.60	102.32	101.52
67	5.3	0.8	86.39	95.14	99.81	101.93	102.65	102.74	102.55	102.06	100.87
68	5.4	0.9	89.88	97.17	100.88	102.44	102.85	102.77	102.43	101.68	99.98
69	5.5	1	92.79	98.81	101.72	102.82	102.99	102.75	102.22	101.12	98.79
70		Cell AZ49	=K*((gl-gC)^2-(gl-AL23)^2-AL49)								

Contour plots of the system-level attribute, its variance, and the resulting value to the customer are shown in Figure 15.7, Figure 15.8, and Figure 15.9, respectively. The presence of nonzero variance reduces the value of Y in the domain from 22.1 to 21.22. If finer detail is desired for picking off the point for the maximum in customer value, sections can be plotted from the data in Table 15.11, as shown in Figure 15.10. The peak in Figure 15.10 is slightly higher for the $x_2 = 5.5$ slice and is located around $x_1 = 4.5$. The target, of course, is not controlled by the position where value is a maximum but where value minus cost is at a maximum, assuming investment is not a function of x_1 and x_2.

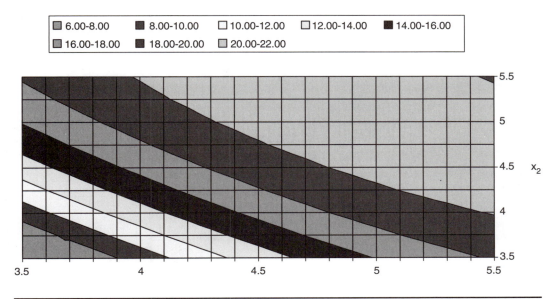

| ■ 6.00-8.00 | ■ 8.00-10.00 | □ 10.00-12.00 | □ 12.00-14.00 | ■ 14.00-16.00 |
| ■ 16.00-18.00 | ■ 18.00-20.00 | □ 20.00-22.00 | | |

Figure 15.7 Contour plot of the system-level attribute, *Y*.

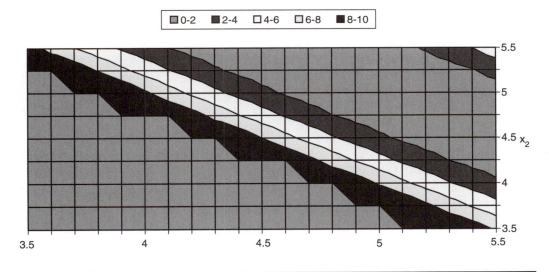

| ■ 0-2 | ■ 2-4 | □ 4-6 | □ 6-8 | ■ 8-10 |

Figure 15.8 Contour plot of variance of *Y* across the domain of interest.

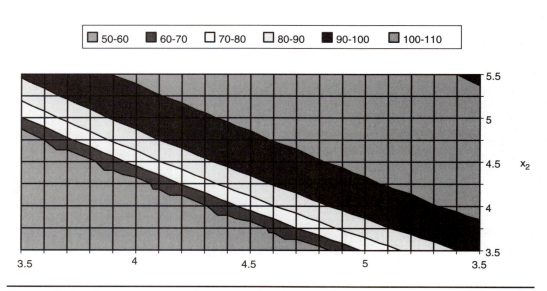

Figure 15.9 Contour plot of value across the domain of interest.

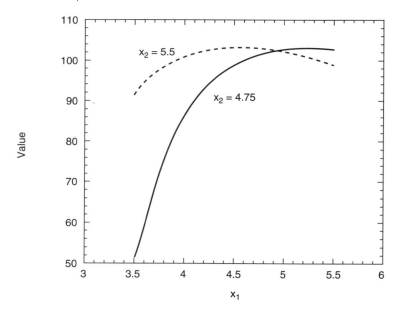

Figure 15.10 Plot of value versus x_1 across two sections, $x_2 = 4.75$ and $x_2 = 5.5$, for improved identification of the point of maximum value.

15.5.2 Robust Design Using RSM

A different situation arises when the control factors are not noisy but uncontrollable noise exists in production from other sources, for example from fluctuations in temperature, tool wear, and variations in material properties. These noise factors can be introduced into an RSM experiment as elements in the noise array through physical means or through the use of computer simulation. In this manner, Taguchi's robust design method becomes the basis for the RSM experiment. The major difference between this approach and the POV just described is that replications are made at each point of the CCD as dictated by the noise array. This also lessens the need to increase the number of replications for the baseline (center point) trial versus any other point. The problem reduces to one of the types considered in Chapter 10, 12, or 13, depending upon the nature of the distribution except for the fact that the RSM attributes are continuous.

An example of the design and the solution array for a robust RSM experiment based upon a two-main-effect CCD is shown in Table 15.12 Four replications per trial were simulated as shown in Table 15.13 The average and sample variance for the trials were computed as Y and SVAR, respectively. The lambda and XI coefficients are shown in Table 15.14 along with their single-tail PWEs computed, respectively, from Satterthwaite's approximate *t*-test and the *F* test method. The population values for the lambda and Xi coefficients are listed in Table 15.15.

The solution matrix in Table 15.12 is seen to be unbalanced for factors 11 and 22, so the *F* test for the XI coefficients is only approximate. The question is how approximate? The answer to this question was obtained using Monte Carlo simulation as follows:

1. The population means (YPOP) and standard deviations (SDPOP) were generated from the lambda (LAMPOP) and Xi (XIPOP) coefficients chosen for the populations listed in Table 15.15.

2. Five random samples per trial were taken from normal populations for the trials using the Excel function = NORMINV(RAND(),YPOP,SDPOP). The sample means and the variances for each trial were recorded, and XI coefficients and their PWE were computed for each factor.

3. A total of 2000 simulations were run.

4. For each simulation, the XI coefficients were computed, saved, and plotted on separate normal probability plots.

5. If the individual *F* test PWE is robust with respect to the solution matrix being unbalanced, the percentages given by the intercepts for the XI coefficients on the normal probability plots should compare favorably with the PWE values computed from the population coefficients.

The normal probability plots of XI1 and XI22 are shown in Figure 15.11 and Figure 15.12, respectively, with the horizontal lines pointing to the PWE intercepts computed from the coefficients for the populations given in Table 15.15. There is excellent agreement for XI1, which had a balanced row. This is expected because its *F* test PWE is exact. The intercept PWE of 5.8% for XI22 versus its *F* test value of 5.0%, although not exact, suggests

Table 15.12 Design matrix, solution matrix, and diagonal of the covariance matrix for the CCD design having two main effects.

Trial	Base 0	A 1	B 2	AB 12	A^2 11	B^2 22
1	1	0.0000	0.0000	0	0	0
2	1	1.0000	1.0000	1	1	1
3	1	1.0000	-1.0000	-1	1	1
4	1	-1.0000	1.0000	-1	1	1
5	1	-1.0000	-1.0000	1	1	1
6	1	1.4142	0.0000	0	2	0
7	1	0.0000	1.4142	0	0	2
8	1	-1.4142	0.0000	0	2	0
9	1	0.0000	-1.4142	0	0	2

		1	2	3	4	5	6	7	8	9	COV
Base	0	1.000	0.000	0.000	0.000	0.000	0.000	0.000	0.000	0.000	1.000
A	1	0.000	0.125	0.125	-0.125	-0.125	0.177	0.000	-0.177	0.000	0.125
B	2	0.000	0.125	-0.125	0.125	-0.125	0.000	0.177	0.000	-0.177	0.125
AB	12	0.000	0.250	-0.250	-0.250	0.250	0.000	0.000	0.000	0.000	0.250
A^2	11	-0.500	0.062	0.062	0.062	0.062	0.188	-0.062	0.188	-0.062	0.344
B^2	22	-0.500	0.062	0.062	0.062	0.062	-0.063	0.188	-0.063	0.188	0.344

Table 15.13 Replications, number of replications, average system-level attribute, and sample variance for each trial for the CCD design in Table 15.12.

						z 9	w 6		
REPLICATIONS									
1	2	3	4	5 6 7 8 9 10		n	Trials	Y	
20.72	20.03	19.50	18.96			4	1	19.80	
22.86	23.11	23.58	21.78			4	2	22.83	
19.75	19.60	19.59	19.91			4	3	19.71	
19.38	19.97	20.34	19.74			4	4	19.86	
14.17	14.05	14.14	14.23			4	5	14.15	
21.89	22.60	22.45	21.68			4	6	22.16	
22.48	22.57	22.38	22.08			4	7	22.38	
15.94	16.19	16.10	16.30			4	8	16.13	
16.31	16.18	16.47	15.95			4	9	16.23	

Trials	SVAR
1	0.566
2	0.579
3	0.023
4	0.161
5	0.006
6	0.194
7	0.046
8	0.024
9	0.049

Table 15.14 Lambda and XI coefficients and their single tail PWE.

		LAM	SDij	DFij	t	PWE
Base	**0**	19.8005	0.3762	3.0000	52.6310	7.6E-06
A	**1**	2.1325	0.0686	8.4632	31.0846	6.2E-10
B	**2**	2.1905	0.0612	7.2724	35.7768	1.7E-09
AB	**12**	-0.6487	0.1097	4.9135	-5.9146	0.002
A^2	**11**	-0.3494	0.1953	3.4764	-1.7891	0.086
B^2	**22**	-0.2711	0.1928	3.3107	-1.4059	0.127
LAM	=MMULT(XS,Y)					
SDij	=SQRT(MMULT(XS^2,SVAR/n))					
DFij	=SDij^4/MMULT(XS^4,(SVAR/n)^2/(n-1))					
t	=LAM/SDij					
PWE	=TDIST(ABS(t),DFij,1)					

		XI	Gij	PWE
Base	**0**	2.471	0.349	0.263
A	**1**	-3.045	-1.218	0.023
B	**2**	-3.471	-1.389	0.013
AB	**12**	0.078	0.022	0.484
A^2	**11**	4.548	1.097	0.033
B^2	**22**	5.316	1.282	0.018
XI	=MMULT(XS,-10*LOG(SVAR))			
Gij	=XI/SQRT(50*COV)			
PWE	=FDIST(10^ABS(Gij),n-1,n-1)			

Table 15.15 Population values for the lambda and Xi coefficients.

Factor	LAMPOP	XIPOP
0	20	1
1	2	− 4
2	2	− 4
12	− 0.8	0
11	− 0.5	4
22	− 0.5	4

that the test provides a useful PWE approximation for coefficients having unbalanced rows in the solution matrix.

The computations of the projections for the sample means for Y and its sample variance, s_Y^2, across the domain are shown in Table 15.16 and Table 15.17, respectively. Their respective contour plots are shown in Figure 15.13 and Figure 15.14. The outcomes Y and its variance can be entered into the appropriate expression for $V(Y, s_Y^2)$. Of course, variable cost across the domain needs to be subtracted from the value function to determine the tar-

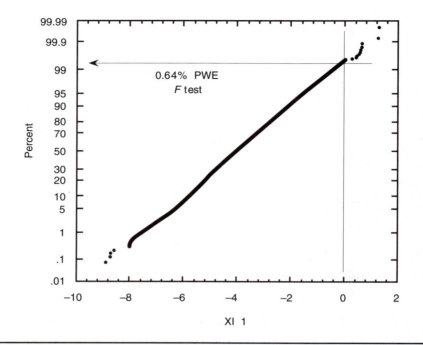

Figure 15.11 Normal probability plot of Monte Carlo simulations for factor XI1 and a comparison of its PWE given by the independent *F* test method using the population XI1 from Table 15.15.

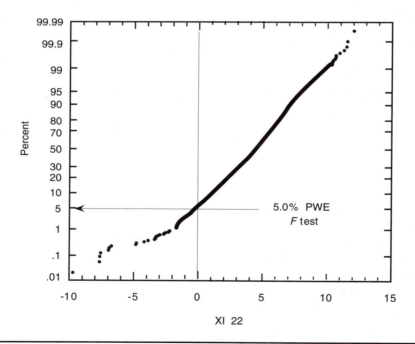

Figure 15.12 Normal probability plot of Monte Carlo simulations for factor XI22 and a comparison of its PWE with the PWE given by the independent *F* test method using the population XI22 from Table 15.15.

Table 15.16 Computation of the system-level attribute Y across the domain of interest.

	AJ	AK	AL	AM	AN	AO	AP	AQ	AR	AS	AT
21			*3.5*	*3.75*	*4*	*4.25*	*4.5*	*4.75*	*5*	*5.25*	*5.5*
22		**CODED**	**-1**	**-0.75**	**-0.5**	**-0.25**	**0**	**0.25**	**0.5**	**0.75**	**1**
23	*3.5*	**-1**	14.21	15.04	15.83	16.59	17.32	18.01	18.67	19.30	19.89
24	*3.6*	**-0.9**	14.55	15.36	16.14	16.89	17.60	18.27	18.92	19.53	20.10
25	*3.7*	**-0.8**	14.89	15.69	16.45	17.18	17.87	18.53	19.16	19.75	20.31
26	*3.8*	**-0.7**	15.22	16.00	16.75	17.46	18.14	18.78	19.39	19.97	20.51
27	*3.9*	**-0.6**	15.54	16.31	17.04	17.73	18.40	19.02	19.62	20.18	20.70
28	*4*	**-0.5**	15.86	16.61	17.32	18.00	18.65	19.26	19.84	20.38	20.89
29	*4.1*	**-0.4**	16.17	16.90	17.60	18.26	18.89	19.49	20.05	20.58	21.07
30	*4.2*	**-0.3**	16.47	17.19	17.87	18.52	19.13	19.71	20.25	20.77	21.24
31	*4.3*	**-0.2**	16.77	17.47	18.13	18.76	19.36	19.92	20.45	20.95	21.41
32	*4.4*	**-0.1**	17.06	17.74	18.39	19.00	19.58	20.13	20.64	21.12	21.57
33	*4.5*	**0**	17.34	18.01	18.64	19.24	19.80	20.33	20.83	21.29	21.72
34	*4.6*	**0.1**	17.61	18.26	18.88	19.46	20.01	20.52	21.01	21.45	21.86
35	*4.7*	**0.2**	17.88	18.51	19.11	19.68	20.21	20.71	21.18	21.61	22.00
36	*4.8*	**0.3**	18.14	18.76	19.34	19.89	20.41	20.89	21.34	21.75	22.13
37	*4.9*	**0.4**	18.40	19.00	19.56	20.10	20.60	21.06	21.50	21.89	22.26
38	*5*	**0.5**	18.64	19.23	19.78	20.30	20.78	21.23	21.64	22.03	22.37
39	*5.1*	**0.6**	18.88	19.45	19.99	20.49	20.95	21.39	21.79	22.15	22.48
40	*5.2*	**0.7**	19.11	19.67	20.19	20.67	21.12	21.54	21.92	22.27	22.59
41	*5.3*	**0.8**	19.34	19.88	20.38	20.85	21.28	21.68	22.05	22.38	22.68
42	*5.4*	**0.9**	19.56	20.08	20.57	21.02	21.44	21.82	22.17	22.49	22.77
43	*5.5*	**1**	19.77	20.27	20.74	21.18	21.58	21.95	22.29	22.59	22.85
44		Cell AL23	=LAM0+LAM1*$AK23+LAM2*AL$22+LAM12*$AK23*AL$22+								
45			LAM11*$AK23^2+LAM22*AL$22^2								

Table 15.17 Computation of the variance across the domain of interest.

	AJ	AK	AL	AM	AN	AO	AP	AQ	AR	AS	AT
47			3.5	3.75	4	4.25	4.5	4.75	5	5.25	5.5
48		**CODED**	**-1**	**-0.75**	**-0.5**	**-0.25**	**0**	**0.25**	**0.5**	**0.75**	**1**
49	3.5	-1	0.0128	0.027	0.048	0.074	0.099	0.112	0.109	0.091	0.066
50	3.6	-0.9	0.0168	0.035	0.063	0.097	0.129	0.147	0.143	0.119	0.086
51	3.7	-0.8	0.0215	0.045	0.081	0.125	0.165	0.188	0.183	0.153	0.11
52	3.8	-0.7	0.0271	0.057	0.102	0.157	0.207	0.235	0.229	0.192	0.137
53	3.9	-0.6	0.0334	0.07	0.125	0.193	0.255	0.289	0.282	0.235	0.169
54	4	-0.5	0.0402	0.084	0.151	0.232	0.307	0.348	0.339	0.283	0.202
55	4.1	-0.4	0.0475	0.099	0.178	0.274	0.362	0.41	0.399	0.333	0.238
56	4.2	-0.3	0.0549	0.115	0.206	0.316	0.418	0.473	0.46	0.383	0.274
57	4.3	-0.2	0.0622	0.13	0.233	0.358	0.472	0.534	0.519	0.433	0.31
58	4.4	-0.1	0.0689	0.144	0.258	0.396	0.522	0.591	0.574	0.478	0.342
59	4.5	0	0.0748	0.156	0.28	0.429	0.566	0.64	0.622	0.518	0.37
60	4.6	0.1	0.0796	0.166	0.297	0.456	0.601	0.68	0.659	0.549	0.392
61	4.7	0.2	0.0829	0.173	0.309	0.474	0.625	0.706	0.685	0.57	0.407
62	4.8	0.3	0.0845	0.176	0.315	0.483	0.636	0.718	0.696	0.579	0.414
63	4.9	0.4	0.0844	0.176	0.314	0.482	0.634	0.716	0.694	0.577	0.412
64	5	0.5	0.0825	0.172	0.307	0.47	0.619	0.698	0.676	0.562	0.401
65	5.1	0.6	0.079	0.164	0.294	0.45	0.591	0.667	0.646	0.537	0.383
66	5.2	0.7	0.0741	0.154	0.275	0.421	0.554	0.624	0.604	0.502	0.358
67	5.3	0.8	0.0681	0.141	0.252	0.386	0.508	0.572	0.553	0.459	0.327
68	5.4	0.9	0.0612	0.127	0.227	0.347	0.456	0.513	0.496	0.412	0.293
69	5.5	1	0.0539	0.112	0.2	0.305	0.401	0.451	0.436	0.362	0.257
70		Cell AL49	=10^(-(XI_0+XI_1*$AK49+XI_2*AL$48+XI_12*$AK49*AL$48+								
71			XI_11*$AK49^2+XI_22*AL$48^2)/10)								

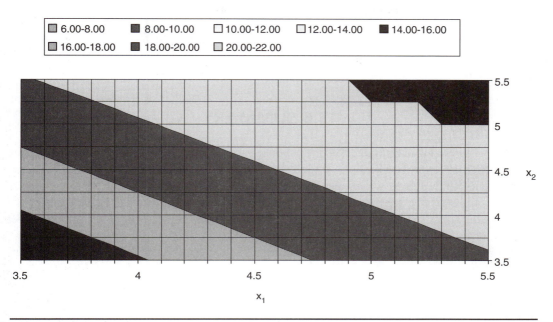

▨ 6.00-8.00	■ 8.00-10.00	☐ 10.00-12.00	☐ 12.00-14.00	■ 14.00-16.00
▨ 16.00-18.00	■ 18.00-20.00	☐ 20.00-22.00		

Figure 15.13 Contour plot of Y across the domain of interest.

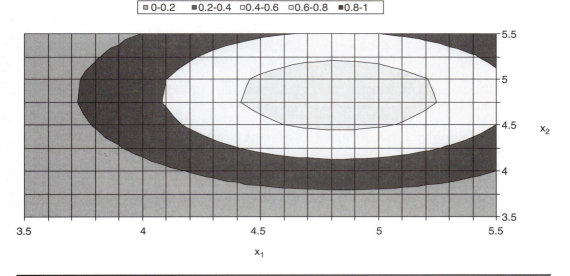

Figure 15.14 Contour plot of variance across the domain of interest.

get location. As $V(Y, s_Y^2)$ is defined for this problem in terms of its *sample* mean and variance, its distribution needs to be evaluated at the target position to determine the confidence level that value exceeds cost. This can be done using the simulation methods discussed in Chapter 10.

15.6 SUMMARY

Response Surface Methods (RSM): Response surfaces map the outcomes of an experiment as a function of several continuous, coded variables across the domain of interest. The Central Composite Design is widely used to develop RSM maps. However, other designs may be more appropriate, depending upon the nature of the problem and the preferences of the investigator. The RSM technique is especially useful in analyzing the outputs from computer experiments.

Strategic RSM: When the outcomes of the RSM experiments are to be used in projecting the optimum attribute levels for maximizing cash flow, separate maps of variance and the mean should be developed for the CTV attributes, which are then combined to map value across the domain. This requires that replications be generated using noise factors in the form of an outer array. The location of the target specification will be the point where value minus variable cost is the greatest provided that the investment level is constant over the domain. The noise factors can also be folded into the design array to provide a full model that includes main effects, noise factors, and their interactions.

REFERENCES

1. G. E. P. Box and N. R. Draper. 1987. *Empirical Model-Building and Response Surfaces.* New York: John Wiley & Sons.
2. G. E. P. Box and D. W. Behnken. 1960. "Some New Three Level Designs for the Study of Quantitative Variables," *Technometrics* 2, pp. 455–475.
3. R. H. Myers and D. C. Montgomery. 2002. *Response Surface Methodology Process and Product Optimization Using Designed Experiments.* New York: John Wiley & Sons, pp. 481–492.
4. M. S. Phadke. 1989. *Quality Engineering Using Robust Design.* Englewood Cliffs, NJ: Prentice Hall, p. 263.
5. D. C. Montgomery, *Design and Analysis of Experiments*, 5th ed. New York: John Wiley & Sons, p. 491.
6. C. F. J. Wu and M. Hamada. 2000. *Experiments Planning, Analysis, and Parameter Design Optimization.* New York: John Wiley & Sons, pp. 444–445.

Appendix A

Constructing Design Matrices

A.1 FACTORS WITH DISCRETE LEVELS (CATEGORICAL FACTORS)

A.1.1 Lambda and Phi Design Matrices

In most strategic experiments, the influence of each control factor is measured relative to a baseline reference state, which, unless otherwise noted, is taken to be trial 1. When there is not a reference state, the factors are measured relative to an artificial state represented by the average outcome of all of the trials. When a specific trial is used as the baseline, the design matrix is referred to as lambda and when the average of all trials is used as the baseline, it is referred to as phi. The estimates for the unknown coefficients are written as

$$\hat{\beta}_{ij} = \begin{cases} \lambda_{ij}, \text{ if a specific trial is the baseline } (q=1 \text{ is default baseline}). \\ \varphi_{ij}, \text{ if the average of all trials is the baseline.} \end{cases} \tag{A.1}$$

and are solved for using the regular least squares (RLS) method. (Note that the "hats" over lambda and phi denoting estimates are dropped for simplicity in notation.) The dummy indices i and j refer, respectively, to the type and discrete level of a factor. The RLS estimates for the base level coefficients for the main effects have the following properties:

$$\lambda_{i0} = 0 \tag{A.2}$$

and

$$\varphi_{i0} = -\sum_{j \neq 0} \varphi_{ij} \tag{A.3}$$

Note, the $j = 0$ levels do not explicitly appear in the matrix form of the RLS solution. The φ_{i0} coefficients must be computed from Equation (A.3) once the others have been determined. Similar relationships hold for the coefficients representing the interactions between factors.[1]

A.1.2 Taguchi and Konishi's Orthogonal Array Representations

Orthogonal arrays form an important subset of experimental designs because they are very efficient in terms of yielding minimum error for a given number of replications per trial. Taguchi and Konishi (TK), for example, have compiled 20 of the more important orthogonal arrays used in robust design experiments.[2] In their representation, the factor levels from 1 to m_i are included in each of the columns for factors of type $i = 1, 2, ...$ However, to take advantage of the significant benefits of matrix algebra in analyzing the outcomes, the single columns for each factor in the TK representation are expanded into $m_i - 1$ columns to form the design matrix, $\mathbf{X}$. Each type of factor i can have an independent number of levels, $m_i \geq 2$.

For illustration purposes, a simple $L_6(2^1, 3^1)$ design having six trials with one factor at two levels and a second factor at three levels is shown in Table A.1 in the TK representation, which counts the factor levels from a base of one.

The first step in converting the TK representation into a lambda or phi representation is to transform the base one representation into a base zero representation by subtracting 1 from the numbers in each column i. The base zero form for the above example is shown in Table A.2.

The design matrix, $\mathbf{X}$, is constructed from the base zero form by first generating a column of ones in the spreadsheet as column 0 for the baseline factor. The lengths of the columns are the same and equal to the number of trials, z. For each off-baseline control factor i having m_i levels, a total of $m_i - 1$ columns with double indexed headings ij are constructed from $j = 1$ to $m_i - 1$. Note that $m_i - 1$ is the largest number appearing in column i of the base zero form.

A -1 is inserted into each cell for each column ij in forming a phi array where a zero appears in column i in the base zero form. Next a 1 is inserted into each cell of column ij where the number j appears in column i of the base zero form, and a 0 is inserted where any other number >0 appears. The phi form for the above example is shown in Table A.3.

Factor 1 has just one column (11) because it has only two levels noted as 0 and 1 in the base zero form. Factor i0 does not appear explicitly, as it can be expressed in terms of the other factors using Equation (A.3). Factor 2 has two columns, 21 and 22, because it has three levels. Where zeros appear in the base zero form, minus ones appear in the phi form. Factor 20 does not appear as an explicit column because from Equation (A.3) it is equivalent to having factors 21 at −1 and factor 22 at −1 simultaneously with each contributing an amount $-\varphi_{21}$ and $-\varphi_{22}$, respectively, to the outcome for the trial. Thus a two-level factor in a phi design will only have -1s and 1s in the column, but factors with more than two levels will have 0s, −1s and 1s in each column. The −1s are present for those rows in which a factor is at its baseline level.

Under column 21, a 1 appears where 1s appeared in column 2 of the base 0 form and zeros appear where 2s appeared. Likewise, under column 22, a 1 appears where 2s

Table A.1 Taguchi and Konishi Representation for $L_6(2^1,3^1)$.

	Factor and level	
Trial	1	2
1	1	1
2	1	2
3	1	3
4	2	1
5	2	2
6	2	3

Table A.2 Base zero form for $L_6(2^1,3^1)$.

	Factor and level	
Trial	1	2
1	0	0
2	0	1
3	0	2
4	1	0
5	1	1
6	1	2

Table A.3 Phi Form for $L_6(2^1,3^1)$.

	0	11	21	22
1	1	−1	−1	−1
2	1	−1	1	0
3	1	−1	0	1
4	1	1	−1	−1
5	1	1	1	0
6	1	1	0	1

Table A.4 Lambda form for $L_6(2^1,3^1)$.

	0	11	21	22
1	1	0	0	0
2	1	0	1	0
3	1	0	0	1
4	1	1	0	0
5	1	1	1	0
6	1	1	0	1

appeared in column 2 of the base zero form and zeros appear where 1s appeared in column 2. The main effect columns for the lambda design matrix can be constructed from the main effect columns of the phi form by replacing the minus ones in the phi form by zeros as a result of Equation (A.1). The lambda form of the $L_6(2^1,3^1)$ is shown in Table A.4. A lambda form design matrix always has only zeros and ones in each column.

The entry in row q for the pairwise interaction column $ijkl$ is constructed by multiplying the value in row q of column ij times the value in row q of column kl. Triplet $ijklmn$ interactions are constructed by multiplying column ij times column kl times column mn.

A.1.3 Example: Conversion of TK $L_9(3^4)$ to X Matrix

Consider transforming the TK $L_9(3^4)$ array to a lambda design and then to a phi design. The TK design, named TFORM in the spreadsheet, is shown in Figure A.1 and converted into the base zero design (=TFORM-1) in Figure A.2. If a FF design were contemplated for factors with three levels, then only the first two main effects could be investigated using nine trials. The reason for this is that the other columns would be used for the interactions between the two main effects. Consequently, if the interactions do exist, they will *confound* the results for all of the main effects. Thus an orthogonal array should not be used if interactions are believed to be important. Taguchi's rule of thumb for handling interactions is that the main effects are usually dominant over interactions and the use of the orthogonal array allows a relatively rapid and efficient means for screening their contribution. A con-

Standard form

TFORM

Trial	1	2	3	4
1	1	1	1	1
2	1	2	2	2
3	1	3	3	3
4	2	1	2	3
5	2	2	3	1
6	2	3	1	2
7	3	1	3	2
8	3	2	1	3
9	3	3	2	1

Base zero form

BZFORM

Trial	1	2	3	4
1	0	0	0	0
2	0	1	1	1
3	0	2	2	2
4	1	0	1	2
5	1	1	2	0
6	1	2	0	1
7	2	0	2	1
8	2	1	0	2
9	2	2	1	0

Figure A.1 TK (name TFORM) and base zero forms for the $L_9(3^4)$ array.

firmation experiment to verify that interactions were minimal should follow the main effects only experiment. If the confirmation experiment does not validate the results forecast, additional experimental trials will be needed, as discussed in Chapter 11.

The transformation from the base zero form to the lambda form of the design matrix (XLAM) is shown in Figure A.2, and the transformation to the phi form of the design matrix (XPHI) is shown in A.3. Note, only zeros appear in trial 1 in Figure A.2, except for the baseline column where there is always a 1. When a 0 appears in column ij, it signifies that level j is not present. If zeros appear across each of the levels for a factor in a row, the factor is at its baseline level, $j = 0$. For the phi array, minus 1s in column ij signifies that the baseline level $j = 0$ is present and a 0 simply signifies that level j is not present for the trial but another off-baseline level is.

The ellipse noted as A, which highlights the 2 in row 7 of column 1 in the base zero form in Figure A.2, splits into a 0 in row 7 of column 11 and a 1 in row 7 of column 12 in the lambda array. However, ellipse B highlighting the 0 in row 5 of column 4 splits into a pair of 0s in the lambda array. The 2 highlighted by ellipse A for the phi design in Figure A.3 splits in the same manner as in the lambda array, but the 0 highlighted by ellipse B splits into a pair of minus ones.

The covariance matrix, XCLAM, for the lambda form shown in Figure A.4 was constructed by taking the inverse of the multiplication of the transpose XTLAM times XLAM. Note that column 0 (as well as row 0) has nonzero elements, which means that the baseline is not orthogonal to the off-baseline coefficients because they are measured relative to the baseline. The filled double diagonal is caused by the fact that the levels for the same factor are not independent. If one level of a factor is present for a trial, then the other levels cannot be present.

The covariance matrix, XCPHI, for the phi form in Figure A.5 was constructed by taking the inverse of the matrix multiplication of the transpose XTPHI times XPHI. Note that the nonzero, double diagonal again appears.

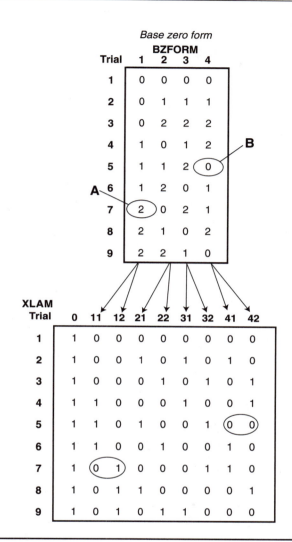

Figure A.2 Development of lambda form (XLAM) for the $L_9(3^4)$ array from base zero form.

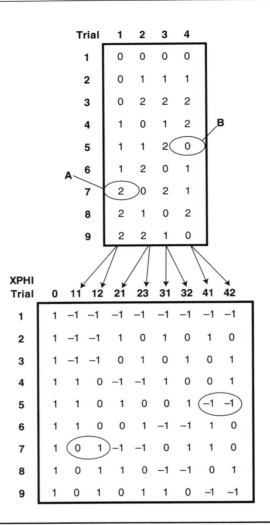

Figure A.3 Development of phi form (XPHI) of the $L_9(3^4)$ from base zero form.

XCLAM	0	11	12	21	23	31	32	41	42
0	1	−1/3	−1/3	−1/3	−1/3	−1/3	−1/3	−1/3	−1/3
11	−1/3	2/3	1/3	0	0	0	0	0	0
12	−1/3	1/3	2/3	0	0	0	0	0	0
21	−1/3	0	0	2/3	1/3	0	0	0	0
23	−1/3	0	0	1/3	2/3	0	0	0	0
31	−1/3	0	0	0	0	2/3	1/3	0	0
32	−1/3	0	0	0	0	1/3	2/3	0	0
41	−1/3	0	0	0	0	0	0	2/3	1/3
42	−1/3	0	0	0	0	0	0	1/3	2/3

Figure A.4 The lambda form of the covariance matrix for the $L_9(3^4)$ array.

XCPHI	0	11	12	21	23	31	32	41	42
0	1/9	0	0	0	0	0	0	0	0
11	0	2/9	-1/9	0	0	0	0	0	0
12	0	-1/9	2/9	0	0	0	0	0	0
21	0	0	0	2/9	-1/9	0	0	0	0
23	0	0	0	-1/9	2/9	0	0	0	0
31	0	0	0	0	0	2/9	-1/9	0	0
32	0	0	0	0	0	-1/9	2/9	0	0
41	0	0	0	0	0	0	0	2/9	-1/9
42	0	0	0	0	0	0	0	-1/9	2/9

Figure A.5   The phi form of the covariance matrix for the $L_9(3^4)$ array.

The solution matrices for the lambda and phi forms are shown in Figure A.6 and Figure A.7, respectively. Note that the lambda form, XSLAM, is balanced in that for each positive element in each row, there is a negative element that is equal in absolute value. This is not true for XSPHI. However, it is true for phi arrays when all of the factors have two levels.

A.1.4 Transforming Coefficients : Phi to Lambda and Lambda to Phi

The lambda and phi coefficients are linearly related, because they are coupled to the same outcome:

$$\mathbf{Y} = \mathbf{X}_\lambda \lambda = \mathbf{X}_\varphi \varphi \qquad (A.4)$$

Thus it follows that

$$\lambda = \mathbf{T}_\lambda \varphi \qquad (A.5)$$

For a square $\mathbf{X}$ matrix, the $\mathbf{T}_\lambda$ matrix that couples the two sets of coefficients is given by

$$\mathbf{T}_\lambda = \mathbf{X}_\lambda^{-1} \mathbf{X}_\varphi \qquad (A.6)$$

The inverse relationship is given by

$$\varphi = \mathbf{T}_\lambda^{-1} \lambda = \mathbf{T}_\varphi \lambda \qquad (A.7)$$

XSLAM	1	2	3	4	5	6	7	8	9
0	1	0	0	0	0	0	0	0	0
11	−1/3	−1/3	−1/3	1/3	1/3	1/3	0	0	0
12	−1/3	−1/3	−1/3	0	0	0	1/3	1/3	1/3
21	−1/3	1/3	0	−1/3	1/3	0	−1/3	1/3	0
23	−1/3	0	1/3	−1/3	0	1/3	−1/3	0	1/3
31	−1/3	1/3	0	1/3	0	−1/3	0	−1/3	1/3
32	−1/3	0	1/3	0	1/3	−1/3	1/3	−1/3	0
41	−1/3	1/3	0	0	−1/3	1/3	1/3	0	−1/3
42	−1/3	0	1/3	1/3	−1/3	0	0	1/3	−1/3

Figure A.6   Solution matrix for the lambda form.

XSPHI	1	2	3	4	5	6	7	8	9
0	1/9	1/9	1/9	1/9	1/9	1/9	1/9	1/9	1/9
11	−1/9	−1/9	−1/9	2/9	2/9	2/9	−1/9	−1/9	−1/9
12	−1/9	−1/9	−1/9	−1/9	−1/9	−1/9	2/9	2/9	2/9
21	−1/9	2/9	−1/9	−1/9	2/9	−1/9	−1/9	2/9	−1/9
23	−1/9	−1/9	2/9	−1/9	−1/9	2/9	−1/9	−1/9	2/9
31	−1/9	2/9	−1/9	2/9	−1/9	−1/9	−1/9	−1/9	2/9
32	−1/9	−1/9	2/9	−1/9	2/9	−1/9	2/9	−1/9	−1/9
41	−1/9	2/9	−1/9	−1/9	−1/9	2/9	2/9	−1/9	−1/9
42	−1/9	−1/9	2/9	2/9	−1/9	−1/9	−1/9	2/9	−1/9

Figure A.7   Solution matrix for the phi form.

The general RLS form given by

$$\mathbf{T}_\lambda = \left[\mathbf{X}_\lambda' \mathbf{X}_\lambda \right]^{-1} \left[\mathbf{X}_\lambda' \mathbf{X}_\varphi \right] = \mathbf{X}_{S,\lambda} \mathbf{X}_\varphi \tag{A.8}$$

must be used if the design matrix is not square. The $\mathbf{T}_\lambda$ and $\mathbf{T}_\varphi$ matrices for this problem are shown in Figures A.8 and A.9.

A.1.5 Constructing Two-Level Orthogonal Arrays

Two-level OAs are widely used in experiments. However, it is tedious and error prone to enter a large design matrix into a spreadsheet cell by cell. Fortunately, several shortcuts can be made in entering two-level design matrices that become particularly helpful for large designs. The starting point for a two-level OA having z trials is the array of main effect factors for the FF design having z trials. The first column in Table A.5 lists the number of main

	0	11	12	21	22	31	32	41	42
0	1	−1	−1	−1	−1	−1	−1	−1	−1
11	−0	2	1	0	0	0	0	0	0
12	−0	1	2	0	0	0	0	0	0
21	0	0	0	2	1	0	0	0	0
23	0	0	0	1	2	0	0	0	0
31	0	0	0	0	0	2	1	0	0
32	0	0	0	0	0	1	2	0	0
41	0	0	0	0	0	0	0	2	1
42	0	0	0	0	0	0	0	1	2

Figure A.8 The T_λ matrix for transforming the phi coefficients to the lambda coefficients.

	0	11	12	21	22	31	32	41	42
0	1	1/3	1/3	1/3	1/3	1/3	1/3	1/3	1/3
11	0	2/3	−1/3	0	0	0	0	0	0
12	0	−1/3	2/3	0	0	0	0	0	0
21	0	0	0	2/3	−1/3	0	0	0	0
23	0	0	0	−1/3	2/3	0	0	0	0
31	0	0	0	0	0	2/3	−1/3	0	0
32	0	0	0	0	0	−1/3	2/3	0	0
41	0	0	0	0	0	0	0	2/3	−1/3
42	0	0	0	0	0	0	0	−1/3	2/3

Figure A.9 The T_φ matrix for transforming the lambda coefficients to the phi coefficients.

Table A.5 Type and number of interactions for OAs with all factors having two levels.

Number of FF main effects	Number and type of interaction						Number of main effects for saturated design	Number of trials
a	ab	abc	abcd	abcde	abcdef	abcdefg		
2	1	0	0	0	0	0	3	4
3	3	1	0	0	0	0	7	8
4	6	4	1	0	0	0	15	16
5	10	10	5	1	0	0	31	32
6	15	20	15	6	1	0	63	64
7	21	35	35	21	7	1	126	127

effects for a series of two-level designs for a range of z from 4 to 127, as noted in the right-most column. For example, column ab lists the number of combinations of pairwise inter-actions, abc lists the number of triplet interactions and so forth. A breakdown of the types of interactions and their number are also shown.

The process for generating a general $L_z(2^{(w-1)})$ design from scratch begins with the main effects for the 2^2 FF phi design shown in the upper left potion of Table A.6 under

Table A.6 Generation of two-level OAs using a spreadsheet.

Row	B	C	D	E	F	G	H	I	J	K	L	M	N	O	P	Q	R	S	T
19					a	b	ab						a	b	c	ab	ac	bc	abc
20		Trial		0	11	21	31				Trial	0	11	21	31	41	51	61	71
21		1		1	-1	-1	-1				1	1	-1	-1	-1	-1	-1	-1	-1
22		2		1	-1	1	1				2	1	-1	-1	1	-1	1	1	1
23		3		1	1	1	-1				3	1	-1	1	1	1	1	-1	-1
24		4		1	1	-1	1				4	1	-1	1	-1	1	-1	1	1
25											5	1	1	-1	-1	1	1	-1	1
26											6	1	1	-1	1	1	-1	1	-1
27											7	1	1	1	1	-1	-1	-1	1
28											8	1	1	1	-1	-1	1	1	-1

Row	B	C	D	E	F	G	H	I	J	K	L	M	N	O	P	Q	R	S	T
30			a	b	c	d	ab	ac	ad	bc	bd	cd	abc	abd	acd	bcd	abcd		
31	Trial	0	11	21	31	41	51	61	71	81	91	10,1	11,1	12,1	13,1	14,1	15,1		
32	1	1	-1	-1	-1	-1	-1	-1	-1	-1	-1	-1	-1	-1	-1	-1	-1		
33	2	1	-1	-1	-1	1	-1	-1	1	-1	1	1	-1	1	1	1	1		
34	3	1	-1	-1	1	1	-1	1	1	1	1	-1	1	1	-1	-1	-1		
35	4	1	-1	-1	1	-1	-1	1	-1	1	-1	1	1	-1	1	1	1		
36	5	1	-1	1	-1	-1	1	-1	-1	1	1	-1	1	1	-1	1	1		
37	6	1	-1	1	-1	1	1	-1	1	1	-1	1	1	-1	1	-1	-1		
38	7	1	-1	1	1	1	1	1	1	-1	-1	-1	-1	-1	-1	1	1		
39	8	1	-1	1	1	-1	1	1	-1	-1	1	1	-1	1	1	-1	-1		
40	9	1	1	-1	-1	-1	1	1	1	-1	-1	-1	1	1	1	-1	1		
41	10	1	1	-1	-1	1	1	1	-1	-1	1	1	1	-1	-1	1	-1		
42	11	1	1	-1	1	1	1	-1	-1	1	1	-1	-1	-1	1	-1	1		
43	12	1	1	-1	1	-1	1	-1	1	1	-1	1	-1	1	-1	1	-1		
44	13	1	1	1	-1	-1	-1	1	1	1	1	-1	-1	-1	1	1	-1		
45	14	1	1	1	-1	1	-1	1	-1	1	-1	1	-1	1	-1	-1	1		
46	15	1	1	1	1	1	-1	-1	-1	-1	-1	-1	1	1	1	1	-1		
47	16	1	1	1	1	-1	-1	-1	1	-1	1	1	1	-1	-1	-1	1		
48							=-$D32*E32												
49								=-$E32*F32											
50									=-F32*G32										
51										=-$D32*K32									
52																=-E32*M32			
53																	=-D32*Q32		

columns 0, 11, and 21. (For two-level designs the double index notation could be dropped.) The $L_4(2^3)$ design uses 11, 21, and 31 for the column notations. Column 31 is formed by multiplying −1 times the product of the elements in columns 11 and 21. The ab notation above 31 indicates that the 31 main effect is confounded with the 1121 interaction between a and b, the products of the elements in columns 11 and 21 being identical, except for sign, to the elements in column 31. Similarly, the main effect 11 is confounded with the 2131 interaction. Main effect 21 is confounded with the 1131 interaction. The L_8 design to the upper right is formed by (1) doubling the area under the 11 and 21 columns in Table A.6, (2) replicating the off-baseline portion of the L_4 array in this area, (3) changing the column indices to 21 and 31, respectively, and (4) adding a new column 11 of four −1s followed by four 1s. The remaining columns 41, 51, 61, and 71 are formed by multiplying the respective main effect columns according to the FF column indices shown. This process for doubling the size of the design is repeated in going from the L_8 to the L_{16} design.

Each of the designs is segmented into FF main effects and interactions, which are entered by multiplication of appropriate columns to the left. The multiplications used for the L_{16} design are shown at the bottom of Table A.6. Note the use of $ signs so that the expression could be dragged across. This same process can be used to build 32, 64, 128, etc. designs as desired. It minimizes the chances of making improper keystrokes and relieves the tedium of having to key in entries on a cell by cell basis. Once an all main effect phi design has been generated, it can easily be converted into the lambda form using an IF statement to convert the −1s to 0s in another region of the spreadsheet. This lambda matrix can then be copied and placed at its desired location.

A.2 CONTINUOUS VARIABLES

In addition to the discrete levels considered above, factors can also be continuous or mixed with some being discrete and others being continuous. Consider the case in which all of the variables, x_i, are continuous. The general form for the RLS solution (see Appendix C for the RLS solution) for continuous, singly subscripted main effects can be written for trial (q) as

$$\hat{Y}(q) = \hat{\beta}_0 + \hat{\beta}_1 x_1(q) + \hat{\beta}_2 x_2(q) + \hat{\beta}_{11} x_1^2(q) + \hat{\beta}_{22} x_2^2(q) + \hat{\beta}_{12} x_1(q) x_2(q) + ... \quad (A.9)$$

The first column, column 0, in the design matrix would again be a column of ones. It follows that the elements in row (q) for column 1 would be $x_1(q)$. The elements in column 22, for example, would be $X_2^2(q)$ and so forth.

It is usually advantageous computationally and in assessing the relative strength of factors on the outcomes to transform the continuous variable $x_i(q)$ to the coded variable $X_i(q)$. The most common form of the transformation is made using the relation

$$X_i(q) \equiv \frac{x_i(q) - \bar{x}_i}{\bar{x}_i} \quad (A.10)$$

in which the term $\bar{x}_i$ is the average of $x_1(q)$ over the trials (q). Instead of the mean value coding represented by Equation (A.10), a transformation can also be made by taking the terms

Trials	0	1	11
1	1	3	9
2	1	5	25
3	1	1	1
4	1	4	16
5	1	7	49

Average = 4

Figure A.10 An uncoded experimental design and outcomes Y for a continuous variable x_1.

Trials	0	1	11
1	1	−0.25	0.0625
2	1	0.25	0.0625
3	1	−0.75	0.5625
4	1	0	0
5	1	0.75	0.5625

Figure A.11 The mean value coded design array generated from the uncoded design in Figure A.10.

$\bar{x}_i$ equal to the value for the baseline for the x_i if the coefficients and their significance are to be measured relative to the baseline. When this is the case, a central composite design (see Chapter 15) offers an advantage in precision because the central point is the baseline.

An uncoded design for a single continuous variable $x_1(q)$ is shown in Figure A.10 having columns for the baseline, linear, and quadratic terms. The mean value coded form for this design is shown in Figure A.11.

REFERENCES

1. H. E. Cook. 1997. *Product Management: Value, Quality, Cost, Price, Profits, and Organization.* Amsterdam: Kluwer, p. 369.
2. G. Taguchi and S. Konishi. 1987. *Taguchi Methods Orthogonal Arrays and Linear Graphs.* Livonia, MI: ASI Press.

Appendix B

Bonferroni Method for Converting PWE to EWE

The standard Type I pairwise error (PWE) or p-value (see Chapter 4) between a pair of states provides a false level of confidence when multiple off-baseline factors are being evaluated. As a result, the PWE should be transformed to an experiment-wise Type I error as an aid in making a more informed decision about the significance of the outcomes.

Fortunately, there is a simple way of doing this due to Bonferroni. Consider the 10 simulated outcomes measured relative to a baseline condition as shown in Figure B.1, the sample size being three. The population means and variances of 10 and 1, respectively, were the same for all of the alternatives as well as the baseline except for alternative 6, which had a population mean of 12. The simulated mean in Cell H9 was generated using the spreadsheet expression

$$\text{Cell H9} = \text{NORMINV(RAND(),\$E9,\$F9)} \quad\quad\quad\quad \text{(B.1)}$$

This expression was then dragged across and down to generate the other replications.

The difference between the means for the alternatives and baseline listed in Cell L10 was computed using the expression

$$\text{Cell L10} = \text{AVERAGE(H10:J10)-AVERAGE(\$H\$9:\$J\$9)} \quad\quad\quad\quad \text{(B.2)}$$

This expression was pulled down to generate the L10:L19 column. For convenience, the population statistics (which of course were known) were used to set the boundaries of the critical region (see Section 4.1.3). The standard deviation of the difference between the two population means is given by

$$\sigma = \text{SQRT}((1^2 + 1^2)/3) = 0.816 \quad\quad\quad\quad \text{(B.3)}$$

The computation of this expression is shown in Cell F24 in Figure B.2. The NORMINV function is used in Cell F26 to set a 1% single-tail critical region to the right. This yields a 99% confidence level for the mean of an alternative being greater than the baseline.

	C	D	E	F	G	H	I	J	K	L
6								=NORMINV(RAND(),\$E9,\$F9)		**Alternate mean**
7			**POPULATION**			**Replications**				**Less**
8			**Mean**	**SD**		**1**	**2**	**3**	**Y**	**Baseline mean**
9	**Baseline**	0	10	1		8.27	7.40	10.16	8.61	
10	**Alternative**	1	10	1		10.14	8.91	10.15	9.73	1.124
11	**Alternative**	2	10	1		9.84	9.45	8.75	9.35	0.739
12	**Alternative**	3	10	1		11.61	11.80	10.01	11.14	2.530
13	**Alternative**	4	10	1		10.08	9.55	10.01	9.88	1.271
14	**Alternative**	5	10	1		9.89	6.87	11.53	9.43	0.822
15	**Alternative**	6	12	1		12.02	12.05	12.54	12.20	3.591
16	**Alternative**	7	10	1		10.90	11.37	9.50	10.59	1.979
17	**Alternative**	8	10	1		9.75	11.91	9.96	10.54	1.930
18	**Alternative**	9	10	1		11.48	9.13	10.35	10.32	1.716
19	**Alternative**	10	10	1		7.52	10.71	10.50	9.58	0.970

Figure B.1 Simulation of the assessments of 10 alternatives versus a baseline using a sample size of three.

	B	C	D	E	F	G	H	I
22								
23					**POPULATION**			
24			SD Difference Two Means=		0.816	=SQRT((1^2+1^2)/3)		
25								
26			Start of 0.01 critical region=		11.899	=NORMINV(1-0.01,E9,F24)		
27			Distance from population mean=		1.899	=F26-E9		
28								
29			Start of 0.001 critical region=		12.523	=NORMINV(1-0.01/10,E9,F24)		
30			Distance from population mean=		2.523	=E9-F29		
31								
32			Intercept + one standard deviation from origin=		16%	=1-NORMDIST(10+F24,10,F24,1)		

Figure B.2 Setting of bounds for single-tail critical region using population statistics.

However, as there are 10 paired comparisons (10 alternatives different from the baseline) to be made, the number of Type I errors per the experiment is increased by a factor of 10 versus the null hypothesis of none being different from zero. Thus the boundary for the critical region should be set at one tenth of the PWE level or 0.1%. This was computed in Cell F29. The computation in Cell F32 illustrates a useful rule when using normal probability plots, which is if a vertical line is drawn such that it intersects the line through the normal plot at 16%, the value of the parameter, g, given by the intercept on the x-axis is one standard deviation from the mean on the low side. If a vertical line is drawn such that the intercept is at 84% (=100-16), the value of g is one standard deviation above the mean. This rule is predicated on the distribution being normal.

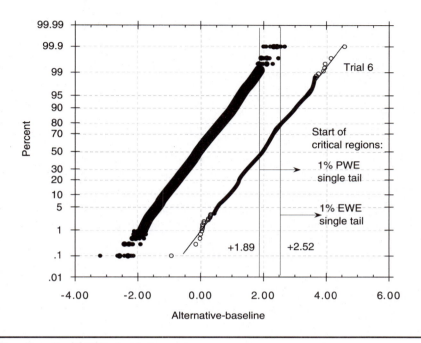

Figure B.3 Results of 500 simulations.

The results of 500 Monte Carlo simulations are shown in Figure B.3. The differences between the means of the alternatives and the baseline mean are seen to lie along a line through zero for all of the alternatives except for alternative 6 (trial 6). To the right of the vertical line at 1.89, there will be on average 0.01×500 points per each of the nine alternatives whose populations did not differ from the baseline. However, per experiment there will be a total of $9 \times 0.01 \times 500$ points or 0.09 per experiment.

If the 1.89 line were set as the boundary of the critical region for inferring that an alternative has a population mean greater than the baseline, there would be an average of nine Type I errors in every 100 experiments. In other words, the Type 2 error rate of 9% would be almost 10 times what would be expected from the PWE assessment. Moreover, the Type I error level and the critical region are assessed based upon the null hypothesis that no alternative is different from the baseline. If this had actually been the case for our experiment (i.e., alternative 6 having the same population statistics as the baseline), the percentage of Type I errors per experiment would have been 10%, not 1%.

Bonferroni's conversion of PWE to EWE is one of simply multiplying the PWE, as computed from the t statistic for example, by the number of alternatives considered. If the total number of unknowns considered were w, which includes the baseline as an unknown, then the conversion of the computed PWE to EWE is given by

$$EWE = [w - 1]PWE \qquad (B.4)$$

Bonferroni's conversion is rigorous in the limit when all of the variation from baseline is random noise and conservative when this is not the case. It can also be applied in a stepwise manner. For example, if seven off-baseline coefficients were evaluated and two were deemed significant after multiplying their PWE by seven, the correction factor for the remaining coefficients should be adjusted to 5 as the null hypothesis has been rejected for the two deemed significant. In other words, only the remaining five need to be judged against the null hypothesis of random noise.

Combinations of factors are also of interest. Consider the outcomes from an L8(2^7) experiment, there being 21 (= 7 × 6/2) distinct pairs. If all variation arises from random error, a 5% combination-wise error (CWE) for pairs will lead to a 1.05 EWE (21*0.05). It is better, however, to assess first the significance of each factor *individually* based upon their individual EWE. The combination of factors found significant and favorable on an individual basis can then be considered for production after the confidence level for the combination has been evaluated strategically (see Chapter 10) against one or more bottom-line metrics such as cash flow and market share. This approach bypasses the need to make a conversion of CWE to EWE.

Appendix C

General Aspects of Regular Least Square Solution

C.1 INTRODUCTION

Let $Y(q)$, the average outcome for trial (treatment) q, be linearly related to the independent variables $X_{ij}(q)$, $X_{ijkl}(q)$, ... The dummy index $i = 1, 2, ...$ denotes the type of factor (variable) under consideration and $j = 1, 2, ...$ denotes the level of the factor. The $X_{ij}(q)$, $X_{ijkl}(q)$, ... represent discrete (categorical) variables and are expressed as 0s and 1s for so-called lambda designs or as −1s, 0s, and 1s for phi designs. The variables can also be continuous in which case the main effects have single subscripts. The number of trials q range from 1 to z.

Discrete and continuous variables can also be mixed in a design. For a discrete automotive variable, $i = 1$ could refer to engines and $j = 1, 2, 3$ could refer to engines having 4, 6, and 8 cylinders. Terms with double indices ij represent main effects and terms with four indices $ijkl$ represent interactions between pairs of main effects with $X_{iklj}(q) = X_{ij}(q)X_{kl}(q)$. An interaction between three factors would be written as $X_{ikljmn}(q) = X_{ij}(q)X_{kl}(q)\,X_{mn}(q)$. In what follows, the expressions will be written for a discrete model.

C.2 MINIMIZING MODEL ERROR

The average outcome for trial q is defined in the usual way by summing over the $r = 1$ to $n(q)$ replications and dividing by $n(q)$:

$$Y(q) \equiv \bar{Y}(q) = \frac{1}{n(q)} \sum_{r=1}^{n(q)} Y(q,r) \tag{C.1}$$

The $Y(q)$ are elements of the $z \times 1$ column matrix (vector) **Y**. The general problem can include m multiple outcomes for each trial in which case **Y** would represent a $z \times m$ matrix.

The linear model for $Y(q)$ is written as

$$Y(q) = \beta_0 X_0(q) + \beta_{11} X_{11}(q) + \beta_{21} X_{21}(q) + ... + \beta_{kl} X_{kl}(q) + ... \beta_{ijkl} X_{ijkl}(q) + e$$

The above expression in matrix form becomes

$$Y(q) = \left[\mathbf{X}(q)\right]\left[\boldsymbol{\beta}\right] + \mathbf{e}$$

$$= \left[X_0(q) \quad X_{11}(q) \quad X_{21}(q) ... \quad X_{ijkl}(q)\right]\begin{bmatrix} \beta_0 \\ \beta_{11} \\ \beta_{21} \\ \vdots \\ \beta_{ijkl} \end{bmatrix} + e(q) \qquad \text{(C.2)}$$

The term $e(q)$ is the zero-mean, random error between the outcomes and the model for the outcomes for trial (q). The full set of linear simultaneous equations for all $q = 1$ to z trials is written as

$$\mathbf{Y} = \mathbf{X}\boldsymbol{\beta} + \mathbf{e} \qquad \text{(C.3)}$$

The expanded form of Equation (C.3) is given by

$$\begin{bmatrix} Y(1) \\ Y(2) \\ Y(3) \\ . \\ . \\ . \\ Y(z) \end{bmatrix} = \begin{bmatrix} X_0(1) & X_{11}(1) & X_{21}(1) & ... & X_{kl}(1) \\ X_0(2) & X_{11}(2) & X_{12}(2) & ... & X_{kl}(2) \\ X_0(3) & X_{11}(3) & X_{12}(3) & ... & X_{kl}(3) \\ . & . & . & ... & . \\ . & . & . & ... & . \\ . & . & . & ... & . \\ X_0(z) & X_{11}(z) & X_{12}(z) & ... & X_{kl}(z) \end{bmatrix}\begin{bmatrix} \beta_0 \\ \beta_{11} \\ \beta_{12} \\ . \\ . \\ . \\ \beta_{kl} \end{bmatrix} + \begin{bmatrix} e(1) \\ e(2) \\ e(3) \\ . \\ . \\ . \\ e(z) \end{bmatrix}$$

The unknown coefficients β_{ij} are the elements of the column matrix β. They are estimated by minimizing the total error given by the sum of the squares of the individual trial errors

$$e_{Total}^2 = \sum_{q=1}^{z} e^2(q)$$

which requires that the partial derivative of the sum of the squares of the error

$$e_{Total}^2 = \sum_{q=1}^{z}\left[Y(q) - \sum_{ij}X_{ij}(q)\beta_{ij}\right]^2 \qquad \text{(C.4)}$$

with respect to each β_{ij} be equal to zero. The partial derivative of Equation (C.4) is given by

$$\frac{\partial e^2_{Total}}{\partial \beta_{ij}} = -2 \sum_{q=1}^{z} \left[Y(q) - \sum_{kl} X_{kl}(q) \beta_{kl} \right] X_{ij}(q) \tag{C.5}$$

This relationship, after setting the partial derivative to zero and rearranging, can be written as

$$\sum_{kl} \alpha_{ijkl} \hat{\beta}_{kl} = \gamma_{ij} \tag{C.6}$$

The coefficients have been given a hat to signify that they represent the regular least square (RLS) estimates for the true coefficients. Equation (C.6) represents a linear set of w equations in w unknowns. In order to solve for the $\hat{\beta}_{ij}$, their number w must be less than or equal to the original number of *independent* equations. The set of equations can be written in explicit matrix form as

$$\begin{bmatrix} \alpha_{00} & \alpha_{011} & \alpha_{012} & \cdots & \alpha_{0mn} \\ \alpha_{110} & \alpha_{1111} & \alpha_{1112} & \cdots & \alpha_{11mn} \\ \alpha_{120} & \alpha_{1211} & \alpha_{1212} & \cdots & \alpha_{12mn} \\ \cdot & \cdot & \cdot & \cdots & \cdot \\ \cdot & \cdot & \cdot & \cdots & \cdot \\ \cdot & \cdot & \cdot & \cdots & \cdot \\ \alpha_{mn0} & \alpha_{mn11} & \alpha_{mn12} & \cdots & \alpha_{mnmn} \end{bmatrix} \begin{bmatrix} \hat{\beta}_0 \\ \hat{\beta}_{11} \\ \hat{\beta}_{12} \\ \cdot \\ \cdot \\ \cdot \\ \hat{\beta}_{mn} \end{bmatrix} = \begin{bmatrix} \gamma_0 \\ \gamma_{11} \\ \gamma_{12} \\ \cdot \\ \cdot \\ \cdot \\ \gamma_{mn} \end{bmatrix} \tag{C.7}$$

The first matrix, defined as α, in Equation (C.7) is square ($w \times w$) and its elements are computed from the relationship

$$\alpha_{ijkl} = \sum_{q=1}^{z} X_{ij}(q) X_{kl}(q) \tag{C.8}$$

For simplicity, possible interaction terms in α have not been shown. The column matrix to the right of the equal sign in Equation (C.7), defined as γ, has w rows and its elements are given by

$$\gamma_{ij} = \sum_{q=1}^{z} X_{ij}(q) Y(q) \tag{C.9}$$

The summation on the RHS of Equation (C.8) involves two columns, *ij* and *kl,* in the design array **X.** The elements in each row *(q)* are multiplied together and the resulting products are summed. These operations are equivalent to multiplying the transpose of column *ij* times column *kl.* Similarly the summation on the RHS of Equation (C.9) is equal to the transpose of column *ij* times the column matrix **Y.** Thus $\alpha = \mathbf{X}'\mathbf{X}$ and $\gamma = \mathbf{X}'\mathbf{Y}$.

The condensed matrix notation for the system of equations is given by

$$\alpha\hat{\beta} = \gamma \tag{C.10}$$

After both sides are multiplied by $[\mathbf{X}'\mathbf{X}]^{-1}$, the RLS solution is obtained:

$$\hat{\beta} = [\mathbf{X}'\mathbf{X}]^{-1}\mathbf{X}'\mathbf{Y} \tag{C.11}$$

Strictly speaking, the matrix $[\mathbf{X}'\mathbf{X}]^{-1}$ is the variance-covariance matrix for $\sigma^2 = 1$. It is always square $(w \times w)$ and symmetric. Here the matrix $[\mathbf{X}'\mathbf{X}]^{-1}$ will be called the covariance matrix $\mathbf{X}_C$ (XC) and $[\mathbf{X}'\mathbf{X}]^{-1}\mathbf{X}'$ will be called the solution matrix $\mathbf{X}_S$ (XS). The terms XC and XS in parentheses are the names given to the covariance and solution matrices in the spreadsheet. The element of $\mathbf{X}_S$ in row *ij* and column *q* is written as $\omega_{ij}(q)$.

C.3 VARIANCE OF THE COEFFICIENTS

The value for a specific coefficient is computed from the equation

$$\hat{\beta}_{ij} = \sum_{q=1}^{z}\omega_{ij}(q)Y(q) \tag{C.12}$$

As this expression is linear in terms of the statistically independent averages $Y(q)$ for the trials, it follows that the variance of factor $\hat{\beta}_{ij}$ is

$$s_{ij}^2 = \sum_{q=1}^{z}\omega_{ij}^2(q)\left[\frac{s^2(q)}{n(q)}\right] \tag{C.13}$$

where $s^2(q)$ is the sample variance for trial *q*. The terms $s^2(q)$ and $n(q)$ are elements in the column vectors named SVAR and n, respectively, in the spreadsheet. The spreadsheet expression for the $w \times 1$ column vector for s_{ij}^2 (VARij) can be written as

VARij=MMULT(XS^2,SVAR/n)

The square root of the factor variance s_{ij}^2 given by s_{ij} represents the *factor standard deviation.* It is more commonly known as the *standard error* of the factor. When the sample size is constant for the trials and the samples come from populations having a common variance, Equation (C.13) reduces to

$$s_{ij}^2 = s_P^2 \, \text{cov}_{ijij} / n \qquad (\text{C.14})$$

The term s_P^2 is called the *pooled sample variance,* which is named PSVAR for spreadsheet computations. The general expression for s_P^2 is given by

$$s_P^2 \equiv \frac{\sum_q [n(q)-1]s^2(q)}{\sum_q [n(q)-1]} \qquad (\text{C.15})$$

Equation (C.15) represents a df weighted average of the sample variances, the df for the pooled variance itself being

$$v_P = \sum_q [n(q)-1] \qquad (\text{C.16})$$

Thus, when the sample size is constant, the pooled variance is equal to the average of the sample variances and the pooled df is $z(n-1)$. The term cov_{ijkl} is the element in row ij and column kl of the covariance matrix $\mathbf{X}_C$, its diagonal elements being cov_{ijij}.

When the sample variances in Equation (C.13) do not come from populations having a common variance (the usual case), the df associated with the variances have a form due to Satterthwaite:[1]

$$v_{ij} = \frac{\left[s_{ij}^2 \right]^2}{d_{ij}} = \frac{s_{ij}^4}{d_{ij}} \qquad (\text{C.17})$$

where

$$d_{ij} = \sum_{q=1}^{z} \frac{\omega_{ij}^4(q)s^4(q)}{n^2(q)[n(q)-1]} \qquad (\text{C.18})$$

The spreadsheet expression for d_{ij} (Dij) is the $w \times 1$ array given by

Dij=MMULT(XS^2,(SVAR/n)^2/(n-1))

C.4 THE DIFFERENCE BETWEEN TWO STATES AND ITS VARIANCE

The difference $\hat{Y}(R, R*)$ between two projected outcomes represented by the states R and $R*$ can be written as

$$\hat{Y}(R, R*) = \hat{Y}(R) - \hat{Y}(R*) \tag{C.19}$$

where

$$\hat{Y}(R) = \sum_{ij} c_{ij}(R)\hat{\beta}_{ij} \tag{C.20}$$

Thus, it follows that

$$\hat{Y}(R, R*) = \sum_{ij} c_{ij}(R, R*)\hat{\beta}_{ij} = \mathbf{C}\hat{\beta}' \tag{C.21}$$

where $\mathbf{C}$ is a $1 \times w$ general contrast vector connecting the two states. Its elements are given by

$$c_{ij}(R, R*) = c_{ij}(R) - c_{ij}(R*) \tag{C.22}$$

After Equation (C.12) has been substituted for β_{ij} in Equation (C.21), the variance of $\hat{Y}(R, R*)$ becomes

$$Var(\hat{Y}(R, R*)) = \sum_{ij}\sum_{kl}\left\{c_{ij}(R, R*)c_{kl}(R, R*)\sum_{q}\omega_{ij}(q)\omega_{kl}(q)\frac{s^2(q)}{n(q)}\right\} \tag{C.23}$$

When the population variances are common for the trials and the sample size constant, Equation (C.23) reduces to the familiar form found in most textbooks:

$$Var(\hat{Y}(R, R*)) = \frac{s_P^2}{n}\mathbf{C}[\mathbf{X'X}]^{-1}\mathbf{C}' \tag{C.24}$$

except for the replacement of the population variance σ^2 by the pooled sample variance.

When the samples do not come from populations having a common variance, the general expression given by Equation (C.23) needs to be evaluated. The computations involved can be greatly simplified by breaking the operations into several steps. The first is to form a new matrix $\mathbf{X_{SS}}$, which is equal to the transpose of $\mathbf{X_S}$ times $\mathbf{C}$:

$$\mathbf{X}_{SS} = \mathbf{X}_{S}'\mathbf{C}$$

The elements of $\mathbf{X}_{SS}$ are given by

$$\omega_{ij}(R, R^*, q) = c_{ij}(R, R^*)\omega_{ij}(q)$$

Equation (C.23) can thus be written as

$$Var(\hat{Y}(R, R^*)) = \sum_{q}\left\{\sum_{ij}\omega_{ij}(R, R^*, q)\left[\sum_{kl}\omega_{kl}(R, R^*, q)\right]\right\}\frac{s^2(q)}{n(q)} \qquad \text{(C.25)}$$

The term in braces in Equation (C.25) is defined as $\psi(R, R^*, q)$, which is equal to the square of the sum of the elements down column q in the $\mathbf{X}_{SS}$ matrix:

$$\psi(R, R^*, q) = \left[\sum_{ij}\omega_{ij}(R, R^*, q)\right]^2 \qquad \text{(C.26)}$$

The $\psi(R, R^*, q)$ form the elements of a new matrix, $\mathbf{X}_{\psi}$ (PSIQ). This $1 \times z$ row matrix has one element for each experimental trial q. These steps can now be combined into a single spreadsheet operation to compute $\mathbf{X}_{\psi}$ directly using the expression

$$\text{PSIQ} = \text{TRANSPOSE(MMULT(TRANSPOSE(XS),CRR))^2} \qquad \text{(C.27)}$$

in which CRR is the name for the $w \times 1$ contrast vector $\mathbf{C}$. The variance for $\hat{Y}(R, R^*)$ in Equation (C.25) is computed by multiplying the row vector $\mathbf{X}_{\psi}$ having elements $\psi(R, R^*, q)$ by a column vector having elements $s^2(q) / n(q)$:

$$s^2_{\hat{Y}(R,R^*)} = \sum_{q=1}^{z}\psi(R, R^*, q)\frac{s^2(q)}{n(q)} = \text{MMULT(PSIQ,SVAR/n)} \qquad \text{(C.28)}$$

Equation (C.28) is simply a more general form for the variance than that given by Equation (C.13), which was written for a specific outcome when there was only one nonzero coefficient, $c_{ij} = 1$. It follows by inspection of Equations (C.17), (C.18), and (C.28) that Satterthwaite's df for the variance of $\hat{Y}(R, R^*)$ is given by

$$v(R, R^*) = \frac{\left[s^2_{\hat{Y}(R,R^*)}\right]^2}{d(R, R^*)} \qquad \text{(C.29)}$$

where

$$d(R,R^*) = \sum_{q=1}^{z} \frac{\psi^2(R,R^*,q)s^4(q)}{n^2(q)[n(q)-1]} = \text{MMULT(PSIQ\textasciicircum2,(SVAR/n)\textasciicircum2/(n-1))} \tag{C.30}$$

After the results of Equations (C.28) and (C.30) are substituted into Equation (C.29), the expression for the df becomes:

$$v(R,R^*) = \text{MMULT(PSIQ,SVAR/n)\textasciicircum2/MMULT(PSIQ\textasciicircum2,(SVAR/n)\textasciicircum2/(n-1))} \tag{C.31}$$

An application of Equation (C.31) is shown in Table 9.11 in examining the statistics for the differences between two states.

C.5 THE *t* STATISTIC AND SIGNIFICANCE OF AN OUTCOME

When the populations from which samples were taken have a common variance, the following two expressions represent a *t* statistic:

$$t = \begin{cases} t_{ij} = \dfrac{\hat{\beta}_{ij}}{\sqrt{s_{ij}^2}} \\ \\ t(R,R^*) = \dfrac{\hat{Y}(R,R^*)}{\sqrt{s_{\hat{Y}(R,R^*)}^2}} \end{cases} \tag{C.32}$$

The first expression is the *t* statistic for the *ij* coefficient measured relative to the baseline for the experimental design and the second expression is the *t* statistic for the difference between two states. They represent approximate *t* statistics when the populations from which the samples were taken do not have a common variance, the df being given by Equations (C.17) and (C.29) for t_{ij} and $t(R,R^*)$, respectively.

The significance of an outcome can be computed from its *t* statistic if the populations from which the samples were taken were normally distributed or approximately so. The spreadsheet computation for the single-tailed, pairwise error (PWE) is given by:

$$e_{PWE} = TDIST(ABS(t), \text{df}, 1) \tag{C.33}$$

If the two-tailed error is of interest, replace the 1 in Equation (C.33) by a 2.

C.6 CONFOUNDING OF MAIN EFFECTS WITH INTERACTION TERMS

Consider the problem of the outcomes computed for main effects being affected (confounded) by interaction terms using a $L_9(3^4)$ OA, Table C.1. This OA is a saturated design in that the number of unknowns equals the number of experimental trials. The simulated outcomes contain a strong 1221 interaction, which leads to confounding errors (aliasing) when computing the λ_{ij} coefficients with the main effects model.

The only λ_{ij} coefficients (LAM) in Table C.1 that are correct are those for 0, 11, 22 and 41. All the others should be zero but are not due to confounding by the 1221 interaction. The sources of confounding are discovered by constructing the confounding array:

$$\mathbf{X}_{CF} = \mathbf{X}_S \mathbf{X}_{FF}^*$$

(C.34)

The matrix $\mathbf{X}_{FF}^*$ consists of the $\mathbf{X}$ matrix plus all of the columns for the interactions of interest between the main effects. (No additional rows are added.) The size of $\mathbf{X}_{FF}^*$ can become cumbersome if all interactions are included. For the design array in Table C.1, the pairwise interactions alone generate an additional 22 columns. The rows for $\mathbf{X}_{CF}$ have the *ij* indices for the main effects, whereas the columns have these same indices plus the interactions *ijkl* and so on. Only a portion of the full confounding array for the $L_9(3^4)$ OA is shown in Table C.2. A one in row *ij* for column *ij* signifies that the main effect interacts with itself. Since there is no new information in the main effect columns, they can be dropped from $\mathbf{X}_{FF}^*$. A zero in row *ij* for column *kl* denotes that the two main effects do not confound, in that a change in the contribution from one does not affect the other. Likewise a zero in row *ij* for column *klmn* denotes that the presence of an ignored but real *klmn* interaction does not affect main effect *ij*. A nonzero entry of an amount *x* in row *ij* denotes that the *klmn* interaction of size θ contributes an amount $x\theta$ to the *ij* main effect.

Table C.1 Lambda form of the $L_9(3^4)$ OA along with the columns for sample size, sample variance, sample mean, and lambda coefficients.

	S	T	U	V	W	X	Y	Z	AA	AB	AC	AD	AE	AF	AG	AH
14	Trial	0	11	12	21	22	31	32	41	42	n	SVAR	Y			LAM
15	1	1	0	0	0	0	0	0	0	0	5	1	5		0	5.00
16	2	1	0	0	1	0	1	0	1	0	5	1	5		11	3.00
17	3	1	0	0	0	1	0	1	0	1	5	2	5		12	1.00
18	4	1	1	0	0	0	1	0	0	1	5	2	8		21	1.00
19	5	1	1	0	1	0	0	1	0	0	5	3	8		22	0.00
20	6	1	1	0	0	1	0	0	1	0	5	3	8		31	-1.00
21	7	1	0	1	0	0	0	1	1	0	5	1	5		32	-1.00
22	8	1	0	1	1	0	0	0	0	1	5	2	8		41	0.00
23	9	1	0	1	0	1	1	0	0	0	5	3	5		42	1.00

Table C.2 A portion of the confounding array for the $L_9(3^4)$ OA in Table C.1.

ij	0	11	12	21	22	31	32	41	42	1121	1122	1131	1132	1141	1142	1221
0	1	0	0	0	0	0	0	0	0	0	0	0	0	0	0	0
11	0	1	0	0	0	0	0	0	0	0.33	0.33	0.33	0.33	0.33	0.33	0.00
12	0	0	1	0	0	0	0	0	0	0.00	0.00	0.00	0.00	0.00	0.00	0.33
21	0	0	0	1	0	0	0	0	0	0.33	0.00	-0.33	0.33	0.00	-0.33	0.33
22	0	0	0	0	1	0	0	0	0	0.00	0.33	-0.33	0.00	0.33	-0.33	0.00
31	0	0	0	0	0	1	0	0	0	0.00	-0.33	0.33	0.00	-0.33	0.33	-0.33
32	0	0	0	0	0	0	1	0	0	0.33	-0.33	0.00	0.33	-0.33	0.00	-0.33
41	0	0	0	0	0	0	0	1	0	-0.33	0.33	0.00	-0.33	0.33	0.00	0.00
42	0	0	0	0	0	0	0	0	1	-0.33	0.00	0.33	-0.33	0.00	0.33	0.33

Table C.3 Comparison of the lambda coefficients with the elements in the 1221 column from the confounding array.

	LAM	1221
0	5.00	0.000
11	3.00	0.000
12	1.00	0.333
21	1.00	0.333
22	0.00	0.000
31	−1.00	−0.333
32	−1.00	−0.333
41	0.00	0.000
42	1.00	0.333

The lambda coefficients for the $L_9(3^4)$ OA are compared in Table C.3 with the elements in row 1221 of the confounding array. The size θ of the 1221 interaction for this problem was taken as 3. The values of the confounded main effects are seen to equal ± 1. This follows from the size of 3 chosen for 1221 and the nonzero values of $\pm 1/3$ for 1221 from the confounding array. Because of the possibility of significant interactions being overlooked when using a main effects only design, Taguchi recommends that a confirmation experiment be run to verify the findings.

C.7 RESOLUTION

Experimental designs are classified into different levels of resolution. In resolution III designs, main effects are confounded with pairwise interactions but not with each other. In resolution IV designs, main effects are clear of each other and pairwise interactions. However, pairwise interactions are confounded with each other. In resolution V designs, main effects and pairwise interactions are not confounded with each other, but pairwise effects are confounded by three-way interactions.

Consider, for illustration, the phi design in Table C.4 constructed from the L8(2^4) SDW (see Appendix F for SDW descriptions), which has four main effects and three interactions. Factor 41 is placed in the last column with the expectation that it will not interact strongly with the other main effects. The FF* and confounding matrices for this design, Table C.5, show that if the 1141 coefficient is not negligible, it will confound with the 2131 coefficient. This interaction makes it a resolution IV design. The lambda form for this design is shown in Table C.6. Its FF* and confounding matrices, Table C.7, show that it is a resolution III design as the 1141 coefficient will confound with all four main effects.

Table C.4 $L_8(2^4)$ phi design with three interactions.

Trial	0	11	21	1121	31	1131	2131	41
1	1	−1	−1	1	−1	1	1	−1
2	1	−1	−1	1	1	−1	−1	1
3	1	−1	1	−1	−1	1	−1	1
4	1	−1	1	−1	1	−1	1	−1
5	1	1	−1	−1	−1	−1	1	1
6	1	1	−1	−1	1	1	−1	−1
7	1	1	1	1	−1	−1	−1	−1
8	1	1	1	1	1	1	1	1

Table C.5 The FF* and confounding matrices for the design in Table C.4.

FF*

	1121	1131	2131	1141
1	1	1	1	1
2	1	−1	−1	−1
3	−1	1	−1	−1
4	−1	−1	1	1
5	−1	−1	1	1
6	−1	1	−1	−1
7	1	−1	−1	−1
8	1	1	1	1

Confounding

	1121	1131	2131	1141
0	0	0	0	0
11	0	0	0	0
21	0	0	0	0
1121	1	0	0	0
31	0	0	0	0
1131	0	1	0	0
2131	0	0	1	1
41	0	0	0	0

Table C.6 $L_8(2^4)$ lambda design with three interactions.

Trial	0	11	21	1121	31	1131	2131	41
1	1	0	0	0	0	0	0	0
2	1	0	0	0	1	0	0	1
3	1	0	1	0	0	0	0	1
4	1	0	1	0	1	0	1	0
5	1	1	0	0	0	0	0	1
6	1	1	0	0	1	1	0	0
7	1	1	1	1	0	0	0	0
8	1	1	1	1	1	1	1	1

Table C.7 The FF* and confounding matrices for the design in Table C.6.

FF*

	1121	1131	2131	1141
1	0	0	0	0
2	0	0	0	0
3	0	0	0	0
4	0	0	1	0
5	0	0	0	1
6	0	1	0	0
7	1	0	0	0
8	1	1	1	1

Confounding

	1121	1131	2131	1141
0	0	0	0	0
11	0	0	0	0.5
21	0	0	0	−0.5
1121	1	0	0	0
31	0	0	0	−0.5
1131	0	1	0	0
2131	0	0	1	1
41	0	0	0	0.5

This may seem confusing, as the phi and lambda forms are for the same basic experimental design of four main effects and three interactions. The only difference is that the reference point for the phi coefficients is the average of all of the trials and the default reference point for the lambda coefficients is trial 1, but any other trial could be chosen. Is the phi form better because it avoids confounding with the pairwise interactions? Not for the problem at hand. For strategic experiments, the coefficients are measured relative to trial 1, in which case lambda and phi give the same result. (They, of course, give the same result for the difference between *any* two states.)

Roughly speaking, for fractional factorial experiments, the phi form minimizes the confounding of main effects with pairwise interactions relative to the lambda form. The downside is that the phi form increases the degree of confounding when computing the differences between states. For example, when using the lambda form, a change from baseline $(1,0,0, \ldots)$ to the state $(1,1,0,0, \ldots)$, no interactions need to be accounted for explicitly. When representing this change using the phi form, there are a host of interactions already at trial 1 $(1,-1,-1,-1, \ldots)$ many of which change in going to the alternate state $(1,1,-1,-1, \ldots)$. From the point of error generation in evaluating differences between states, the phi form confounding of 1141 with 2131 is no less serious than the lambda form confounding of 1141 with the four main effects.

The issue of interactions in many respects is a tempest in a teapot. Simply put, if certain interactions are known to be important, then design the experiment so they are measured. If interactions are not expected to be important, then evaluate additional main effects and run a confirmation experiment to verify the results.

REFERENCE

1. F. E. Satterthwaite. 1946. "An Approximate Distribution of Estimates of Variance Components," *Biometrics Bulletin* 2, pp. 110–114.

Appendix D

Monte Carlo Analysis of a Binomial Distribution Problem

In Chapter 12 the variance of $Ln(p)$ for the binomial distribution problem was computed using the Taylor expansion approximation. It is instructive to check the accuracy of the findings using Monte Carlo simulation. Moreover, the exercise illustrates a general, lookup-table approach that can be used when the Taylor expansion and the normal distribution assumption are poor approximations due to a small sample size.

The results of 600 Monte Carlo simulations for the lambda coefficients (LAMSIMij) and their standard deviations (SDMC) are shown in Figure D.1. At the top of Figure D.1 are the means and standard deviations for the normal probability plots. The SDij in Table 12.14 and the SDMC in Table D.1 are in good agreement, as are the two sets of lambda coefficients. The plots of the simulations in Figure D.1 are linear, which provides strong support for the assumption that the lambda coefficients are normally distributed over a fairly wide range. Nevertheless, the t distribution was used with a conservative sample size of 30 to compute the PWE because the number of simulations was not large enough to confirm linear behavior below 1% and above 99%.

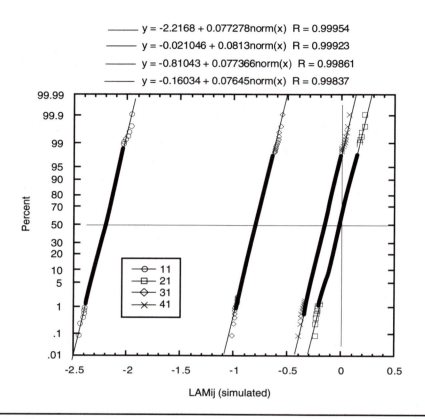

———— y = -2.2168 + 0.077278norm(x) R = 0.99954
———— y = -0.021046 + 0.0813norm(x) R = 0.99923
———— y = -0.81043 + 0.077366norm(x) R = 0.99861
———— y = -0.16034 + 0.07645norm(x) R = 0.99837

Figure D.1   Normal probability plots of the 600 simulations for each factor.

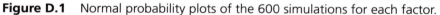

Table D.1   Computation of the EWE for the coefficients using Monte Carlo simulation. The results here should be compared to those in Table 12.14.

		TRANSPOSE LAMSIMij	TRANSPOSE SDMC	tMC	PWEMC	EWEMC
0	0	-0.41	0.044	-9.30		
A	11	-2.22	0.078	-28.74	1.09E-23	0
B	21	-0.02	0.081	-0.30	3.82E-01	1.53
C	31	-0.81	0.077	-10.64	5.26E-12	0.00
D	41	-0.16	0.077	-1.95	3.06E-02	0.12

D.1 STEP 1: CONSTRUCT LOOKUP TABLE FOR RANGE OF POSSIBLE DEFECT POPULATIONS

The five-step process used in constructing the Monte Carlo analysis is shown from Table D.2 through Table D.6. Only the first 10 rows are shown in each table. Table D.2 lists in each column the individual number of defects Y_p (array name PMEAN) across the three sigma ranges for the populations for each of the eight experimental trials. The eight numbers (array name ThreeSig) in row 2 across columns Q through X of Table D.2 (45, 36, etc.) represent values that are three standard deviations on the low side of the mean of each trial. The expression for ThreeSig is given by

$$\text{ThreeSig} = 3 * \text{SQRT(TRANSPOSE(p)} * (1 - \text{TRANSPOSE((p))} * \text{NP}$$

where N_p (NP) is the population size, which can be made arbitrarily large. For convenience, it is taken to be equal to 1000. The numbers in the first line of the enumerated list in Table D.2 were computed using the expression

$$\text{ROUND(TRANSPOSE(p)} * \text{NP} - \text{ThreeSig}, 0)$$

which generates a value for the number of defects that is approximately three standard deviations from the expected mean of the distribution, $p(q)N_p$, for trial q. The remainder of

Table D.2   Range of possible values for the number of bad parts in the populations (N_p) for each trial. Only the first 10 rows of the list are shown.

	P	Q	R	S	T	U	V	W	X
1		ThreeSig=3*SQRT(TRANSPOSE(p)*(1-TRANSPOSE(p))*NP)							
2		45	36	45	45	27	16	18	16
3	NP			Sample size n =		1000			
4	1000				PMEAN				
5			first row =ROUND(TRANSPOSE(p)*NP-ThreeSig,0)						
6			1	2	3	4	5	6	7	8
7	1	614	136	610	313	65	14	21	15
8	2	615	137	611	314	66	15	22	16
9	3	616	138	612	315	67	16	23	17
10	4	617	139	613	316	68	17	24	18
11	5	618	140	614	317	69	18	25	19
12	6	619	141	615	318	70	19	26	20
13	7	620	142	616	319	71	20	27	21
14	8	621	143	617	320	72	21	28	22
15	9	622	144	618	321	73	22	29	23
16	10	623	145	619	322	74	23	30	24

the lookup table was computed simply by adding a one to form the number in each new row. If computation speed were not an issue, a single column from 0 to 1000 could be used for all of the trials.

D.2 STEP 2: CONSTRUCT CUMULATIVE DISTRIBUTION TABLE

Given the value of vector of sample means (SMEAN) for the trials computed from the expression

$$SMEAN=TRANSPOSE(p) * n$$

the cumulative distribution, κ, is listed in Table D.3 as a function of the defect *populations* represented by the array variable PMEAN in Table D.2. The κ were computed from the spreadsheet expression

$$1-BINOMDIST(SMEAN,n,PMEAN/NP,1)$$

The last argument in the expression for BINOMDIST is a logical value; a one returns the required cumulative distribution and a zero returns the frequency distribution.

Table D.3 Cumulative distribution values for κ for the populations in each of the trials given the sample number of defects for the trials. Only the first 10 rows of the list are shown.

	Y	Z	AA	AB	AC	AD	AE	AF	AG
3		**SMEAN=TRANSPOSE(p)*n**							
4		659	172	655	358	92	30	39	31
5		Binomial Cumulative Distribution =1-BINOMDIST(SMEAN,n,PMEAN/NP,1)							
6		1	2	3	4	5	6	7	8
7	1	0.0015	0.0005	0.0015	0.0011	0.0004	0.0001	0.0001	0.0001
8	2	0.0018	0.0008	0.0018	0.0013	0.0007	0.0002	0.0003	0.0002
9	3	0.0022	0.0011	0.0022	0.0017	0.0010	0.0005	0.0007	0.0007
10	4	0.0027	0.0014	0.0027	0.0021	0.0016	0.0013	0.0015	0.0016
11	5	0.0033	0.0020	0.0033	0.0026	0.0024	0.0031	0.0031	0.0037
12	6	0.0040	0.0026	0.0040	0.0032	0.0036	0.0065	0.0058	0.0075
13	7	0.0048	0.0035	0.0049	0.0039	0.0053	0.0126	0.0104	0.0142
14	8	0.0058	0.0046	0.0059	0.0048	0.0076	0.0229	0.0176	0.0252
15	9	0.0069	0.0060	0.0071	0.0059	0.0107	0.0388	0.0284	0.0417
16	10	0.0083	0.0078	0.0084	0.0071	0.0149	0.0618	0.0437	0.0654

D.3 STEP 3: ALGORITHM FOR PICKING POINTS FROM CUMULATIVE DISTRIBUTION LIST

The expressions listed in column AH of Table D.4 represent the computations used column AI. These are dragged across to generate the expressions for the other columns. The computations in Table D.4 are initiated in row 5 with the selection of a random number between 0 and 1 for each trial. If this number is below the first cumulative distribution value in Table D.3, it is set to this value in row 6. The expression in row 7 represents a special boundary condition, row 8 being the general expression dragged down to complete the computations. The resulting fraction is compared to each value for the cumulative distribution for the same trial in Table D.3. The logical If statements enter a value of 0 or FALSE(=0) into each cell when there is no match and enter the population value for Y_p when there is a match. The variable Y_p, which is a whole number, is tracked in the computations instead of the fractional results for κ because it provides greater clarity in checking for errors in the computations. Finally, the value for the match is transferred to row 4 of the spreadsheet at the top of the table by summing all of the outcomes down a given row as the only nonzero value in the sum is the value that was selected for the population.

Table D.4 Random numbers are generated for the cumulative distributions and a simulated value of the number of bad parts for the population for each trial is selected. Only the first 10 rows of the list are shown.

	AH	AI	AJ	AK	AL	AM	AN	AO	AP
1					Trial				
2		1	2	3	4	5	6	7	8
3									
4	=SUM(AI7:AI81)	659	168	657	364	88	23	37	32
5	=RAND()	0.4800040	0.331159	0.52107	0.637417	0.284882	0.038803	0.298168	0.523856
6	=IF(AI5<Z7,Z7,AI5)	0.4800040	0.331159	0.52107	0.637417	0.284882	0.038803	0.298168	0.523856
7	=IF(AI$6<Z7,Q7,IF(AI$6<Z8,Q8,0))	0	0	0	0	0	0	0	0
8	=IF(AI$6>=Z8,IF(AI$6<Z9,Q9,0))	0	0	0	0	0	0	0	0
9		0	0	0	0	0	0	0	0
10		0	0	0	0	0	0	0	0
11		0	0	0	0	0	0	0	0
12		0	0	0	0	0	0	0	0
13		0	0	0	0	0	0	0	0
14		0	0	0	0	0	0	0	0
15		0	0	0	0	0	23	0	0
16		0	0	0	0	0	FALSE	0	0

D.4 STEP 4: STORAGE OF SIMULATED VALUES FOR THE DEFECT POPULATIONS

The simulated possible values for the population, given the sample number of defects for each trial that are generated in row 4 of Table D.4, are captured and placed in another location in the spreadsheet, row 7 of Table D.5. As logs are taken of the outcomes in Table D.5, methods for working around the possibility of outcomes equal to zero may be needed as discussed in Appendix E. The Monte Carlo simulations were run by capturing the repeated outcomes in row 7 of Table D.5 and placing them sequentially in the rows underneath.

Table D.5 Capture of the simulations for each trial. Only the first 10 rows of the list are shown.

	AY	AZ	BA	BB	BC	BD	BE	BF
5	**1**	**2**	**3**	**4**	**5**	**6**	**7**	**8**
6	=$AI$4	=$AJ$4	=$AK$4	=$AL$4	=$AM$4	=$AN$4	=$AO$4	=$AP$4
7	659	168	657	364	88	23	37	32
8	684	159	637	338	76	38	48	32
9	665	184	678	374	92	31	33	35
10	679	164	678	380	84	31	48	38
11	653	192	637	345	84	32	35	40
12	669	174	659	379	93	31	38	35
13	675	171	681	337	96	31	41	35
14	685	170	671	367	97	31	44	25
15	688	174	678	359	88	31	33	37
16	674	189	684	375	92	27	48	30

D.5 STEP 5: COMPUTATION OF THE SIMULATED LAMBDA COEFFICIENTS

The lambda coefficients for $Ln(\kappa)$ were computed as log of the simulated Y_p populations divided by $n = 1000$ using the expression

$$TRANSPOSE(MMULT(XS,TRANSPOSE(LN(AY7:BF7/10^3))))$$

These coefficients were placed in row 7 across columns BI through BM, which are shown in Table D.6. The standard deviations (SDMC) of the 600 outcomes for each factor were

Table D.6 Computation of the individual simulated lambda coefficients for each simulation and the computation of the resulting means (LAMSIMij) and standard deviations (SDMC) for the coefficients. Only the first 10 rows of the list are shown.

	BH	BI	BJ	BK	BL	BM	BN
4		0	A (11)	B (21)	C (31)	D (41)	
5	SDMC	0.044	0.078	0.081	0.077	0.077	=STDEV(BI8:BI610)
6	LAMSIMij	-0.408	-2.216	-0.021	-0.811	-0.161	=AVERAGE(BI8:BI1063)
7	=TRANSPOSE(MMULT(XS,	-0.448	-2.328	0.058	-0.861	-0.118	
8	TRANSPOSE(LN(AY7:BF7/NP))))	-0.422	-2.143	0.013	-0.798	-0.249	
9		-0.376	-2.288	-0.044	-0.727	-0.213	
10		-0.448	-2.177	0.121	-0.808	-0.192	
11		-0.427	-2.225	-0.023	-0.667	-0.251	
12		-0.408	-2.233	-0.003	-0.770	-0.180	
13		-0.383	-2.183	-0.011	-0.841	-0.197	
14		-0.357	-2.267	-0.064	-0.926	-0.073	
15		-0.370	-2.269	-0.024	-0.735	-0.270	
16		-0.406	-2.280	0.039	-0.892	-0.044	

computed and are shown in row 5 of the spreadsheet. The average down each column yields the simulated mean values for the lambda coefficients, which are listed in row 6 of the spreadsheet, name array LAMSIMij. The results for LAMSIMij were transferred to the first column of Table D.1, and the results for SDMC were transferred to the second column of Table D.1.

Appendix E

Monte Carlo Analysis of a Poisson Distribution Problem

The Poisson distribution problem in Chapter 12 is reevaluated here using the Monte Carlo simulation. The steps in the process are similar in many respects to those for the lookup Monte Carlo used for the binomial distribution in Appendix D. Normal probability plots of the simulation outcomes are shown in Figure E.1. The mean values and standard deviations are listed above the plots.

E.1 STEPS 1 AND 2: COMBINED LOOKUP AND CUMULATIVE DISTRIBUTION TABLES

The computations in support of the simulations are listed in Table E.1 through Table E.7. The steps used in the process are described in the remainder of Appendix E.

Given the sample means for the trials, the possible values for the defect populations are listed as the column array PMEAN in Table E.1. A single column could be used as opposed to use of a separate column for each trial for the binomial distribution in Appendix D because the differences in the expected ranges for the defects between the trials were less. The cumulative distributions for each of the trials are shown for the first five trials in Table E.1. The sample means (SMEAN) for each trial shown in row 4 represent the transpose of Y from Table 12.17.

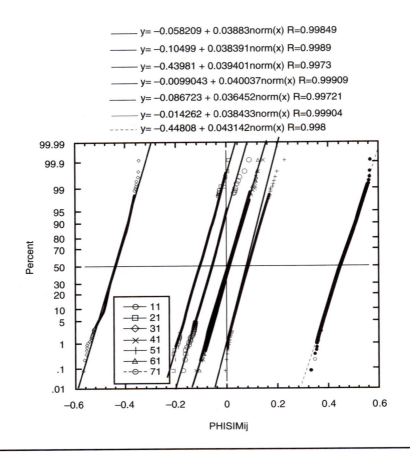

——— y= −0.058209 + 0.03883norm(x) R=0.99849
——— y= −0.10499 + 0.038391norm(x) R=0.9989
——— y= −0.43981 + 0.039401norm(x) R=0.9973
——— y= −0.0099043 + 0.040037norm(x) R=0.99909
——— y= −0.086723 + 0.036452norm(x) R=0.99721
——— y= −0.014262 + 0.038433norm(x) R=0.99904
- - - - - y= −0.44808 + 0.043142norm(x) R=0.998

Figure E.1 Normal probability plots of the simulated phi coefficients.

Table E.1 Values for the cumulative distributions for trials 1 through 5 as a function of the number of defects (PMEAN) in the population shown in the first column.

	E	F	G	H	I	J
3	Trial	**1**	**2**	**3**	**4**	**5**
4	SMEAN	16.3333	8.6667	8.3333	46.3333	12.0000
5						
6	PMEAN		=1-POISSON(SMEAN,PMEAN,1)			
7	1	8.9E-16	1.1E-06	1.1E-06	-2.2E-16	6.4E-11
8	2	5.6E-11	2.4E-04	2.4E-04	1.1E-16	2.1E-07
9	3	2.2E-08	3.8E-03	3.8E-03	1.1E-16	1.6E-05
10	4	1.1E-06	2.1E-02	2.1E-02	-2.2E-16	2.7E-04
11	5	2.0E-05	6.8E-02	6.8E-02	7.8E-16	2.0E-03
12	6	1.7E-04	1.5E-01	1.5E-01	-2.2E-16	8.8E-03
13	7	9.6E-04	2.7E-01	2.7E-01	1.6E-15	2.7E-02
14	8	3.7E-03	4.1E-01	4.1E-01	1.9E-15	6.4E-02
15	9	1.1E-02	5.4E-01	5.4E-01	-1.3E-15	1.2E-01
16	10	2.7E-02	6.7E-01	6.7E-01	-2.0E-15	2.1E-01

E.2 STEP 3: ALGORITHM FOR PICKING POINTS FROM CUMULATIVE DISTRIBUTION LIST

Table E.2 shows the computations used for each trial to generate the random numbers used set equal to the cumulative distribution for each trial. These cumulative distribution values were then used to select a representative value for the population mean. The summing algorithm used for the binomial distribution in Appendix D was also used here to pick the simulated population mean from each column (see row 6 of the spreadsheet).

Table E.2 Random selection of the cumulative distribution for each trial and the resulting values for the population mean.

	W	X	Y	Z	AA	AB
1						
2						
3	=RAND()	0.878089	0.271582	0.416194	0.65104	0.07263
4						
5	=SUM(X7:X206)	21	7	8	49	8
6	=IF(X$4>F7,IF(X$4<F8,$E7),0)	FALSE	FALSE	FALSE	FALSE	FALSE
7		FALSE	FALSE	FALSE	FALSE	FALSE
8		FALSE	FALSE	FALSE	FALSE	FALSE
9		FALSE	FALSE	FALSE	FALSE	FALSE
10		FALSE	FALSE	FALSE	FALSE	FALSE
11		FALSE	FALSE	FALSE	FALSE	FALSE
12		FALSE	7	FALSE	FALSE	FALSE
13		FALSE	0	8	FALSE	8
14		FALSE	0	0	FALSE	0
15		FALSE	0	0	FALSE	0

E.3 STEP 4: STORAGE OF SIMULATED VALUES FOR THE DEFECT POPULATIONS

As each simulation was generated, the results for the population defects in row 6 of Table E.2 were automatically copied and pasted in row 7 at another location in the spreadsheet shown in Table E.3. As logarithms are taken of the simulated outcomes, outcomes equal to zero require special handling. For this particular problem, any outcome of zero was simply changed to an outcome of one, which had no appreciable effect as the sample means were such that zeros rarely appeared. Another way to work around this issue would be to add a smaller number such as 0.1 to every simulated value.

Table E.3   Copy and collection of simulated values for the defect populations.

	AO	AP	AQ	AR	AS	AT
5		1	2	3	4	5
6	=IF(X$6=0,1,X$6)	21	7	8	49	8
7		20	11	6	40	19
8		13	5	6	51	15
9		23	11	5	49	16
10		9	10	11	40	11
11		12	9	7	45	13
12		14	11	7	47	17
13		13	13	9	57	11
14		18	10	8	39	18
15		18	8	6	44	11
16		12	11	8	43	8

E.4 STEP 5: COMPUTATION OF THE SIMULATED PHI COEFFICIENTS

After 600 simulations were run, the results in Table E.3 were averaged in groups of three as shown in Table E.4 to simulate the role of the sample size of $n(q) = n = 3$. Strictly speaking, this process should precede by averaging simulations 1,2,3 then 4,5,6 and so forth. Practically speaking, this is too laborious for the limited gain in rigor. Instead, the averaging was done for simulations 1,2,3 then 2,3,4 then 3,4,5 and so forth, which was convenient in that one formula could be written and then dragged down to compute the rest. This process also generated three times as many points making for a smoother curve on plotting the results. Once the averaging was completed, the phi coefficients for each simulation were computed as shown in Table E.5. The average value for each coefficient (PHISIMij) was determined along with the standard deviations computed by the Monte Carlo process (SDMC) for the coefficients, listed in rows 5 and 6 respectively in Table E.5.

Table E.4   Averaging of the defect populations by threes.

	CQ	CR	CS	CT	CU	CV
6		1	2	3	4	5
7	=AVERAGE(AP7:AP9)	18.66666667	9	5.6667	46.667	16.667
8	=AVERAGE(AP8:AP10)	15	8.6666667	7.3333	46.667	14
9	=AVERAGE(AP9:AP11)	14.66666667	10	7.6667	44.667	13.333
10		11.66666667	10	8.3333	44	13.667
11		13	11	7.6667	49.667	13.667
12		15	11.333333	8	47.667	15.333
13		16.33333333	10.333333	7.6667	46.667	13.333
14		16	9.6666667	7.3333	42	12.333
15		14	8.3333333	8.3333	43.667	10
16		13	9	8	44.333	10.333

The outcomes for the Monte Carlo process are summarized in Table E.6. They are seen to be close to the values using the Taylor expansion approximation in Chapter 12.

Table E.5 Computation of the phi coefficients for each row in Table E.4 and the computation of the overall averages, PHISIMij, in row 6 and standard deviations, SDMC, in row 5.

	DI	DJ	DK	DL	DM	DN
4		0	11	21	31	41
5	SDMC	0.038	0.038	0.040	0.039	0.037
6	PHISIMij	-2.910	-0.058	-0.111	-0.439	0.008
7	=TRANSPOSE(MMULT(XXS,	-2.921	-0.049	-0.132	-0.413	0.065
8	TRANSPOSE(-LN(CR7:DG7))))	-2.881	-0.036	-0.116	-0.456	0.028
9		-2.882	-0.035	-0.101	-0.431	0.012
10		-2.900	-0.066	-0.106	-0.406	-0.058
11		-2.911	-0.019	-0.107	-0.417	-0.093
12		-2.941	-0.017	-0.106	-0.376	-0.074
13		-2.902	-0.006	-0.095	-0.425	-0.011
14		-2.858	-0.061	-0.084	-0.421	0.027
15		-2.839	-0.056	-0.110	-0.471	0.055
16		-2.854	-0.093	-0.083	-0.484	0.041

Table E.6 Computation of EWE (EWEMC) of the PHISIMij coefficients as computed from the Monte Carlo simulation results. The df (DFij) used of 25.3 was taken from Table 12.18.

	TRANSPOSE PHISIMij	TRANSPOSE SDMC	tMC	PWEMC	EWEMC
0	-2.910	0.0379	-76.857	0	
11	-0.058	0.0380	-1.520	0.071	1.06
21	-0.111	0.0403	-2.750	0.005	0.08
31	-0.439	0.0387	-11.356	0.000	0.00
41	0.008	0.0366	0.228	0.411	6.16
51	0.082	0.0378	2.165	0.020	0.30
61	0.018	0.0383	0.465	0.323	4.85
71	0.452	0.0380	11.884	0.000	0.00
1121	0.026	0.0376	0.697	0.246	3.69
1131	-0.142	0.0360	-3.930	0.000	0.00
1141	0.042	0.0385	1.102	0.141	2.11
2131	-0.018	0.0409	-0.441	0.332	4.97
2141	0.311	0.0382	8.129	0.000	0.00
3141	-0.117	0.0415	-2.818	0.005	0.07
3151	-0.015	0.0378	-0.404	0.345	5.17
112131	0.018	0.0385	0.475	0.319	4.79

TRANSPOSE PHISIMij	=TRANSPOSE(PHISIMij)	**PWEMC**	=TDIST(ABS(tMC),DFij,1)
TRANSPOSE SDMC	=TRANSPOSE(SDMC)	**EWEMC**	=15*PWEMC
tMC	=TRANSPOSE(PHISIMij)/TRANSPOSE(SDMC)		

Appendix F

Use of SDWs and Templates on CD-ROM for Analysis Automation

The process for Level 1 analysis is well automated using software packages such as MINITAB, Design Expert, and SAS. However, they do not treat important aspects of strategic experiments for Levels 2, 3, and 4. Consequently, more than 40 Strategic Design Workbooks (SDWs) have been developed to partially automate the analysis for some of the more common experimental designs. These are listed in Table F.1. Templates have also been generated to aid in the development of other designs (see Table F.2). For completeness, several aspects of Level 1 analysis are also included in the SDWs. As fresh designs are created, they can be added to the user's SDW library. The SDWs and templates are included on the CD-ROM with this book.

Table F.1   Incomplete list of Strategic Design Workbooks.

1 L4(2^3)	**15** L16(2^15)	**29** L9(2^1,3^3)
2 L4(2^3) PHI	**16** L32(2^31)	**30** L9(2^2,3^3)
3 L8(2^4) PHI	**17** L32(2^31) PHI	**31** L12(2^3,3^1)
4 L8(2^4) 3 int	**18** L9(3^2) FF	**32** L12(2^4,3^1)
5 L8(2^4) 3 int PHI	**19** L9(3^2) FF PHI	**33** L12(2^4,3^1) PHI
6 L8(2^7)	**20** L9(3^4)	**34** L18(2^1,3^7)
7 L8(2^7) Lognormal	**21** L9(3^4) Lognormal	**35** L16(4^1,2^12)
8 L8(2^7) Binomial	**22** L16(4^5)	**36** L12(3^1,4^1) FF
9 L8(2^7) Poisson	**23** L25(5^6)	**37** L12(3^1,4^1) FF PHI
10 L8(2^3) FF	**24** L27(3^3) FF	**38** L12(4^1,3^1,2^1)
11 L12(2^11)	**25** L32(2^31)	**39** L20(5^1,2^8)
12 L16(2^5) 3 int	**26** L32(2^31) PHI	**40** L20(5^1,2^8) Lognormal
13 L16(2^5) 10 int	**27** L6(2^2,3^1)	
14 L16(2^8) resIV	**28** L8(4^1,2^4)	

Each SDW includes worksheets dedicated to one element of the analysis. Users, of course, have the full flexibility and transparency afforded by the spreadsheet and can modify any SDW to generate different output computations and plots to suit personal taste. If multiple attributes are being considered, a separate SDW for each should be used as each attribute will have a different value curve. The results for each attribute can then be combined into a summary workbook.

F.1 DESCRIPTION OF THE SDW WORKSHEETS

The computations performed by each of the worksheets in a typical SDW are described below in the order in which they typically appear. The first seven worksheets examine the influence of the factors on mean and variance. The remaining worksheets examine the influence of the factors on value and CIQ using Monte Carlo simulation.

Design and Outcomes

This worksheet contains the design matrix (X), the solution matrix (XS), and a column vector representing the *diagonal* of the unit variance covariance matrix (COV). Up to 10 replications per trial can be entered, and the number of replications can vary from trial to trial. Rose-colored backgrounds identify cells in the worksheet for data entry. The sample means (Y) and variances (SVAR) are computed automatically from the replications as are the number of replications per trial, n. A default model named YMODEL is computed in the LAM Coefficients worksheet by setting to zero those coefficients whose EWE exceeds the significance level ALPHALAM, which is entered by the user in the Lambda Coefficients worksheet. YMODEL is copied and placed in the Design and Outcomes worksheet beside Y to ease comparisons.

A second default model named SVARMODEL is computed for SVAR in the XI Coefficients worksheet by setting to zero those XI coefficients whose EWE exceeds the significance level ALPHAXI which is entered by the user in the XI Coefficients worksheet. This model is copied and placed in the Design & Outcomes worksheet beside SVAR. The pooled sample variance, PSVAR, and R^2 are computed automatically. For simplicity, all of the expressions used in the computations use LAM as the name for the coefficients for the mean even if a phi design is being evaluated. This should cause minimal confusion, as it is clear from the design matrix if a phi or lambda design is being used.

Level 1

This worksheet computes the significance of the coefficients for the mean using the pooled sample variance and pooled df. If only one replication per trial is made, the analysis must be made using the LOF worksheet. The lambda coefficients (LAM) are duplicated from the LAM worksheet. A default, reduced set of coefficients (REDLAM_1) is also constructed for Level 1 by setting to zero those coefficients whose Type I EWE error exceeds the value set for level 1. The model named YMODEL_1 is computed from these coefficients.

LOF

This worksheet computes the significance of the coefficients of the mean using the lack of fit (LOF) variance between the model with $w < z$ and actual outcomes. (This worksheet is not included in every SDW.) Weaker factors are systematically eliminated from the model by entering 0s in their rows in the column vector KEEP, as described in Section (7.6). A reduced set of coefficients (KEEPLAM) is then constructed and an estimated pooled variance (SSLOFvar) is computed. This LOF variance is compared to the pooled variance (PSVAR) using the standard F ratio test. A *large* Type I error is good in that it indicates that the two variances are similar and that the LOF model is about as good as can be expected, considering the error in the measurements.

Contrasts

This worksheet computes the difference and PWE significance between any two states using the general form for Satterthwaite's df and approximate t test described in Appendix C.

XI Coefficients

This worksheet computes the coefficients of -10 times the base 10 log of the sample variances. A default set of coefficients is constructed (REDXI) based upon the Type I error entered for these coefficients (ALPHAXI). The experiment-wise errors are computed by interpolation when the sample size is not constant. As discussed above, the default set is used to construct the default model (SVARMODEL), which is placed in the Design and Outcomes worksheet adjacent to sample variances (SVAR). The user can modify the default set for the coefficients as desired. Note that the first entries in the MIN and MAX PWE columns are partially disguised to denote that the Bonferroni transform of PWE to EWE does not apply to the baseline.

Variance Direct

When examining the influence of the factors on variance, it can be insightful to compute also the coefficients for variance instead of the logarithm of variance. Coefficients determined in this manner can be analyzed for significance using the distribution generated by Monte Carlo simulations, but they should not be summed together to project the variance for a combination of factors. Although this worksheet is not present in all SDWs, it can be copied and pasted easily from one SDW to another.

LAM Coefficients

This worksheet computes the coefficients of the means and their significance using Satterthwaite's df and approximate t test. As discussed above, a default set of coefficients (REDLAM) is constructed by setting those coefficients to zero whose EWE exceeds the Type I error (ALPHALAM) set by the user. The resulting significant factors are used to construct the default model (YMODEL), which is placed in the Design and Outcomes worksheet adjacent to sample means (Y). The user can modify the default set of REDLAM coefficients as desired. Note that the first entry in the PWE column is partially disguised to denote that the name PWE for the column does not include the baseline (first entry). Likewise the EWE is computed differently for the baseline and off-baseline coefficients.

Variance Mean & CIQ Simulation

This worksheet simulates the ranges for the population means and variances which are then transformed into simulations for value and the CIQ (CIQSIM1). Lambda coefficients for -10 times the log base 10 of the CIQ are then computed as a column vector (LAMSN1), which is transposed to a row to aid in making repeated Monte Carlo simulations. The distributions from the simulations are used to assess the strategic significance of the coefficients. If the attribute is of the NIB1 type, the user needs to enter a 1 for the scalar variable named SF and the value for the target specification, gT. If it is not NIB1, the user needs to enter a 0 for SF and any value including 0 for gT. *The other parameters used to define the value curve are entered in the Value Curve Plotter worksheet.*

Value for Special Vector

This worksheet sets up the Monte Carlo simulation process for constructing the distribution for the difference in value between an arbitrary state and baseline. The outcomes can be considered as "strategic contrasts." It is an extension of the previous worksheet, which sets up the simulation process for the individual coefficients for the CIQ. Repeated Monte Carlo simulations allow the distribution to be generated. Before running the simulations, the user needs to enter 1s and 0s for the special vectors for variance (XIVECTOR) and for the mean (LAMVECTOR). The signs and significance of the coefficients are given for both XI and LAM to aid in the choice of the coefficient combinations for evaluation. Hierarchical rules should be followed when selecting which coefficients are to be used for the mean and variance.

Value Equations

Some SDWs have this worksheet, which contains several of the value model expressions pasted in it as objects. The expressions can be copied and placed elsewhere in the worksheet for convenience in displaying the algebraic forms of the value equations alongside the spreadsheet computations. The same expressions also appear in the Value Curve Plotter worksheet.

Value Curve Plotter

This worksheet is used to enter the parameters that define the value curve for the problem at hand. The resulting values are used in computing the CIQs and values in other worksheets. Plots of the value curve, the CIQ, and the loss of value due to variation are also generated. The user needs to develop the appropriate range for the value curve by selecting the origin for g (gSTART) and the increment in g (gINC). End points should be selected for the range where value is positive to avoid singularities.

Table F.2 SDW templates.	
1 CCD Template	**5** OP5 Template
2 Normal Template	**6** OP6 Template
3 Lognormal Template	**7** OP7 Template
4 OP4 Template	**8** OP8 Template

F.2 SDW TEMPLATES

The CCD template listed as #1 in Table F.2 is for CCD designs having two factors. The Normal Template is the template for normally distributed variables and the Lognormal template is for lognormally distributed variables. The five templates OP4 through OP8 are used to analyze the signal portion of signal/response experiments having four to eight signal levels, respectively. These templates are used in conjunction with the Normal or Lognormal templates for analyzing the influence of the control factors on the coefficients for the orthogonal polynomials.

Appendix G

Derivation of the Individual *F* Test for the Influence of Factors on Log Variance

The derivations of Equation (9.5) and its counterpart, Equation (9.2),[1] begin with the expression for the sample variance statistic:

$$s^2(q) = \frac{\sigma^2 \chi^2}{v} \tag{G.1}$$

for an arbitrary trial q. The sample size $n(q) = v + 1$ for the trials is assumed constant. The natural logarithm of Equation (G.1) is given by

$$Ln(s^2(q)) = Ln(\sigma^2) + Ln\left(\frac{\chi^2}{v}\right) \tag{G.2}$$

For the null hypothesis that the samples are taken from normally distributed populations having a common variance, σ^2, the expression for the off-baseline coefficients given by Equation (9.4) becomes

$$\xi_{ij,Ln} = -\sum_q \omega_{ij}(q) Ln\left(\frac{\chi^2}{v}\right) \quad ij \neq 0 \tag{G.3}$$

Equation (G.3) displays a well-known result, which is that the off-baseline coefficients are represented by a statistic that is independent of the population variance when the null hypothesis of a common population variance for the trials is imposed. A new statistic, Z_{ij}^*, is defined in terms of $\xi_{ij,Ln}$ and its standard deviation $\sqrt{E(\xi_{ij,Ln}^2)}$:

$$Z_{ij \neq 0}^* \equiv \frac{\xi_{ij,Ln}}{\sqrt{E\left(\xi_{ij,Ln}^2\right)}} \tag{G.4}$$

If the solution matrix is balanced for the off-baseline coefficients in the sense that for each $\omega_{ij}(q) < 0$ there is a $\omega_{ij}(q') = |\omega_{ij}(q)|$, it follows that the expected value of $\xi_{ij,Ln}$ is given by

$$E\left(\xi_{ij,Ln}^2\right) = \frac{\sigma_{Ln(\chi^2/v)}^2}{2} \sum_q \omega_{ij}^2(q)$$

$$= \frac{\sigma_{Ln(\chi^2/v)}^2}{2} \, cov_{ijij} \tag{G.5}$$

where

$$\sigma_{Ln(\chi^2/v)}^2 \equiv E\left(\left[Ln\left(\frac{\chi^2}{v}\right)_q - Ln\left(\frac{\chi^2}{v}\right)_{q'}\right]^2\right)$$

It follows from Equations (G.4) and (G.5) that

$$Z_{ij\neq0}^* \equiv \frac{\xi_{ij,Ln}}{\sqrt{\dfrac{\sigma_{Ln(\chi^2/v)}^2 \, cov_{ijij}}{2}}} \tag{G.6}$$

The need to compute the variance $\sigma_{Ln(\chi^2/v)}^2$ can be bypassed by using the results for $E(\xi_{ij,Ln})$ from a readily solved, simple problem represented by an experiment having only two trials, a baseline (trial 1) and alternative (trial 2). This results in two simultaneous equations given in matrix form by

$$\begin{bmatrix} 1 & 0 \\ 1 & 1 \end{bmatrix}\begin{bmatrix} \xi_{0,Ln} \\ \xi_{11,Ln} \end{bmatrix} = \begin{bmatrix} Ln(s_1^2) \\ Ln(s_2^2) \end{bmatrix} \tag{G.7}$$

The solution to Equation (G.7) for the $\xi_{ij,Ln}$ is given by

$$\begin{bmatrix} \xi_{0,Ln} \\ \xi_{11,Ln} \end{bmatrix} = \mathbf{X}_S \begin{bmatrix} Ln(s_1^2) \\ Ln(s_2^2) \end{bmatrix}$$

where

$$\mathbf{X}_S = \begin{bmatrix} 1 & 0 \\ -1 & 1 \end{bmatrix} \tag{G.8}$$

is the solution matrix. Thus it follows for $\xi_{11,Ln}$ that

$$\xi_{11,Ln} = Ln(s_2^2) - Ln(s_1^2)$$

$$= Ln\left(\frac{s_2^2}{s_1^2}\right) \tag{G.9}$$

Summation of the squares of the elements $\omega_{11}(q)$ from $q = 1$ to 2 for factor 11 (summation of the squares of the elements across the second row of the solution matrix) yields $\text{cov}_{1111} = 2$. For the null hypothesis that the sample variances came from populations having a common variance, the usual F statistic for this problem is given by the ratio of the two sample variances:

$$F \equiv \frac{s_1^2}{s_2^2} \tag{G.10}$$

The ratio of the two sample variances in Equation (9.14) is computed and substituted into Equation (G.10) to yield

$$F \equiv F_{11} = \exp\left(\xi_{11,Ln}\right) \tag{G.11}$$

From Equations (G.6) and (G.11), it follows that F_{11} for this problem can be written as

$$F_{11} = \exp\left(Z_{11}^* \sqrt{\sigma^2_{Ln(\chi^2/v)}}\right)$$

which can be generalized to the form

$$F_{ij} = \exp\left(Z_{ij}^* \sqrt{\sigma^2_{Ln(\chi^2/v)}}\right) \tag{G.12}$$

for an arbitrary off-baseline factor ij for any experimental design that satisfies the three conditions described in Section 9.2. Substituting the RHS of Equation (G.6) for Z_{ij}^* in Equation (G.12) yields

$$F_{ij} = \exp\left[\frac{\xi_{ij,Ln}}{\sqrt{\text{cov}_{ijij}/2}}\right]$$

which is equivalent to Equation (9.5), after replacing $\xi_{ij,Ln}$ by its absolute value to adhere to the convention of computing the F ratio as a number greater than or equal to unity.

REFERENCE

1. H. E. Cook. 1997. *Product Management Value, Quality, Cost, Price, Profit, and Organization.* Amsterdam: Kluwer, pp. 360–362.

Appendix H

Bits for Drilling Printed Circuit Vias

The manufacturing process for printed circuit boards involves drilling holes called "vias" into the boards using steel drill bits (bits) having diameters of the order of 0.01 inch. The vias are plated to form electrical connections between layers. The bits are highly susceptible thermal loading, as much of the frictional heat diffuses into the bit from the less conductive polymer. Bit breakage is expensive, as the circuit board has to be scrapped.

ITT, which received an order from the Navy to build a quantity of circuit boards at a cost of up to $600 each, found it impossible to meet its production quota due to breakage. Faced with this problem, Frank Montmarquet of ITT used a series of robust design experiments to discover the material and geometrical factors for markedly improving bit life.[1, 2] The initial screening experiment, based upon an OA, showed that the percentage of cobalt carbide in the bit was a dominant factor. This finding supports the view that bits used in this application need good high-temperature strength. Follow-on experiments identified additional factors for improving bit life.

The purpose here is to re-examine the initial screening experiment within the framework of strategic experimentation. The outcomes found by Montmarquet for bit life are reproduced here as Table H.1. Also shown is the $L_8(2^5)$ outer array for the five noise factors that were not controllable in production but that were controllable during the experiment. These included factors such as feed rate, backup material, and number of layers in the board. Testing was suspended if a bit survived after having drilled 3000 vias. It is clear from Table H.1 that the noise factors for the first column provided a relatively benign environment, as 9 out of 16 survived 3000 holes, the right censored limit. The $L_{16}(4^1, 2^{12})$ design matrix (inner array) is shown in Table H.2. Factors A2, A3, and A4 represented increasing amounts of cobalt carbide over the baseline level, A1. Control factor "e" (11,1) was a dummy factor with no actual changes being made as a result of its moving from one level to the other. The last column is for the interaction between D2 and E2. All of the other two-level factors involved changes in bit geometry including radial rake, helix rake, flute length, and point style.

Table H.1   Noise array and bit lifetimes.

Q	-1	1	1	-1	-1	1	1	-1
P	-1	1	-1	1	-1	1	-1	1
O	-1	-1	1	1	1	1	-1	-1
N	-1	-1	1	1	-1	-1	1	1
M	-1	-1	-1	-1	1	1	1	1
Trial	**1**	**2**	**3**	**4**	**5**	**6**	**7**	**8**
1	1280	44	150	20	60	2	65	25
2	2680	125	120	2	165	100	795	307
3	2670	480	762	130	1422	280	670	130
4	2655	90	7	27	3	15	90	480
5	3000	440	480	10	1260	5	1720	3000
6	2586	6	370	45	2190	36	1030	16
7	3000	2580	20	320	425	85	950	3000
8	800	45	260	250	1650	470	1250	70
9	3000	190	140	2	100	3	450	840
10	3000	638	440	145	690	140	1180	1080
11	3000	180	870	310	2820	240	2190	1100
12	3000	612	1611	625	1720	195	1881	2780
13	3000	1145	1060	198	1340	95	2509	345
14	3000	970	180	220	415	70	2630	3000
15	3000	3000	794	40	160	50	495	3000
16	680	140	809	275	1130	145	2025	125

Table H.2 $L_{16}(4^1,2^{12})$ lambda design matrix. Factor "e" (11,1) was blank.

	Base	A2	A3	A4	D2	B2	C2	F2	G2	H2	I2	E2	J2	BLANK e	L2	D2xE2
Trial	**0**	**11**	**12**	**13**	**21**	**31**	**41**	**51**	**61**	**71**	**81**	**91**	**10,1**	**11,1**	**12,1**	**2191**
1	1	0	0	0	0	0	0	0	0	0	0	0	0	0	0	0
2	1	0	0	0	0	0	0	0	1	1	1	1	1	1	1	0
3	1	0	0	0	1	1	1	1	0	0	0	0	1	1	1	0
4	1	0	0	0	1	1	1	1	1	1	1	1	0	0	0	1
5	1	1	0	0	0	0	1	1	0	0	1	1	0	0	1	0
6	1	1	0	0	0	0	1	1	1	1	0	0	1	1	0	0
7	1	1	0	0	1	1	0	0	0	0	1	1	1	1	0	1
8	1	1	0	0	1	1	0	0	1	1	0	0	0	0	1	0
9	1	0	1	0	0	1	0	1	0	1	0	1	0	1	0	0
10	1	0	1	0	0	1	0	1	1	0	1	0	1	0	1	0
11	1	0	1	0	1	0	1	0	0	1	0	1	1	0	1	1
12	1	0	1	0	1	0	1	0	1	0	1	0	0	1	0	0
13	1	0	0	1	0	1	1	0	0	1	1	0	0	1	1	0
14	1	0	0	1	0	1	1	0	1	0	0	1	1	0	0	0
15	1	0	0	1	1	0	0	1	0	1	1	0	1	0	0	0
16	1	0	0	1	1	0	0	1	1	0	0	1	0	1	1	1

Table H.3 Replications computed as $Ln(1/x)$, sample size (n), and ML estimates of the mean and standard deviation for samples taken from a normal distribution.

												z	w
												16	15
	Replications (leave blank if no entry)											*ML Estimates*	
Trial	1	2	3	4	5	6	7	8	9	10	n	mean	stddev
1	-7.15	-3.78	-5.01	-3.00	-4.09	-0.69	-4.17	-3.22			8	-3.891	1.715
2	-7.89	-4.83	-4.79	-0.69	-5.11	-4.61	-6.68	-5.73			8	-5.040	1.952
3	-7.89	-6.17	-6.64	-4.87	-7.26	-5.63	-6.51	-4.87			8	-6.230	1.008
4	-7.88	-4.50	-1.95	-3.30	-1.10	-2.71	-4.50	-6.17			8	-4.013	2.095
5	-8.01	-6.09	-6.17	-2.30	-7.14	-1.61	-7.45	-8.01			8	-6.304	2.948
6	-7.86	-1.79	-5.91	-3.81	-7.69	-3.58	-6.94	-2.77			8	-5.044	2.199
7	-8.01	-7.86	-3.00	-5.77	-6.05	-4.44	-6.86	-8.01			8	-6.570	2.151
8	-6.68	-3.81	-5.56	-5.52	-7.41	-6.15	-7.13	-4.25			8	-5.814	1.213
9	-8.01	-5.25	-4.94	-0.69	-4.61	-1.10	-6.11	-6.73			8	-4.845	2.695
10	-8.01	-6.46	-6.09	-4.98	-6.54	-4.94	-7.07	-6.98			8	-6.445	1.099
11	-8.01	-5.19	-6.77	-5.74	-7.94	-5.48	-7.69	-7.00			8	-6.805	1.184
12	-8.01	-6.42	-7.38	-6.44	-7.45	-5.27	-7.54	-7.93			8	-7.121	0.974
13	-8.01	-7.04	-6.97	-5.29	-7.20	-4.55	-7.83	-5.84			8	-6.675	1.287
14	-8.01	-6.88	-5.19	-5.39	-6.03	-4.25	-7.87	-8.01			8	-6.703	1.726
15	-8.01	-8.01	-6.68	-3.69	-5.08	-3.91	-6.20	-8.01			8	-6.808	2.517
16	-6.52	-4.94	-6.70	-5.62	-7.03	-4.98	-7.61	-4.83			8	-6.028	1.006

The reciprocal lifetimes are the strategic variables of <u>choice</u> for this problem because the added part cost due to bit breakage is equal to $N_H C_D (1/x)$, Equation (13.2). For this problem, the fully accounted costs for bit breakage, C_D, is set equal to $600, the cost of a scrapped board. The actual value for N_H is not known here and is set conveniently to one, which results in the computation of the added part cost per via drilled in the board. The natural logarithms of the reciprocal lifetimes, listed in Table H.3, fit the shapes of a normal distribution and a Weibull distribution almost equally well. For simplicity, the distribution of $Ln(1/x)$ is assumed normal. Replications highlighted by the rectangular boxes were for suspended tests. The means and standard deviations were determined using repeated applications of the ML estimate worksheet for samples taken from a normal distribution shown in Table H.4. The analysis shown is for trial 15 with the log likelihood target at n = 8.

For a lifetime x, the fraction of drills failed is given by

$$1\text{-NORMDIST}(Ln(1/x),\text{MEAN},\text{StdDev},1)$$

the fraction not failed being given by one minus failed, the expression in cell AC38. The ML estimates for the means and the square of the standard deviations were set equal to Y and SVAR, respectively, in the SDW Design and Outcomes worksheet. Note, by taking the reciprocal values, the right censored lifetimes appear on the left.

Table H.4 Worksheet for generating ML estimates for the mean and standard deviation for trial 15 for the log of the reciprocal lifetimes, $Ln(1/x)$.

	AA	AB	AC	AD	AE	AF	AG	AH	AI	AJ	AK	AL
30							Replication					
31			1	2	3	4	5	6	7	8	9	10
32		Lifetime	-8.006	-8.006	-6.677	-3.689	-5.075	-3.912	-6.205	-8.006		
33		Suspended="S"	S	S	F	F	F	F	F	S	F	F
34			0	0	1	1	1	1	1	0	1	1
35												
36												
37		Fail	0.1415	0.1415	0.1583	0.0735	0.1251	0.0818	0.1540	0.1415	0.0041	0.0041
38		Suspended	0.3170	0.3170	0.5208	0.8924	0.7545	0.8751	0.5948	0.3170	0.9966	0.9966
39												
40			0.3170	0.3170	0.1583	0.0735	0.1251	0.0818	0.1540	0.3170	0.0041	0.0041
41												
42			n	LN(Likelihood)			ML est.					
43			3	-4.141								
44			4	-6.751		MEAN	-6.808	2.517	StdDev			
45			5	-8.830								
46			6	-11.334								
47			7	-13.205								
48			8	-14.353								
49			9	-19.855								
50			10	-25.356								
51												
52			AC37	=NORMDIST(AC32,MEAN,StdDev,0)								
53			AC38	=NORMDIST(AC32,MEAN,StdDev,1)								
54			AC40	=AC34*AC37+(1-AC34)*AC38								
55			AC43	=LN(PRODUCT(AC40:AE40))								
56			AC44	=LN(PRODUCT(AC40:AF40))								

The influence of the factors on log variance as measured by the ξ_{ij} coefficients (XI) for this problem are shown in Table H.5, as taken from the Variance Coefficients worksheet for the SDW. Although none of the off-baseline factors are seen to be significant at 0.1 EWE, main effects L2 and E1 (-E2) are most favorable for reducing variance in the log transformed data set.

The outcomes of the analysis of the factors on the mean (LAM) taken from the Lambda Coefficients worksheet are shown in Table H.6.

The two factors for the higher cobalt carbide levels, A3 and A4, are seen to be highly significant in making the log of the reciprocal lifetime more negative (the direction for improving bit life).

The strategic portions of the analysis given in Table H.7 and Table H.8 were taken from the Value Mean & Simulation worksheet. It was necessary to modify this worksheet as the function needed, Equation (13.2), is not provided by the standard form used for value curves. Thus the expression for the CIQ replaced by the fully accounted cost CD(=$600)

Table H.5   Outcomes for XI coefficients.

				MIN(n)		MAX(n)		Averaged		
		XI	Gij	PWE	EWE	PWE	EWE	PWE	EWE	SIGXI
Base	0	-4.68	-0.66	0.03	0.03	0.03	0.03	0.03	0.03	significant
A2	11	-1.90	-0.38	0.14	1.91	0.14	1.91	0.14	1.91	NOT
A3	12	1.58	0.32	0.18	2.50	0.18	2.50	0.18	2.50	NOT
A4	13	0.50	0.10	0.39	5.40	0.39	5.40	0.39	5.40	NOT
D2	21	1.25	0.25	0.23	3.26	0.23	3.26	0.23	3.26	NOT
B2	31	0.61	0.17	0.31	4.31	0.31	4.31	0.31	4.31	NOT
C2	41	0.68	0.19	0.29	4.01	0.29	4.01	0.29	4.01	NOT
F2	51	-1.65	-0.47	0.09	1.25	0.09	1.25	0.09	1.25	NOT
G2	61	1.87	0.53	0.07	0.92	0.07	0.92	0.07	0.92	NOT
H2	71	-1.86	-0.53	0.07	0.93	0.07	0.93	0.07	0.93	NOT
I2	81	-1.37	-0.39	0.13	1.84	0.13	1.84	0.13	1.84	NOT
E2	91	-3.50	-0.70	0.02	0.34	0.02	0.34	0.02	0.34	NOT
J2	10,1	-0.20	-0.06	0.43	6.07	0.43	6.07	0.43	6.07	NOT
e	11,1	0.90	0.25	0.23	3.20	0.23	3.20	0.23	3.20	NOT
L2	12,1	3.03	0.86	0.01	0.13	0.01	0.13	0.01	0.13	NOT
D2xE2	2191	2.24	0.32	0.18	2.50	0.18	2.50	0.18	2.50	NOT

ALPHAXI 0.1

Table H.6   Outcomes for LAM coefficients.

ALPHALAM 0.1

		LAM	SDij	DFij	t	PWE2	EWE	SIGLAM
Base	0	-3.891	0.606	7.0	-6.42	0.00	0.00	significant
A2	11	-1.140	0.498	42.6	-2.29	0.01	0.19	NOT
A3	12	-1.511	0.424	36.7	-3.57	0.00	0.01	significant
A4	13	-1.760	0.434	42.4	-4.05	0.0001	0.00	significant
D2	21	-0.980	0.399	36.3	-2.45	0.01	0.13	NOT
B2	31	-0.032	0.327	75.6	-0.10	0.46	6.46	NOT
C2	41	-0.432	0.327	75.6	-1.32	0.10	1.33	NOT
F2	51	0.363	0.327	75.6	1.11	0.14	1.89	NOT
G2	61	0.240	0.327	75.6	0.73	0.23	3.25	NOT
H2	71	0.531	0.327	75.6	1.63	0.05	0.76	NOT
I2	81	-0.452	0.327	75.6	-1.38	0.09	1.19	NOT
E2	91	-0.209	0.511	41.5	-0.41	0.34	4.79	NOT
J2	10,1	-0.619	0.327	75.6	-1.90	0.03	0.43	NOT
e	11,1	-0.096	0.327	75.6	-0.29	0.38	5.39	NOT
L2	12,1	-0.543	0.327	75.6	-1.66	0.05	0.70	NOT
D2xE2	2191	0.849	0.653	75.6	1.30	0.10	1.38	NOT

Table H.7 One simulation of ranges for population variance and population average of 1 / x.

Trials	LPOPVARSIM	RN2	tSIM	LPOPYSIM	POPVARSIM	POPYSIM
1	1.5	0.7	0.6	-3.5	1.36E-02	0.1
2	6.5	0.3	-0.7	-5.5	7.43E+00	0.1
3	2.1	1.0	3.3	-5.1	2.49E-03	0.0
4	12.7	0.5	0.0	-4.0	3.09E+07	9.9
5	4.8	0.1	-1.3	-7.7	3.61E-03	0.0
6	2.7	0.6	0.2	-4.9	1.30E-02	0.0
7	1.4	0.6	0.2	-6.4	3.39E-05	0.0
8	1.4	0.8	0.9	-5.4	2.25E-04	0.0
9	10.4	0.6	0.3	-4.6	1.14E+05	1.9
10	1.2	0.7	0.6	-6.2	2.77E-05	0.0
11	1.7	0.7	0.6	-6.6	5.57E-05	0.0
12	0.7	0.9	1.2	-6.7	2.77E-06	0.0
13	2.0	0.7	0.7	-6.4	1.46E-04	0.0
14	5.5	0.0	-1.9	-7.9	9.17E-03	0.0
15	7.0	0.6	0.3	-6.5	2.67E+00	0.0
16	0.5	0.6	0.2	-6.0	6.62E-06	0.0

Table H.8 One simulation of the ranges for the CIQ and the lambda coefficients for −10 times the log of the CIQ.

Trials	fvSIM1	ktSIM1	VIDEAL	VALUESIM1	CIQSIM1	CD 600 =-(0-CD*POPYSIM)		LAMSN1
1	1.10E+00	304.3	12.2	6.85E+00	3.73E+01	Base	0	-15.7
2	8.80E-01	304.3	12.2	-2.25E+03	6.32E+01	A2	11	13.5
3	1.21E+00	304.3	12.2	1.13E+01	1.11E+01	A3	12	11.2
4	-2.96E+03	304.3	12.2	-9.41E+09	5.92E+03	A4	13	13.5
5	1.22E+00	304.3	12.2	1.11E+01	3.20E+00	D2	21	0.9
6	1.19E+00	304.3	12.2	7.94E+00	1.79E+01	B2	31	-3.8
7	1.22E+00	304.3	12.2	1.22E+01	2.01E+00	C2	41	2.0
8	1.22E+00	304.3	12.2	1.21E+01	5.21E+00	F2	51	-7.5
9	-1.04E+02	304.3	12.2	-3.47E+07	1.12E+03	G2	61	0.0
10	1.22E+00	304.3	12.2	1.22E+01	2.13E+00	H2	71	-10.3
11	1.22E+00	304.3	12.2	1.22E+01	2.06E+00	I2	81	0.2
12	1.22E+00	304.3	12.2	1.22E+01	1.02E+00	E2	91	-5.8
13	1.22E+00	304.3	12.2	1.21E+01	2.84E+00	J2	10,1	4.1
14	1.22E+00	304.3	12.2	9.37E+00	3.64E+00	e	11,1	1.3
15	1.15E+00	304.3	12.2	-8.02E+02	2.91E+01	L2	12,1	8.2
16	1.22E+00	304.3	12.2	1.22E+01	1.96E+00	D2xE2	2191	2.1

times the simulated reciprocal lifetimes (POPYSIM) for each trial (see the expression at top of Table H.8). The four columns that used the standard form for the value curve were left unchanged but a pattern was laid over them to avoid misinterpretation.

The simulated coefficients (LAMSN1) for -10 log of the CIQ were computed using the spreadsheet expression

$$LAMSN1=-MMULT(XS,10*LOG(CIQSIM1)).$$

A total of 1000 simulations were run, and the distributions for the three most significant coefficients are shown in Figure H.1. The median intercepts for factors A3(12), A4(13), and L2(12,1) were found to be 7.51, 7.77, and 7.42, respectively. The finding that factor 12,1 was the most significant is surprising at first. However, inspection of Table H.5 and Table H.6 shows that this factor was favorable and borderline significant for reducing the log variance of the Ln transformed lifetimes and it was favorable for reducing the reciprocal Ln lifetimes but not deemed significant. Nevertheless, these two results combine favorably enough on transforming back to the projected means for the reciprocal lifetimes to make factor 12,1 the best factor in reducing costs associated with bit breakage.

The individual median cost savings for factors A3(12), A4(13), and L2(12,1) determined from the distributions shown in Figure H.2, were found to be $48, $44, $47. The slight improvement of factor A3 over A4 for the cost savings is due to the fact that factor

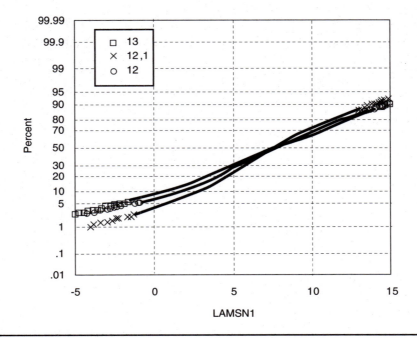

Figure H.1 Distributions for LAMSN1 for three most significant factors.

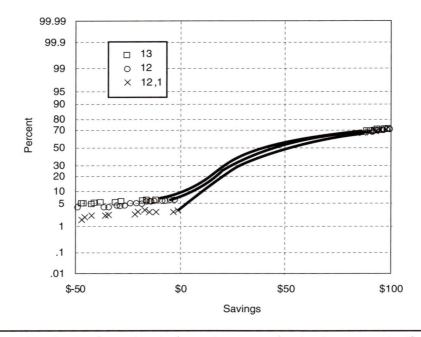

Figure H.2 Distribution for savings in $ per via per part for the three most significant factors.

A3 is projected to have larger reduction in variance (larger XI) as shown in Table H.5. Although the concentration of cobalt carbide and point geometry were found to be very important, other factor levels had expected values that were favorable but their EWE levels were high. In this situation, favorable factors not deemed significant can be programmed for production use if they do not add to variable cost.

This median projected cost saving for combining factors A4 and L2 is $59, eliminating most of the projected median added cost of $63 for the baseline bit (taken here as trial 1) per via drilled. Nevertheless, cost savings opportunities of up to $4 per via drilled remain according to the analysis given here. Montmarquet identified additional bit design changes for improving durability, which were validated in follow-on experiments.

As the experiment was dominated by main effects, it is useful to examine the strategic significance levels of each of several of the best trials relative to the baseline trial 1. The reason for this is that the significance level computed this way includes the contributions from all possible interactions between main effects for the trial. The distribution for savings for trial 16 is shown in Figure H.3. The main effects for this trial include factors A4 and L2. The PWE intercept of approximately 1% needs to be multiplied by 14 to convert to EWE, making it only borderline significant. The median is $63, which is close to the median projected above of $59 for the condition of baseline plus A4 and L2. A similar plot (not included) for trial 12 cost savings versus baseline has a PWE of 0.4% and a median of $67.

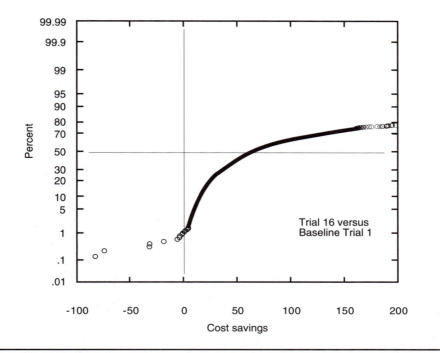

Figure H.3   Projected cost savings for trial 16 versus baseline trial 1.

REFERENCES

1. F. Montmarquet. November 1988. *Printed Circuit Drill Bit Design Optimization Using Taguchi Methods, 0.013 Diameter Bits.* Sixth Symposium on Taguchi Methods, Dearborn, MI: American Supplier Institute, pp. 207–216.
2. C. F. J. Wu and M. Hamada. 2000. *Experiments Planning, Analysis, and Parameter Design Optimization.* New York: John Wiley & Sons, pp. 546–547.

Appendix I

Point Estimates for the Variance of the SN Ratio

As discussed in Chapter 12, Monte Carlo simulation is the approach recommended for evaluating the strategic significance of the factors on SN_Ω, the signal to noise ratio for the CIQ. Nevertheless, useful but approximate point estimates of the variance of the SN_Ω can be made using Taylor expansions. These approximations are accurate when the sample size is large and the standard deviation small. When this is not the case, they provide order of magnitude estimates, which can be used to check the outcomes of the Monte Carlo simulations and to provide insight regarding the influence of sample size.

From Equations (2.8) and (5.14) for the NIB1 problem, it follows for a normally distributed population that the SN_Ω can be expressed as (using natural logs of the CIQ to facilitate analysis)

$$SN_{\Omega,NIB1}(\mu, \sigma^2, q) \equiv \left[\frac{10}{Ln(10)}\right] Ln\left(\frac{\mu^2(q)}{k_T g_T^2(q)\sigma^2(q)}\right)$$

$$= \left[\frac{10}{Ln(10)}\right]\left[Ln\left(\mu^2(q)\right) + Ln\left(\frac{1}{\sigma^2(q)}\right) - Ln\left(k_T g_T^2(q)\right)\right] \tag{I.1}$$

The point estimate of the variance based upon the Taylor expansion (see Section 4.2) is given by

$$VAR(SN_{\Omega,NIB1}) \cong \left[\frac{10}{Ln(10)}\right]^2 \left[\frac{4s^2(q)\left[n(q)-1\right]}{g^2(q)n(q)\left[n(q)-3\right]} + \frac{2}{n(q)-1}\right] \tag{I.2}$$

The population values for $\mu^2(q)$ and $\sigma^2(q)$ in Equation (I.1) were treated as statistics by replacing them with Equations (5.21) and (5.17), respectively. The following substitutions were also made: $VAR(t) = v(q) / [v(q) - 2]$; $E(\chi^2) = v$; and $VAR(\chi^2) = 2v$.

The approximation in Equation (I.2) (after being divided through by $[10/Ln(10)]^2$) for $n(q) = 5$ and $g(q) = 10$ is compared in Figure I.1 as a function of the sample standard devi-

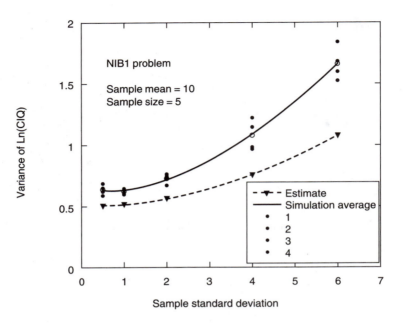

Figure I.1 Simulated versus estimated variance of the *Ln*(CIQ) for the NIB1 problem for a sample size of 5.

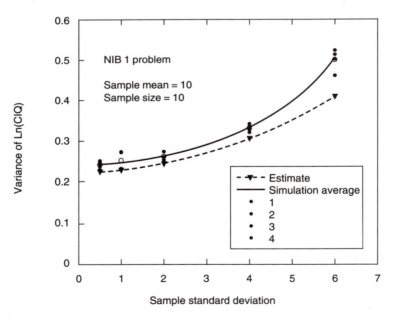

Figure I.2 Simulated versus estimated variance of the *Ln*(CIQ) for the NIB1 problem for a sample size of 10.

ation is $s(q)$ to the same variance determined by computer simulation. Four separate 1000 simulations were made for each point so that the variation in the simulation could also be observed. The comparison for $n(q) = 10$ is shown in Figure I.2, where the comparison of the estimate to the simulated results are seen to be reasonably good for standard deviations of 2 and below, but biased to the low side. Thus, the approximation represented by Equation (I.2) will be reasonably accurate when the sample size $n(q)$ is 10 or greater and the standard deviation is 1/5 or less than the absolute value of the mean.

The signal to noise ratio for the NIB2 problem with the CIQ defined by Equation (5.7) for $\gamma = 1$ is given by

$$SN_{\Omega,NIB2}(\mu,\sigma^2,q) \equiv \left[\frac{-10}{Ln(10)}\right] Ln\left(k_T^*\left[\left(\mu(q) - g_I\right)^2 + \sigma^2(q)\right]\right) \tag{I.3}$$

For the same approximation used to derive Equation (I.2), it follows that

$$E\left(\chi^2\right) = v \tag{I.4}$$

The outcomes for the NIB2 approximation in Equation (5.7) (after being divided through by $[10/Ln(10)]^2$) for $n(q) = 5$ and $g(q) - g_I = 10$ are compared to the simulation of this expression in Figure I.3 as a function of the sample standard deviation $s(q)$. Again, four separate 1000 simulations were also made for each point. The comparison shows bet-

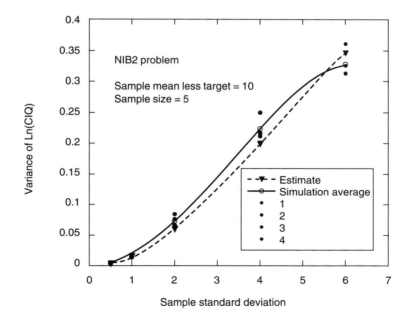

Figure I.3 Simulated versus estimated variance of the Ln(CIQ) for the NIB2 problem for a sample size of 5.

ter agreement than might be expected for this relatively small sample size of five. For a sample size of $n(q) = 10$, which is not shown, the estimated and simulated results are in good agreement.

The distributions for SIB g and for $g = 1/x$ for LIB x can often be approximated by a normal distribution when $g(q, r)$ is transformed to $Ln(g(q,r))$, in which case the $g(q, r)$ are said to be lognormally distributed. For this class of problems for $\gamma - 1$, -10 times the base 10 log CIQ is given by Equation (I.3) for $g_I = 0$ and the Taylor expansion approximation for the variance is given by

$$
VAR(SN_{\Omega,\text{lognormal}}) \cong \left[\frac{10}{Ln(10)}\right]^2 \left[\frac{g^4(q)}{\left[g^4(q) + s^2(q)\right]^2}\right] \times
$$

(I.5)

$$
\left[\frac{4s_{Ln}^2(q)\left[n(q) - 1\right]}{n(q)\left[n(q) - 3\right]} + \frac{s_{Ln}^4(q)}{n(q) - 1}\left\{2 + \frac{1}{2}\left[2\exp\left(s_{Ln}^2(q)\right) - 1\right]^2 + 4\left[2\exp\left(s_{Ln}^2(q)\right) - 1\right]\right\}\right]
$$

In Equation (I.5), $g(q)$ is the sample mean (untransformed) and $s^2(q)$ is the sample variance (untransformed) for trial (q). Note, the untransformed means and variances are not statistically independent. The term $s_{Ln}^2(q)$ is the sample variance for the normally distributed $Ln(g(q,r))$. A check of Equation (I.5) for $Ln(g(q)) = 2$ found it to be in reasonable agreement with simulated results for $VAR(SN_{\Omega,\text{Lognormal}})$ for sample sizes of 10 or greater and $s_{Ln}^2(q) \leq 0.4$.

Index

A

acceleration performance value curve, 24–26

action plans, system level, 16

aliasing, 305

American Supplier Institute, 122

analysis, levels of. *See* levels of analysis

architecture, system, 48–51

arrays

  orthogonal. *See* orthogonal arrays (OAs)

  outer, 98–100, 104

attributes

  collinearity between, 38

  critical to value. *See* critical to value (CTV) attributes

  ideal, 43

  larger is better, 24, 43, 86–88, 231

  nominal is best, 24, 43, 85–88, 104, 195

  non-negative, 215

  smaller is better. *See* smaller is better (SIB) attributes

  value and, 8, 11, 62, 78

axiomatic design, 3

B

Bartlett's test, 149

BBD (Box-Behnken design), 258

Bernoulli trials, 74, 207

binomial distributions

  application to smaller is better problem, 207–211

  error in neutral price for, 80–81

  generally, 74–75

Monte Carlo analysis, 311–317

for non-negative, random, physical variables, 195, 215

black belts, 1–2

Bonferroni method, 125, 129–130, 293–296

bootstrapping, 116

bottom-line metrics analysis, 202–207

Box-Behnken design (BBD), 258

breakeven time, 4, 13

business environment, changes over time, 5–6

C

case studies. *See* examples

cash flow

  confidence levels, 8

  as metric, 4

  projecting, 12, 13, 15, 60–61, 168–170

CB (Cournot/Bertrand) pricing model, 3–4, 52–54

CCD (central composite design), 258, 280, 292

CCD template, 329

censored tests, 227, 229

central composite design (CCD), 258, 280, 292

Central Limit Theorem, 66–67, 83

central point in central composite design, 258

chaos, 5–6

chi-square distribution, 70–71

CIQ (cost of inferior quality). *See* cost of inferior quality (CIQ)

circuit board vias example, 335–343